N

INSTINCT IN MAN

IN THE LIGHT OF RECENT WORK IN
COMPARATIVE PSYCHOLOGY

RONALD FLETCHER

SCHOCKEN BOOKS • NEW YORK

TO MY
MOTHER AND FATHER
WITH GRATITUDE

This edition is published by arrangement
with International Universities Press, Inc.,
the publishers of the original edition, 1957.

First SCHOCKEN PAPERBACK edition 1966

CONTENTS

PREFACE TO THE PAPERBACK EDITION

THIS edition is appearing at a time when other commitments prevent me from considering any large-scale revision. It is almost ten years, however, since the first publication of the book, and consequently I would not like it to appear without some brief mention of work that has been undertaken since that time. Hence this preface. I would like, too, to explain certain aspects of the standpoint of the book to those new readers who may be reached by this paperback edition.

When this book was written, the concept of 'instinct' was widely declared to be 'dead.' I thought that this widespread view was untrue, and that the arguments on which it rested were confused, ill-informed, and far too dogmatic. The object of this book was, therefore, to reconsider the concept and to argue for its reinstatement as an essential and fundamental concept in psychology.

It was clear that a great deal of experimental work on the nature of instinctive experience and behaviour was continuously being undertaken despite the supposed 'death' of the concept. In fact, there has never been any break in this work at all. It has been continuous from the turn of the century—in the hands of scholars like Lloyd Morgan, L. T. Hobhouse, and William McDougall; among biologists such as E. S. Russell in the early thirties; and in the work of the 'Comparative Ethologists' which began about the mid-thirties and continues to flourish today. Also, other schools of psychology—such as that of Freud—were extremely influential, and yet it did not seem to be sufficiently realised that the whole of Freud's interpretation and explanation of the vicissitudes experienced during the development of the human personality, and the 'mental mechanisms' which came into operation to deal with the resulting anxiety, rested firmly upon an 'instinct theory' too. It seemed not to be realised that if it were claimed that human nature was devoid of pressing instinctual demands, the whole Freudian theory of the human personality fell to the ground. In short, there seemed to be a good deal of confusion about the several aspects of the subject. Also, it seemed to me that—whatever dangers and possible fallacies might attend the *concept* of instinct—the *facts* the concept sought to indicate and explore (i.e., that in all animal species, including man, there were certain regular correlations of anatomical structure, neuro-physiological functions, elements of experience, and elements of behaviour, which were established in large part by heredity and not by any means entirely by learning) were undeniable; and that the investigation of the nature and extent of instinctual experience and behaviour in all animal species was therefore fundamental and indispensable for any satisfactory comparative psychology. I therefore reviewed the earlier theories of instinct and tried to relate them with the work of the Comparative Ethologists and the ideas of Freud in order to arrive at the best statement of a contemporary theory of instinct. And I then suggested some implications of this theory for certain directions of research in psychology, social philosophy, and sociology.

It is for the reader to decide to what extent the argument of the book is successful; but it does appear that much of the work which has been undertaken during the past ten years has been such as to support it. The concept of 'instinct' is not dead yet. Or, if it is, it shows a surprising amount of vitality for a ghost! A great deal of experimental work is now based upon it, and is flourishing more than ever before.

In particular, the comparative study of patterns of animal behaviour that has come to be called 'Comparative Ethology'—employing ever more rigorous experimental methods—has expanded very considerably during the past ten years. Professor Konrad Lorenz and his colleagues continue their work (of the kind that is reported in Chapter IV) at the Max Planck-Institut für Verhaltensphysiologie. In Britain, Professor N. Tinbergen, Professor Robert Hinde, and Professor W. H. Thorpe exert an ever growing influence, and continue to produce work that amply supports and justifies the use of the concept. Most of the advances made during the period, together with detailed bibliographies, can be found in *Current Problems in Animal Behaviour* (Cambridge University Press, 1961) edited by W. H. Thorpe and O. L. Zangwill; in the revised edition of *Learning and Instinct in Animals* by W. H. Thorpe (Methuen, London & Harvard University Press, Cambridge, Mass., 1963); and in a useful and informative article by Thorpe entitled 'Progress and Prospects in Ethology' (in *The Cell and the Organism* edited by J. A. Ramsay and V. B. Wigglesworth, Cambridge University Press, 1961).

Three particular developments of this work are worth noting.

The first is its extension by very carefully informed *amateur* investigations. Tinbergen especially, in one of his books—in *The Study of Instinct,* I believe—emphasised the fact that amateurs could still make very useful contributions to the subject by undertaking systematic observations of animal behaviour and carefully describing them. This field of activity has grown enormously and has been productive of many worthwhile studies—perhaps especially in the study of the behaviour of birds. There are many examples, but one book is especially entertaining and describes the enjoyment and excitement, as well as the scientific nature, of such work: *Key to a Bird's World* by Terry Gompertz (Michael Joseph, London, 1966).

The second development is the extension of such studies to the behaviour of primates; to those species whose patterns of experience and behaviour can be compared much more closely and readily with the experience and behaviour of man. Very recently (1965) a Mammal Behaviour Study Unit was set up at the London Zoo. This is directed by Dr. D. Morris, and many lines of research into the behaviour of monkeys and apes in particular (but also that of jackals, wolves, and other animals) are being undertaken by his team of researchers. But the research that has become most prominent during recent years has been that undertaken by Professor Harry Harlow of the University of Wisconsin at the Regional Primate Research Center there.

During a period of more than seven years, Professor Harlow has studied the effects of maternal and social deprivation among monkeys. He has described the extent to which a close, affectionate, protective relationship with a mother, or a mother-substitute, is a factor of the utmost importance for the normal growth and maturation of monkeys, and the extent to which the absence of such a relationship gives rise to identifiable abnormalities of behaviour and quite specific and predictable incapacities for adult social life. Young monkeys cling closely to their mothers—or a dummy substitute—and use their mother as a basis of security from which gradually to explore the world about them, and as a refuge to which they can immediately and safely return if they encounter danger. And if young monkeys *lack* this early security and refuge, they come to manifest 'neurotic' behaviour patterns remarkably like our own. For example, they clasp their heads and bodies in their arms and legs and rock to and fro; they pace restlessly backwards and forwards, or round and round in circles; they sit passively and gaze vacantly into space; and sometimes, says Professor Harlow, "this is accompanied by a bizarre movement in which one arm gradually rises as if detached from the body, while the wrists and fingers become flexed and closed into a fist—a pattern similar to that seen in schizophrenic human patients, where it has been given the name of 'waxy flexibility' . . ." Monkeys which lack this secure mother-relationship also behave with exaggerated aggression, and they are often unable to form 'normal' social relationships later in their lives. They show little 'friendship' for companions; they rarely develop normal heterosexual behaviour; and females tend, if they have offspring, to ignore or abandon them.

This research—of which students of psychology will be well aware —is clearly of the greatest interest. It appears to demonstrate unquestionably the importance of innate patterns of experience and behaviour for the understanding and explanation of patterns of learning and maturation, and it is clearly very relevant to our studies of human experience and behaviour. Some of Harlow's experiments are described in *Determinants of Infant Behaviour,* edited by Brian Foss (Vol. 1, Methuen, London, 1961). Similar studies covering a wider range of primate behaviour are to be found in *Primate Behaviour,* edited by I. deVore (Holt, Rinehart & Winston, New York, 1965).

This leads to the third development of importance: the application of these studies of instinct to the understanding of human nature, and to the exploration of human problems. It is worth noting, for example, that the Mammal Behaviour Study Unit set up in London was supported by the World Health Organization for the investigation of the natural forms of birth control that some animal species seem to have achieved. This knowledge, it is thought, might well be of relevance in dealing with the problems of human population growth. But more particularly, the findings of Comparative Ethology in the field of animal behaviour are coming to be applied quite systematically and seriously to the understanding of the growth, maturation, and patterns of learning and personality development of human beings. The most prominent scholar in this field is undoubtedly Dr. John Bowlby, and his work has given rise to great controversy. He has attempted to study the importance for individual personality development of close, affectionate, and secure relationships between parent and child. Like Harlow, he claims that when children suffer early deprivation of this affection and security, they too are likely to develop patterns of anxious and abnormal behaviour; and barriers are likely to be created in their personalities which prevent, or make very difficult, the subsequent achievement of normal and effective adult relationships of a sexual kind; of a more general affectionate kind; and even of responsible and affectionate parenthood. All this, again, can be seen to be very closely related to all that Freud has to say about the nature and development of the human personality. And, indeed, Dr. Bowlby continues to claim that there is the most intimate and important theoretical relationship between the concepts of ethology and the concepts of Freud—a view that (as will be seen later) is also strongly argued in this book.

All in all, then, I do not think that the thesis of this book requires any important amendment in the light of subsequent work. On the contrary, such work seems strongly to support it, and there seems every reason to suppose that the reconsideration of the nature of instinct and the bringing together of the work of the ethologists and psycho-analytic theory, which is suggested here, is likely to provide a useful and fertile basis for research.

In addition to this brief mention of recent directions of work, there are one or two reasons for the standpoint I have adopted in the book that I would like to explain to American readers in particular.

It will be seen that I am strongly opposed to 'Behaviourism.'

Writing on this subject of 'instinct' between about 1945 and 1957, I wished to take issue strongly with certain trends and influences of American psychology which then seemed very powerful. Perhaps, at a distance in Britain, I was wrong about these trends. Perhaps I over-emphasised or over-estimated their power. But they were in the fore-front of my mind, and therefore I think it would be a good thing to explain them. One of these was the increasing narrowness of the way in which 'Comparative Psychology' was interpreted. The image of American experimental psychology which was then dominant in Britain was very aptly reflected in the satirical principle stated by a psychologist who is quoted later in these pages: "The more I see of men—the more I study rats!" There seemed to be only one kind of creature in the animal kingdom! The broad range of comparative psychology seemed in danger of being lost. Secondly, a very extreme—and, to my mind, philosophically false—notion of 'Behaviourism' seemed to be narrowing the subject matter of psychology to a point where it had nothing to do with human experience and where the science of psychology itself was no longer necessary. J. B. Watson, of course, had been the most extreme exponent of this, but the kind of position he had adopted and promulgated seemed to be very wide-spread. The attack upon the concept of 'instinct' had been in large part an attack from the 'behaviourist' standpoint. Consequently, in my attempted defence of the concept of 'instinct' I felt it necessary to offer a rebuttal of Behaviourism. On this question of Behaviourism itself, I still feel as strongly now as I did then, but there are one or two points I would like to make very clear.

Two formulations of a behaviouristic position must be distin-guished—one limited, one extreme. On the one hand, it may be claimed that all hypotheses in psychology must be formulated in such a way as to permit of empirical test, and that the conditions of empirical test must have behavioural reference, since elements of 'experience,' as such, cannot be 'observed' let alone quantified and measured. There is much to be said by way of argument about this limited formulation, but I want to make perfectly clear that I would not wish to quarrel unduly with it. It is the second, and more extreme formulation of 'Behaviourism' that I still think must be completely rejected: that since elements of 'experience' are not amenable to observation or measurement, they should not enter into the sphere of psychology at all; or indeed—taking it to the Watsonian extreme— that we have no testable grounds for even maintaining that 'experience' 'exists,' and one is being something of a mediaeval occultist in even bothering to reflect, conjecture, and form hypotheses about it. This statement of Behaviourism seems to me totally unwarranted, untrue, and dangerous. It may be noticed, firstly, that if it is true, it rules 'psychology' out of existence. *Psych*ology is only required as a science if we are aware of something we call the *psyche*—certain attributes to which we refer as 'mind,' 'feeling,' 'thinking,' 'perception,' etc.— about which we are driven to ask questions and about which we seek knowledge. If elements of experience of this kind do not exist, or cannot permit of systematic exploration, and if patterns of observed behaviour and their neuro-physiological bases are all we are able to study, then we can manage quite well with the sciences of biology and physiology. People who adopt the extreme Behaviourist position ought not to call themselves 'psychologists' at all. However, the fact that Behaviourism disposes of psychology does not prove that it is false.

A second point I cannot accept is that it is possible even to observe and describe behaviour adequately, let alone understand and explain it fully, without reference to elements of experience and meaning. So that the idea that we can have a science of behaviour wholly denuded of the imponderables of experience is, I think, false. Thirdly, I think that this extreme Behaviourism can be misleading and stultifying for the development of psychology as a science. It can be misleading in that it can lead students to prize the quest for *scientific exactitude* higher than the quest for the *full appreciation of the subtlety of the subject matter whose many dimensions they should be seeking to understand and explain*. Scientific exactitude, of course, is of great importance, but it is not an end so important as to warrant a vast oversimplification of the subject matter with which it is supposed to deal in order that it may be attained. This is, in fact, to be directly *un*scientific. To put it another way: if we are not careful, the desire to be scientifically exact can be in danger of making us empirically naive. We may become prepared to entertain, to see, to acknowledge only what we can be scientifically exact about; whereas we ought to be acquainting ourselves in the fullest way possible with *all the subtleties of our subject matter* and seeking the *most appropriate* concepts and techniques for enunciating and testing our hypotheses *as precisely as is possible.*

Somewhere, Tinbergen says that a science does not advance by limiting its subject matter to what can be handled by its existing concepts and technical apparatus, but only by confronting what are, at present, the important and baffling imponderables, and seeking *new* concepts and *new* techniques of investigation that will render them amenable to systematic exploration. In this sense, for example, the concepts of Freud—formulated to grope towards a systematic understanding of the complex vicissitudes and changes of the human personality as the individual grows to maturity in the context of his material and social environment—may be far more fruitful for the furtherance of psychological research and for the further enrichment of our knowledge of human nature, human learning, and human adjustment than, say, a reward-punishment-reinforcement theory of learning which can be quantitatively measured by administering food pellets or electric shocks to rats—even though, at present, the hypotheses arising from Freud's concepts are extremely difficult to subject to crucial conditions of test.

However, in this preface I do not want to enter fully into the argument. I only want to clarify in a preliminary way some of the reasons why I adopted a forthright position in this book.

This explains, too, why I decided not to try to take a certain range of American psychology into account. The work of C. L. Hull, B. F. Skinner, Z. Y. Kuo, E. C. Tolman, R. M. Yerkes, some of the work of D. O. Hebb and of L. Carmichael on maturation, and of many others, is all relevant to the questions I raised—and I have been criticised for having neglected to consider it. This is certainly a shortcoming of my treatment. And it is a simple fact that, though I am familiar with much of this work, I am certainly not sufficiently informed about all of it to take it completely into account. But, apart from my own limitations, there were two other reasons why I decided not to attempt it. The first is that one simply cannot do everything in one book—and I found it a large enough task to assess critically, and to relate, the several fields of work I was especially interested in bringing together. The second reason was that I thought it better to make my argument stark and clear, rather than to try and qualify it too much. The supposed destruction of the concept of 'instinct' had been so overwhelmingly accepted, and was so fashionable, that I felt it better, for controversy's sake, to give a hard, clear knock back.

The matter can be put very simply. When writing the book, I

realised fully that it would be running completely against the current of many points of view which had come to be accepted in psychology —especially in American psychology—during the past few decades, and I therefore wished to argue the case as clearly and forcibly as was possible.

Now that the book is appearing in paperback form it is likely to reach many more university teachers and students in America, and it is for this reason that I want my approach to be clearly understood.

The kind of reception of the book I would most like, and most hope for, is no more than that its argument should be considered seriously.

Ronald Fletcher,
University of York.
May 1966.

PREFACE TO THE FIRST EDITION

THIS book is an altered and considerably shortened version of a thesis of the same title which was submitted for the Doctorate in Philosophy in the University of London. The alterations necessary in fitting the manuscript for publication have resulted in the fact that some points (not all of central importance) do not receive as much emphasis, or substantiation, as I would have liked; and on one or two of these points I would like to make a few observations.

(1) Swings of fashion, and indulgence in heated and often superficial polemics, are as common (and harmful) in academic thought, as in most other areas of human experience. The literature embodying the study of human motivation during the past five decades is an extremely good example of this. Originally, I went to some lengths to demonstrate that—underlying the apparent disagreement between the various systems of explanation based upon the concepts of 'instinct', 'need', 'drive', 'reflex' and 'chain-reflex'—there was, in fact, fundamental agreement about the elements of human experience and behaviour involved; and that this basic agreement had been hidden or vitiated by the polemical defence of extremes. Here, I can only assert that this is so. The reader can, however, test this assertion for himself, by studying, say, the work of McDougall, Lewin, Allport, and Watson—taking care to dig beneath the concepts used, to the inter-related facts of physiology, experience, and behaviour, to which they refer. Similarly—to mention a closely related problem—many critics have claimed that great disagreement exists between the lists of instincts, or basic motives, presented by various psychologists. This is a curious and astonishing claim. For if care is taken to keep in mind the *mode of classification* employed by each psychologist, these lists can be seen to manifest a far greater degree of *agreement* than of disagreement. This, again, the reader can test, by gathering together several of the lists of basic motives and systematically comparing them.

(2) Though I have attempted to vindicate the views of many of the older psychologists—such as William James, Lloyd Morgan, L. T. Hobhouse, James Drever, and others—I am not satisfied that I have emphasised the value of their work as much as it deserves. I am among those who believe that the line between science and philosophy has been too sharply and naïvely drawn during recent decades, and that—in the study of psychology and sociology in particular—philosophical competence is highly desirable, indeed essential. Most of the earlier psychologists mentioned in Part (1) were possessed of a sound

philosophical background, and a study of their work serves as a healthy corrective to much of the naïve 'scientism' which is a danger at the present time. A particular regret is that it proved necessary to eliminate an extensive section on the work of Hobhouse dealing with his attempt to devise a classification of 'levels of mental development' to serve as a basis for Comparative Psychology and Comparative Sociology. This had to be discarded because it moves too much into the sphere of intelligence and sociological theory, and too far from the study of Instinct proper, which, after all, is our central concern here. For the wider purposes of Comparative Psychology, however, it is of great value. Readers who are interested in this matter will find the most condensed statement of Hobhouse's views in the early chapters of his book *Development and Purpose*.

(3) Since this book covers a wide range of material, and since it aims at synthesis, I have felt it necessary to give quotations from the many authors as evidence of their own points of view. When one is strongly inclined towards synthesis, one tends to interpret the ideas of others all too easily in the direction of one's own inclination, leaving the reader with the difficulty of deciding whether the apparent agreement is really there, or whether it is simply the outcome of the present author's zeal. I have tried, therefore, to make it perfectly clear what the many points of view, in fact, are; and to demonstrate that they do, in fact, supplement each other and contribute to a comprehensive theory.

(4) Finally, I would like to emphasise the importance I have come to attach, after much careful study, to the views of Freud. Much nonsense is talked at the present time to the effect that Freud is 'out of date'. It is very difficult to believe that such critics have studied Freud meticulously. A full study of psycho-analytic theory, and those other theoretical positions which have sprung from it, persuade one that Freud himself remains the most profound and reliable theorist of them all. Freud has a cavalier manner of going about his speculations which is intensely irritating sometimes; but one learns, after much acquaintance with his thinking, that his integrity and his scientific rigour are reliable, and thoroughly to be admired. More than most other writers of the 'depth-psychology' schools, he is always attempting to correlate his own propositions with those parallel propositions which, to the best of his knowledge, are reliably established in the neighbouring sciences of biology and physiology. Neither is Freud so open to criticism from the cultural or sociological point of view as is commonly supposed. The fact is, I think, that the world is full of critics who have never taken pains to read the work they criticise. Many

critics of Freud can never have turned more than a few of his pages. Fashion and polemics again! The serious student, at least, must avoid this kind of position. The person who studies Freud chronologically and systematically will discover (a) that there is a surprising amount which seems outrageous and which he must reject, but (b) that there is an even more surprising amount which, after all his criticism, he must retain. And during this process of working argumentatively through the changing pattern of Freud's ideas, he will find himself equipped, at last, with a mode of interpreting human experience which is the most profound and illuminating in the whole of psychology, and which is most suggestive and useful in the wider context of social theory. In Chapter VI, Freud's views are treated critically, and I have had to concentrate as much as possible on what he has to say about Instinct. Even so, I think that this chapter might prove useful to the reader as an introduction to Freuds' whole system of thought.

ACKNOWLEDGEMENTS

I would like to express my gratitude to Professor Morris Ginsberg, to whom, most of all, I am indebted. I do not know to what extent he is in agreement with all the conclusions of this book, but I count it a great privilege that, throughout the writing of it, I was able to avail myself of his criticism and his advice.

Grateful acknowledgements for the use of certain published material are due, also, to the following authors and publishers:

Dr. N. Tinbergen and the Clarendon Press, Oxford (for three illustrations and quotations from *The Study of Instinct*); Dr. Ernest Jones (for quotations from *Psycho-Analysis and the Instincts*); The Hogarth Press and the Institute of Psycho-Analysis (for quotations from the English translations of Freud's works); Professor Konrad Lorenz, Methuen & Co., and Cambridge University Press (for quotations from *King Solomon's Ring* and *Physiological Mechanisms in Animal Behaviour* respectively); Dr. Rudolf Brun, Benno-Schwabe, Switzerland, and International Universities Press, New York (for quotations from *General Theory of Neurosis*); Dr. W. H. Thorpe and the *Bulletin of Animal Behaviour* (for quotations from 'The Modern Concept of Instinctive Behaviour'); E. A. Armstrong, J. Gray, and Cambridge University Press (for quotations from *Physiological Mechanisms in Animal Behaviour*); J. Bowlby and Blackwell Scientific Publications Ltd., Oxford (for quotations from *Prospects in Psychiatric Research*); G. W. Allport, Holt & Co. New York and Constable & Co. (for quotations from *Personality: A Psychological Interpretation*); E. B. Ford and Watts & Co. (for quotations from *Scientific Thought in the Twentieth Century*); H. Kalmus and Penguin Books Ltd. (for quotations from *Genetics*); A. R. Lindesmith, A. L. Strauss, and the *American Journal of Sociology* (for quotations from *Comparative Psychology and Social Psychology*); William James and Macmillan & Co. (for quotations from *Principles of Psychology*); James Drever and Cambridge University Press (for quotations from *Instinct in Man*); L. T. Hobhouse, Macmillan & Co., and Chapman & Hall (for quotations from *Mind in Evolution* and *Morals in Evolution* respectively); W. McDougall and Methuen & Co. (for quotations from *An Introduction to Social Psychology*); C. Lloyd Morgan and Macmillan & Co. (for quotations from *The Interpretation of Nature*); E. S. Russell and Arnold & Co. (for quotations from *The Behaviour of Animals*); Watts & Co. (for quotations from Thinkers Library editions of Darwin's works); M. Ginsberg and Methuen & Co. (for quotations from *Studies in Sociology*); G. E. Coghill and

14   INSTINCT IN MAN

Cambridge University Press (for quotations from *Anatomy and the Problems of Behaviour*); D. Katz and Longmans, Green (for quotations from *Animals and Men*); L. L. Bernard and Holt & Co., New York (for quotations from *Introduction to Social Psychology*); and Professor Cyril Burt, to whose views, as expressed in the symposium 'Is the Doctrine of Instincts Dead', I have referred at several points.

R. FLETCHER.

Bedford College,
University of London.
November 1956.

CHAPTER I

INTRODUCTION

THE task which we here propose is the re-investigation of the concept of 'Instinct', and the consideration of the extent to which this concept is of use in the study of human experience and behaviour.

Perhaps no concept in Psychology has raised such a long and detailed controversy as has that of Instinct, and, for many, the whole question is a closed book. In American psychological literature in particular the word instinct has been carefully avoided,[1] and terms such as 'need' and 'drive' have superseded it. In view of this widespread tendency to regard instinct as a dead and useless concept, it is necessary to give some preliminary indications as to why it is thought that the concept merits reconsideration, and—as we shall insist—re-instatement in the study of motivation.

1. *The Universe of Discourse of Psychology*

In the first place it must be emphasised that Psychology as a science is concerned not only with the study of human beings. The universe of discourse with which it is concerned is 'the positive study of experience and behaviour', and it involves therefore a study not of man alone but of the experience and behaviour (in so far as this is possible) of all living creatures. In a word, Psychology involves the comparative study of all animal species. It would be considered extremely inadequate if Biology (to mention another, closely related, science) were to concentrate simply upon the study of the human species, and it is clear that the extent of its established knowledge, even with regard to man alone, would be severely restricted if it did so. Yet there is a tendency in psychology, especially in America, to concentrate upon the study of man and the higher mammals which are closely related to him. That the narrowness of this concentration, and its attendant dangers, are beginning to be recognised in America may be seen in an article by A. R. Lindesmith and A. L. Strauss entitled 'Comparative Psychology

---

[1]See, however, 'A Symposium on Heredity and Environment', *Psychological Review*, 1947.

and Social Psychology'[1], in which they claim that this attitude is leading
to a 'return to anthropomorphism'. Quoting Lloyd Morgan's Law of
Parsimony: 'In no case may we interpret an action as the outcome of the
exercise of a higher psychical faculty, if it can be interpreted as the outcome of the exercise of one which stands lower in the psychological scale'[2],
they suggest that the present tendency among psychologists is to accept
just the reverse principle: 'Never interpret the behaviour of lower
animals in terms of relatively simple psychological functions generally
admitted to exist in lower animals, if it is at all possible to interpret behaviour in terms of superficially similar but relatively complex psychological functions generally believed to exist only in man.' This is an over-
statement, but it serves to point out the danger to which they wish to
direct attention. They also quote T. S. Schneirla as saying: '. . . the
true comparative aspects of the science (Psychology) have been progressively minimised the more investigations have been focused upon mamm-
alian subjects and upon problems close to the human level.'

That the recognition of the wider 'universe of discourse' of Psychology, and the value within it of comparative studies, are of importance
can be seen by considering the plain implications of the theory of
evolution. That man has evolved from some pre-human form of life,
that he and the other present-day primates have only recently diverged
from a common primate stock, that the experience and behaviour of man
is similar to that of the higher animals in many respects: all these facts,
which are fairly generally accepted, imply a continuity of animal and
human development.

Darwin tells us: 'It is notorious that man is constructed on the same
general type or model as other mammals. All the bones in his skeleton
can be compared with corresponding bones in a monkey, bat, or seal.
So it is with his muscles, nerves, blood-vessels, and internal viscera. The
brain, the most important of all the organs, follows the same law . . .
Bischoff, who is a hostile witness, admits that every chief fissure and fold
in the brain of man has its analogy in that of the orang. . . .'[3]

Similarly, with regard to the *experience* of man and animals, Darwin
says: '. . . man and the higher animals, especially the primates, have
some few instincts in common. All have the same senses, intuitions, and
sensations, similar passions, affections, and emotions, even the more
complex ones, such as jealousy, suspicion, emulation, gratitude, and
magnanimity; they practise deceit and are revengeful; they are sometimes susceptible to ridicule, and even have a sense of humour; they feel

[1] *American Journal of Sociology* (November, 1952).
[2] C. Lloyd-Morgan, *Introduction to Comparative Psychology*, p. 59.
[3] Charles Darwin, *The Descent of Man*, p. 5.

wonder and curiosity; they possess the same faculties of imitation, attention, deliberation, choice, memory, imagination, the association of
ideas, and reason though in very different degrees.'[1]

It may be considered that this passage is saturated with anthropomorphism, but *The Descent of Man* and *The Expression of the Emotions
in Man and Animals* are filled with empirical observations which Darwin
offers in support of his contention. The theory of evolution, therefore,
suggests the probability that a knowledge of animal processes—of experience and behaviour as well as of structure and physiology—would
throw light upon human experience and behaviour.

There is, however, one point which we should note in accepting the
suggestions arising from the theory of evolution. If the doctrine of
Emergent Evolution is right, we must take care not to adopt too naïve a
notion of the 'continuity' of development between species. This doctrine
suggests that new mutations may bring into being a species which is
qualitatively different both from other species and from the species from
which it is derived. If this is so, then it may be incorrect to attempt to
reduce our account of any such emergent level to the explanatory terms
which are adequate for the levels below or above it. We have, therefore,
a notion of 'levels' of development, each of which may manifest qualitatively unique features and which may require an account different
from the explanations we can give of other levels. This theory was
stressed in particular by Lloyd Morgan, and we find it re-emphasised in
the altogether 'warning' article by Lindesmith and Strauss which we
have previously mentioned. Again, they quote Schneirla: 'The principle
of levels has come into current usage through a recognition of important
differences in the complexity, the degree of development, and the inter-
dependent organisation of behavioural functions through the animal
series. The evidently superior properties that appear on a new level of
organization are . . . functional properties arising from a new system of
organization which differs in given ways from "lower" and "higher"
systems.' This point does not affect what we have said about the importance of comparative studies, nor does it lead us to doubt the theory
of evolution. It merely warns us not to regard the 'continuity' of the
evolutionary process in too naïve a way. With this point in mind we can
still have confidence (because of what is already known about related
species) in the probability that a knowledge of animal processes will
throw light upon human experience and behaviour, though we must
always treat the comparative studies of different species with great care.

It is this comparative study of animal experience and behaviour and
the implications of the theory of evolution which provide our first reason

[1] *The Descent of Man*, p. 87.

for maintaining that the concept of instinct is indispensable in comparative psychology. 'By far the greater part of the behaviour of animals',
E. S. Russell tells us, 'falls into the category of instinctive action; only in
the higher vertebrates does adaptive or intelligent behaviour play any
great role.'[1] In studies ranging from the simplest to the most complicated
animal organisms, we are confronted by patterns of behaviour, often
amazing in their intricacy and in their apparent purposiveness, which,
whilst being well-adapted to the satisfaction of the needs of the organism
in its particular environment, and with regard to the several situations
which it encounters in this environment, can be performed without any
previous experience of this environment and of these situations. Such
behaviour appears, in many cases, to be so perfect on its first appearance,
that many observers have felt themselves compelled to regard it as
evidence of the divine purpose in nature.[2] The degree of rigidity or
plasticity of this behaviour varies from the lower to the higher species in
the evolutionary scale; the criterion of 'lower' and 'higher' being here
simply the degree of complexity of organisation. Thus, among the
insects, such behaviour is not greatly modified throughout the life
history of the individual, nor is it capable of any great degree of modification. In the higher vertebrates, however, behaviour can be modified
during the course of individual experience, though it is by no means
altogether plastic; and in man, behaviour is so variable as to have persuaded some observers that it involves no instinctive elements at all.

With regard to this question of the varying degrees of modifiability
of behaviour, we must mention an important point which is stressed by
Darwin, William James, and L. T. Hobhouse. Hobhouse makes it clear
that instinct and intelligence cannot be regarded as two separate and
mutually exclusive features. The *presence* of intelligence (which we might
call provisionally the capacity to vary responses effectively when faced
by unusual situations) does not by any means imply the *absence* of instinctive experience and behaviour, nor does it imply that the latter is
completely supplanted or overruled. Coupled with this observation, we
must note the point made by both Darwin and William James: namely,
that *there is no inverse ratio between instinct and intelligence.* Darwin
points out that, among the insects, those which possess 'the most

[1] E. S. Russell, *The Behaviour of Animals*, Chapter V, p. 90.
[2] In this connection, we might quote an interesting illustration from *Masterman Ready*
by Captain Marryat which is mentioned by Hobhouse in *Mind in Evolution*: 'Instinct in
animals, William', continued Mr. Seagrave, 'is a feeling which compels them to perform
certain acts without previous thought or reflection; this instinct is in full force at the moment
of their birth; it is the guidance of the Almighty's hand unseen; it was therefore perfect in
the beginning, and has never varied. The swallow built her nest, the spider its web, the bee
formed its comb, precisely in the same way four thousand years ago as they do now.'

wonderful instincts are certainly the most intelligent'.[1] William James makes the same point and goes on to maintain that man has, in fact, *more* instinctive tendencies than any other species.[2] This latter assertion is dubious and obviously requires qualification, but, whether it is true or not, we must recognise the value of the underlying point which is made. It does *not* follow from the fact that we find *intelligence* in an animal, or a species, that there is an *absence* of *instinctive* elements. This is a point of importance.

However, since we are maintaining that the concept of instinct is indispensable in the comparative study of experience and behaviour, let us give one or two examples of the kind of behaviour with which we are confronted.

The larva of the Capricorn Beetle, which, Fabre tells us, is as unimpressive in appearance as a 'bit of intestine', burrows into the trunk of an oak tree when it is as slim as 'a tiny bit of straw'. For three years it burrows its way through the inner depths of the tree, gradually increasing in size to the thickness of a man's finger. By ingenious experiments, Fabre has studied the details of this creature's behaviour until it finally emerges as a fully developed beetle.[3] Throughout this period, the creature eats its way through the oak, the wood passing through its body into the tunnel behind; and it is in contact with no other creature, even of its own kind. But what happens at the end of this period? Fabre was able to prove that the fully developed beetle could not, by its own efforts, escape from the tree when only three-quarters of an inch of wood separated it from the outside. Concluding that the larva itself must in some way prepare for the exit of the fully developed beetle, Fabre then studied the preparations for the pupa stage. Though it has never ventured near the outside of the tree before, the larva now makes its way to the bark. Sometimes it burrows through the bark and leaves an opening, but more often it leaves a very thin film of the bark unbroken. Then it retreats some distance down its tunnel and hollows out, in the side of this, a large chamber. This chamber, it must be noted, is not a closely-fitting one, adapted to the *present* size of the larva, but is sufficiently large to accommodate the developed beetle and to give some room for the action of its legs. The larva then constructs a cover, or door, to the entrance of the chamber. A pile of woody refuse is left outside, and inside the larva prepares a concave cover of chalky white substance which consists of carbonate of lime and an organic cement, and is disgorged from the stomach. When this door is completed, the larva proceeds to rasp the sides of the now sealed-off chamber, covering the floor

[1] *The Descent of Man.*   [2] *Principles of Psychology.*
[3] See J. H. Fabre, *The Wonders of Instinct*, Chapter IV.

with a soft down, or wood-wool, formed by the minute shreds of wood. This down is then applied to the walls, forming a continuous felt at least a millimetre thick. When this task is finished, the larva sheds its skin and becomes a pupa, and its position is always such that its head is pointing towards the door of the chamber. This position is itself important, since the mature beetle has a stiff horny structure and could not possibly turn round in the chamber if by any chance the larva had taken up the wrong or reverse position. When the beetle is ready to leave the tree, it has before it only the white concave cover which can easily be pushed aside, and a pile of loose refuse. The spacious passage before it leads it, without chance of mistake, to the exit, where it has, at most, only the very flimsiest film of bark to gnaw through.

Here, performed by a creature which looks no more than a 'bit of intestine', is an example of intricate behaviour which appears to be pregnant with foresight for the later stages of its own development, but which cannot possibly be learned from others, since it has been in contact with none! How are we to account for such behaviour?

A second example of such apparently purposive behaviour can be seen in the reproductive behaviour of a more complicated organism: the three-spined stickleback.

From the moment of hatching until the manifestation of reproductive behaviour, the stickleback has associated only with the young of its own age and with its father, and after becoming independent it has only seen individuals in neutral condition, either males or non-pregnant females. In the spring, the increase in the length of day brings the male stickleback into a condition of reproductive motivation. This drives it to migrate into shallow fresh water and to undertake a kind of random, searching, exploratory behaviour. Within a certain territory a nest is constructed which is more or less tubular and built in a depression of the sandy bottom with bits and pieces of stems, roots, and leaves. The underside of the male's body now has a vivid red colouration. Any other male who enters his territory is driven off, with specific fighting movements. When a female, with swollen abdomen and an upward-tilted posture is seen, the male swims towards her in a zig-zag fashion. Then he swims away from her in the direction of his nest. If the female follows him he swims down to his nest and points inside it with his nose, whereupon the female goes inside. The male then performs a quivering motion, prodding the abdomen of the female with his nose, and, as a result of this action, the female spawns. The male fertilises the eggs and thereafter takes care of them, performing periodical fanning motions with his fins which keep the eggs adequately supplied with oxygen.

This is a simple description of the stickleback's reproductive behaviour. A more detailed account will be given later, when we consider N. Tinbergen's experimental work.[1] Even this, however, is sufficient to indicate the apparently purposive nature of this behaviour, which is common to all male sticklebacks, which is admirably adapted to the needs of the stickleback and its young, but which is *not learned*.

Innumerable instances of such complicated behavioural processes—which cannot possibly be learned—could be quoted.

It seems absolutely necessary, then, that we should employ, here, the concept of instinct, and, in order that the observed facts of such behaviour should be fully covered, the concept must include at least the following elements. Instinctive experience and behaviour must involve some *internal condition* disposing the organism to react to specific objects in the environment. This 'selectivity' of response can be accounted for only if some *specific perception* is appropriate to particular responses, having the effect of directing the attention and activity of the organism. In the absence of learning, these internal conditions and these appropriate perceptions must be considered *innate*. When there has been no possibility of learning the appropriate motor-responses, we must also assume an *innate and specific pattern of behaviour*. This complex of closely related features of experience and behaviour is also seen to be *common to members of a species*, at least of the same sex.

These criteria of instinctive experience and behaviour are not intended at this stage to be exhaustive. They are simply *some* of the criteria which seem to be necessary. It will be noted, for example, that no mention has yet been made of the question of emotion and its place in instinct-experience, and this is a question of some difficulty which will be discussed later.

We have seen, however, that the concept of instinct, embracing at least the several criteria we have mentioned, is essential to give even the most rudimentary account of much of the observed behaviour of animals. Since this concept is indispensable for the study of such a wide range of animal species, it would seem unwise to reject it from the outset in our study of human experience and behaviour. The implications of evolutionary theory lead us to suppose that it is at least probable that we should find some elements of instinctive experience and behaviour in man. It is hardly likely that, of all the species in existence, man alone is born with no such instinctual heritage. The best procedure would seem to be to utilise this concept which is so necessary in our study of the rest of the animal world, and then, if it should prove to be of little use in the

[1]See pp. 132-134 ; also *The Study of Instinct* by N. Tinbergen.

study of man, to reject it. This would seem better than to reject it on the *a priori* grounds that man's behaviour is so plastic and complicated that the doctrine of instincts cannot possibly apply. It might be pointed out that the complex activity of insects—say a society of ants or bees— appears to be wonderfully purposive and intelligent at first sight. But detailed study shows that this is not the case. The intelligence which actually takes place is infinitely less than appears on the surface.

2. *Needs, Drives, and Reflexes are Components, or Features, of Instinctive Experience and Behaviour as a whole*

A second reason why it would seem better to retain the concept of instinct rather than to supersede it by 'need', 'drive', or 'reflex' and 'chain-reflex', is that these latter elements are only components of instinctive experience and behaviour as a whole. An organism is born into a fairly specific environment (what the biologist calls its 'habitat' or its 'ecological niche') with particular needs which are to some extent peculiar to its own species. The internal conditions and experience of these needs drive the organism to react to specific objects in the environment, and the organism inherits certain anatomical structures with their 'functional correlates' or behavioural reactions which are employed in the activity necessary for the satisfaction of these needs. In any instinctive action, all these features of experience and behaviour are closely correlated in one process of behaviour which, whilst being well-adapted to the environmental situation, is not learned. It is true that, in conceptual analysis, we can dissect any such instinctive activity into 'need', 'drive', 'behaviour-pattern', 'reflexes', and other components. But it is hard to see what can be gained by substituting any one of these components for the concept of instinct as a whole. It might be said, for example, that a certain organism has a sexual need. But it is clear that such a statement would tell us nothing about the other closely related experiential and behavioural features which, in the case of most animal species, always, in fact, accompany the satisfaction of this need.

It would seem to be the best procedure, then, to retain the concept of instinct—implying the innately established relationship of these various features in one unlearned experiential and behavioural process. In the study of man, we may well find that some of the features of instinctive experience and behaviour permit of a high degree of modification, whilst others may not be so modifiable. Thus, we shall probably find, as McDougall suggests, that the *perception* involved in some instinctual experience may, as an outcome of the many associations arising during the course of individual experience, be considerably broadened and modified; or that the *overt behavioural reactions* may change and vary with experience and learning. But this will emerge as our study proceeds. At the outset, however, we cannot *presuppose* that the nature of man, as distinct from the rest of the animals, does *not* involve elements of instinctive experience and behaviour, and, since the concept of instinct is applicable to such a comprehensive degree in the study of the animal world, we must not reject it in the study of man until we find that it is of little use in that connection.

3. *Instincts and Learning Processes*

A third reason which seems to support the retention of the concept of instinct is that the processes of learning in the individual may be very closely connected with, and directed and influenced by, the instincts. Our reasons for supposing this will be discussed in detail later, but it is clear from the outset that all learning is, in fact, a modification of innate endowment, and consequently a knowledge of the innate endowment of any given species is a necessary pre-requisite for any knowledge of the nature and extent of its learning processes. For some time there has been a tendency for the study of motivation and the study of learning to drift apart—to such an extent that, nowadays, they are almost considered separately.[1] This separation is of doubtful value, and we shall suggest later than the *affective* elements of experience are of fundamental importance for the learning processes, and that a good many of our conceptual distinctions between the 'perceptual', 'cognitive', and 'affective' aspects of experience require a good deal of re-thinking. Most of the experimental work on Learning can be seen to involve motivational factors—as, for example, rewards and punishments in Trial and Error Learning, or the setting of a goal in order to observe elements of 'Insight' which might arise during the efforts to attain it. Similarly, a study of instinct must soon encounter the necessity of noting the modifications of the initial behaviour-patterns which are subsequently shown.[2] The recent work in Comparative Ethology indicates, as we shall see, that learning processes are often very closely related to the instincts. We shall also suggest that the Psycho-Analytic account of instinct in man has a great deal of importance to say in this connection.

At this point, however, we may at least suppose that much learning takes place in close relation to the efforts, on the part of the individual, to secure the satisfactory performance of the instincts, and this probability seems to justify an investigation of the nature and number of the instinctual processes at work and their relation to the nature and direction of the learning processes.

[1]The recent book 'Learning and Instinct in Animals' by Dr. W. H. Thorpe is a notable exception to this.

[2]If only for the purpose of distinguishing between 'innate, unlearned', and 'acquired, learned', components of behaviour.

4. *Instincts and Social Behaviour*

A fourth reason why it seems preferable to retain the concept of instinct is the possibility that a knowledge of the instinctive tendencies in man, and of closely related learning processes, may be of use in the explanation of human social behaviour. Here, again, the concepts of 'need' and 'drive' might leave out many features of importance. We could say that men have the need for political security, but this would not be sufficient to tell us why, for example, children tend to follow the political views of their parents, or why masses of people can be emotionally swayed by some often-presented political symbol such as a flag, a national anthem, or the huge portrait of a political leader. It may be, however, that a knowledge of the instinctual tendencies in man, and especially of the ways in which they affect closely related learning processes, would be of some help in this direction. This is not to say that a knowledge of the instinctive processes in man could ever be expected to provide a *complete* account of social behaviour. It is clear that many other sociological factors would have to be taken into account for this. But it seems likely that an inquiry into the nature of instinctual experience in man would serve to throw at least some light on social behaviour, whereas a mere statement of needs or drives would leave much of importance out of the picture.

This point may be better emphasised if we think of Freud's treatment of 'The Instincts and their Vicissitudes'. For Freud maintains not only that powerful instincts exist in man, but also that the vicissitudes which they undergo in relation to necessitous features of the physical and cultural environment result in certain fairly well-defined 'mental-mechanisms', which are not themselves learned since they are largely unconscious processes, but which can be regarded as modes of adaptation to the demands of the environment and which are said to be common to human beings owing to the very nature of their instinctual endowment and the similarity of the conflicts which they must meet. Thus, Freud postulates such 'mechanisms' as 'displacement', 'identification', 'introjection', 'symbolisation', 'condensation', 'sublimation', and so on. This view, it is clear, has a very important bearing on the relation between the instincts and the learning processes, and if Freud is right in postulating certain instincts and such closely related mechanisms of adjustment to stress, this knowledge will be of much greater value for the explanation of social behaviour than would a list of needs or drives which failed to take them into account.

5. *Recent Work in Comparative Ethology*

A fifth reason for reconsidering the concept of instinct is that (from about the early 1930s) there has been a striking amount of new experimental work in the study of animal behaviour with particular reference to the investigation of instinct. In this work the concept of instinct has been firmly established and has been given, at last, what has been called 'scientific respectability'. Part of our discussion will consist of a review of this work, and an attempt to assimilate it into the older body of work on instinct.

6. *Instincts in Psycho-Analysis*

A final preliminary reason to support our reconsideration of the concept of instinct is the fact that a theory of the instincts plays a very important part in psycho-analytic theory, and both Freud and Ernest Jones continually assert in their writings the great importance of the subject for Psychology. The theory of instincts in Psycho-Analysis has remained in a peculiar isolation from the theoretical writings on instinct of the other psychologists. This may have been due to some element of antagonism towards Psycho-Analysis; or to the fact that the Psycho-Analytic theory emerged from the study of abnormal cases and clinical observations; or, possibly, because the terminology of Psycho-Analysis is so strikingly different from that of the other schools of Psychology, thereby making any blending of the two spheres of work appear very difficult. On the other hand, it may have been due to Freud's sheer lack of attention to findings in Comparative Psychology. Whatever the reason may be, it remains true that there is a curious gap between instincts as discussed by Freud, and instincts as discussed by the other instinct-theorists. Another part of our discussion, therefore, will consist of a critical account of the theory of the instincts in Psycho-Analysis, and an attempt to consider it in relation to both the earlier views on instinct and the recent views arising from the work in Comparative Ethology.

7. *Summary of the Task Proposed*

The last full-scale discussion of the place and value of the concept of Instinct in Man was that undertaken by Professor James Drever in his book of that name, and this was a thorough-going psychological account of instinct. Drever tells us that it had been his original intention to include a consideration of the writings of Freud and Jung, but that he had later decided not to do so. In a paper written later, on 'The Classification of Instincts' (1924), he makes the following remarks: 'In reviewing the older classifications at the present time, there are two main groups of facts or considerations to be kept in view. The one group comprises the facts revealed by the various methods of modern psycho-pathology, especially the methods of Freud and his school; the other group is related to the development of biological research, and the results achieved. These facts and considerations must be kept in view, but it by no means follows that the principles underlying the older classifications must in all cases be entirely set aside.'

These remarks summarise admirably the task we propose. On the one hand we shall review the findings of the recent studies in Comparative Ethology. On the other hand we shall do our best to assess the findings of Psycho-Analysis. But, like Drever, we shall adopt the view that much that was put forward in the older discussions of instinct remains of value.

PART ONE

———————————— ————————

THE EARLIER VIEWS
ON INSTINCT

CHAPTER II

THE EARLY 'DOCTRINE OF INSTINCTS'

Our object in this chapter and the next is twofold: (1) to elucidate the chief criteria of instinct, and other general points, on which there was substantial agreement among the earlier writers; (2) to enumerate exhaustively the criticisms of this early 'doctrine of instincts', and to see to what extent these criticisms have been met. This will enable us to frame a clear statement of the early 'doctrine of instincts'. With this statement clearly in mind, we shall be in a much better position to discuss the recent work in Ethology and the account of instinct given in Psycho-Analysis.

1. *The Earlier Writers*

(1) *Charles Darwin*. The study of instinct can be traced far back into the history of thought, as James Drever in particular has shown, but we are justified in regarding the work of Darwin as the most important turning-point in the history of the subject.[1]

In *The Origin of Species*, Darwin devotes a whole chapter to Instinct, not with the aim of giving a full account of instinct, but in order to show that the facts of instinct do not stand in the way of the theory of natural selection, but rather tend to support it. Thus, he claims that the instincts of a species, as well as the characteristic physical structure of a species, come into being as a result of 'numerous, slight, spontaneous variations' (what we would now term 'mutations') and the effects of natural selection.

Though he does not attempt a definition of instinct, some of his remarks approach such a definition. 'An action, which we ourselves require experience to enable us to perform, when performed by an animal, more especially by a very young one, without experience, and

---

[1]Perhaps Herbert Spencer's view of instinct as a 'compound reflex' also deserves treatment here. But our aim is not to be historically exhaustive. For the purpose of clarifying the earlier views on instinct, reference to the work of Darwin and that of a few subsequent writers is adequate.

when performed by many individuals in the same way, without their knowing for what purpose it is performed, is usually said to be instinctive.'

Darwin, however, is very quick to qualify this remark. 'But I could show', he says, 'that none of these characters are universal.' Firstly, he points out that learning and intelligence often accompany instinctive behaviour. In his own words: 'A little dose of judgment or reason . . . often comes into play, even with animals low in the scale of nature.' Secondly, he maintains that instincts are not absolutely invariable in the members of a species, but that they vary among individuals. And thirdly, he points out that instincts are not necessarily perfect in their function of adapting the creature to its environment, but that their blindness and rigidity often result in mistakes.

Darwin's importance lies not so much in what he himself said about instinct, but in the widespread influence of his theory of variations and natural selection upon the later study of instinct. For it cannot be too often emphasised that all the subsequent accounts of instinct were undertaken with this evolutionary hypothesis in mind, and can be understood only in the context of the evolutionary process.[1]

We see here, then, the first main point on which all the post-Darwinian writers on instinct were agreed: namely, that the instinctive experience and behaviour of any particular species is (like the physical structure peculiar to the species) an outcome of the evolutionary process; is determined, that is to say, mainly by spontaneous variations and the operation of natural selection. With this commonly agreed context of the evolutionary process in mind, we can turn to the accounts of instinct presented by certain of the writers who developed the suggestions of Darwin.

(2) *William James*. In *The Principles of Psychology*, published in 1890, William James defines instinct as: 'the faculty of acting in such a way as to produce certain ends, without foresight of the ends, and without previous education in the performance.' He adds: 'Instincts are the functional correlatives of structure. With the presence of a certain organ goes, one may say, almost always a native aptitude for its use.'

Other features of instinctive behaviour are indicated in his subsequent remarks. With regard to the underlying *neuro-physiological organisation*, he says: 'the nervous system is to a great extent a preorganized bundle of such (instinctive) reactions—they are as fatal as sneezing, and as exactly correlated to their special excitants as it is to its own.' With

[1]It might be noted that *all* the writers we shall consider in this chapter refer, at some point, to the work of Darwin.

regard to the *perceptual feature* of instinctive reactions, James tells us that: 'in the animal it is a particular sensation or perception or image which calls them forth.'

James is more inclined to a 'mechanistic' account of instinctive behaviour than are the other writers we shall consider. 'The actions we call instinctive all conform to the general reflex type; they are called forth by determinate sensory stimuli in contact with the animal's body, or at a distance in his environment.' Nevertheless, this mechanistic approach seems to be modified in his subsequent treatment, though it is never explicitly changed. Later, for example, James appears to accept a threefold classification of the movements of infants: into impulsive, reflex, and instinctive—which would seem to imply some necessary difference between reflex and instinctive actions. As a matter of fact, James is rather loose in his use of these terms, at some points in his argument using the word 'impulse' as being almost synonymous with that of 'instinct', whilst at other times he obviously regards the 'impulse' as one feature only of the 'instinct' as a whole. His assertion, for example, that man has more instincts than any other animal seems to rest really on his conviction that man has more 'impulses' than any other animal.

However, that James' treatment is not so mechanistic as his explicit statements would lead us to suppose can be seen when he makes the point that instincts are not always blind or invariable. 'Every instinctive act, in an animal *with memory,*[1] must cease to be "blind" after being once repeated, and must be accompanied with foresight of its "end" just so far as that end may have fallen under the animal's cognizance.'

Two points may be noted here.

Firstly, James introduces into his account of instinct-experience not only an element of perception or sensation, but also an element of *cognition.* This is an important point, suggesting that one innate feature of instinctive *experience* is that of a primary awareness of the *significance* of a certain perception, or of a certain object, with regard to the inner tension experienced by the organism at that time. It is this cognitive element, this primary awareness of the significance of some object in the environment, which, together with subsequent experience and memory, makes possible the gradual acquisition of a foresight of ends, and of an awareness of the relevance of certain actions as the means of achieving these ends. We shall see that this element is dealt with by later writers under the heading of 'instinct-meaning' or 'instinct-interest', and that it is a point of great importance for any psychological account of instinct.

The second point of importance which James makes here is that,

[1]Our emphasis.

though the first performance of an instinct has had no previous experience to guide it, there may be an element of learning even in this first performance which may be gradually, or quickly, developed with further repetitions of the experience. Two points are really implicit in this. The first is that, given an innate cognitive element, the learning process may be very closely and significantly related to the earliest performances of an instinct.[1] The second point is simply that the instincts of an animal may permit of modification by learning from the very outset. James is careful to make it clear, however, that this point does not necessarily apply to all creatures. 'An insect that lays her eggs in a place where she never sees them hatched must always do so "blindly"; but a hen who has already hatched a brood can hardly be assumed to sit with perfect "blindness" on her second nest. Some expectation of consequences must in every case like this be aroused; and this expectation, *according as it is that of something desired or of something disliked*, must necessarily either reinforce or inhibit the mere impulse.' The attention we have drawn to the 'expectations of something desired or of something disliked' in this last quotation, indicates another point of importance which James introduces implicitly here: namely, that the *affective* aspects of experience are of the utmost importance in the learning processes. But this point we must merely indicate here, postponing a full discussion until later.

Concluding on this point, James says: 'No matter how well endowed an animal may originally be in the way of instincts, his resultant actions will be much modified if the instincts combine with experience, if in addition to impulses he have memories, associations, inferences, and expectations, on any considerable scale.'

We must restrict ourselves now to only three of the further observations made by James.

The first point is that the instinctive tendencies in an animal can be in conflict with each other, thus giving the *impression* of intelligence. Thus a hungry bird may simultaneously be impelled to peck at grain in the farmyard and to 'freeze' or seek shelter at the sight of a bird of prey overhead. The creature exhibiting such conflicting instinctive tendencies: 'loses the instinctive *demeanour* and *appears* to lead a life of hesitation and choice . . . not, however, because he has no instincts—rather because he has so many that they block each other's path.' James applies this point to man, who, he says, compared with the animals, 'possesses all the impulses that they have, and a great many more besides'. Reason, according to James, cannot inhibit any particular impulse, but it may make inferences which excite the imagination and release impulses acting in the opposite way, and thus, he concludes: 'though the animal

[1]See p. 147, 'The Learning Processes'.

richest in reason is also the animal richest in instinctive impulses too, he never seems the fatal automaton which a *merely* instinctive animal must be.'

The last two points we shall consider are those which William James calls the 'Two Principles of Non-Uniformity', and he gives them this name because he believes that it is by these two principles that instincts may be *masked* in the life of the mature animal.

The first is the 'law of inhibition of instincts by habits'. 'When objects of a certain class elicit from an animal a certain sort of reaction, it often happens that the animal becomes partial to the first specimen of the class on which it has reacted, and will not afterward react on any other specimen.'

This might be regarded as a special case of what James has already spoken of as a learning process which is closely related to the earliest performances of the instinct. What James has in mind mainly when making this point, however, is that once an instinctive reaction has resulted, say, in the selection of one particular mate, or the construction of one particular 'home', this selection tends to narrow the range of the instinctive activity to these selected objects. 'Each of these preferences carries with it an insensibility to *other* opportunities and occasions—an insensibility which can only be described physiologically as an inhibition of new impulses by the habit of old ones already formed.' Or, again, 'a habit, once grafted on an instinctive tendency, restricts the range of the tendency itself, and keeps us from reacting on any but the habitual object, although other objects might just as well have been chosen had they been the first-comers'. We might note here that James regards both instinctive activity and habit as possessing a similar degree of rigidity; that he thinks they are often closely and significantly related; and that habit in a sense moulds or determines the direction of the subsequent instinctive activity of the organism, and tends to render the organism insensitive to other objects in the environment which, originally, would have been equally likely to call forth its instinctive activity. In this account of the habituation of an organism to a particular object of instinctive activity we can see a simple version of what McDougall later describes as the formation of 'sentiments'.

The second 'Principle of Non-Uniformity' which James puts forward is the 'Law of Transitoriness'. 'Many instincts ripen at a certain stage and then fade away.' This law, James tells us, does not apply to all instincts. Thus, hunger persists throughout the individual's lifetime. The example which he gives to illustrate this 'law' is that of sucking in young mammals, which is ripe at birth and leads to the habit of taking the breast, but which, with weaning, disappears.

We may take this point as an indication of the fact that instincts emerge with the growth and maturation of the individual, and that when instincts are said to be innate or inherited this does not mean, by any means, that they are all held to exist, as a given 'set' of instincts, manifested at birth. Certain instincts will be of greater importance at certain stages of development, and may not be so important at either earlier or later stages. They may, indeed, as James says, 'fade away' at a later age. And here, James makes another point of importance in connection with this 'transitoriness' of the instincts.

He suggests that these periods of importance of certain instinctive tendencies imply certain 'periods of importance' for learning, and that a knowledge of such periods is of great value and importance to the educator. 'If, during the time of such an instinct's vivacity, objects adequate to arouse it are met with, a *habit* of acting on them is formed, which remains when the original instinct has passed away; but if no such objects are met with, then no habit will be formed; and, later on in life, when the animal meets the objects, he will altogether fail to react, as at the earlier epoch he would instinctively have done.' This point is mentioned since it is particularly apt in view of the 'Critical Period Hypothesis' which has arisen from the recent ethological work and which we shall discuss in detail later.[1] It is of interest to note how James treats this question when speaking of the life of human beings. Having enumerated the instincts in man, he goes on to say:

'In a perfectly-rounded development every one of these instincts would start a habit toward certain objects and inhibit a habit towards certain others. Usually this is the case; but, in the one-sided development of civilised life, it happens that the timely age goes by in a sort of starvation of objects, and the individual then grows up with gaps in his psychic constitution which future experience can never fill. Compare the accomplished gentleman with the poor artisan or tradesman of a city: during the adolescence of the former, objects appropriate to his growing interests, bodily and mental, were offered as fast as the interests awoke, and, as a consequence, he is armed and equipped at every angle to meet the world. Sport came to the rescue and completed his education where real things were lacking. He has tasted of the essence of every side of human life, being sailor, hunter, athlete, scholar, fighter, talker, dandy, man of affairs, etc., all in one. Over the city poor boy's youth no such golden opportunities were hung, and in his manhood no desires for most of them exist. Fortunate it is for him if gaps are the only anomalies his instinctive life presents; perversions are too often the fruit of his unnatural upbringing.'

[1]See p. 149, 'The Critical Period Hypothesis'.

(3) *C. Lloyd Morgan*. Lloyd Morgan defines instinctive behaviour as: 'comprising those complex groups of co-ordinated acts, which, though they contribute to experience, are, on their first occurrence, not determined by individual experience: which are adaptive and tend to the well-being of the individual and the preservation of the race; which are due to the co-operation of external and internal stimuli; which are similarly performed by all members of the same more or less restricted group of animals; but which are subject to variation, and to subsequent modification under the guidance of individual experience.'

This definition contains the basic features mentioned by both Darwin and William James. It is, however, largely a biological definition, the psychological points being implicit rather than explicit. Nonetheless, three psychological points are in evidence: (1) that instinctive *experience* is spontaneous and unlearned, (2) that its arousal is dependent partly upon internal factors and partly upon 'external stimuli'—which implies some inner condition disposing the organism to react to certain 'appropriate perceptions', and (3) that instinctive experience and behaviour permit of modification during the course of, and in the light of, individual experience.

This mixture of both a biological and a psychological definition of instinct raises a point which Lloyd Morgan considers to be of importance. He explicitly maintains, throughout his work, that Comparative Psychology, and particularly 'Genetic Psychology' which traces the origin and growth of experience and behaviour, must, of necessity, adopt a 'hybrid universe of discourse'. Firstly, the attempt to trace any continuity of experience and behaviour between parent and offspring inevitably involves the bridge of gene-transmission in reproduction, which can be stated only in bio-physiological terms. Secondly, even in the study of the individual there are, on the one hand, the behavioural responses to various features of the environment and the physiological processes of the organism which are involved, and, on the other hand, the essentially psychological (i.e. experiential) features of such behavioural and physiological processes: perception, cognition, conation, emotion, and the like. Ideally, Lloyd Morgan suggests, these require independent accounts, and, strictly speaking, constitute two 'universes of discourse': the bio-physiological and the psychological. The question of any *causal* relations between the two is an extremely difficult one, and therefore the best approach is that of regarding the one set of phenomena as being *closely correlated* with, or as being *concomitants* of, the other. Thus, when giving a *psychological* account of instinct-*experience*, we can correctly speak of the *physiological concomitants* of this experience, thereby denoting those physiological processes which are found to be highly correlated with these particular features of experience, without committing ourselves to any strictly causal statement. This position, it seems, is one which we must still hold, though we shall comment on it later.

Lloyd Morgan was subsequently criticised, especially by Drever, with regard to this point, but Drever's criticism was not that such a notion of 'concomitancy' was untenable (indeed he agrees that this notion is the expedient and correct one), but that Lloyd Morgan, in adopting this idea of a hybrid universe of discourse, often confused the two aspects in his treatment, speaking confusingly of psychological features in bio-physiological terms and vice versa. To give an example: we find Lloyd Morgan distinguishing between instinct and intelligence in the following way. Instinctive behaviour 'is dependent entirely on how the nervous system has been built up through heredity, under the mode of racial preparation which we call evolution'. Intelligent behaviour is partly dependent on the way in which the nervous system has been built up through heredity, but 'depends also on how the nervous system has been modified and moulded in the course of that individual preparation, which we call the acquisition of experience'. These statements, of course, could be defended, but Drever's point, which must be conceded, is that the statements are couched in essentially physiological terms though referring, especially in the second case, to psychological (experiential) features. To restrict ourselves to the statement on intelligence, it is true, as Drever points out, that: 'It would include under intelligent behaviour the most unintelligent and unconsciously formed habits, like habits of speech and gesture. On the other hand it is very doubtful how far we can regard what is essentially intelligent in intelligent behaviour as due to the acquisition of experience.' Apart from such inconsistencies in his detailed treatment, however, Lloyd Morgan's insistence upon the recognition of a 'hybrid universe of discourse' in psychology, and upon the notion of 'concomitancy', seems to be well-founded.

We must restrict ourselves now to a consideration of three other features of Lloyd Morgan's treatment which are particularly noteworthy: (1) his conception of 'the primary tissue of experience', (2) his conception of 'instinct-meaning', and (3) his distinction, within the sphere of intelligence, between intelligent control on the perceptual plane, and intelligent control on the conceptual and ideational plane.

Lloyd Morgan holds that the instinctive tendencies of an individual are the outcome of the evolutionary process of the species, and arise spontaneously in the individual's own life history as initial unlearned contributions to 'behaviour-experience'. Illustrating this by reference to a moor-hen which is startled by the appearance of a puppy at the pondside, causing it to dive (though it has never experienced this reaction before, and has never had any opportunity of learning it), he suggests that the new factors comprised by this instinctive reaction, performed for the first time, are as follows: (1) There is a specific presentation (clearly implying a specific perception) differing from previous presentations. (2) There is a new response, affording new data to 'behaviour-experience'. And (3) there is a hitherto unfelt quality of emotional tone. These factors are: 'all coalescent into one felt situation.' And this new instinct-experience constitutes an element of the 'primary tissue of experience'.[1] Elsewhere,[2] in making the same point, Lloyd Morgan indicates his view on the place of consciousness in instinct. Stating again that the instinct depends wholly on how 'the automatic centres have been built up through heredity' and that its initial occurrence in the individual is independent of previous experience, he says: 'But the automatic centres are in closest possible touch with the differentiated control system which is the organ of experience. And the performance of an instinctive act so stimulates the centres of intelligent control as to afford the primary data of experience. In this sense, instinctive behaviour is probably accompanied by vivid consciousness.' The great importance to genetic psychology of the study of instinct, Lloyd Morgan thinks, is this fact: that an instinctive situation is presented to the individual consciousness as a 'primary unit-complex of experience' which is independent of any guidance in terms of the individual's own experience. We have seen above the factors which he thinks are involved in this 'primary unit-complex'. 'Psychologists', he says, 'analyse the instinctive situation. But I conceive that it is presented to consciousness as one developing whole. And the mode of its development is an organic legacy; it is essentially a flow of physiological process in the automatic centres; but it entails a flow of consciousness in the differentiated centres of intelligent control; and this flow of consciousness in its entirety, within a given situation, I am disposed to regard as a primary datum in individual development.'

Individual experience begins with the occurrence of a number of 'primary unit-complexes' of behaviour and experience, which 'run together, overlap, coalesce, and unite synthetically to form a primary body of experience', and the first occurrences of the instincts are not an outcome of individual experience or learning. Lloyd Morgan lays great stress, however, on the fact that this is so only for the *first* performance of the instincts, and here he introduces his concept of 'instinct-meaning'.

It may be that on the *second* and all subsequent performances of an instinct certain modifications of behaviour may be made in the light of

[1]'The Natural History of Experience', *British Journal of Psychology*, vol. iii (1909).
[2]*The Interpretation of Nature.*

the individual's past experience. The objects towards which the instinctive behaviour is directed will, after the first occurrence of the instinct, acquire 'meaning' for the individual in terms of his earlier experience.

We may recall here the view of William James that: 'every instinctive act, in an animal *with memory*, must cease to be "blind" after being once repeated, and must be accompanied with foresight of its "end" just so far as that end may have fallen under the animal's cognizance.' Lloyd Morgan is making essentially the same point, and he too makes the same qualification as James, saying that this acquisition of 'instinct-meaning' applies to 'those animals whose subsequent behaviour is under intelligent guidance; for it is clear that this first performance may afford the means of acquiring the necessary experience for such guidance'.

The following is the simple incident which Lloyd Morgan gives to illustrate this point.

'A chick, in virtue of its instinctive tendencies, pecks at a small moving insect—a lady-bird—seizes it, throws it on one side, shakes its head, and wipes its bill on the ground. That is the way the situation develops. On the following day it sees such an insect, and may run towards it; but it does not take it into the bill, though it may perhaps wipe its bill upon the ground. The lady-bird has acquired meaning, and in accordance with this meaning the behaviour of the chick is modified.'

'Instinct-Meaning', in Lloyd Morgan's view, is very closely related to the *affective* element in experience. Objects acquire meaning in terms of 'felt satisfaction'. These elements of satisfaction and dissatisfaction which play such a large part in the acquisition of 'meaning' are termed the 'psychological values' as distinct from the purely biological 'survival values'.[1]

Then, considering the role of intelligence as being the modification of behaviour in accordance with the psychological values, Lloyd Morgan goes on to distinguish intelligence on the *perceptual* level from intelligence on the *conceptual and ideational level.*

[1] *The Interpretation of Nature*, p. 120: 'One can ... scarcely too strongly emphasise the fact that in passing from biological responses and reactions in the sphere of instinct, as above defined, to intelligent behaviour founded on experience, we introduce a wholly new but supplementary order of values—values not only in terms of organic survival, but also in terms of conscious satisfaction. That situation which has afforded pleasure or has been attended with some form of satisfaction is redeveloped when occasion arises through the presentation of its earlier stages. But that situation which has led to painful results, or some form of discomfort, is not redeveloped. If the earlier stages be presented, the unsatisfactory behaviour is inhibited. The two sets of values—survival values and satisfaction values—are, however, so often and of necessity so predominantly consonant—their inter-relations are so many and so close—that we are apt to forget that they are logically distinct. Physiology, as such, knows nothing whatever of those pleasure-pain values which for the psychologist are essential. They form no part of the ideal construction of physiology: they are dominant factors in the ideal construction of psychology.'

Modifications occurring on the *perceptual* plane are always on essentially practical lines; always closely connected with active behaviour. The individual becomes 'accustomed' to experiencing and behaving in particular ways in certain situations, and, during his continuing experience of them, becomes more and more aware of the ends of these actions and more familiar with the behavioural means of achieving them satisfactorily. But, at this level, it is simply a matter of 'growing used to the situations' and being able to modify behaviour slightly when the situations differ slightly on subsequent occasions. As yet, no element of conceptual knowledge enters, and Lloyd Morgan believes that all animal, and a great deal of human learning takes place upon this plane.[1]

By contrast, intelligent control on the *conceptual* and *ideational* plane involves systematic knowledge, or, as Lloyd Morgan puts it, 'an ideal or schematic construction'. '. . . when situations are viewed from the standpoint of a system of knowledge, their salient features have not only "meaning" for practical behaviour, but also "significance" in relation to that system. They are apperceived as particular examples which illustrate some general scheme or principle.' Intelligent activity at this level is that of identifying, comparing and contrasting, analysing, inferring, generalising, and so on. It deals with the material of perceptual experience but now within a certain framework of concepts, ideas, and logical interrelationships, and is able to refine still further the 'meanings' which have been acquired on the level of perceptual experience. 'Just as the instinctive factor provides data which intelligence deals with so as to shape it to more adaptive ends, so does the perceptual factor provide the more complex data which, through ideational process, are raised to a yet higher level in rational conduct.'

On the perceptual plane, then, we are concerned with modifications of behaviour-experience in accordance with acquired 'meanings' of objects in relation to certain felt impulses and to feelings of satisfaction and dissatisfaction (psychological values), whereas, on the conceptual-ideational plane this perceptual experience itself is considered critically and analytically in terms of concepts, ideas, ideals, and their relationships within a systematic scheme of thought.

Lloyd Morgan attempts to clarify his distinction by reference to a game of golf, and his illustration is worth noting.

'For most of those who simply play with more or less success but without troubling their heads about the theory or science of the game, their skill is so far on the perceptual plane. How the golf ball lies, the look of the course for an approach shot, the slope of the green for one's putt; all these are full of "meaning" for the practised player. As the

[1]*The Interpretation of Nature*, p. 127.

result of previous experience, each immediately suggests that requisite response in play. There is a direct association between such a situation in the game and the appropriate action. Skill depends on a body of experience begotten of constant practice, and a man may be a first-rate exponent without having any systematic knowledge in terms of which he can explain how and why and on what principles he acts in this or that particular way. It is simply the net result of having so acted in hundreds of similar situations. And the most skilful player is the one whose action is the natural and spontaneous outcome of the circumstances of the moment. The successful driver at golf walks up to the tee, takes his line, and smacks the ball a couple of hundred yards. . . .'

This is an example of intelligent control on the perceptual plane. Lloyd Morgan continues:

'Now let us suppose that he wants to know, for his own satisfaction or to explain to others, how the game should be played. . . . What must he do? He has to analyse the strokes into the component movements which he has hitherto felt or seen as unity-wholes. He compares the stance and swing of professionals and scratch men. Amid many idiosyncrasies he finds certain essentials in each case that he can accept as a model. These he selects from the non-essentials. By abstraction and generalisation he reaches general principles. . . . He has added to his practical experience a system of knowledge. This he could never have reached without analysis, comparison, generalisation, and the application of abstract principles to the concrete case. This involves not merely perceptual but ideational and conceptual process.'

Lloyd Morgan implies that perceptual intelligence (whilst it is purely such, as in animals other than man) remains, even though it may become intricate and well-adjusted, essentially a process of *adaptation* to the given environment. Conceptual and ideational intelligence, on the other hand, makes possible a process of *transformation* of the environment. This has a bearing on what subsequent writers (whose work we shall consider) have had to say as to the importance, in human life, of the social environment, or the 'social heritage'.

'One of the most important features of ideational and conceptual process, is that it not only involves new relations with the environment, but creates a new environment in which these relationships obtain. Perceptual intelligence is, in the main, receptive and representative of a natural environment which takes form independently of the exercise of its influence. Only in a limited degree are its products in behaviour so applied as to modify and enrich that natural environment. . . . But it is a characteristic feature of ideational process that it is constantly, to a much larger degree, embodying the products of its rational thought in concrete form so as to constitute part of the physical surroundings. Our books, our art-galleries, our museums; our railways, steamships, and electrical appliances; all the multifarious products of what we call civilization; what are they but an environment in which the results of ages of human thought are embodied.' 'To an extent only foreshadowed in the animal world does man both create and select his own milieu. And this is the key-note of the higher human evolution as contrasted with that which obtains among the lower animals. It involves a transference of evolution from the organism to the social environment.'

(4) *L. T. Hobhouse.* The ideas of Hobhouse and Lloyd Morgan are strikingly similar. Hobhouse, indeed, acknowledges his debt to Lloyd Morgan in the sphere of animal psychology, and his distinction between various grades of mental development is very similar to the distinction which Lloyd Morgan makes between the perceptual and the conceptual and ideational levels of intelligent control. In the work of Hobhouse, however, this latter question is carried out much more thoroughly, and whereas Lloyd Morgan simply points out that social processes become of great importance where human conceptual and ideational activity is concerned, Hobhouse investigates the question much further and undertakes wide comparative studies on the strictly sociological level. His books provide a coherent discussion of the evolutionary process as a whole with particular reference to the growth and development of mind (in the context of correlated levels of social organisation) and its significance for the future of human social development. With this wide range of study in mind, it can be seen that any summary we can give of the treatment of Hobhouse must be, at the best, an inadequate sketch. All we can do is to concentrate on what he has to say about instinct, in order to elucidate, for our own purposes, the main points which he makes.

In view of some of the criticisms of this earlier work on instinct which we shall be considering later, we might note, first of all, the careful approach which Hobhouse makes to the subject. In our first chapter we mentioned the quotation from Captain Marryat's book which Hobhouse uses to illustrate the older view of instinct as indicating 'the guidance of the Almighty's hand unseen'. Hobhouse comments upon this quotation as follows:

'It may be said to be the breakdown of this conception which made animal psychology possible as a science. As soon as it was seen that instinct, like other animal functions, rested upon conditions many of which can be assigned, that it does not spring into existence all at once in full perfection, but is subject, like other features of organic life, to growth and change and possibly to decay, that it is not always perfect or unerring, that no impassable gulf severs it from intelligence, but rather that intelligence first arises within the sphere of instinct—when instinct was thus brought into relation with more commonplace facts, the awe and mystery surrounding it were dissolved, and the central feature of animal psychology became susceptible of scientific treatment. No one supposes that all instincts are explained, or are easy to understand in the present stage of our knowledge. The central conception of instinct itself is not as clearly defined as might be desired. But instinct is no longer a mysterious faculty which may at once be set down as a sufficient explanation of anything in the behaviour of animals that we do not understand. Instinct cannot do anything and everything. It has limits even if we have difficulties in drawing them with precision. And secondly, its territory is not apart, but strictly continuous with other powers of organised beings. Instinct, in short, is a product of evolution. It presides at a certain phase, and has, all in due order, its beginning, its rise, its culmination, and its decline.'

It is important to notice this care with which Hobhouse introduces the study of instinct. The idea that instinct is some 'mysterious faculty' is rejected; is shown to be redundant and scientifically useless. The concept of instinct is used to denote a certain feature of animal behaviour, which, far from being all-sufficient as an explanation of animal behaviour, itself requires explanation. Hobhouse is also well aware that a full account of the causal factors underlying the manifestation of instinct in animal behaviour is not available in his time. Nonetheless, he is quite well aware that such causal factors must exist and that studies of them should be undertaken. In short, the concept of instinct is held to denote a central feature of animal behaviour which must be taken into account and which is helpful in explanation, but which itself requires further analysis.

Hobhouse defines instinct in the following manner.

'Just as the hereditary structure may determine a reflex response, which performs a function without intelligence or purpose, so it may determine a tension of feeling guiding a train of sensori-motor acts—and indeed of structural and reflex acts along with them—and persisting till a result of importance to the organism is attained. . . . Among the higher animals, but particularly among the most developed insects, there are long trains of intricately adjusted actions, which can be conclusively shown to be independent of any intelligent apprehension of their ultimate end, though they may use a measure of dawning intelligence . . . in executing certain steps. These form the instincts proper, and of their genesis we can only repeat what has been said of reflexes and of structure in general. They arise from variations, the original source of which is unknown, but which depend for their permanence on their suitability to the requirements of the species. . . .'

Hobhouse also regards instinctive behaviour as being a 'functional correlate' of inherited structures, (as do the earlier writers we have mentioned). 'If a structure can arise through heredity under the influence of natural selection, so also can the function which such a structure performs, and instinct, upon this view, is nothing but the specific function of a definite inherited structure. The evolution of wings is not a separate process from the evolution of flying.' 'But', he goes on to say, 'to complete the account of the relation between structure and function, we should require a knowledge of the molecular structure of the nervous system of which we are as yet only at the beginning.'

Here again we see that Hobhouse was clearly aware of the necessity of investigating the underlying causes of instinctive behaviour, though the state of knowledge did not permit it in his time.

Distinguishing between compound reflex and instinct, Hobhouse stresses the 'conative' element as being one of the most important criteria of the instinct. Admitting that some instincts approach the compound reflex type, he points out that there are 'cases in which the "instinct" exhibits a more special adaptation of reflexes, which postulates a certain control of action by the persistent requirements of the organism.' 'Instincts recede from the compound reflex type as the persistent internal disposition (i.e. felt as a "craving") influences the response. Where there is by heredity a certain setting determining reflexes in a special way, there is an instinct which is distinguishable from a compound reflex. The instinctive act is no longer one which follows with perfect uniformity from a certain stimulus. It follows from the stimulus only if it is appropriate to the setting of the organism at the time.'

Thus Hobhouse maintains that a certain persisting inner tension with its underlying physiological conditions, which the animal feels as a craving, is an important criterion of instinct, and that, though certain mechanical reflexes may form part of the appropriate sensori-motor act, these would not be brought into play in this particular way unless the persisting inner tension and internal conditions were present. In this way Hobhouse indicates the importance of an inner 'spontaneous' factor of instinctive experience and behaviour which is to a large extent independent of external stimuli. 'The instinct is thus in part independent of stimulus. It needs objects in order to work itself out, but it is not entirely set in motion by the influence of those objects.' The tension arises and persists internally, prompting the animal to act in relation to certain appropriate objects whereby the tension will be reduced; and in this train of actions mechanical reflexes play a part. This particular point regarding the combination of inner spontaneous factors on the one hand, and actions which involve certain fixed reactions to external stimuli on the other, will later be seen to be highly relevant to recent experimental work, and it is therefore worthwhile to quote a particular passage from Hobhouse which is peculiarly apt and anticipatory.

'The setting itself may be called forth by external stimuli, as when sexual passion is aroused by the presence of a particular female. But it also develops normally in the life of the organism according to the stage of its growth, or it may be according to such general outward changes as are involved in the coming round of the season. Thus, like impulsive action, the "setting" of the instinctive act arises from internal causes, for which reason the true instinct may be regarded as a kind of synthesis of the impulsive and the reflex type of action—the internally initiated and the externally regulated.'

The insight in Hobhouse's conception will be more fully appreciated when we discuss the ethological account of instinct in Chapter IV. For the present we must merely take note of it.

On the question of the place of consciousness in instinct-experience, Hobhouse speaks very tentatively, but suggests that at least two elements of consciousness can be 'referred to the response of hereditary structure to stimulus'. One is *sensation*, which is 'the conscious accompaniment of a response to stimulus by the nerve structure'. The other is *feeling*, which is 'the conscious state associated with certain responses of the physical structure determined in the first instance by heredity'. Feeling 'is more conspicuously connected with response, since it is generally if not necessarily and essentially associated with important muscular reactions affecting not only the 'voluntary' muscles but those of the viscera'.

With regard to the perceptual feature of instinctive experience, Hobhouse says that the instinctive action 'is at least a response to a stimulus of a complicated kind'. The animal responds 'not to a series of simple sense stimuli, but to the changing phases of a complex situation'. 'By the "situation" here is meant those objects in the immediate surroundings that have a bearing on the attainment of a particular end, and operate on the sense organs of an animal.[1] The influence which we have to ascribe to the situation implies the existence of an abiding internal state of the organism which deals with it, adjusting action to its changing phases. . . . Just as the reflex excitability is the correlative of the sense-

[1]Compare with what is said by the Ethologists about the 'Perceptual World' of each animal species in Chapter IV.

stimulus, so this relatively permanent state, which dominates many reflexes, is the correlative of a combination of circumstances, or a "situation". It is this relatively permanent state', Hobhouse concludes, 'directing a series of actions towards a definite result, that we call Instinct.'

There are certain other points which Hobhouse stresses, and which he supports by a great deal of experimental evidence drawn from various writers. These are: 'that instinct is not always perfect in its working; that it does not proceed on an unchangeable model; that it is on occasion applied mistakenly, uselessly and injuriously; that it is often incomplete at birth, and requires development; and that at any rate, among the higher animals, it is so interwoven with intelligence that the two factors become exceedingly difficult to disentangle.'

Hobhouse goes on to discuss the relations between instinct and intelligence in the framework of a classification of 'levels of correlation' or 'levels of mental development'. His treatment is very comprehensive and detailed, bringing within its range all kinds of mental activity: from that of the simplest living organism to that of the most complex human society. Unfortunately, we must leave this aspect of his work untouched, as any worthwhile discussion of it would take us too far from our central task of considering the nature of instinct. Two things only might be said.

Firstly, Hobhouse regards instinct as the highest level of mental development established by heredity and co-existent conditions (typical environmental circumstances) combined. It involves a definite correlation of anatomical structures, physiological processes, and features of experience and behaviour, which is established by heredity; which manifests a certain degree of plasticity in encountering co-existent conditions in the individual's experience; and which makes provision for the future (of which the individual has had no experience, and can have no clear conscious apprehension). It can be regarded as a correlation of trains of action in subservience to the vital needs of the organism, and it should be emphasised that the *conative* element (the persisting internal conditions, felt subjectively as a craving) is regarded as the central feature of instinct—lending unity and persistence to the train of actions until a certain end-state is attained.

Secondly, Hobhouse is persuaded that instinct is certainly an important element in *human* experience. Higher levels of mental development do not, and cannot, *supersede* the hereditary basis of human nature. No matter how intricate intelligent control becomes, it must always rest upon the massive mode of correlation established by heredity. The hereditary basis of all generations of human beings is essentially the same (though it is always conditioned by particular Social Traditions) and any intelligent moulding of social conditions and social life has to take it into account. The broader ends of human life are therefore set by the instincts—although Hobhouse would not say that these were the *only* ends of human activity.

This is Hobhouse's general position, but his views on the place of instinct in man must be qualified by two final points.

Whilst believing that the permanent basis of human life is instinctive, Hobhouse conceives the instincts in man as being of the nature of innate promptings, cravings, or determining tendencies, which are specific in themselves but which do not comprise fixed inherited motor-patterns of behaviour. The actual overt pattern of behaviour which is manifested in efforts to satisfy these promptings is not automatically given, to the same degree as in the lower animal species, but depends largely upon the experience and intelligent control of the individual and also *upon the complex influences of the social tradition into which he is born and within which he lives*.

In this way, Hobhouse recognises the plasticity of human nature, and emphasises the importance of the *Social Tradition* as a determining influence upon human behaviour. It is to be noted that to accept the instinctive basis of human nature is *not* to deny the facts of cultural diversity.

Finally, we might close this account of the treatment of Hobhouse with a quotation which shows quite clearly that, whilst supporting the doctrine of instincts, he does not by any means regard the individual simply as an *aggregate* of separate instincts or innate tendencies.

'. . . the whole vaguer mass of the social feelings are in their basis hereditary. But we are not guided merely by instinct, because the power of looking at life as a whole brings our various dispositions and tendencies into relation with one another. We are not to conceive the hereditary endowment of man as consisting in a number of separate instincts so much as in the temperament and character, that basis or background of life which, suffused as we grow up with experience, tends to determine how we will take things, how we will regard fresh experience and weave it into the whole of our life. Reason and will are with us as hereditary as any capacity to feel or any tendency to physical or mental response to particular stimulus, and it is a mistake to found human psychology on a row of separate instincts that may be variously combined. What we should emphasise rather is the element of heredity which forms the substructure of all our thought, feeling, and action.'

(5) *William McDougall.* McDougall's work on the subject of instinct achieved a much wider popularity (indeed, notoriety) than did the work of the previous psychologists. Three facts may account for this. (1) His account of instinct was very largely a *psychological* account; i.e. framed mainly in experiential terms, which involved more points of controversy than the mere statement of the biological facts of instinct in the lower organisms would have done. (2) His treatment, especially in his book *Social Psychology*, was directed predominantly to the study of *human* instincts, and it is, of course, in connection with the question of instinct in *man* that most of the controversy has arisen. And (3) his views were presented in a compact conceptual scheme, the very simplicity of which may, on the one hand, have made his work readable and popular with lay readers, and, on the other, may have aroused the ire of professional psychologists who, confronted with the great complexity of human experience and behaviour, were rather chary of simple answers. Whatever may be the truth of this, it is certain that much criticism directed against the theory of instincts was, in fact, only applicable to McDougall and could not legitimately be brought against other writers in this field. This will be more apparent later. For the present, however, it is important to note only that the doctrine of instincts does not stand or fall with the views of McDougall.

Having said this, we must also say that McDougall himself has often been misunderstood and misrepresented, and many of the criticisms brought to bear on his work have been not only inadequate but also completely irrelevant. On the whole, we would hold that the work of McDougall has stood up well to the continuous and rigorous criticism which has been directed against it, and it would be tempting to give a detailed 'apologia' for his views. This, however, cannot be attempted here.

McDougall believes that 'The human mind has certain innate or inherited tendencies which are the essential springs or motive powers of all thought and action . . .', and these innate tendencies he calls 'Instincts'. We can get an adequate idea of what he means by this concept by considering two quotations.

Firstly, he tells us that the term 'instincts' denotes: '. . . certain innate specific tendencies of the mind that are common to all members of any one species, racial characters that have been slowly evolved in the process of adaptation of species to their environment and that can be neither eradicated from the mental constitution of which they are innate elements nor acquired by individuals in the course of their lifetime.'[1]

[1] *Social Psychology*, p. 20.

Secondly, we have his often-quoted definition of an instinct: '. . . an inherited or innate psycho-physical disposition which determines its possessor to perceive, and to pay attention to, objects of a certain class, to experience an emotional excitement of a particular quality upon perceiving such an object, and to act in regard to it in a particular manner, or, at least, to experience an impulse to such action.'[1]

If we dissect these statements, we find that, for McDougall, an instinct comprises the following features:

(a) It is inherited, *not* learned.
(b) It is common to all members of a species. (We might add: 'of the same sex'.)
(c) It persists throughout the lifetime of the individual.
(d) It involves a certain inner tension or disposition, which has a physiological basis but which is also experienced as a felt tension.
(e) It involves a particular perception which is in some way appropriate to, or significant for, this tension, and leads to the directing of attention to the particular object perceived.
(f) It involves a particular emotional excitement with regard to this perceived object.
(g) It involves a felt impulse to act in a particular way in relation to this perceived object, and
(h) It most probably leads to the performance of a particular appropriate action.

We must add two further points in order to do justice to this very brief condensation of McDougall's views.

Firstly, whilst maintaining that the instincts are not themselves learned, McDougall lays emphasis upon the fact that certain features of the instincts can be *modified* by learning: to a relatively small degree in the case of the lower organisms, but to a considerable degree in the higher animals and man. Thus, by the associations resulting from experience, the *perception* exciting the instinctive behaviour can be modified, and, by the learning of alternative modes of action, the *motor-activity* involved in the instinctive behaviour can be modified.

Secondly, whilst maintaining that the instincts 'cannot be eradicated from the mental constitution of which they are innate elements', McDougall does not hold that they persist throughout the lifetime of the individual *in their original form*. During the course of experience, the primary emotions become merged and 'compounded' into much more complex emotional states, and these emotional dispositions tend to become organised in systems about the various objects, and classes of

[1]*Social Psychology*, p. 25.

objects, that excite them. Such systems of emotional tendencies, McDougall, following A. F. Shand, calls the 'Sentiments'.

There are two legitimate criticisms of McDougall.

Firstly, he has been charged with coupling each primary emotion too rigidly to specific instincts, as, for example: 'The Instinct of Flight —and the Emotion of Fear', or 'The Parental Instinct—and the Tender Emotion'. It is evident at once that such a classification gives far too simple an account of the relationship between instinct and emotion. We feel the tender emotion, for example, in situations other than those involving the parental instinct, and it is a matter of common observation that some features at any rate of the parental instinct involve feelings far removed from the tender emotion.

Secondly, critics have pointed out that there is some inconsistency in McDougall's classification of the instincts. We have seen how McDougall defines an instinct. Having enumerated what he considers to be the chief human instincts in the light of this definition, and having found that there are some tendencies which he considers to be innate but which do not fit in with his definition, he postulates a second category of 'General Innate Tendencies' such as Sympathy, Suggestibility, Imitation, and Play. Play is not regarded as an instinct by McDougall because there are many varieties of play and not all of these have the same permanent nucleus of emotion (which is, in McDougall's terms, a necessary criterion of an instinct), nor do they embody an innate impulse to some specific end. But, we might argue, is not Curiosity also directed to a variety of situations, often with various ends in view, and often accompanied by a different emotional tone? Why, then, should Curiosity be regarded as an instinct, and Play not? This criticism is well-founded, and it is not difficult to point out other inconsistencies in McDougall's classification. It is not, however, a seriously damaging criticism, and James Drever was able to amend McDougall's classification without great difficulty.[1]

We can now mention some of the points arising in McDougall's work which are not, as a rule, given special attention, and we might note also those points which are of particular interest with reference to the recent work in Comparative Ethology.

The explicit purpose of McDougall's inquiry is to provide a psychology which will serve as a reliable basis for the social sciences. Impatient with the barrenness of the psychology of conscious states, associationism, and the like, McDougall claims that it is a study of the dynamic, impulsive side of man's nature which is indispensable for social psychology. He maintains, further, that it is only a comparative and

[1]See p 64.

evolutionary psychology that can provide the basis for a study of
motivation; and such a study, he thinks, could not have been adequately
undertaken before the science of Biology had been established. Stressing the importance of the work of Darwin, McDougall tells us that he
is attempting to follow up this work, attempting: 'to refine upon his
(Darwin's) first rough sketch of the history of human motives.'

McDougall's aims in undertaking the study of instinct are therefore
very clear.

It is important to dwell a little upon certain aspects of McDougall's
views on the *modification* of instinctive behaviour, since he has often
been misrepresented as holding hard and fast to the permanence (and
all-sufficiency for explanation) of the primary instincts and ignoring the
wide differences of human behaviour to be found in various cultures.

It must be emphasised that nowhere does McDougall deny the
influence of different cultural backgrounds upon human behaviour.
Part of his task, he tells us, is: 'to show how, under the influence of the
social environment, they (the instinctive tendencies) become gradually
organised in systems of increasing complexity, while they remain unchanged as regards their most essential attributes'.[1] Whilst holding that
the instinctive tendencies are 'probably common to men of every race
and of every age', he says: 'These primary innate tendencies . . . are
favoured or checked in very different degrees by the very different social
circumstances of men in different stages of culture.'[2] In the light of these
remarks it is quite misleading to suggest that McDougall does not grant
the great influence upon behaviour of differing social processes.

But McDougall has something more definite to say about the ways
in which instinctive tendencies are modified in the higher animals and
in men.

'While it is doubtful[3] whether the behaviour of any animal is wholly
determined by instincts quite unmodified by experience, it is clear that
all the higher animals learn in various and often considerable degrees to
adapt their instinctive actions to peculiar circumstances; and in the long
course of the development of each human mind, immensely greater
complications of the instinctive tendencies are brought about, complications so great that they have obscured until recent years the essential
likeness of the instinctive processes in men and animals. These complications of instinctive processes are of four principal kinds, which we
may distinguish as follows:

'(1) The instinctive reactions become capable of being initiated, not
only by the perception of objects of the kind which directly excite the

innate disposition, the natural or native excitants of the instinct, but also by ideas of such objects, and by perceptions and by ideas of objects of other kinds.[1]

'(2) The bodily movements in which the instinct finds expression may be modified and complicated to an indefinitely great degree.

'(3) Owing to the complexity of the ideas which can bring the human instincts into play, it frequently happens that several instincts are simultaneously excited; when the several processes blend with various degrees of intimacy.

'(4) The instinctive tendencies become more or less systematically organised about certain objects or ideas.'

McDougall gives a detailed account of each of these modes of modification.

Sufficient has been said, however, to show that McDougall nowhere adopts the view that the whole of human activity can be explained by simply enumerating a set of human instincts; and that he is not only aware of, but actually attempts to state in detail, how the native tendencies of men are modified during the course of their individual experience. We have made it clear, too, that—whilst he does not investigate in detail the nature of social conditioning—he is, nonetheless, well aware that differences in human behaviour are brought about by the complex influences of differing cultural traditions.

Whilst holding that the instincts can be modified in various ways, McDougall thinks, however, that the *affective* feature of the instincts remains permanent and unmodified throughout experience. Thus, discussing the instinct of 'pugnacity', he tells us that: '. . . one exercises but little, if any, control over the violent beating of the heart, the flushing of the face, the deepened respiration, and the general redistribution of blood-supply and nervous tension which constitute the visceral expression of the excitement of this instinct and which are determined by the constitution of its central affective part.' The visceral changes involved in any particular instinctive tendency, when aroused, remain the same throughout life; and the accompanying emotional experience, similarly, is held to be unmodified.[2]

We must confine ourselves, now, to what McDougall has to say about the several features of instinct, and what he considers to be the chief criterion of instinctive experience and behaviour. This will be of use when we come to deal with the criticisms of the doctrine of instincts,

[1]E.g. Contiguous perceptions; objects closely associated, in experience, with the original excitant; and objects very similar to the original excitant.
[2]*Social Psychology*, p. 36.

and will be relevant to many of the points made by the Comparative Ethologists.

In his early chapter on the nature of instincts, McDougall says:

'. . . the psycho-physical process that issues in an instinctive action is initiated by a sense-impression which, usually, is but one of many sense-impressions received at the same time; and the fact that this one impression plays an altogether dominant part in determining the animal's behaviour shows that its effects are peculiarly favoured, that the nervous system is peculiarly fitted to receive and to respond to just that kind of impression.[1] The impression must be supposed to excite, not merely detailed changes in the animal's field of sensation, but a sensation or complex of sensations that has significance or meaning for the animal; hence we must regard the instinctive process in its cognitive aspect as distinctly of the nature of perception, however rudimentary.[2] In the animals most nearly allied to ourselves we can, in many instances of instinctive behaviour, clearly recognize the symptoms of some particular kind of emotion such as fear, anger, or tender feeling; and the same symptoms always accompany any one kind of instinctive behaviour, as when the cat assumes the defensive attitude, the dog resents the intrusion of a strange dog, or the hen tenderly gathers her brood beneath her wings. We seem justified in believing that each kind of instinctive behaviour is always attended by some such emotional excitement, however faint, which in each case is specific or peculiar to that kind of behaviour. Analogy with our own experience justifies us also in assuming that the persistent striving towards its end, which characterizes mental process and distinguishes instinctive behaviour most clearly from mere reflex action, implies some such mode of experience as we call conative, the kind of experience which in its more developed form is properly called desire or aversion, but which, in the blind form in which we sometimes have it and which is its usual form among the animals, is a mere impulse, or craving, or uneasy sense of want. Further, we seem justified in believing that the continued obstruction of instinctive striving is always accompanied by painful feeling, its successful progress towards its end by pleasurable feeling, and the achievement of its end by a pleasurable sense of satisfaction.'

We may note also that McDougall postulates that such instinctive experience and behaviour probably has a specific neuro-physiological basis. 'Just as a reflex action implies the presence in the nervous system of the reflex nervous arc, so the instinctive action also implies some

[1] See the discussion of 'Sign-Stimuli' and 'Innate Releasing Mechanisms' in Chapter IV.
[2] See the 'Instinct-Meaning' of Lloyd Morgan, and the 'Instinct-Interest' of Drever.

enduring nervous basis whose organisation is inherited, an innate or inherited psycho-physical disposition, which, anatomically regarded, probably has the form of a compound system of sensori-motor arcs.'[1]

But, to return to the previous passage: we have seen how McDougall describes the three main features which he considers to be characteristic of instinct: the specific appropriate perception (with some element of 'cognition' and 'instinct-interest'); the specific craving, or conation, directing behaviour towards a certain end; and the specific emotion. Towards the end of this passage the inadequacy of his treatment of 'emotion' becomes clear when it is seen that he introduces into his discussion at least three kinds of affective experience. First, he postulates a *specific* emotion accompanying the particular sequence of actions. Second, he postulates the 'conative' aspect of the experience. And third, he postulates feelings which are consequent upon whether or not the instinctive action is carried out to its successful conclusion: painful feeling in the case of obstruction and thwarting; pleasurable feeling in unobstructed activity; and the 'pleasurable sense of satisfaction' when the end is achieved. It is clear from this that McDougall's account of the affective features of instinct-experience requires a much more detailed analysis than he offers.

In this same chapter, however, McDougall gives a very clear exposition of what he considers to be the chief distinguishing feature of instinctive activity, and it is worth our while to take note of this. But before quoting what McDougall has to say, it may be noted that, from the publication of *The Energies of Men* in 1932, he had adopted the use of the term 'Propensity', and it is important to realise that this did not signify in the slightest degree a rejection either of the term 'instinct' or of the theory of the instincts which he had previously put forward. By the use of the term 'propensity', McDougall merely wished to emphasise and make perfectly clear, as we shall see from his following remarks, what he considered to be the *chief* distinguishing feature of instinctive experience and behaviour. The idea that the adoption of this word meant, in any way, a change in McDougall's theoretical position, or that it led to any kind of confusion in his thinking, is simply absurd.

'It seems clear that we should regard the central part of the instinctive disposition as both affective and conative in function, as responsible both for the emotional or feeling quality of the instinctive response (with the corresponding system of visceral and other innervations which determine what we call the expressions of the emotion) and for the conative experience, with the setting of the goal, with the continued

[1] *Social Psychology*, p. 25, and compare with the discussion of the 'Hierarchical Organisation of the Nervous System' in our account of Comparative Ethology, Chapter IV.

direction of the striving towards that goal, no matter what forms of bodily movement may be used in the course of such striving.

'It is this central part of the instinct, both affective and conative in function, which we need to distinguish and define as clearly as possible; and since we can properly and very advantageously regard it as a functional unit of structure, we need for it some special designation. I have, therefore, proposed to speak of this central part of the innate disposition which is an instinct as a *propensity*. . . .

'Under this terminology we recognise in any instinct of the typical and fully developed kind, a central core, the propensity (more technically to be called the conative-affective disposition or, more shortly, the affective disposition, or affective core of the instinct) as well as, on the motor side, some motor mechanism (or complex of motor mechanisms in the highly complex chain-instincts, such as that of the famous Yucca Moth) through which the conative tendency most readily expresses itself; and, on the afferent or receptive side, some one or more cognitive dispositions by means of which the animal is able to perceive the objects that evoke and guide its instinctive striving. The cognitive disposition like the motor mechanism, is in some cases very simple, and in others very complex and multiple. And it is of the first importance, for the understanding of the formation of the sentiments and of all the organisation of our affective life, that the propensity (the central affective-conative core of each instinct) seems capable of functioning in relative independence of both the cognitive and the motor parts of the total instinctive disposition; readily acquiring functional relations with other cognitive dispositions and with other motor mechanisms than those with which it is innately and directly linked in the racial constitution.

'And this central core or propensity, having once attained its full development by a process of spontaneous maturation, seems to maintain its native properties and functions relatively unchanged throughout the life of the creature; while the cognitive disposition may undergo very great elaboration and differentiation; and the motor mechanisms may (in man to an unlimited extent, but in the animals to a very small extent only) undergo that kind of development which we call the acquisition of skills.'[1]

This passage makes it absolutely clear that, for McDougall, the most important distinguishing feature of instinctive experience and behaviour is the persisting 'conative-affective' core.

This emphasis is of the utmost importance in the controversy over

[1] *Social Psychology*, p. 502.

the theory of instincts. If this point of emphasis had been clearly under-stood throughout, it is doubtful whether the controversy over the question of instinct in man would have been anywhere near so prolonged and intense as in fact it was. Misunderstanding the importance of this emphasis, and consequently conceiving the concept of instinct put for-ward by these earlier writers as always comprising rigid motor mechan-isms, many writers rejected the 'instincts' with scorn only to re-introduce them—*in precisely the sense in which McDougall describes them above*—under the heading of 'drives'.

This point deserves driving home. Let us, then, in order to establish this point beyond all doubt, look at McDougall's explicit rejection of the identification of 'instincts' with 'motor mechanisms'.

Having pointed out that, in instinctive behaviour, the animal makes use of a large number of inborn motor mechanisms 'each of which gradually takes the shape common to all members of the species, by a process of maturation which is but little influenced by the circumstances of the animal and little by the animal's own activities', McDougall insists that the identification of any instinct with a particular motor mechanism is erroneous. He puts forward two points in support of this contention.

'First, one instinct may impel an animal to a series of activities in which it employs in turn two or more such motor mechanisms or, in some cases, well nigh its entire array of such mechanisms. Secondly, two or more instincts may in turn impel the animal to use the same motor mechanisms. Especially is this true of those motor mechanisms which subserve locomotion. The bird may use his powers of flight in the course of migration, of mating, of fighting, of escape from danger, of building his nest, of pursuing his prey. . . . How absurd, then, to pretend that an instinctive action is nothing more than the activation of a pre-formed motor mechanism of particular pattern!'[1]

McDougall's conception of the instinct is clearly the same as that put forward by Hobhouse and other writers we have considered: that is, as being a correlation of various features of experience and behaviour established by heredity—in which a persistently recurring craving with its underlying neuro-physiological conditions employs various sensori-motor actions and reflexes until a certain end, in relation to appropriate objects in the environment, is attained. All we wish to stress here is that, for McDougall, the most important distinguishing feature of the instinct is its innate 'conative-affective' core—and *not* any fixed, particular motor mechanisms.

[1] *Social Psychology*, p. 415.

We may note finally (1) McDougall's view on the relation between instinct and intelligence, and (2) the way in which he regards the concept of instinct, and why he thinks that it is necessary.

(1) McDougall's conception of the relation between instinct and intelligence is very similar to that expressed by Hobhouse.

'The separation of instinct and intelligence is effected by a misleading process of abstraction. In reality, instinctive action everywhere displays that adaptability to special circumstances which is the mark of intelligence; instinct is everywhere shot through with intelligence, no matter how constantly, in how routine a fashion, a particular mode of instinctive behaviour may be repeated. Where the routine-specialised behaviour suffices, there no special adaptation of the inborn mode of action is made; but where the inborn mode of action does not suffice for the attainment of the natural goal of the instinct, there some adaptation, or some effort at adaptation, is made. And intelligence, on the other hand, works always in the service of some conation, some tendency, some desire, or intention, rooted in and springing from our instinctive constitution.'[1]

(2) In his supplementary chapter: 'Recent Light on the Instincts of Man', McDougall remarks on the way in which he regards the concept of instinct; why the concept comprises the several features he assigns to it, and why it is necessary.

'Instinct is a general conception to which we are led in our endeavour to interpret by a common principle the various forms of unlearned activity displayed by man and animals.

'When we array these forms of activity and seek their common objective characters, we find seven which seem to mark them as distinct in kind from all processes of the inorganic world and as expressive of mind, of hormic, or, in the widest sense, purposive action or striving. These objective marks of purpose may be enumerated as follows: *First*, a certain spontaneity of movement, a power of initiative. *Secondly*, a tendency to persistence, whether the movement concerned is apparently spontaneous or is initiated by some physical stimulus falling on the organism from without. *Thirdly*, variation of kind or of direction of the persistent movements. *Fourthly*, the cessation of the movements when, and not until, they result in the attainment of the goal, in effecting a change of situation of a particular kind. *Fifthly*, the movements commonly seem to anticipate, or to prepare in some manner for, the new situation which they themselves tend to bring about. *Sixthly*, repetition of the situation that has evoked the train of movements, evokes again a

[1] *Social Psychology*, p. 421.

similar train of movements, but the movements so evoked commonly show, as compared with those of the former occasion, some degree of improvement in respect of efficiency, i.e. in respect of speed, accuracy, or nicety of adjustment. *Seventhly*, the purposive action is in a sense a total reaction, that is to say, it is an activity in which the whole organism takes part so far as is necessary; the energies of the whole organism seem to be bent towards the one end, all other concurrent processes within it being subordinated to the major or dominant system of hormic activity.'[1]

On all essential points, McDougall gives an account of instinct which is in close agreement with that of the earlier writers we have considered. It was, nonetheless, his treatment which had the merit of bringing the whole subject of motivation and instinct into the foreground of discussion and controversy in psychology; and we hope to show that, in the main, McDougall's work has stood the tests of criticism well, and is to a great extent supported by the most recent experimental work.

(6) *James Drever*. In his book *Instinct in Man*, published in 1917, Drever emphasises the fact that the psychological study of instinct in man was by no means entirely a post-Darwinian phenomenon. Really, he makes two points here. He is concerned to show that a great deal of the insight into the instinctual side of human nature shown by earlier philosophers and 'introspective psychologists' is still of use. And, secondly, he argues that much of the post-Darwinian work on instinct was unfortunate and misleading, especially with regard to its estimation of the place of instinct in human experience, because of its predominantly bio-physiological and mechanistic slant. As indicated during our discussion of Lloyd Morgan, Drever spends a great deal of effort in emphasising that the bio-physiological account and the psychological account of Instinct are concerned with two essentially different 'universes of discourse'. Each makes necessary reference to the other; is 'concomitant' to the other; but neither can be described or explained in terms of the other. Drever says:

'This constant emphasis upon the contrast between the psychological and the biological point of view would not be necessary were it not for the fact that the prevailing view of Instinct, during the last generation or so, has been the biological, the result being that we have become accustomed to oppose animal behaviour to human behaviour, regarding the one as typically instinctive, the other as typically intelligent, and also to maintain that the instincts and instinctive tendencies of human nature

[1]*Social Psychology*, p. 411.

are insignificant. Had the psychologist been clear as regards the psychological nature of instinct, this position could not have developed. For, though perceptual experience is more and more overlaid by the higher mental processes, it always underlies them, and, though control of primitive impulse becomes more and more complex, it is always a control by that which draws its controlling force, ultimately and fundamentally, from primitive impulses, never a control "ab extra".'

If we take the fixed and rigid motor mechanisms which seem to be a feature of the instinctive behaviour of the lower organisms as being the chief criteria of instinct, then it is clear that we shall conclude that the instinctive equipment of man is insignificant. But if, on the other hand, we take, as McDougall, Hobhouse, etc., have emphasised, the *conative* feature—the congenital cravings leading to the persistence and variation of behaviour until a certain end is reached—as being the essential criterion of instinct, then it is obvious that our view of the place of instinct in human nature will be vastly different. It is important to realise that Drever is by no means wishing to belittle the biological account of instinct when he speaks in this way. On the contrary, he stresses the fact that both the biological account and the psychological account are equally necessary and important. The only thing he insists upon is that the distinct nature of the two studies should be clearly recognised.

His discussion of this point leads Drever to give both a biological and a psychological definition of instinct.

He words the biological definition as follows:

'As a factor determining the behaviour of living organisms, Instinct, physiologically regarded, is a congenital predisposition of the nervous system, consisting in a definite, but within limits modifiable, arrangement and co-ordination of nervous connections, so that a particular stimulus, with or without the presence of certain co-operating stimuli, will call forth a particular action or series of actions; this predisposition, biologically regarded, is apparently due to the operation of natural selection, and determines a mode of behaviour, which secures a biologically useful end, without foresight of that end or experience in attaining it.'

Drever's main concern is to give a psychological account of instinct, and several chapters are devoted to this task. It is in his entire treatment, and not in any simple definition, that we should look for his conception of the psychological aspects of instinct. We can, however, isolate two brief definitions he gives of instinct-experience, which will have to suffice here. In his introductory chapter, he says: 'Provisionally, we understand by Instinct an innate impelling force guiding cognition, accompanied by interest or emotion, and at least partly determining action.'[1] Later, he tells us: 'Psychologically, the only possible interpretation of instinctive behaviour seems to be in terms of specific impulse determining specific act, on presentation in perceptual consciousness of a specific situation.'[2]

Much of Drever's treatment is similar to that of the writers we have already considered, and of these similar features of his work we can merely make very brief mention, reserving our main attention for the points connected with the question of 'emotion', on which Drever makes a real advance on the previous writers.

'Instinct-Experience', Drever holds, is essentially that of perceptual consciousness and contains (1) a felt impulse, (2) a visually apprehended object or situation, and (3) a feeling of 'interest' or 'worth-whileness', passing into 'satisfyingness'.

There is no strict dichotomy between instinct and intelligence, Drever thinks.

'. . . actions are called instinctive when what we may call the potency of experience is low, intelligent, when it is high. But psychologically Instinct and Intelligence cannot be placed in opposition. The potency of experience will vary with the degree of intelligence. But the degree of intelligence is simply the degree of "psychical integration". The primary "psychical integration" is the integration of instinct and sensation in the rudimentary and fundamental experience of a determinate conscious impulse, defined by a perceived situation or object, and correlated with a feeling, which we may for the present describe as "worth-whileness".'

Experience always involves instinct and intelligence in varying degrees—at various levels of 'psychical integration'—and the simplest case of perceptual experience is that of instinct: comprising a felt impulse, the perception of a situation, and a *feeling* of interest or worth-whileness.

Drever makes much of this latter point, emphasising that, even in the most rudimentary instinctive experience, such a feeling of interest is present. This is an elaboration of Lloyd Morgan's conception of 'instinct-meaning', and Drever stresses more emphatically that this interest or worth-whileness is essentially an *affective* element, and, also, that it is a given, innate, element of instinct-experience, and is thus the basis for subsequent learning. 'This interest it is not quite correct to call an interest in the visually apprehended object, nor an interest qualifying the impulse. It is essentially a *feeling* dependent upon the whole relation of impulse to object. . . . It is the very core of the (instinct-) experience itself. We define then primary meaning as the feeling of relation between an object or a situation and an impulse towards that object or situation, that feeling being best described as interest or "worth-whileness".'

[1] *Instinct in Man*, p. 20.   [2] *Ibid.* p. 107.

Perhaps the most interesting and suggestive part of Drever's account lies in his discussion of the place of emotion in instinct-experience. Two points of importance are made, both of which constitute an advance on the previous writers.

It is while carrying out his discussion of 'instinct-interest' or the feeling of worth-whileness, that Drever is led directly into the problem of emotion. In so far, he argues, as instinctive behaviour takes its normal, unobstructed course, and the feeling of worth-whileness passes over into the feeling of 'satisfyingness' (i.e. when the inherited motor mechanisms are adequate in the situation and meet with success in attaining the instinctual end), then no emotion arises. But if this activity is checked or thwarted in any way, then a tension arises, a tension which, in feeling, is an emotion. There are elements of feeling in this tension which are different from the original feeling-experience from which the tension arises, and this can be explained, Drever holds, by viewing these new feeling elements as the outcome of the *urgency* of the particular impulse which is temporarily denied its normal sequence of activity and its consequent satisfaction. The function of the emotion, then, is to *reinforce* the impulse, and to lead to persistent and more varied behaviour in order to overcome the particular obstruction; it entails a certain modifiability of behaviour when unusual circumstances are encountered by the organism. Nonetheless, when this urgency is very great, Drever points out that one characteristic of emotion aroused to a high pitch of intensity is its *ineffectiveness* in securing the end of the thwarted impulse. It is here that Drever makes a suggestion which is of extreme interest, and which we wish to emphasise.

One circumstance under which such tension must be expected to arise, is when there is no inherited provision of precise reactions appropriate to particular situations; i.e. when automatic behaviour-mechanisms are *not* established by heredity. Biologically regarded, the survival value of *precise* reactions to *particular* situations is strictly limited to animals confined to a stable and not too complex 'ecological niche'. The capacity for *adaptation* to a changing and complex environment, or to various environments, however, also has a distinct and substantial biological advantage, but this requires *plasticity* of reaction; it requires the *lack* of fixed inherited motor-mechanisms appropriate to particular situations, and it most probably involves, therefore, some *delay* of reaction, and some consequent feeling of 'tension', whilst adequate adaptation or learning is taking place. In the higher animals and man, we should expect to find, then, and we *do* find, signs of emotional development going along with degrees of plasticity of reaction.

This is a most important point, and it can be seen at once that it brings this account of instinct very closely into line with the treatment of Freud, suggesting that the apparent gulf between this early doctrine of instincts and the Psycho-Analytic theory of the instincts is not so wide as we have been prone to think. It is clear that the emphasis which Drever places upon the element of 'tension' in the instinctual experience of man is very significant in the light of the Freudian emphasis upon 'anxiety' and 'the heightening of the whole cathectic process' which is the outcome of the nervous system's task of 'binding' the instinctual excitations. The importance of this point is that it gives us a sound biological reason for believing that—quite apart from any 'Super-Ego' formation, or any form of social conditioning and subsequent repression of impulses—*some* degree of tension, emotion, or anxiety is necessarily involved in the instinctual experience of man by virture of his hereditary endowment: inheriting, as he does, certain congenital cravings or persistently recurring impulses, but few appropriate motor-mechanisms whereby, as is the case among the lower organisms, these impulses can automatically find their outlet and their satisfaction. In this point we can see the intriguing possibilities of an integrated theory of the instincts, embracing both animal and human psychology, and satisfactorily bringing together the work of these earlier psychologists and that of the Psycho-Analytic school. We shall in fact attempt the statement of such an integrated theory later.

Since we consider this a point of great importance, however, and since it does not seem to have been followed up as thoroughly as it might have been, let us see what Drever himself has to say about it in his chapter on 'Instinct and Emotion'. It may be noted, in the following passage, how suggestive the point is, also, for Comparative Psychology.

'This arrest of the impulse may arise from a variety of circumstances, but, as we have seen, in the case of the human being one set of circumstances is specially important. With many instinctive impulses, and, among these, some of very great significance, there is no provision in the organism, by means of any neural pre-arrangement, for that particular course of action which will meet the particular individual case. . . . It follows that there must be at least momentary arrest of the impulse, while the particular course of action is being intelligently determined—intelligently, if only on the perceptual level.

'If this is a valid explanation of the instinct-emotion, then we ought to find in a comparative study of the instincts of animals, representing different stages or levels of intelligence, that, in the case of certain instincts, the development of the emotional element in instinctive behaviour proceeds "pari passu", on the whole, with the dropping out of inherited special adjustments for particular reactions to particular situations. And this is apparently what we do find. Romanes has discussed the emotional manifestations of organisms at different levels,[1] and though, as he points out, the inference to the emotional life of animals "necessarily becomes of less and less validity as we pass through the animal kingdom to organisms less and less like our own", we cannot fail to be struck by the fact that the manifestations of emotion become rarer and rarer, and more and more ambiguous, as we descend the scale, and as instinctive activities become more and more fixed and definite. First the self-feelings disappear, then the emotions connected with the distinctively social instincts, then curiosity, and finally we are left with fear and anger, even these disappearing in the lowest.

'What appears to be the biological function and significance of emotion would lead us to expect precisely this phenomenon. Biologically the function of emotion is to reinforce impulse and interest. This reinforcement will be necessary in two cases, either where an obstacle must be surmounted, or where a more or less prolonged course of trying to find the appropriate reaction is necessary, owing to the fact that no neural pre-arrangement provides for the precise action in a particular case. In the first set of circumstances, in addition to the appropriate emotion, whatever that may be, anger generally develops as a further reinforcement. In the second, anger will not meet the needs of the situation, since only actions of a certain kind will satisfy the impulse and interest involved, and only the appropriate emotion can secure such actions.'[2]

The second point of interest in Drever's treatment of emotion arises during the course of his criticism of McDougall. McDougall, we may remember, analyses the instinct-experience into three features: the perceptual and cognitive, the affective, and the conative; but later merges the latter two in his conception of the 'propensity' or 'conative-affective core' of the instinct. This is the feature of instinctive experience and behaviour which McDougall thinks persists unmodified, but we have seen that he mentions several affective elements of the instinct-experience which were unaccounted for in terms of this 'emotion'. Drever disagrees that 'emotion' can be regarded as the essential affective element in the instinct-experience, and points out that in some cases the satisfactory performance of the instinct involves little or no emotion, whilst, at the other extreme of a high intensity of emotion, the organism

[1]Drever's reference: Romanes, *Animal Intelligence*, pp. 45, 155, 204, 242, 270, 329, 334; *Mental Evolution in Animals*, Chapter XX; *Mental Evolution*, p. 341.
[2]*Instinct in Man*, p. 160.

is rendered ineffective in attaining its object. He proposes that the essential affective element of instinct-experience is the instinct-interest, or feeling of worth-whileness, and that this is not, as such, emotional, but becomes emotion only when the action undertaken for the satisfaction of the interest is suspended or checked. This, says Drever, best accounts for the facts when we are considering those instinctive activities which manifest no pronounced emotion. On the other hand, he agrees with McDougall that in some cases the emotion is the predominant characteristic of the whole instinct-experience, as for example, in the 'fear' or the 'fighting' instincts. From this, Drever concludes that, in the human being and the higher animals, at any rate, there are at least two types of instinct to be taken into account.

Drever's view, then, is that the 'instinct-interest' is essentially and invariably a feature of instinctive activity (we may remember that this is 'the feeling of significance dependent upon the whole relation of impulse to object'), whereas the element of emotion is not. The instinct-interest, normally, is accompanied by behaviour which results in the satisfactory attainment of the object of the interest. The emotion is that tension arising from an arrest of the impulse, or from the denying of that activity leading to the satisfaction of the interest. Nonetheless, though the emotion is not an invariable feature of *all* instinctive activity, there are at least *some* instincts, of great importance in both human and animal life, of which, under normal conditions, an emotion is one of the most prominent characteristics. A distinction must be made, therefore, between those instincts which approximate to the 'pure' type, and those which are characteristically 'emotional'. Thus, Drever's differences with McDougall do not, as he admits, lead to such a great disagreement in results after all. 'The important point', says Drever, 'is that the great instincts of human nature have all their accompanying and typical emotion.'

This fact (that typical emotions characterise some of the more important instincts in the higher animals and man) is then coupled by Drever with his previous point, that, in these cases, no particular motor-mechanisms are established by heredity in relation to particular situations. This can be seen in his comments on the 'fear' instinct.

'In the first place, the emotion "fear" is integrally connected with the instinctive responses to a "danger" situation. In the second place, though originally in the history of the race these responses may have represented specific responses to specific perceived situations, and therefore separate instincts,[1] in the human being, and in the higher

---

[1]And, in this case, being separate instincts, the previous analysis of 'instinct-interest' leading to tension or emotion in conditions of obstruction and thwarting, would hold.

animals, they represent the multiple response of a single instinct, which is quite properly called fear, and which is normally, or usually, emotional, just because of the multiple response.'

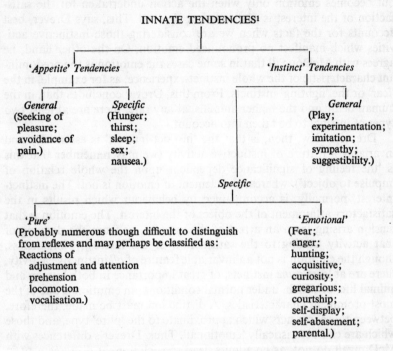

'We are compelled . . . to recognise, with McDougall, that some of the most important instincts of the human being, as well as of the higher animals, are of the "emotional" type, that is to say, are not merely of the nature of specific responses to specific situations, but specific only as to the kind of situation, the emotional accompaniment, and the end secured by the response, and, as regards the first and third of these, specific in varying degrees.'

The instincts of man, according to Drever, must be divided into at least two groups: those characterised by specific responses to specific situations, like sucking; and those consisting of tendencies specific in varying degrees with regard to the situation and response, but always quite specific with regard to the accompanying emotion. Like McDougall, Drever has to distinguish, also, a group of general innate tendencies—such as play, imitation, and the like—which can hardly be

[1] *Instinct in Man*, p. 169.

said to be specific at all, with regard to either situation or response, and which have no specific emotion associated with them. These general tendencies, Drever says, do not normally determine specific ends or interests, but attach themselves to the ends and interests determined by the specific tendencies, more especially those of the 'emotional' group. A further distinction is made between the groups already mentioned and the 'appetite tendencies' which are characterised by a feeling of uneasiness and restlessness, which, in a sense, occurs before the particular impulse which it determines, as, for example, in the experience of hunger. These distinctions which Drever makes for the purposes of classification will all be seen to be highly relevant to the new work in Comparative Ethology, and, since we shall be attempting our own classification of the instincts in man in the light of this recent work, we might note the brief scheme (*see opposite page*) which Drever presents, as a ground for comparison.

(7) *Morris Ginsberg*. Although known mainly as a sociologist, Professor Ginsberg, has, throughout his career, concerned himself with psychology, and especially with its bearing upon social theory. In his book *The Psychology of Society*, and in two later papers, he presents us with definitions of instinct which summarise admirably the findings of the earlier writers.

In the paper 'The Place of Instinct in Social Theory', he outlines the features of instinctive experience and behaviour as follows:

'. . . the term Instinct covers those forms of behaviour consisting of a series of interrelated acts which (1) are directed towards an end or goal, (2) exhibit a certain adaptability and persistence with varied effort which might connote intelligence, but which (3) are performed in circumstances in which, in the absence of experience and taking into consideration the level of mentality otherwise attained by the organism in question, there can be no knowledge of the end nor deliberate and conscious contrivance on the part of the individual. For example, the activities involved in nest-building are complex, varied, and adapted to their surroundings—yet we cannot attribute to the bird at its first performance a knowledge of the end in the sense of the completed nest. We can only describe its behaviour by assuming an impulse towards an unknown goal innately determined which persists until the end is achieved. The impulse must not be conceived as a force or animistic spirit acting 'upon' the organism; it is simply what the animal feels while the instinct is operative, and which lends persistence, unity and continuity to the series of efforts involved. Further, the instinct is not a mere pattern of behaviour or 'motor mechanism'. We must assume a persistent conation regulating and sustaining a course of action and rendering it adaptive and variable within limits.'

Again:

'. . . instincts are impulses innately determined to pursue certain ends. In the simplest forms the ends are unforeseen and the patterns of behaviour whereby they are realised relatively fixed and uniform. There appears to be always, however, at least sensori-motor action rendering possible a certain adaptation of the inborn patterns to the requirements of the situation. Instinctive behaviour has unity and persistence and some degree of prospective reference, or forward direction, and this differentiates it from reflex action. As intelligence develops the ends come more clearly into consciousness and the relation of the means required for their fulfilment to the ends are grasped more and more articulately. But though the plasticity of behaviour is thereby indefinitely increased, the impulses remain, and the ends of life, however system- atised, retain as their central core something of the original impulses. The urge of the instincts has feeling tone, but is not as such emotional, and there does not appear to be the precise relation between instinct and emotion that Professor McDougall claims for the primary instincts.'

A third clear definition of Instinct is given in the paper on 'Emotion and Instinct'.

'By instinct I understand a series of reflex or sensori-motor acts held together by an underlying mood or feeling of tension, which persists until the end of the series is attained. Instinct is not a mere concatenation of reflexes. There must be in instinct a continued interest, sustaining, directing, and guiding the inherited typical reactions. There must be something, in fact, which accounts for the persistence with varied effort characteristic of such behaviour as is exemplified, for example, in instinctive hunting. The function of the feeling of interest, which may be characterised negatively as one of tension, and positively as one of worth-whileness, is to prompt and sustain action until the tension is relieved, in other words, to make possible persistence with varied effort. The function of emotion, it is now suggested, is to reinforce such per- sistence, while increasing the plasticity of the behaviour requisite for dealing with the situation.'

We can see, within these definitions, the major points made by Lloyd Morgan, Hobhouse, and Drever, and it is of interest to note that everything in them could have been drawn from the literature on Instinct without reference to McDougall. Whilst not wishing in the least to disparage McDougall's work, it is necessary to point out to those who equate 'the theory of instincts' with McDougall that all the major points which arose from the study of instinct can be found, clearly stated, and adequately illustrated by empirical observations and experiments, in the work of other writers.

Ginsberg's analysis of the relation between instinct and emotion is much more thorough than that of McDougall. In essentials, however, his conclusions are in agreement with those of Drever, though he goes further in giving an analysis of the different phases of emotional experience and in pointing out that the nature of the emotions and the circumstances under which they arise are not necessarily exhaustively accounted for in any statement of their relation to the instincts.

Ginsberg (like Hobhouse) also emphasises the importance of the *Social Tradition* as a determinant of human behaviour, and this serves to drive home the point that thinkers who supported the theory of instincts by no means held that this provided a *complete* explanation of human experience and behaviour. We have seen that not a single writer who supported the early theory of instincts denied the importance of the social environment as a determining influence upon human behaviour. On the contrary, all admitted it.

We are now in a position to present a summary account of the early views on Instinct, drawn from the writers whose work we have discussed. For the purpose of clarity, we shall set out this account systematically, making each point separately and distinctly.

2. *A Summary Statement: The Early 'Doctrine of Instincts'*

The Doctrine of Instincts can best be stated in the form of an answer to two questions.

(A) Among animals, especially among those species low in the evolutionary scale but also among the higher species, which, in processes of learning do not seem to manifest a very high degree of intelligence, we find numerous examples of complicated trains of behaviour which seem well adapted to those situations which are normally encountered in the 'ecological niche' of the species, which seem to be periodically and recurrently directed towards specific features of the environment and towards the attainment of a certain 'end-state', and which, though they may be modified to some extent in the light of subsequent experience, are performed with a surprising degree of perfection without previous experience; without any previous possibility of learning on the part of the individual. Such trains of unlearned behaviour and the particular acts which they comprise are very similar, if not identical, in all members of the same species, at least, of the same sex. How are we to account for such behaviour?

(B) In view of the evolutionary hypothesis which views human experience and behaviour as being to some degree continuous with animal experience and behaviour: to what extent are the features of such behaviour discernible and of importance in the nature of man?

In reply to question (A):

(1) The theory of evolution postulates that the structural characteristics of existing species have been brought into being by a long process of heredity and hereditary change, depending upon (i) mutations, and (ii) the process of natural selection. It is now held that not only the structural characteristics of species, but also:

(a) the complex *internal processes* (nervous, visceral, chemical, muscular) of the organism;

(b) certain uniform, automatic behaviour-mechanisms called *Reflex Actions*;

(c) certain actions better fitted for particular, directed modes of adaptation, called *Sensori-motor Actions*;

(d) certain features of experience, accompanying and arising from the complex internal processes, called *Persistent and Recurring Impulses*, or *Cravings*, and also less specific feelings of uneasiness and restlessness, called *Appetites*, which persist in the organism and lead to the utilisation, in a certain behavioural sequence, of the above-mentioned types of action, until a certain 'end-state' is attained and the craving relieved;

(e) certain other features of experience—called *Emotions*—which follow upon the frustration of these impulses, and which lead to the reinforcement of them, and to a greater plasticity in the employment of behavioural responses;

(f) certain definite *modes of perception* which seem to be specifically related to, and adapted to, these impulses and certain appropriate objects in the organism's environment;

(g) a certain feature of experience called '*Instinct-Interest*' or '*Instinct-Meaning*', which is conceived as the feeling of the whole relation between felt impulse, appropriate object, and behavioural means, and which is held to be an elementary 'cognition', and

(h) certain *capacities* for subsequent *intelligent control*;

are brought into being by heredity, and by the same process of evolution.

These internal physiological conditions; these various kinds of motor-activity—which may be regarded as 'functional correlates' of structures; and these various features of experience—perceptual and cognitive, conative and affective; are also (as is the inherited structure of the organism) held to be common among the members of a species, at least, of the same sex.

(2) The trains of unlearned behaviour which we find among animals are therefore accounted for as being the manifestations of these inherited features of structure, physiological process, behaviour, and experience, when the animal encounters the various situations of its environment; and the concept which is used to describe the way in which these features are related in any such manifestation of experience and behaviour is the Instinct. The Instinct is simply a concept used to denote a certain correlation of these various features; a correlation which, well-adapted in all its aspects to the normal situations of the environment, is established by heredity, and which can therefore account for the trains of unlearned behaviour which we observe in animals without entailing assumptions of individual experience and consequent learning.

The Instinct is held to comprise:

(*a*) *Internal Physiological Features*. These are the internal neuro-physiological conditions which form the basis of the behavioural and experiential features. The early 'Doctrine of Instincts' has little to say in this connection, excepting in a hypothetical form such as we have noted during our discussion of the various writers. Whilst these writers were well aware of the existence and importance of these features, the state of knowledge in their time precluded any detailed positive statement as to their nature.

(*b*) *Behavioural Features*. (i) A sequence of actions—sometimes of long duration—which leads to a specific end (i.e. sexual courtship and mating, nest-building, migration) and which, whilst comprising reflex actions and sensori-motor actions, shows a unity and complication which cannot be accounted for in terms of an associative 'addition' of these type-reactions alone.

(ii) A persistence of such behaviour, and, further, an increase in the complexity and variability of such behaviour, when the animal encounters any unusual obstacle which prevents it from attaining that 'end-state' to which its activity appears to be directed.

(iii) A cessation of such behaviour when this 'end-state' is attained.

(*c*) *Experiential Features*. (i) A perceptual feature, which indicates a sensitivity to specific elements of the environment which are appropriate to the instinct-experience of the moment, and which renders the animal relatively insensitive to other features in the perceptual situation even though, in fact, it is capable of perceiving them. Coupled with the persistently recurring impulse and the 'instinct-interest' mentioned below, this 'selective' perception gives the appearance, in the animal's behaviour, of 'concentration', or the 'narrowing of attention' to certain objects in the environment.

(ii) A craving, or persistently recurring impulse, which continues until a specific 'end-state', which relieves the craving or satisfies the impulse, is reached through behaviour.

(iii) A feeling of the significance of the whole relation between specific craving and specific perception which is termed the 'instinct-interest', and which can best be described as a feeling of worth-while-ness. This is an elementary 'cognitive' feature, even though it is an element of feeling, and it is relevant to what we shall have to say later on the importance of the 'affective' aspects of the learning processes.

(iv) A feeling of heightened tension, termed Emotion, arising when the normal instinctual activity is obstructed, and leading the animal to increase its efforts to carry out this behaviour successfully, and to increase the variability of its responses by the employment of other elements of its equipment of motor-reactions; but which may, in its most extreme form, render the behaviour of the animal completely undirected and ill-adapted to the situation.

(3) It is held that, among the simplest animals, the correlation of these several features is very closely and rigidly established by heredity. The instincts are, therefore, among these species, very specific, and comprise rigid and definite motor-mechanisms closely correlated with the instinctive impulse and the appropriate perception, and, in the situations encountered in the normal 'ecological niche', they are usually well-adapted. Because of their highly invariable nature they tend to become maladaptive when there are any unusual changes in these situations, and they are consequently regarded as being relatively 'blind', leading often to error. Among these lower species, emotion is held to play a very small, and among the lowest, a negligible part in instinctive experience and behaviour. As we come to the study of animal species higher in the evolutionary scale, however, it is held that (a) motor-responses and perceptions are less closely and rigidly correlated with the specific innate impulses by heredity, and (b) that, correspondingly, the emotional element of the affective experience becomes more prominent, having now a positive biological function to serve, and is of greater importance in leading the animal to persist in and vary the behaviour necessary to reach the appropriate 'end-state'.

(4) In view of the above points, and also because of our knowledge of the modifiability of perception and motor-response, *it is the conative-affective element of instinctive experience and behaviour which is regarded as the most central distinguishing feature of Instinct*. It is this feature which, throughout the whole range of species, gives unity and persistence to the features of behaviour which, whether rigidly correlated by heredity, or to some extent variously selected in the light of individual experience, are utilized in attaining the appropriate 'end-state'.

(5) It is held that the capacity for intelligent control, inherited in varying degrees by various species, comes into play in connection with the experience and activity of the instincts. The writers on Instinct discriminated between several levels of intelligent control, and, briefly, it is held that among the lower species intelligence may be almost negligible, or capable of only very minor adjustments in connection with the reactions involved in immediate activity, but that, among the higher species, intelligence becomes capable of grasping the relations between impulses, ends, and behavioural means, on the perceptual level, and finally, in the case of man, achieves a much more refined knowledge of these relations on the conceptual and ideational level. Instinct and Intelligence are therefore not regarded as being separate and distinct from each other, but as mingling modes of correlation, the one determined by heredity, and the other coming into play, within this given context, during the course of individual experience. All experience involves instinctual and intelligent elements, mingled in various degrees. It should also be added that intelligent control is conceived as developing from the original 'instinct-interest' in the light of 'feelings of satisfaction or dissatisfaction' encountered during the course of individual experience.

(6) Besides maintaining that behaviour may be modified by means of various degrees of intelligent control, it is held that instinctive experience and behaviour are also conditioned by habit-formation and by sentiment-formation, thus centring the instinctive activity of the animal, and the human being, about certain objects, and rendering it relatively insensitive to other objects of the same kind.

(7) It is held that, though inherited, the instincts are by no means present, in the sense of being mature, at birth, but that they emerge with the growth and maturation of the individual, so that certain instincts will be important, perhaps predominant, at one stage of growth and not at another; though some instincts are held to persist throughout the

lifetime of the individual. It is also held that, even though some instincts seem to 'fade away' after their particular period of importance, yet they may have an influence upon the later experience of the individual.

(8) Whilst the instincts of an animal are held to be specific—that is to say, they are distinguishable as to the specific craving, the specific appropriate perception, and the specific behavioural sequence—it is not held that the individual can be regarded as a mere 'aggregate' of them. The individual is regarded as a unity, a whole, with a complex experience, the elements of which have some kind of central order, or integration, which integration is furthered by intelligence. Thus, more general concepts such as 'temperament' and 'character' are used to denote the more pervading tendencies of the experience and behaviour of the individual as a whole. Nonetheless, the instincts remain distinguishable and specific within the complex of individual experience and behaviour. They exert a determining tendency on behaviour, and, when arising and activating the individual, they tend to bring the attention and efforts of the individual as a whole to bear upon that behaviour which is necessary to gratify them.

In reply to question (B):

(1) It is held that instinctual experience and behaviour *is* discernible, and *is* of great importance in the nature of man.

(2) In this instinctual experience and behaviour of man, two features of instinct—the perceptual feature, and the equipment of motor-responses—are not rigidly established by heredity; nor are they closely correlated with the specific cravings, or the 'conative-affective cores' of the instincts, by heredity. Both these features are held to be highly modifiable and dependent to a great extent upon experience and learning. At the same time, it is held (1) that there are at least some simpler instincts which appear to comprise well-defined motor-responses, and (2) that even in the more intricate behavioural sequences which are the outcome of experience and learning, there are at least some behavioural responses which are specifically related to certain 'cravings' and which are not wholly learned.

(3) *It is the conative-affective feature of instinctive experience and behaviour which is held to be of basic importance in the nature of man.* Certain distinguishable cravings, or periodically recurring and relatively persistent impulses, prompting behaviour and the exercise of intelligence

towards the attainment of specific and appropriate ends, are certainly inherited by man, and emerge in each individual during the course of growth and maturation. These inherited impulses are, it is held, common to all members of the human species, at least, of the same sex.

(4) In accordance with the hypothesis that it is of distinct biological advantage to possess the capacity of adaptation to considerable and varied environmental changes, rather than to be rigidly confined to a narrow 'ecological niche'; in view of the highly modifiable nature of certain features of human experience and behaviour as mentioned above; and in view, also, of the longer period of infancy and utter dependence upon parents of the offspring of the higher vertebrates, and especially of man; it is held that:

(a) The sequences of behaviour, and the motor-responses involved, employed by the human individual in gratifying his instinctual cravings are noted for their *plasticity*, and (1) are largely dependent upon processes of learning which take place during the period of infancy and youth, and (2) permit of great modification by the individual himself in accordance with the circumstances peculiar to his own experience.

(b) Because of the lack of automatic and well-adapted behavioural responses in the innate endowment, the element of emotion plays a greater part in the instinctual experience of man than it does in that of the animals. On the one hand, tension or emotion arises because the instinctual impulses are experienced, with all their forcefulness, in the absence of any automatic, appropriate motor-responses, and a measure of delay and suppression is involved whilst the behaviour which will give gratification is learned. On the other hand, there are certain instincts in man of which the emotion is the dominant element, as, for example, in fear, and it has been suggested that these, too, are the outcome of the non-specificity of the relations between impulses, perceived situation, and motor-response in man. In such cases, an instinctual tendency involves multiple responses, and it has been suggested that the emotion, here, *is* so dominant and important *because* of the multiplicity of possible responses and the fact that none of them are automatic, thus rendering a certain degree of selection necessary in relation to the particular situation. Apart from these two features of the place of emotion in human instinctual experience and behaviour, emotion also arises in man, as in the animals, when normal instinctual activity is obstructed or thwarted.

(5) It is held that the instincts lay down the basic and permanent ends of human activity, and that human intelligence is employed

predominantly in so ordering behaviour as to achieve the satisfactory attainment of these ends. In the main, the writers we have considered seem to hold the view that probably all the ends of human activity, no matter how complex, are ultimately traceable to the instincts, but, as a qualification to this, it is pointed out by both Hobhouse and Ginsberg that, whilst the complexity of human activity may be based upon the ends set by the instincts, it appears, nonetheless, that at least *some* further ends arise which cannot be explained entirely in terms of the instincts: as, for example, the desire for truth, the insistence upon 'scientific integrity' in inquiry, and so on. All these writers are agreed, however, that the major ends of human activity are rooted in the instincts.

(6) It is held, finally, that: since human individuals always live within particular social contexts, and are from the beginning of their lives subjected to many and varied social influences; and also because of the modifiability of human behaviour and the capacity for intelligent control which has been mentioned earlier; the *Social Tradition* is a factor of the utmost importance in shaping their behavioural responses and moulding their attitudes to various features of personal and social life. Thus, though the instinctual endowment of man is held to be common to all members of the species, setting the major common ends of all human activity, it is also held that the manifest details of individual and social behaviour will differ from society to society, or from social group to social group. Thus, whilst stressing the importance in human nature of instinctual experience and behaviour, the 'Doctrine of Instincts' by no means holds or implies that a knowledge of this instinctual endowment is sufficient for an explanation of all the complexities of individual and social life. Obviously, for these wider questions, much more than a theory of instincts is required.

*   *   *   *   *

This, then, is the early 'Doctrine of Instincts'. We have seen that, far from being a theory which asserts something arbitrary and unsupported about human nature, it is a theory worked out to give as satisfactory an account as is possible of that unlearned experience and behaviour which can be observed throughout the whole range of animal species; that it arose really in the context of Comparative Psychology with the theory of evolution in mind; and that it was on the strength of the theory of evolution that features of instinctive experience and behaviour, so common in other animal species, were looked for, and, according to these writers, found, in the nature of man.

With these early views clearly in mind, we can now turn to consider the criticisms which were levelled against them.

CHAPTER III

CRITICISMS OF THE EARLY 'DOCTRINE OF INSTINCTS'

In all, there seem to be ten such criticisms, and they will be dealt with in accordance with their degree of relevance and importance.

1. *The Behaviourist Criticism*

The criticism offered by the Behaviourists was the most radical and extreme of all the criticisms we shall have to consider. Since it exerted such a wide and pernicious influence upon subsequent psychology, especially in America, we shall discuss it at some length.

The Behaviourist view in its most extreme form was expounded by Watson, and can be formulated in the following way.

First, we are given two basic assertions:

(1) We have no right to posit perceptions and feelings in the animals or persons we are observing. In so far as we are scientific, we must take into account only those stimuli and responses which are strictly observable.

(2) Similarly, we have no right to introduce into our explanations such immaterial concepts as 'motives' or 'purposive tendencies'.

Given these two propositions, Watson argues, it can be said that: 'There is no such thing as the inheritance of temperament, capacity, mental constitution or mental characteristics . . .' and, '. . . all that is inherited is a pattern reaction, the separate elements of which are movements principally of the striped muscles.' All that is inherited is a number of reflexes. These, from the very outset of the individual's life are subjected to processes of conditioning which are continuous and complex, and which give rise to 'Compound-Reflexes'. Consequently: 'all so-called instinctive behaviour is really learned behaviour.' The intricate sequences of action which have been termed instinctive by the writers we have considered, are really the outcome of a long process of learning, taking place throughout the course of the individual's development.

The Behaviourists support their argument by reference to the 'Law of Parsimony'—which was stated by Lloyd Morgan (though not, of course, with any reference to Behaviourism)—and which holds that one should always adopt that explanation which is simplest and makes fewest assumptions.

The Behaviourists claim that all observable behaviour can be explained adequately in terms of reflexes and the process of conditioning ; that this avoids all the dubious assumptions (of perception, conation, instinct-interest, etc.) which the concept of instinct involves ; and that Behaviourism is, therefore, the most economical, besides being the more scientific, theory.

Such a naïve Behaviourist criticism would not nowadays be advanced.

Even without detailed argument, it is obvious that such a theory does not account at all adequately for the observed facts of experience and behaviour which the concept of instinct tries to embrace. The examples given in our opening chapter of the behaviour of the larva of the Capricorn Beetle, and the reproductive behaviour of the male stickleback (and many similar examples could be given [1]), reveal the quite spontaneous manifestations of well-adapted behavioural responses when the creature is facing a situation *for the first time*, and when there has been *no possibility of previous learning*. The simplest laboratory conditioning of a reflex takes time, and, it might be noted, is established in connection with a felt need in the animal and an association with a certain end which gives satisfaction (e.g. in the case of Pavlov: hunger/bell/presentation of food), and therefore a complicated chain-reflex sufficient to account for behaviour as intricate as that of the reproductive behaviour of the stickleback would require an appreciable length of time to allow for the conditioning to take place. But observation and experiment show that the animal—when in a condition of sexual motivation *for the first time*, and when faced with a particular situation *for the first time*—responds with a well-adapted sequence of actions which cannot possibly have been learned.

Thus, merely from a simple observation of the behavioural facts, the explanation of extreme Behaviourism seems completely far-fetched; and this, it may be noted, without taking into consideration at all the question as to whether there are any elements of *experience* accompanying such sequences of action.

We might also point out that the notion of 'conditioning' alone is not sufficient as an explanation of the process of learning with which the Behaviourists seek to oppose the doctrine of instincts.

[1] See the example of young trap-door spiders quoted by E. S. Russell in *The Behaviour of Animals* (Arnold, 1934), pp. 96-97.

Modern learning theory has moved far away from the supposed sufficiency for explanation of such mechanical conditioning or associationism, and there were always psychologists who recognised its inadequacy. Behaviourist theory not only fails to take into account the observed facts embodied in the Instinct theory, but also, whilst claiming that the sequences of action previously attributed to instinct can be better explained in terms of learning, it fails to give an adequate account of such learning.

Criticisms have been directed against (1) the primary assertions concerning the self-imposed limits of observation and method, and (2) the over-simplified physiology upon which the reduction of all behaviour to conditioned 'chain-reflexes' is based.

(1) Concerning the first point, Watson feels that to include features of 'perception' and 'feeling' in any description of observed behaviour is to 'introduce an air of mediaeval occultism'. Professor Burt, however— and we agree wholeheartedly with him—has suggested that to explain behavioural processes completely in terms of the movements of 'striped muscles', with no mention of 'perceiving', 'striving', and the like, is *more* occult, and not less.[1] The dangers of anthropomorphism are real enough, and we must beware of them, but it is going to a great extreme in opposition to a possibility of error, to adopt a position which denies the very existence of subjective experience. Indeed, by so doing, Behaviourism rules itself out altogether as a *psychological* theory. *Biology* can describe for us the behaviour of animals in relation to the various features of their respective habitats. *Physiology* can describe for us all the internal processes which are concomitant with these behavioural reactions. And if the Behaviourist theory is right—what else is required? If there is no such thing as subjective experience—sensation, feeling, striving, thinking, and the like—then there is no need for *Psychology!* Considerations such as these reveal the utter absurdity of Behaviourist theory. Behaviourism can be regarded as a positive regression in the history of Psychology.[2]

Let us see what McDougall, who admits the existence of subjective feelings, has to say about the element of 'striving' in instinctive behaviour.

---

[1] 'Is the Doctrine of Instincts Dead', Symposium, *British Journal of Educational Psychology* (1941-43).

[2] Some thinkers argue that Behaviourism had, at least, the merit of emphasising the need for close observation and experiment. This is true—but, even here, one cannot see why it should have been considered that these earlier writers were in need of such persuasion. They were, in fact, empiricists, and took into account, explicitly, all such empirical knowledge of animal behaviour as was available to them. Lloyd Morgan and Hobhouse were, indeed, pioneers of experimental psychology.

'We are justified in assuming the conative aspect of the psychical process', he says, 'because all instinctive behaviour exhibits that unique mark of mental process, a persisting striving towards the natural end of the process. That is to say, the process, unlike any merely mechanical process, is not to be arrested by any sufficient mechanical obstacle, but is rather intensified by any such obstacle and only comes to an end either when its appropriate goal is achieved, or when some stronger incompatible tendency is excited, or when the creature is exhausted by its persistent efforts.[1]'

Surely there is no harm in accepting the existence of subjective feelings, so long as we do *not* conclude that this constitutes a satisfactory *causal* explanation of the whole process of behaviour?

Here, the question always arises as to whether it is legitimate to attribute 'purposive tendencies' to animals in their behaviour. No harm can be done if the word 'purpose' is used in order to *describe* the facts, not necessarily to *explain* them. Instinctive actions terminate in a certain end. Until this end is reached, the creature persists in its conative efforts. Once this end is reached, the activity ceases. Used descriptively, the term 'purpose' merely signifies the sequence of behaviour towards an end, and in this sense it can be observed; it is objective. 'Purpose' could also mean 'consciously apprehended purpose', but it need not be held that such a 'conscious apprehension' of the end of action necessarily exists in instinctive behaviour.

At the same time we must point out that there are no grounds for holding that *some* kind of awareness of the end, that is to say the feeling of significance of some particular object in connection with a certain felt craving, does *not* exist in instinctive experience and behaviour. Without labouring the point, we have seen that the assumption of an element of 'instinct-interest' or 'instinct-meaning' in instinctive experience makes sense of the subsequent modification of behaviour by means of intelligent control; makes intelligible the way in which intelligence arises in the service of the instincts; and we have seen that, ultimately, intelligence may achieve a comprehensive grasp of the relations between craving, appropriate end, and behavioural means. When this stage is reached—as in the conceptual and ideational knowledge of man, and perhaps on the perceptual plane among the higher animals—activity can legitimately be said to be purposive from the conscious, subjective point of view as well as from the objective point of view, though it is still directed towards an end set by instinct.

However, we can agree that though the term 'purpose' can be used from the purely objective point of view, the imputation of 'subjective purpose' must be treated with the greatest care, though, as we have seen, there are cases in which it would be quite correct to do so.

E. S. Russell,[1] who also believes that it is quite impossible to give an adequate description of animal behaviour without taking into account features of experience, makes this point very clearly.

After giving examples of elvers swimming steadily and persistently up the River Severn, and salmon swimming upstream, 'breasting the current and leaping turbulent falls', Russell goes on to say that these examples 'serve to illustrate what is the most characteristic feature of behaviour as directly observed, namely, that the animal tries or strives to do something specific, that it seeks to achieve some end, to satisfy some need. It is not in the least necessary to assume that it is conscious of the end pursued, that it represents to itself the goal and the means of reaching it. . . . We need make no hypothesis at all about the animal's inner experience, but we must accept the direct observational evidence that, in the examples quoted and in thousands of others, behaviour is, objectively considered, directed towards an end.'

Supporting this view, Russell stresses the fact that behaviour is often part of a long-range cycle of events in which one action leads to the next until the end is reached. 'Each stage in the chain or cycle is unintelligible to us except in relation to what has gone before, and, more particularly, to what is yet to come. Such cycles have a temporal unity, extending often over months of time, just as a simple conative action has unity of short temporal range.' The best example of this is the breeding cycle in birds.

'Here we have in many cases selection of territory by the male, warding off of intruders, the attraction of a mate, courtship, sexual union, the building of a nest, egg-laying, brooding, the feeding of the young until they can fend for themselves; parallel with these events are cyclical changes in the reproductive organs. . . .'

'The remarkable thing about the whole intricate cycle is that each step is anticipatory . . . of the stages yet to come. Territory is selected with a view to the needs of the young that are to be born a month or two later. The nest is built in readiness for the eggs to be laid, and of a size sufficient to accommodate the fledglings. All goes on *as if* the pair of birds planned their course of action with foresight of its end. It is, of course, extremely doubtful whether they do foresee the ultimate end or aim of their actions; their behaviour is mainly instinctive, independent of previous experience, and to a considerable extent stereotyped and invariable.'

[1]*The Behaviour of Animals*, Chapter I, p. 3.

In these examples we see evidence of that 'provision for the future' which the earlier writers pointed out, which is characteristic of instinctive experience and behaviour, and which is established by heredity, and not by previous experience on the part of the individual.

In the light of these arguments, the Behaviourists' primary objection to the introduction of perceptions, feelings, and purposive tendencies, into the description of observed behaviour is untenable and must be rejected. No adequate description (let alone explanation) of behaviour can be given without taking them into account, and, whilst the inner experiences of these features cannot themselves be directly observed, a good deal of evidence for their existence can, in fact, be directly observed.

(2) The Behaviourist criticism has also been met with regard to its insistence upon the inheritance only of isolated, differentiated reflexes as the basis of individual development, and the explanation of all subsequent behavioural processes in terms of conditioning. It has been pointed out (*a*) that the facts of instinctive experience and behaviour cannot be described adequately in terms of reflexes alone, and (*b*) that the stress upon independent reflexes as the basic units of behaviour is far too naïve and does not receive support from physiological research.

Instinctive behaviour essentially comprises, among other things, a craving, a persistently recurring impulse, which is closely correlated with the direction, the persistence, and the unity of a certain sequence of actions. In such instinctive activity, the whole organism is involved. The attention and efforts of the animal as a whole are concentrated upon this action in relation to certain features of a complex situation. Simple reflex-actions, in contrast with this, are mechanical, automatic, and effortless; they are type-reactions (over which the individual has little or no control) to simple, single stimuli; and, finally, they do not involve the attention or activity of the whole organism, but are *partial* reactions. Whilst we may be conscious that a reflex action has in fact occurred, consciousness has practically nothing to do with its activation. There is no need to labour this distinction, as we have already seen in our discussion of the earlier writers that the distinction was quite clearly recognised by them.

There is now a good deal of experimental evidence in support of the view that there is no set of isolated reflexes at birth, but that, from the beginning, even before birth, the organism is *active* as well as *re-active*[1]; that innate behaviour comprises factors which are 'spontaneous' (the outcome of the complex internal processes of the organism) besides

[1] As Hobhouse puts it: the individual is a 'going concern' and not entirely dependent upon external stimuli for its activation.

those factors which are re-active to external stimuli. The work of Coghill[1] on the growth and development of the nervous system in Ablystoma, the Axolotl larva, in relation to the development of its first co-ordinated movements such as swimming and walking, illustrates this.

Coghill found, firstly, a close correlation between the growth of the nervous system and the appearance of more complicated behavioural reactions, and secondly, that behaviour was, from the beginning, a unified or integrated activity. Early limb movements were found to be an integral part of the total action of the animal, and only later acquired any independence. Coghill tells us: 'The local reflex of the arm is not a primary or elementary behaviour pattern of the limb. It is secondary, and derived from the total pattern by a process of individuation.' He goes on to show how walking develops out of swimming. '. . . movement of the trunk in walking is nothing more nor less than the swimming movement with greatly reduced speed. . . .' Walking, then, does not arise by the combination of separate limb reflexes; the limb-movements are at first integrated with the trunk-movements, and only later acquire some measure of independence. The process of growth and development generally, and the development of behaviour, is essentially one of differentiation within a whole.

The idea that the reflex-arc is the basic unit of behaviour, and that all behaviour can be accounted for in terms of such reflexes and their subsequent conditioning, is *not*, therefore, supported by the facts of development. Behaviour does not appear to be the outcome of the addition or combination of originally separate reflexes.

E. S. Russell[2] emphasises that 'in the intact animal, as is now generally recognised, there is no such thing as pure reflex action in normal behaviour; all so-called reflexes are parts of co-ordinated, and generally . . . directive actions, and they cannot be understood until their relation to the objective aim of the whole action is known. . . .' During the course of his discussion of this point, Russell gives two illuminating examples to show the inadequacy of the 'reflex'—'chain-reflex' postulate.

Quoting from W. A. Kepner, he gives an illustration of a pure reflex action in an *organ* of 'Planaria', divorced from its living association with the rest of the animal.

'When we examine the reflex conduct of an incomplete organism or organ the suggestion of choice in the conduct becomes nil. Dr. Arnold Rich and I observed that, by destroying certain neural centres of "Planaria albissima", its proboscis would undergo auto-amputation. The proboscis then freed would swim about as an independent organism

[1] *Anatomy and the Problem of Behaviour*, 1929.   [2] *The Behaviour of Animals*, p. 12.

ingesting and swallowing every small object that it would encounter. But in this reflex conduct it displayed no choice. Swallow it had to; so that if we placed small particles of glass in its path, these would be taken in. The proboscis would even turn upon the body of which it had formed an organized part and eat its way through from one side to the other. When this organ is under the normal inhibitory control of the animal, as a whole, it displays a very evident faculty of choice in that it nicely chooses between food and non-food. In normal life, therefore, we have the proboscis of Planaria displaying choice, whereas it is only when it is detached from its body proper that it shows a purely mechanical reflex in which no choice is apparent.'[1]

No example could better illustrate the difference between a 'pure reflex' working autonomously, and when working as part of the integrated action of the organism as a whole. Russell, however, also puts forward a much simpler observation, which, in spite of its simplicity, is equally damaging to any theory of behaviour which rests only upon initial reflex actions and their subsequent conditioning.

'A blackbird picks up a worm in its beak, and, if it is feeding itself, swallows it. This *might* be a purely reflex train of events. But if it is foraging for its family it does *not* swallow the worm, though on the reflex theory swallowing ought to follow automatically from the stimulus of the worm in the mouth. It keeps the worm in its beak and perhaps hunts for more before taking it back to the nest. The objective aim or "purpose" of the activity controls its detailed course, inhibits the normal swallowing reflex, if reflex it be.'

In view of these many objections and the evidence which has been presented in support of them, we can regard the Behaviourist criticism of the Doctrine of Instincts as being conclusively refuted. It is, indeed, difficult to see how the Behaviourist position ever had the vogue and exercised the influence it did, especially in view of the work of the earlier writers we have considered. All these writers were perfectly well aware of the importance of the physiological and the behavioural aspects, as well as of the excperiential aspects, of the facts of innate experience and behaviour which they attempted to describe with the concept of Instinct. In the work of Hobhouse, for example, the complex internal processes of the organism, and the reflex action, were all given due consideration and their due place in his treatment of the various levels of correlated action. How the naïvety of the Behaviourist approach could ever have been considered more 'scientific' and reliable than this

[1] W. A. Kepner, *Animals Looking into the Future*, quoted by Russell.

earlier work is a mystery, and seems, now, quite incomprehensible. One can only conclude that this earlier work was not studied with the detailed care that it deserved, and that the stimulus of McDougall's simple and forthright statement and the heated reaction which it called into being, precluded a study of other writers in the field.

2. 'The Hypostatization of Concepts'

The second criticism can be framed as follows:

'The Doctrine of Instincts commits the fallacy of the hypostatization of concepts, and of assigning to them, thereby, the power of causality.'

This criticism arises from the fact that such terms as 'the sexual instinct' or the 'fighting instinct' are considered to be class-names denoting certain correlated sequences of physiological facts, attendant experiences, and trains of behaviour. They are merely descriptive concepts, and to regard them as being, in any sense, discrete 'entities' or 'things' is an error. The error is increased by speaking as though these 'entities' actually *caused* the sequences of physiology, experience, and behaviour, of which, initially, they were simply the descriptive concepts. This error leads (*a*) to the assertion of obscure but essentially trivial propositions, which, when analysed, are shown to consist of the mere repetition of one statement, and (*b*) to a state of sterility in psychology, when processes are thought to be explained when, in fact, they have simply been named—leaving all the actual causal factors of the process undiscovered. In this way the psychology of Instinct commits the same error as that of the older Faculty Psychology which explained behavioural processes simply by saying that 'faculties' were possessed by the agent, and that these 'faculties' *caused* these behavioural processes.[1]

In order to be perfectly clear on this point, we might attempt an illustration of it. Thus, closely following the definition of an instinct proposed by McDougall, we might say:

'The sexual instinct', let us say of a certain species of bird, 'is a psycho-physical disposition determining the female bird to perceive and pay attention to the display of plumage of the male bird, to experience an excitement of a particular quality on perceiving it, and to adopt a certain sequence of behaviour in courtship and mating, or, at least, to experience an impulse to act in this way.'

'The sexual instinct', this criticism says, is our descriptive concept which denotes the correlation of all these features of experience and behaviour. Now, it is argued, if we are asked: 'How does the female bird come to manifest this kind of experience and behaviour in courtship and

[1] The clearest statement of this criticism is to be found in 'Faculty Psychology and Instinct Psychology' by G. C. Field, *Mind*, 1921.

mating?'—it is pointless to answer that it is 'caused by the sexual instinct' or that it is 'due to the operation of the sexual instinct', since, at the outset, we have used the term 'the sexual instinct' simply to indicate these features of experience and behaviour. Such an answer, when analysed, would be seen to consist of the same proposition stated twice. We should be saying: 'ABC is caused by X (which = ABC).' Our answer would in no sense constitute an explanation. And, the criticism goes on, if such answers are taken to be satisfactory as analyses of the causal factors in question, then the effect will be to bring experimental inquiry to a full-stop. This verbal usage will give the impression that the causal factors *are*, in fact, adequately known, when all that we have done is simply to give *names* to the observed facts which require explanation.

Such then is the second criticism advanced against the use of the concept of Instinct. We find Thorndike saying: 'The old use of the term instinct was akin to the faculty psychology that was satisfied to explain events by naming their unknown causes', and, after suggesting that this older usage still persists, Thorndike informs us that: 'There are no such magical instincts.'

Before replying to this criticism, it must be admitted that the danger of sterility following upon such a naïve usage of the concept of Instinct as a form of explanation does seem to have been very real, and many psychologists were led to rebel against the use of the concept for this reason alone. We find Katz saying in 1937: 'The concept of need in comparison with that of drive has the advantage of being nearer to reality, and assuredly is much less encumbered with hypotheses than is the concept of instinct. For the present it is, of course, impossible to work in animal psychology without the postulation of instincts, because they are necessary for the classification of certain forms of behaviour, but all those who understand the situation complain of the irritating sterility of this concept in any approach to new problems. . . .'[1] We shall find, too, that the revival of the experimental study of instinct in the 1930's followed upon the re-formulation of the concept by Konrad Lorenz. To the extent that this criticism warned psychologists of the dangers inherent in a careless verbal usage of the concept of instinct, and therefore insisted that the causal factors underlying innate experience and behaviour remained to be discovered, it was of real value.

Whether the earlier writers on instinct were guilty of this charge of hypostatisation is a different matter. For all of them, the concept of instinct denoted a certain correlation of features of physiological process, experience, and behaviour, which were adapted to certain features

[1]Katz, *Animals and Men*.

of the organism's normal environment, and which were established by heredity. Each specific instinct was named in accordance with the normal 'end-state' of the particular sequence of behaviour. Thus, the 'sexual instinct' was that which terminated in courtship and sexual mating, the 'parental instinct' was that which terminated in the care of the young. The concept, therefore, could correctly be called a descriptive concept. None of these writers, however, conceived these instincts as being 'mysterious entities' which *caused* the features of experience and behaviour which they actually comprised.[1] *All* of them stated that the instincts came into being, as did the physical structures of species, through the process of evolution: that is to say, they were the *effect* of heredity, mutations, and the process of natural selection. To this extent, then, all these writers attributed the instincts of any species to the same underlying causes which the biological theory of evolution postulates in order to account for the physical structures of various species. Similarly, all were aware that the concept of instinct comprised (*a*) neuro-physiological facts, (*b*) behavioural facts, and (*c*) facts of experience. Perceiving the difficulty of establishing any strictly causal relationships between the physiological and behavioural facts on the one hand and the facts of experience on the other—neither of which could be described adequately in terms of the other—we have seen that these writers postulated the notion of '*concomitancy*'. They were, at this stage, not prepared to postulate definite causal relationships between the two levels, though they assumed that such relationships were there to be discovered. They were, in fact, extremely careful on this point.

When we regard the concept of instinct in this way (as comprising features of several orders of phenomena), we can see that it is of the nature of a collective or compendious term. Within the concept of instinct itself, we might find physiologists who would be inclined to say that the internal physiological conditions comprised the chief causal factor of instinct, and that 'experiential' factors were wholly dependent upon these and had no *causal* efficacy in their own right. On the other hand, psychologists might be found who would say that it was the 'perception' of a completely unusual situation which *caused* a disordered and ill-adapted sequence of behaviour to take place, which then *caused* certain visceral changes which finally *caused* the experience of emotion. Thus, perhaps many kinds of causal relationships might be held to obtain between the various features of physiological process, experience, and behaviour which the concept of instinct comprises, and we shall see that much of the recent experimental work

[1]We may recall Hobhouse's specific rejection of this, p. 42.

really consists of breaking down the concept of instinct into its several features and attempting to elucidate the detailed relationships which hold between them. However, our point here is simply to show that the early writers were in fact aware of the complexity of the causal relations involved. We may remember the care with which Lloyd Morgan and Drever stressed the difficulty involved in elucidating these causal relationships, and the very careful approach to this whole question made by Hobhouse which we quoted in particular anticipation of this criticism.[1]

McDougall is really the only writer who might be charged with this particular fallacy, but even with McDougall it is more the outcome of careless terminology than any fundamental mistake as to the facts. Thus, McDougall defines an instinct as '. . . a psycho-physical disposition *which determines* . . .' and then he lists the various components of instinctive experience and behaviour. But if we were to change these words very slightly, to read: '. . . a psycho-physical disposition *comprising* . . .' and then enumerated the same components, the error would be removed. And it is true to say that McDougall really regards the instinct as a descriptive concept; that, as we have said above, he regards these 'psycho-physical dispositions' as being correlations of physiological, behavioural, and experiential features established by heredity.

Our last chapter should have made it clear that the earlier writers objected as much as do their critics to regarding the instincts as being 'mysterious faculties' with which animals were endowed, and which accounted for their behaviour. We have seen how Hobhouse says that it was the breakdown of this conception which 'made animal psychology possible as a science'. And we can find similar observations in the work of McDougall. We find him saying, for example: 'Contemporary writers of all classes make frequent use of the words "instinct" and "instinctive", but, with very few exceptions, they use them so loosely that they have almost spoilt them for scientific purposes. . . . The actions of animals are popularly attributed to instinct, and in this connection instinct is vaguely conceived as a mysterious faculty, utterly different in nature from any human faculty, which Providence has given to the brutes because the higher faculty of reason has been denied them.' After giving examples of such usage, McDougall says: 'they justify the statement that these words "instinct" and "instinctive" are commonly used as a cloak for ignorance when a writer attempts to explain any individual or collective action that he fails, or has not tried, to understand.'[2]

In assessing this second criticism, we can say that it was of value in

[1]See pp. 41-43.   [2]*Social Psychology*, pp. 18-19.

pointing out the dangers attendant upon a mistaken satisfaction with the concept of instinct as comprising an adequate *causal* analysis of instinctive experience and behaviour. The charge against the writers on instinct themselves, of the hypostatisation of concepts, however, is seen to be a very dubious one. Only McDougall seems to be at all guilty of it, and even in his case, the matter seems more one of verbal carelessness than a serious misinterpretation of the facts.

3. *The Organism cannot be regarded simply as an 'Aggregate' of Separate Instincts*

This third criticism can be formulated as follows:

'The Doctrine of Instincts tends to regard the instincts as a number of separate entities, and to regard the organism as a whole as being simply an 'aggregate' of these entities. This will not do. The organism as a whole cannot be regarded merely as a sum of separate bits of experience and behaviour, but must be regarded, from the very beginning, as possessing a certain unity in its growth and development.'

This objection is clearly related to the charge of hypostatisation, and, here again, it is levelled mainly at the treatment of McDougall. It is true that McDougall's treatment sometimes gives the impression that the instincts are regarded as a number of self-subsistent sources of energy of which the organism is merely the sum. 'The disposition of a person is the sum of all the innate dispositions or instincts with their specific impulses or tendencies. . . .'[1] And the analogies he uses are sometimes unfortunate. 'Directly or indirectly the instincts are the prime movers of all human activity. . . . Take away these instinctive dispositions with their powerful impulses, and the organism would become incapable of activity of any kind; it would lie inert and motionless like a wonderful clockwork whose mainspring had been removed or a steam-engine whose fires had been drawn.'[2]

There is no doubt, then, that McDougall's treatment does sometimes suggest that the instincts are a set of irreducible forces which determine practically everything, and that the individual is simply the sum of these forces. We have tried to show that, when his work is studied in detail and all his various qualifications are noted, this impression of the rigidity, separateness, and unmodifiability of the instincts is not in fact carried out in an extreme way, and is certainly not intended; nonetheless it is true that much of what he has to say gives the impression to which this objection is raised. We must therefore regard this as a legitimate criticism of McDougall. We cannot, however, regard

[1] *Social Psychology*, p. 102.   [2] *Ibid.* p. 38.

it as a legitimate criticism of the Doctrine of Instincts as a whole. None of the other writers regarded the organism as a 'simple aggregation of separate instincts' in this way. Reference may be made to the statement of Hobhouse (p. 46).

Let us be quite clear, however, what is being admitted here. We have accepted the objection which says that the instincts cannot be regarded as a set of self-subsistent entities, irreducible 'bits', of which the organism is a simple collection or aggregate, whilst denying that, apart from McDougall, any of the earlier writers did in fact regard them in this way.

But let us be clear that this point in no way controverts the view of the specificity of the instincts! It merely emphasises that, specific though they are, they cannot be regarded as irreducible entities or as being in any sense self-subsistent, and that the organism is something *more* than a simple addition of them.

Let us press this question further, and consider in what way we can regard the instincts as being specific, without committing the error which has just been outlined. Just as we have pointed out (in our argument against the view that isolated reflexes form the basic units of behaviour) that the organism is from the beginning an 'active' process of growth and development and that the more or less independent reflexes gradually crystallise during the course of this development by a process of differentiation within the whole; so we must take the view that the instincts, too, cannot be regarded as irreducible units, but that they also are specific correlations of physiological, behavioural, and experiential features which gradually crystallise, or become differentiated, during the process of growth and maturation. To take an example, the new hormonal factors and the new physical changes which characterise the onset of the secondary sexual characteristics in human development, are concomitant with the arousal of specific experiential and behavioural features in the individual. These physiological, behavioural, and experiential features are *specific;* they are distinguishable from other correlations of such features in the individual, as, for example, those underlying hunger, thirst, fear, sleep, and so on. In this way, we can regard the instincts as being specific, but, at the same time, as being differentiations which are gradually established during the course of the growth and maturation of the individual organism as a whole.

We may hold the view, then, that the instincts are specific, distinguishable elements in the experience and behaviour of the individual without committing the error either of regarding them as self-subsistent entities, or of regarding the organism as a simple aggregate of them.

The earlier writers did in fact regard the specificity of the instincts in this way, and therefore this third criticism is not relevant to them.

Before leaving this criticism, we might mention one final point without elaborating upon it at this stage. This is: that, *psychologically* speaking, the view that the individual is, throughout the course of growth and development, a nicely integrated whole may be every bit as naïve as the view that the individual is simply an aggregate of separate instincts. Because of points we have mentioned earlier, the instinctual demands of the human being will, necessarily, be attended with certain degrees of tension and anxiety, and the emerging Ego of the individual may experience situations of the most severe conflict whilst seeking to establish satisfactory modes of behaviour. Whilst agreeing with this third objection, therefore, we must nonetheless point out that we could not accept any sweeping assertion from the opposite view (i.e. that, in all cases, individual development is characterised by an orderly, central integration, within which the instincts emerge in due order and nicely fulfil their appropriate functions) without qualification. The process of individual development, especially from the point of view of the individual's *experience*, cannot be as simple as either of these views supposes.

4. *Each Instinct cannot be said to have a Particular Attendant Emotion*

This criticism does not require further discussion here. We have already seen the weakness of McDougall's treatment; the way in which this was quickly recognised by other writers on the subject; and—in the work of Drever and Ginsberg—how it was considerably amended, resulting in a much more satisfactory account of the whole question of the relation between instinct and emotion. Since these writers were themselves supporters of, and contributors to, the doctrine of instincts, this criticism cannot be directed against the theory of instincts as a whole, but, once again, must be regarded as a criticism of McDougall.

5. *The Environmentalist Criticism.* (*Arising from the work of the Cultural Anthropologists*)

This criticism arose from the varieties of behaviour revealed by the studies of different human societies, and from the accompanying discovery that the 'goals' of endeavour and the 'attitudes' of human beings differed and varied in strength from society to society. The material upon which this criticism rests is now very wide and varied, but we may illustrate it briefly from the work of Ruth Benedict[1] and Margaret Mead[2] who might be considered as its chief proponents.

[1]Ruth Benedict, *Patterns of Culture.*
[2]Margaret Mead, *Sex and Temperament in Three Primitive Societies.*

Benedict, in describing and discussing the social behaviour of the Zuñi (Pueblo) Indians, the Kwakiutl Indians, and the Dobu Islanders, shows how widely the behaviour of each of these three groups differs from that of the others, and, also, how the goals of endeavour are different in each. The Zuñi Indian is a well-integrated peace-loving individual who seeks to fit in inconspicuously with the complex cere- monies and social rituals of the community which are so ordered as to minimise friction, discord, and disruption in every aspect of life. The Kwakiutl Indian seeks social prestige above everything else, competing with his fellows in a form of intense rivalry in which success is attained by the strange method of destroying great quantities of property. The man who can destroy most at one of these feasts—to which he has invited his rival—enjoys the highest social prestige. The Dobuan Islander, different altogether from these former types, lives in a society saturated with mistrust and treachery; he goes his own way, guarding his charms (connected with the growing of yams, etc.) secretively and jealously from others; expecting treachery from the other members of his society and always ready to behave treacherously towards them.

Margaret Mead describes the temperament and behaviour mani- fested in the sexual relations of the members of three different societies. Among the Arapesh both men and women are what we would describe as gentle and effeminate; sexual relations are initiated by either sex; and both male and female share equally in the bringing up of the children and in participating in their childrens' activities. Among the Mundu- gumor, on the other hand—whilst, again, there is no evident difference in the temperamental qualities of male and female, and whilst sexual relations are again initiated by either sex—sexual behaviour is charac- terised by its aggressive, hostile, vicious nature; family relations are violently competitive; children must obtrude as little as possible in the life of adults, and, hung in their baskets on the wall, are given only scant attention, being fed quickly and abruptly when they scream with hunger. The Tchambuli come a little closer to what we expect in such relations between male and female from the point of view of our own culture, were it not for the fact that the status and temperament of the sexes are the complete reversal of our own. Here, it is the women who exert initiative and power, who are regarded as the most 'highly-sexed' of the two sexes, who initiate sexual relations. The men in this society, we are told, must be wooed by the women before their desire is aroused, and exercise their 'effeminate' charms in order to wheedle their wishes from their women-folk.

Such descriptions of human behaviour in societies other than our own are extremely interesting, and Social Anthropology is now in a position to provide us with a wide range of monographs describing human behaviour in the simpler societies. But what is the conclusion arising from such work which can be used as a criticism of the doctrine of instincts? It is, we are told, that the wide variations in human behaviour which anthropological studies reveal, are culturally, or environmentally determined, and *not innately* determined.

But this criticism can be seen to be quite wide of the mark, and rests upon a very superficial interpretation—one might almost assert a very limited reading—of the work of the writers on instinct. We have seen that not a single writer who supported the doctrine of instincts denied (*a*) that the instincts in man were highly modifiable, especially on the 'perceptual' and the 'behavioural' sides, or (*b*) that the particular pattern of behaviour which individuals adopted in pursuing the instinctual ends of activity would be largely determined by the Social Tradition into which the individuals were born and within which they grew to maturity. Indeed, all these writers were quite well aware of this modifiability and of the important influence of the social context, and in the work of Lloyd Morgan, Hobhouse, and Ginsberg, this complex factor is given great stress. We have shown, too, that even McDougall laid stress on the modifiability of the instinctive manifestations, and of the influence upon behaviour of different social settings.

Such a criticism would be legitimate against a theory which proposed to explain all varieties of human behaviour in terms of the instincts, without taking other factors into account. But the doctrine of instincts did not do this. None of the writers who contributed to the theory asserted or expected that the instincts would explain everything; they were merely concerned to show (among other things) that man did in fact inherit certain instincts which set the basic ends of human activity, and that this was a fact of importance which had to be taken into account in any theory of human nature.

Furthermore—and this must be *emphasised* repeatedly—the feature of instinct which was held to be of the greatest importance in man was *not* the *behavioural* feature, but the '*conative-affective*' core of the instinct; the 'craving' or the persistently recurring impulse. These were the instinctual features which were held to be innate in human nature and common to all members of the human species, *not* the *behaviour patterns* which were developed in their service. If the doctrine of instincts maintained that rigid motor mechanisms and behaviour patterns were inherited by man and were common to the human species, then this criticism—which shows that human behaviour differs in different societies—would have some point; but since this was never postulated, but was, in fact, explicitly denied by the writers on instinct, the criticism can be seen to have no point whatever.

Before leaving this point, however, it may be mentioned that those social anthropologists who might be grouped broadly under the name of the 'Culture-Personality' school, are now receiving a good deal of criticism.[1] Two points which have a bearing on the present question might be mentioned. Firstly, it seems probable that the tendency to describe individual personalities in terms of broad cultural uniformities, has gone too far, and it may be that the whole question of the degree to which individual persons are 'conditioned' by their 'culture' has been too readily assumed, rather than demonstrated. The second point is that the emphasis on the varieties of behaviour in different human societies may well have tended to obscure the similarities; similarities not only of 'instinct-experience' (congenital impulses), but even of elements of behaviour. Thus, let us consider behaviour involved in walking, eating, drinking, defecation, sleeping and waking, sexual intercourse, the care of young infants, fear and the avoidance of danger. It would seem that, no matter how varied are the more complicated methods of food-seeking, sanitation, provision for rest and sleeping, the regulation of the relations between the sexes, the bringing up of children, the social methods for avoiding danger, and so on, it remains true, nonetheless, that there are certain basic features of behaviour which are congenital in man and which are necessarily involved in the satisfaction of the congenital cravings, some of which persist throughout his life. Margaret Mead describes for us three varieties of sexual behaviour in three societies, but, we suggest, this merely indicates that the cultural setting exercises its influence upon the behaviour adopted in order to satisfy the instinctual demand which is inherited; and the contributors to the theory of instincts would have no quarrel with this. But if the persisting sexual impulse was not inherited, and if this impulse did not drive men and women to definite fundamental forms of behaviour for its gratification, no 'social conditioning' would ever take place. There would be nothing to 'condition'. No rules regulating sexual relations would be necessary. There would be nothing to regulate. If the Cultural Anthropologists are going to make us doubt the existence of the sexual instinct in man (and the same applies to the other instincts) they must show us not how variously men and women satisfy this instinct in different societies, but a society in which—as an outcome of the determining influence of the social environment—there is no evidence of the sexual impulse, or of the basic forms of sexual behaviour, at all. We can predict that such a society is going to be very hard to find.

[1]See R. Bendix, 'Compliant Behaviour and Individual Personality', *American Journal of Sociology*, November 1952, No. 3, vol. lviii, p. 292.

6. *There is no Stereotyped Behaviour at all in Man*

Since there is no stereotyped behaviour at all among men, some critics have asked, how can we tell whether any human act is, or is not, instinctively determined? If we cannot do this, the concept of instinct is not practically useful.

Two points may be made in reply to this criticism. The first is that, once again, critics have not been clear as to what the writers on instinct have had to say, and the criticism is therefore beside the point. All these writers are agreed that the pattern of motor-responses is highly modifiable in man, and cannot be held to be the chief distinguishing feature of instinct. No matter how variable this overt behaviour is, however, we find that much of it is directed towards those ends which satisfy congenital cravings such as hunger, thirst, sleep, sex, and the like. And it is the *latter* which are conceived to be the chief persisting features of instinct in man. This criticism, like that of the Cultural Anthropologists, is not really relevant.

We might, however, question the assertion made. Is it *true* that there is no stereotyped behaviour at all in man? We suggested in meeting the last criticism that there were probably *some* common features in the behavioural sequences involved in the gratification of instinctual cravings; *some* behavioural reactions, at least, which were common to all men. How do men walk, run, grasp, fight, ward off blows, eat, drink, defecate, urinate, sleep, copulate, feed their new-born offspring? Surely there are *some* features of behaviour in the activities here mentioned which are specifically involved in the satisfaction of innate impulses and cravings and which are common to all members of the species? These will always be involved, it is true, in different social contexts, in wider and variable behaviour-patterns connected with food-seeking or food-production, sanitary arrangements, the construction of dwelling-places, customs and laws of courtship and marriage, methods of child-rearing, and so on. Nonetheless, these common, basic, and necessary features of behaviour remain as definite elements within the cultural complexity. Moreover, they are often more powerfully desired than the details of the institutional fabric of society, and methods of compulsion and punishment have to be employed in order to force human behaviour into the strait-jacket of the social order.

When we are asked, then: How can we tell whether any human act is, or is not, instinctively determined? we can reply in three ways. (1) We can say that the doctrine of instincts does not maintain that stereotyped behavioural reactions are rigidly established by heredity in the case of man, only that certain persistently recurring impulses or cravings are inherited and are of the greatest importance. The question of determining whether a certain human *action* is instinctively determined—in the sense of showing how it is established by heredity—does not strictly arise. The persistently recurring impulses and cravings themselves (hunger, thirst, tiredness and sleep, fear, sexual cravings, etc.) can be shown to be common to all human beings by simple observation. Further, they can be shown to be innate in that they rest upon definite structural and physiological conditions which develop during the course of growth and maturation, and which are not noticeably affected by social 'conditioning'. (2) We can say that at least *some* basic behavioural features connected with the congenital cravings and necessary for their gratification seem to be innate and common to all members of the human species. As to how these can be determined as being innate, we shall have more to say when we consider the work of the ethologists, but it is clear that, in order to prove our point, we should be able to show that the development of such behavioural reactions is closely correlated with growth and maturation, and is not learned. (3) We can say that those sequences of behaviour which terminate in the ends set by the instincts can be said to be *determined* by the instincts to the extent that they are necessarily undertaken *in the service of* the instincts (considered as congenital cravings); but here we would readily agree that the particular detailed patterns of behaviour adopted in any society are very largely determined by other, social, factors which could not be described at all in terms of the instincts. In a later chapter we shall try to classify those human instincts the existence of which we can be reasonably certain in the light of recent work, and, in view of what has been said here, we shall try to include, in this classification, the basic behavioural features which are considered to be involved.

7. *Psycho-Analysis has proved that much previously considered to be Innate is, in fact, Acquired in early life*

It is difficult to see how such a criticism could be advanced by anyone who thoroughly understood the Psycho-Analytic account of the personality, and the large part assigned in it to the instinctual demands. However, the view has been put forward that Psycho-Analysis has shown that many features which were previously considered to be innate were actually acquired in infancy, and that this, therefore, may be true also of the many 'instincts' which have been postulated. Since we shall be considering the Psycho-Analytic theory of the instincts in much detail later, we can merely satisfy ourselves at this point by countering this suggestion by a quotation from Freud himself.[1]

[1] *An Autobiographical Study.*

'When I laid stress upon the hitherto neglected importance of the part played by the accidental impressions of early youth,' says Freud, 'I was told that psycho-analysis was denying constitutional and hereditary factors—a thing which I had never dreamt of doing.'

As we shall see, Freud not only regarded the instincts as being of importance in human life, but insisted increasingly during his career on the utmost importance for Psychology of a satisfactory account of the instincts. A good deal of his work consisted of efforts to achieve such an account, though he frequently expressed dissatisfaction with his own formulations, and remained dissatisfied even in his last written work. For the present it is sufficient to see that this criticism arises from a misinterpretation of the Psycho-Analytic theory.

8. *Whenever we can prove Hereditary Determination we can discover some Obvious Underlying Physiological Structure*

This criticism rests mainly upon the work of Bernard.

We are told: whenever we can prove hereditary determination we can discover some obvious underlying physiological structure, as in the case of the Reflex. This we cannot do in the case of the instincts. Therefore they cannot be said to be innately determined. If, however, we ask: but *how* do we prove hereditary determination?—we shall be told: by discovering some obvious underlying physiological structure. This criticism, then, is simply the assertion of an axiom: namely, that only structures can be inherited.

An obvious reply to this criticism is that we can see no reason why we should accept such a dogmatic axiom. But, before developing this reply, let us see how Bernard treats the question of Instinct on this basis, for he raises other points with which we should deal.

Bernard contends that the acquired elements of character are far more numerous than the inherited ones, and that they are collectively, if not always individually, very much stronger. He stresses the predominance of *habit* as against the importance of *instinct*. He does not, however, dispense with instincts altogether. The 'habit complex is built upon an instinctive foundation', and this consists of certain 'fundamental structural and functional organisations which are basic to the life of the individual and the species'. Bernard's point is not that there is no instinctive foundation in the constitution of the individual, but that this foundation consists of far more numerous 'structural-functional organisations' than those instincts postulated by McDougall and others. For him, an instinct 'must be recognisable as a concretely definable unit-character in the Mendelian sense', and therefore the 'actual instincts are at once much simpler, more elemental, and much more numerous than those set forth in the classifications of McDougall, Thorndike, Woodworth, and others'.

It is difficult to see how any analysis could be more detailed than that of Thorndike who asserts that the 'dynamic realities (determining the behaviour of the organism) are the genes and their environments', and that 'there are probably thousands of genes'. However, Bernard insists upon the great detail of the instinctive mechanisms, and holds that the acquired elements which are built upon these during the course of individual experience are the more predominant and important elements of character.

We could stress the relative *complexity* of instinctive behaviour as against the simple stimulus-response view of the instinct; and insist upon the *conative* feature as being the chief distinguishing feature of instinctive experience and behaviour, but neither of these points need be re-emphasised here. Our reply can be directed against Bernard's emphasis upon *habit*.

The manifestation of an instinctual craving and the behaviour which follows upon it is a process quite distinct from that of habit-formation. Thus, the emerging sexual impulse, becoming strong and persistent with the onset of puberty and the development of the secondary sexual characteristics, is not only universal, but relatively sudden and spontaneous. The attraction which we feel towards the opposite sex is something arising spontaneously within us, and leads to behaviour which, far from being the result of a long process of habituation, is quite new and disruptive of our previous habits.

The young man now feels a need to be with the girl who attracts him at every possible moment. Next week will not do: it must be *tonight*!— and then *tomorrow* night! Instead of arriving home at nine o'clock in the evening, as he has been accustomed to do for years, he now comes home in the early hours of the morning; he simply *cannot* tear himself away from the girl earlier. Such behaviour is so different from his *habitual* behaviour, that his parents are quick to notice it, and are often very disturbed by it, evidently being persuaded that something troublesome and significant is happening. Similarly, this need to be with his girl-friend so often begins to conflict with the outings he has been in the habit of enjoying with friends of his own sex. He feels much more inclined, now, to devote *all* his time to his relationship with the girl; and his interest in these other, habitual, activities wanes conspicuously. This change in his inclinations becomes so intense that he frequently finds himself in conflict with his parents, with the parents of his girl-friend, and with a good many of his former friends whose tastes and activities he now curiously finds to have become dull and pointless.

None of this experience and behaviour is at all comparable to *habit*, which has become almost automatic through long usage. On the contrary, it is a positive disturbance of previous modes of experiencing and behaving. It is quite impossible, then, to describe the emergence of such instinctive experience and behaviour in terms of the acquiring of habits.

Furthermore, it is rash to assume that the 'collective effect of the acquired elements in character' is stronger than that of the inherited instincts. The facts of moral conflict would be hard to explain if we did not assume that the sexual impulse, fear, anger, and the like, were not only persisting and inherent features of our nature, but also were often much more powerful than the restraining habits which we acquired during the course of our experience.

The main question to be asked of this criticism, however, is that which we raised briefly at the outset. Why should we hold that nothing can be inherited but *structures*?

Bernard seems to admit that the functional correlates of structures can be inherited, by his use of the term 'structural and functional organisation', but why should we, at the outset, be precluded from assuming the possibility at least of innate features of *experience* which are closely correlated with the functioning of inherited structures? The stomach of an organism, it would be allowed, is inherited. The particular muscle-contractions which lead the organism to seek and eat food are also inherited. Why then may we not assume that, closely correlated with these muscular contractions, a certain *feeling*, which we call appetite, or *hunger*, is also inherited? It would be difficult to hold that such feelings were *learned*; or that they were habit-complexes built upon a structural-functional foundation. Indeed, it could be held as being highly probable that the learning process only *followed upon* such feelings and the 'interests' connected with them, and that no learning would ever take place *in the absence of* such prior impulse-feelings and interests.

But let us take a different example. Does a male adolescent *acquire the habit* of speaking in a deep voice in place of the high-pitched treble voice that he has *been accustomed* to using during all the previous years of his life? Or is this change a single feature of an innate process which, in human beings, occurs at a particular stage of growth and maturation? The answer to this question is perfectly clear; and this 'break' in the human male voice can be held to be inherited just as a structure (say the larynx) can be held to be inherited. Similarly, we maintain that experiential features such as 'impulses', 'cravings', 'perceptions', and 'emotions', are inherited in precisely the same sense. All these are features of the intrinsic processes of growth and maturation of the organism which are set by the hereditary constitution.

This insistence upon 'structures' as being in some sense the only fundamental *things* which we can reliably observe is reminiscent of a 'discrete physical object' epistemology which has for a long time been looked upon with some degree of doubt, and which, whether its proponents like to admit it or not, involves many metaphysical assumptions which do not stand up well against careful inquiry. In so far as scientists merely disregard these assumptions, or impatiently decline to consider them, their position amounts merely to an assertion of faith that 'concrete, material objects' comprise the fundamental units of their observation and inquiry. Without going into epistemology and metaphysics, however, let us indicate our reasons for holding that the insistence upon the sole importance of 'structures' in accounting for all the processes of heredity, growth, and maturation, is both naïve and inadequate.

We have previously held that we cannot regard isolated reflexes or separate instincts as being in any sense sets of 'things' which comprise the basic units of behaviour, but that we must regard them as specific differentiations which emerge during the process of growth and maturation of the organism as a whole. In the same way, specific *structures* cannot be regarded as independent 'things' or units, but must also be regarded as emerging features of a continuing process of growth. The highly complicated internal processes of the growing organism (which include, we must remember, such intricacies as the changing processes of glandular secretions) cannot be regarded, fundamentally, as a process of interaction between given, independent structures; but the structures themselves must be regarded as gradually differentiated and functionally inter-dependent features of this continuing process.

In holding that the instinct 'must be recognisable as a concretely definable unit-character in the Mendelian sense', it would appear that Bernard is making much too naïve an assumption in thinking that even 'structures' can be so definitely recognised. The impression given by such a position is that each gene is responsible for a particular unit-character, and that each structure or structural-functional organisation can be traced as the outcome of a particular gene, whereas this cannot be done in the case of the 'instincts' as usually postulated. The truth is that we are far from having such a complete knowledge of genetics to determine the truth or falsity of such assertions. The evidence which exists, however, is such as to discountenance the view of a simple 'gene'-'particular structure' relationship in development. Whilst the genes are regarded by geneticists as fundamental and distinct units, there is evidence to show that they do not work independently of each other and that they probably have not single but multiple effects in the developing organism. Thus, E. B. Ford[1] tells us:

[1]'Genetics', *Scientific Thought in the Twentieth Century*, Watts, 1951, pp. 193-213.

'The inheritance of sex suggests that though the genes behave as distinct units in heredity, they are not independent in their working, a consideration which merits brief study. It must first be noticed that each of them, though a distinct entity, has multiple effects, a point which may usefully be illustrated by examples.

'In man, a single gene, which acts as a recessive, produces both deafness and "retinitis pigmentosa", a grave defect of the eyes leading gradually to blindness. The first genetic studies on the fruit-fly "Drosophila melanogaster", subsequently famous in this field, were directed to the difference between flies with the normal red eyes and a recessive variety with white. But the distinction proved to be more fundamental than appeared, and to affect also the colour of one internal organ (the testis sheath) and the shape of another (the spermatheca). In maize a gene which controls the type of starch produced by the plant affects also the rate at which the pollen tubes grow down to fertilize the ovules. These are single instances chosen from a great variety, but a wide generalisation shows that the genes usually, and perhaps always, have multiple effects. For varieties, whether slight or striking, produced by their allelomorphs are less hardy than are the corresponding normal forms—for instance, human albinos not only lack pigment in the skin, hair, and eyes, but have a shorter expectation of life than have ordinary people. Thus there is good reason for thinking that even those genes whose results appear to us trivial or superficial have, in reality, an important influence upon the working of the body.

'Single hereditary units therefore are not restricted to a single type of effect; moreover, they interact with one another to produce the characteristics for which they are responsible. For example, in Asiatic cotton the development of one form of crumpled leaves requires the co-operation of two pairs of allelomorphs, each undetectable alone even when homozygous. While in the fruit-fly "Drosophila melanogaster", the genes for brown and for scarlet eye-colour combine to produce white eyes. Indeed, the effects of any particular gene depend to some extent upon its "genetic-setting", which in some individuals will enhance and in others minimise them.'

The findings of genetics show, then, that even the genes (fundamental inherited units as they appear to be) cannot be strictly regarded as a set of isolated entities or things, each of which is responsible for a single feature of development. Even at this earliest stage, the genetic constitution has a certain developmental unity which is something more than the 'bits' which, from the point of view of our observation, we can discriminate, and into which we can conceptually analyse it. In view of this astonishing picture of the organism's complex conception and development, it is arbitrary to assert that only 'structures' are inherited and of importance, and naïve to regard even 'structures' as being identifiable as 'concretely definable unit-characters'.

In conclusion we can say that this criticism does nothing at all to reveal any fault or weakness in the theory of instincts. It is seen to entail a dogmatic axiom which need not, and from our point of view, cannot be accepted.

9. *The Diversity among the Lists of Instincts*

The concept of Instinct, it is argued, cannot be very useful if, in fact, no one can decide what the instincts are. Since every psychologist presents a different classification, nothing very much can really be known about the matter, and the concept of instinct remains, therefore —whether valid or invalid—of no practical use. Bernard, in particular, has investigated the various classifications which have been offered, and has presented an interesting table showing a statistical analysis of the types of instinct listed by five hundred writers.

It can be seen at once that this criticism is not a very damaging one. It points out the fact that no certainty has yet been reached as to the number of the instinctive tendencies in man; or that no generally agreed mode of classifying the instincts in man has yet been arrived at. This is true enough. But it does not follow that the doctrine of instincts as a whole is therefore to be dispensed with. The fact that no agreement has yet been reached does not mean that the instinctive tendencies of man are not there and will not, with further work, be satisfactorily classified. The criticism merely points to the need for further inquiry. The evidence of such instinctive tendencies is there, but they have not yet been clearly distinguished. We might mention the confusion which reigned in Chemistry when early attempts were made to classify the chemical elements. But, although no one could then agree as to the correct number of elements, today the classification is clear and is agreed upon.[1] Similarly, we may expect an increasing clarity in the analysis of the instincts as investigation proceeds.

Before leaving this criticism another point may be made. It may well be the case that much of the apparent diversity among the lists of instincts rests *not* upon fundamental disagreements as to the facts (though some such disagreement probably exists) but upon the fact that different writers have used different *principles of classification*. To mention but a few examples, Freud does *not* hold that there are only *two*

[1]Somewhere, I think, McDougall makes this analogy.

instincts—the Life Instinct and the Death Instinct—but that all the instinctual tendencies of man can be subsumed under these two (for him) basic headings. McDougall employs a different method of classification, naming the instinctive tendencies in accordance with the observed 'ends' of the various sequences of instinctive behaviour. Thorndike, believing that the instinctive *responses* are more numerous than McDougall's classification suggests, offers a classification which is simply a list of such innate *responses*. It might be held by a critic that Freud postulated the existence of two instincts in man, McDougall thirteen (with the addition of a few minor instincts), and Thorndike forty. Such a statement refers, however, to the *mode of classification* adopted by these writers rather than to any essential disagreement as to the facts. A comparison between the list of McDougall and Thorndike does not reveal any great disagreement as to the kinds of experience and behaviour which can be considered instinctive in man; it merely happens that Thorndike names several 'original responses' which McDougall groups together under the heading of the 'end' in which a sequence of these responses terminates. A close scrutiny of the many lists of instincts will show that the opinions as to which aspects of human experience and behaviour are held to be instinctive are more closely in agreement than is commonly supposed.

10. *The Functional Autonomy of Motives*

The final criticism stems from McDougall's view that *all* human drives derive their energy from the instincts.

'The instinctive impulses', says McDougall,[1] 'determine the ends of all activities and supply the driving power by which all mental activities are sustained; and all the complex intellectual apparatus of the most highly developed mind is but a means towards these ends, is but the instrument by which these impulses seek their satisfaction. . . .'

This is a sweeping assertion that would be difficult either to substantiate or to disprove. But we have already seen that others among the earlier writers, whilst holding that the instinctive impulses laid down the basic ends of human activity, held also that *other* ends arose during the course of individual experience which could not be explained entirely in terms of the instincts. It is therefore no criticism of the doctrine of instincts to say that new or additional motives can be acquired by man. Such a criticism applies only to the sweeping generalisation made by McDougall.

If the criticism arising from the view which we have called 'The Functional Autonomy of Motives' (using the phraseology of Allport)

[1] *Social Psychology*, p. 38.

was simply that men acquire new drives, which are in all probability
socially engendered, and which become self-motivating (in the sense
that they come to have their own peculiar craving, which, though
acquired, compulsively demands satisfaction; as, for example, in the
habit of smoking), then we could accept it; but would point out that
this criticism did not in any sense deny the presence and importance of
the instincts.

In so far as such critics stop here there is no fundamental quarrel
between them and supporters of the doctrine of instincts. The problem
really resolves itself into an empirical question of whether such new and
'autonomous' motives are in fact found in human individuals. The
theory of the 'functional autonomy of motives', however, goes further
than this, and in its more extended form constitutes a definite criticism
of the doctrine of instincts. The chief proponent of this view is G .W.
Allport,[1] and we must first see what he has to say upon the subject.

Allport develops his theory with the object of studying the unique,
developed, individual personality. He feels that too much stress has been
laid upon 'common' qualities or 'common' traits, and that too little
attention has been devoted to the uniqueness of individual personalities.
He wishes to escape the tendency to generalise about 'basic' motives,
and tries to emphasise the uniqueness of the pattern of motives existing
in each individual; and it is whilst doing this that he arrives at his notion
of the 'functional autonomy of motives'. In all mature personalities,
Allport tells us that 'master-sentiments' exist. These have probably
developed from earlier motives arising in earlier situations, but in the
present, adult personality they have a *functional autonomy;* they persist
in the contemporary personality in relation to the individual's *present*
situation. This can be illustrated by one of Allport's examples. A miser
may learn his habits of thrift during a period of poverty, or they may be
a symptom of sexual perversion, but this trait of miserliness persists, and
becomes stronger even, after the compulsion of the necessitous circumstances or the actual causes of the neurosis have been relieved. 'The
activity of the new unit does not depend on the continual activity of the
units from which they develop.' This new principle, Allport maintains,
'renders the old hypothesis of human instincts superfluous '.

On the face of it, the process thus described is not in any way different from that familiar to other psychologists as 'habituation' or 'sentiment-formation'. It is not new to say that a habit or a sentiment, once
established, persists even though the conditions under which it was

[1]G. W. Allport, *Personality: A Psychological Interpretation.* Allport has since modified
the views we criticise here; but it is still necessary for us to see to what extent this insistence
upon the 'Functional Autonomy of Motives' did constitute an effective criticism of the
Theory of Instincts.

formed cease to exist. And it is difficult to see what is added to our knowledge by calling these features 'functionally autonomous'. It was certainly no part of the doctrine of instincts to deny the uniqueness of individual personalities, even though it maintained that all individuals inherited certain definite cravings by virtue of their hereditary constitution. Let us consider Allport's notion of the development of the individual personality in more detail and see on what grounds he concludes that the hypothesis of human instincts is rendered superfluous.

Allport makes use of the concept of 'drive': 'a vital impulse which leads to the reduction of some segmental organic tension. It has its origin in an internal organic stimulus of peculiar persistence, growing characteristically stronger until the organism acts in such a way as to alleviate the accumulating tension.' He is prepared to admit that these may be termed 'instincts' in infancy,[1] and to admit 'the persistence of some instinctive forms of activity throughout life'. The personality of an individual is then: 'the mode of adjustment or survival that results from the interaction of his organic cravings or segmental drives with an environment both friendly and hostile to these cravings, through the intermediation of a plastic and modifiable nervous system.' Allport is prepared to admit (1) nutritional drives or cravings, (2) sexual drives, (3) those drives resulting from 'persistent organic tension involving fear', and (4) anger, or aggressive drives . . . and 'possibly others whose existence is less easy to establish'. After the stage of infancy, however, Allport holds that these primitive segmental drives rapidly diminish in importance and 'are progressively supplanted by more sophisticated types of motive, characteristic of the mature personality'. The 'original drives, instincts, or libidinal strivings of early childhood are quickly overlaid by experience, and organized into a personal system of attributes'. This developed personality is unique to the individual, and Allport regards it as 'essentially a post-instinctive phenomenon'. The detailed effects of learning 'ultimately transform the segmental cravings of infancy into desires having no longer any functional connection with them, but holding in their own right an autonomous place in personal life'. For Allport: 'all motives are contemporary', and whilst they can, at least in theory, be traced back to the segmental drives of infancy, this bond is broken as the individual matures. The tie between the autonomous motives of the adult and the earlier drives or impulses of the child in simply historical, not functional. For any study of the developed human personality, therefore, the hypothesis of instincts and the tracing of their development through the formation of habits, sentiments, and

[1]'Motivation in Personality: Reply to Mr. Bertocci', *Psych. Rev.* 1940, vol. xlvii, pp. 533-554.

the like, during the course of individual experience is superfluous. The contemporary motives of the unique adult personality are functionally autonomous, and we can, Allport says: 'take motives at their face value, assume that they are pretty much what they appear to be.' In putting forward this view, Allport is clearly and openly aware that it is 'obviously opposed to psycho-analysis and other genetic accounts assuming inflexibility in the drives of life.'

In the first place we can see that in his definition of 'drive', and in his admission that at least some such drives are innate, active in infancy, and persistent throughout the individual's life, Allport is in all essentials in agreement with what is held by the doctrine of instincts. As Professor Burt has said: the drive is the instinct under a new name. 'Flung out at the front door, the old instincts are allowed in at the back, after assuming an alias and a slight disguise.'

The difference between Allport's position and that of the doctrine of instincts does not lie here. It lies really in the view that is held as to the relation of the developed personality to its previous process of development, and in the place which is attributed to the 'innate segmental cravings' in the developed personality.

The view held by the writers on instinct is that the instinctive impulses persistently recur throughout the life-time of the individual, though some of these impulses are more important than others during various stages of maturation, and some seem even gradually to 'fade away'; that they become centred about the certain objects and situations in relation to which they have been activated and gratified during the course of the individual's experience, and thus give rise to relatively complex, though stable, habit-formations and sentiments. In this process of personality development, the influences of the social tradition play a significant part so that the sentiments will be established with reference to various features of the social structure. The chief point here, however, is that the theory postulates a continuous process of development, from infancy onwards, in which the instincts, the ends which they set, and the behaviour which issues in their service, play a large and continuing part. The later characteristics of the individual personality are thus held to grow out of these earlier processes, and, because of this, it is held that the earlier processes, considered in relation to the social situations within which they occur, have a determining influence upon the sentiments or 'traits' which are established; and consequently we need to know the facts of this process of development in order to understand fully the contemporary motives of the individual.

Even with regard to this view of the process of personality development, and the part played by the innate drives, Allport is not altogether in disagreement. It is in his view as to the relation between the present personality and this previous process of development that the difference arises. He holds that the later traits and motives are in some sense 'functionally autonomous' from the earlier processes; that, whilst they grow out of the earlier impulses and situations and modes of gratification, they nevertheless in some way *supplant* them. They are then held to be *self-motivating* in the sense of not deriving their present energy or impetus from those earlier drives and situations in the context of which they took shape. They are *contemporary*, and whilst they have a historical connection with the earlier processes, they are now *autonomous* and have no *functional* connection with them.

It is difficult to see what addition to our knowledge this final insistence gives us. Granted that the motives, sentiments, and traits of the adult individual are *contemporary*, it nonetheless remains true that for a full and reliable understanding of them, and for any explanation of them, we need to know that process of development of which they are the result.

The point which is puzzling in Allport's treatment is this distinction between a 'historical' and a 'functional' tie. What is really meant by this distinction? Can all the motives, sentiments, and traits of an individual personality be held to be historically connected with previous constellations of motives and situations and yet be held, somehow, to manifest a contemporary pattern which is functionally quite independent of them? This seems a very curious proposition, and seems to go against all our notions of individual development. It is difficult, too, to know what precisely is meant by *functional* in a sense that would justify, or make feasible, its complete dissociation from the historical pattern of development. There is no reason to suppose that the contemporary motives in the individual are not *both* historically *and* functionally related to his early complexities of experience; and (if we can make this clear) why the 'functional-patterns of motives' in the successive periods of the individual's life are not formatively and significantly related to each other.

Allport is aware that his theory stands in contradiction to the findings of psycho-analysis, and he appears to be quite untroubled by this fact. It would seem, however, that he misrepresents or misconceives the psycho-analytic account of instinct and of the development of the personality; and is led, also, either through his disregard, or his low opinion, of the psycho-analytic findings to exercise too little care in his observations. When he tells us that his theory 'is obviously opposed to psycho-analysis and other genetic accounts assuming inflexibility in the drives of life', he is surely misconceiving the nature of the psycho-analytic account? The account of the extremely 'fluid' nature of the libidinal impulses in their search for gratification, and of the many mental-mechanisms which operate unconsciously in order to meet the instinctual demands for gratification, surely does not maintain *inflexibility* in the drives of life? Similarly, when he suggests that we can 'take motives at their face value, assume that they are pretty much what they appear to be', he is clearly not taking into account the stress which psycho-analysis lays upon the importance of unconscious mental processes and such processes as 'rationalisation'. Allport also seems to ignore the implications which the psycho-analytic theory of neurosis has for the developmental continuity of the individual and for the significance (from the point of view of their formative influence upon adult motives, sentiments, traits, etc.) of *infantile* mental processes, which are very closely related to the activation of the instincts. The principle of 'functional autonomy' is in danger of missing half the picture of the individual personality; and it may well be that these less evident features are among the most significant.

The contention, too, that the developed personality is essentially a 'post-instinctive' phenomenon, cannot be upheld. If Allport is prepared to allow hunger, sex, fear, and anger among his organic cravings, the adult personality can never be said to come *after* these. They are congenital, persistently recurring, and always have to be taken into account. The facts of moral conflict would be difficult to explain if we held that the primary impulses were always nicely tamed during personality development, and did not occasionally erupt and usurp the acquired patterns of conduct and attitude. To assert that the developed personality is 'post-instinctive', does not seem to fit the facts. Any successful theory of personality must in some way account for these sudden and apparently incalculable disturbances of experience and behaviour which often occur unexpectedly in what would appear to be stable, well-established, and reasonably balanced personalities. The doctrine of instincts, coupled with the psycho-analytic account of instinctual repression and its effects, seems much more satisfactory from this point of view than does the principle of the 'functional autonomy of motives'.

To summarise. In so far as this criticism points to the probability that some ends may be acquired by the individual which cannot be fully explained in terms of the instincts, we can agree with it; but still hold, nonetheless, that this is not damaging to the doctrine of instincts. With regard to the more far-reaching criticisms arising from the theory of the 'functional autonomy of motives', we have given reasons to suggest: (a) that much of the theory of 'drives' and their persistence, and the process of personality development giving rise to the formation of habits, sentiments, traits, and developed motives, is in agreement with what the doctrine of instincts maintains, (b) that, since the instincts or drives persist throughout the individual's experience, the developed personality cannot be regarded as 'post-instinctive', but the instincts must be assigned an active part even here, and (c) that the postulation of 'functionally autonomous motives' in the developed individual (1) does not seem to add anything to our knowledge of the development of human motives, (2) does not seem to be supported by any substantial evidence, and (3) is completely opposed to the findings of psycho-analysis, which (if we disagree with them) must be disproved rather than ignored. Indeed, the postulate that adult motives are functionally autonomous, seems to beg the question, and does not appear to constitute any sort of demonstration. It seems clear that such complicated relations as do exist between innate impulses and the process of development of the individual personality, including the gradual establishing of sentiments, traits, and so on, can only be elucidated by a thorough-going genetic psychology such as that implied in the doctrine of instincts and the theory of psycho-analysis.

This review of the criticisms which emerged against the doctrine of instincts shows that none of them was seriously damaging. Many were directed against the work of McDougall alone, and this concentration of attention upon McDougall was unfortunate, since other writers on the subject avoided some of the careless statements which are to be found in his work and which gave impressions which, almost certainly, he did not want to give. Certain of these criticisms were of value as warnings against loose and erroneous ways of using and regarding the concept of instinct. Others, such as the one directed against McDougall's treatment of the relation between instinct and emotion, were seen to have been taken into account by other writers who were themselves contributors to the doctrine of instincts, and they were thus not relevant to the doctrine of instincts as a whole. Several have been shown to be irrelevant, and due to a misconception of what the instinct theory really put forward. It remains true, even so, that the concept of instinct became unfashionable. The criticisms had their effect in spite of their inadequacy. The Doctrine of Instincts was never dead—simply buried.

PART TWO

COMPARATIVE ETHOLOGY AND PSYCHO-ANALYSIS

CHAPTER IV

RECENT WORK IN COMPARATIVE ETHOLOGY[1]

In the early 1930's a significant change in the conceptualisation and in the experimental investigation of Instinct was being initiated by several students of animal behaviour, and especially by Konrad Lorenz. The modern study of animal behaviour, which has come to be known as Comparative Ethology, owes its formulation mainly to Lorenz. The study has developed rapidly, and the literature of the subject grows both in bulk and interest from year to year. Much of this early work was undertaken by a group of zoologists on the continent, and the account of instinct which is presented is predominantly a bio-physiological account. The work has been introduced to students in this country by W. H. Thorpe of Cambridge who has given us a very clear account of the conceptual scheme of Lorenz,[2] and by N. Tinbergen of Oxford who (in his book *The Study of Instinct*) has given us a fascinating review of the whole field. In this chapter we shall consider the ideas of Lorenz and those of Tinbergen. The concepts used by both writers are very similar so that a full account of both would involve a good deal of repetition. For this reason we shall only sketch the ideas of Lorenz, and shall then concentrate on the wider review of Tinbergen for the purpose of giving an adequate summary of what ethology has to say. A treatment of both writers is necessary, in spite of their great similarity, since there are one or two points of difference between them which we consider to be of some importance. What these points are will emerge during our discussion.

1. *Konrad Lorenz: His Chief Concepts*

(1) *Instinct*. When Lorenz speaks of an 'instinct', he means, if we retain for a moment the terminology we have used in our earlier

[1]'Ethology' was the term originally employed by J. S. Mill in Book VI of his 'System of Logic' to designate 'The Science of Character'. Tinbergen's use of the same term has been criticised; but there need be no confusion if we remember that, for him, Ethology always means 'The Scientific Study of Animal Behaviour'.

[2]W. H. Thorpe, 'The Modern Concept of Instinctive Behaviour', *Bulletin of Animal Behaviour*, February 1948. Also: see 'Learning and Instinct in Animals, 1956, and note on p. 344.

chapters, a specific inherited *motor-mechanism*. In each example of true instinctive behaviour there is a 'core of absolutely fixed, more or less complex automatism' and this is the *instinct* proper. Lorenz has shown that such behavioural automatisms are as constant and uniform in any species as are the structural features of the species, and that they are just as useful as structures for purposes of classifying species. The definition of an instinct given by Lorenz is: 'an (1) inherited, (2) specific, (3) stereotyped, pattern of behaviour. It is separated from other types of stereotyped inborn behaviour (kinesis and taxes) by being (4) released complete by, rather than guided by, the environment, and (5) by its tendency to accumulate reaction specific energy. This shows itself by (6) lowering of the threshold for release, and (7) by a tendency to vacuum activity.'[1]

The concepts which appear in this definition are described as follows.

(2) *Reaction Specific Energy*. Each instinct involves the building up of a specific tension in the central nervous system. This specific tension is called the *Reaction Specific Energy*. If the animal is not in the situation appropriate for the release of the instinct (and, consequently, for the release of this Reaction Specific Energy) the energy accumulates.

(3) *Lowering of the Threshold for Release*. This accumulation of the specific energy results in a *lowering of the threshold* of sensitivity to those stimuli which are appropriate to the release of the instinct. The greater the specific tension, the slighter the appropriate stimulus needed to 'set off' the instinct.

(4) *Vacuum Activity*. If this process of accumulation continues for any length of time, a point may be reached at which the instinct will 'go off' in the complete absence of appropriate external stimuli. This manifestation of the instinct in the absence of appropriate stimuli is termed *Vacuum Activity:* denoting the fact that the instinct seems to be *forced* out without being excited by any stimulus.

One or two examples will serve to illustrate the last three concepts.

Lorenz noticed vacuum activities in a starling which, although it was hand-reared and fed artificially, would go through the entire behaviour-pattern of insect-hunting (including catching, killing, and swallowing) when there were no insects there at all. Thorpe kept a hand-reared tawny owl and observed that, after being fed, it would go through all the motions of pouncing upon a living prey, although it had never had the

[1]For this whole analysis of Lorenz's scheme, see Thorpe's *Modern Concept of Instinctive Behaviour*.

experience of dealing with a living mouse. An illuminating example is also quoted by Rudolf Brun.

'I owe to the courtesy of the eminent Zurich lepidopterist, Dr. E. Fischer, a very interesting observation of a thwarted instinct "operating in a void", or "running to waste", in an insect.

'The pupae of a butterfly, *Hoplitis milhauseri F.*, lie in cocoons almost as hard as wood. However, at the head end the pupae possess a special appliance whose purpose is undoubtedly to cut through this hard shell. It consists of a spine on the front of the head, projecting between two ridges. With the help of this device, which somewhat resembles a tin-opener, the pupa cuts a circular hole in the hard shell of the cocoon, making a lid which can be thrown back, so that the butterfly can creep out through the hole. Now, Fischer took two pupae of this butterfly out of their cocoons a few days before they were ready to leave them and laid them on the floor of the breeding cage, where they remained quietly for some days. The insects then perforated the shells of their pupae and crept out of them. But now, instead of immediately beginning, like other butterflies, to develop their wings, the insects ran to the wall of the breeding cage, and there, for about an hour, they made incessant thrusting and circling movements with their now quite unarmed heads, as though they still had to saw through the non-existent cocoons! While they did this the hinder part of the body was stretched out backwards and propped against the floor. If they were disturbed at their task they resumed their strange behaviour the moment they were free to do so. After an hour of this it appeared that the impulse had done enough, and the insects repaired to the roof of the cage in order to develop their wings.'[1]

Thorpe points out that in the prolonged absence of mates birds have been known to manifest display behaviour, and even attempted copulation, towards very inadequate objects. Thus Lorenz tells of a budgerigar which seemed to derive what might be called 'substitute gratification' from displaying to a ping-pong ball.

The reaction specific energy is held to be very closely related to the particular instinct since, once the instinct has been released, some length of time seems to elapse before the instinct can again be stimulated. Time is required for the 're-accumulation' of the specific energy.[2] The evidence also suggests, we are told, that the longer an instinct is dammed up, the greater is its intensity when it is released.

These three characteristics of instinctive reactions are held to denote

[1] *General Theory of Neurosis*, p. 261.
[2] We shall see that not all the ethologists are agreed on this.

the difference between instincts and either simple or chain-reflexes. The instinct *involves* reflexes, but reflexes themselves do not exhibit anything like reaction specific energy.

(5) *Taxes*. Taxes are inherited *orienting* movements. Instincts are held to be different from taxes in that they are *released* but not *guided* by the environmental situation. They are 'set off', it is said, by a kind of 'trigger action'. Once the instinct has been released, the animal seems forced to complete that particular behaviour pattern; to such an extent that, once started, it is sometimes difficult to interrupt the performance. A further difference between instincts and taxes is that, in the case of the instinct, the releasing *stimulus* takes the form of a relatively complex 'gestalt'. The reaction is not to a single simple stimulus, but to a particular *pattern* of stimuli.

(6) *Releaser*. The term 'releaser' denotes that specific 'pattern of stimuli' which is appropriate to the 'setting off' of the instinct.

(7) *Receptory Correlate*. The releaser specific to an instinct is held to 'fit' a *receptory correlate* in the animal's perceptual process or central nervous system. A certain perception seems to have the specific function of releasing a certain reaction specific energy. The animal is 'attuned' to specific features of the environment (as distinct from others which its sensory equipment is equally capable of perceiving) even without previous experience. When a reaction specific energy has been built up, the receptory correlate is activated by the specific perception encountered in the environment, and the particular instinct is thus released. Receptory Correlates are held to be sometimes entirely inborn; sometimes partly inborn and partly the outcome of particular kinds of learning which occur during the earliest operations of an instinct; and sometimes hardly at all due to heredity, and mainly learned.

(8) *Instinctive Behaviour*. Instinctive behaviour is the whole sequence of behaviour of which the instinct proper is the automatic core, and comprises (*a*) the reaction specific energy, resting upon internal physiological processes, (*b*) the 'appetitive behaviour' which takes the form of random, exploratory movements, bringing the animal into that situation in which it will encounter those releasers appropriate to the 'setting off' of the instincts, and, (*c*) the final release of the instinct proper, guided by taxes and adjusted to the particular environmental details by the 'coat of reflexes'.

(9) *A Schematic Representation: W. H. Thorpe.* This pattern of instinctive behaviour, including the above-mentioned components, has been presented schematically by Thorpe. It will be of interest, later, to compare this with a similar schema drawn up by Tinbergen.[1]

INSTINCTIVE BEHAVIOUR

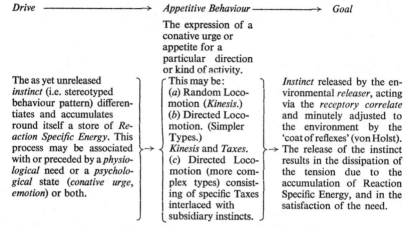

Drive ⟶ *Appetitive Behaviour* ⟶ *Goal*

The expression of a conative urge or appetite for a particular direction or kind of activity.

The as yet unreleased *instinct* (i.e. stereotyped behaviour pattern) differentiates and accumulates round itself a store of *Reaction Specific Energy*. This process may be associated with or preceded by a *physiological* need or a *psychological* state (*conative urge, emotion*) or both.

This may be:
(a) Random Locomotion (*Kinesis.*)
(b) Directed Locomotion. (Simpler Types.)
Kinesis and *Taxes.*
(c) Directed Locomotion (more complex types) consisting of specific Taxes interlaced with subsidiary instincts.

Instinct released by the environmental *releaser*, acting via the *receptory correlate* and minutely adjusted to the environment by the 'coat of reflexes' (von Holst). The release of the instinct results in the dissipation of the tension due to the accumulation of Reaction Specific Energy, and in the satisfaction of the need.

This completes our sketch of the concepts used by Lorenz. The way in which they are used in the experimental study of instinctive behaviour will emerge more fully in our review of Tinbergen's book.

It scarcely needs to be pointed out how close a resemblance these concepts bear to those which we have discussed in the work of the earlier writers. We may recall their postulation of a close correlation between internal physiological processes; specific, persistently recurring impulses or cravings; specific appropriate perceptions; certain sequences of behaviour involving sensori-motor actions and reflexes; and particular 'end-states' in which this sequence of experience and behaviour culminated. But we shall leave detailed considerations of such comparisons until a later chapter.

To leave this skeleton account of the work of Lorenz without mention of other qualities which he possesses, however, would be to give a very false and inadequate impression. Lorenz is more than an exact scientist. He has been called 'the modern Fabre', and is deserving of this comparison. His accounts of animal life reveal a love of animals, and a delight in his relations with them, which Fabre himself showed in his writing on the life of insects. His writing is delightful: matter-of-fact, as

[1]See pp. 132-135.

when he is pointing out the various troubles which must be anticipated by anyone who decides to keep animals—the destructiveness of his monkeys, the stains left on the carpet by his geese; full of humour as when he is describing his 'inverse cage principle' whereby his house (or his child left sleeping on the lawn) is caged off from the animals, who are themselves left in freedom outside, and when his problem is to keep his animals *out* of the cage rather than to keep them enclosed in cages of their own; and, at times, achieving a quality of beauty (for which Fabre's own style was noted) as when he is describing the surrounding district of his home in Altenberg. All this is made more entertaining by Lorenz's gift with the pencil. His numerous drawings add to the delight of his pages. His book *King Solomon's Ring* reveals all these qualities, and the chapter, 'The Perennial Retainers', which deals with his colony of jackdaws is perhaps the most charming and intriguing of all. We shall refer to this chapter, surprisingly enough, when we come to consider the Ethological study of man.

2. *N. Tinbergen: A Review*

(1) *Introductory Comments on Problems and Methods.* Tinbergen opens his account of instinct with several observations on questions of method, and on the relations between ethology and other inquiries into the causes of behaviour. It will be worth our while to note his position on these matters before summarising the content of his work.

The limited purpose of his inquiry is: to investigate the *causal structure* underlying *innate* behaviour; and innate behaviour is defined as 'behaviour that has not been changed by learning process'.

Tinbergen then claims that, whilst there are other studies which contribute to our *understanding* of instinctive behaviour, these studies fall outside the scope of a strictly *causal* analysis. They are (1) the study of *directiveness*, and (2) the study of the *subjective phenomena* which attend innate behaviour. This is a point about which much controversy centres, so that we must understand correctly what Tinbergen has to say about it.

When discussing the *directiveness* of behaviour, Tinbergen readily admits that behaviour is directed to an end, but stresses the fact that to indicate the end of a sequence of behaviour is far from being sufficient as a causal explanation, and the ethologist must therefore persist in his investigation of those causal factors at work in the animal which enable it to perform these directive activities. This is clear enough, and accept-able. We must point out, however, that it would be going too far to say that the 'end' of a sequence of behaviour can have *nothing* to do with the study of causation. Without dwelling upon the point, we have seen that in instinct-experience the 'end' of behaviour may enter, no matter how dimly, as an element of the primary 'instinct-interest', and *may* therefore be a feature of instinctive experience and behaviour which should not be neglected in a *causal* account, especially with regard to the satisfactory explanation of subsequent learning and the modification of behaviour.

On the question of *subjective phenomena*, Tinbergen's position seems, at first sight, to be stated clearly enough, but a closer examination shows that it is not free from ambiguity.

One point he makes is that: 'because subjective phenomena cannot be observed objectively in animals, it is idle either to claim or to deny their existence.'[1] Thus, it would seem that when he says: 'Although the ethologist does not want to deny the possible existence of subjective phenomena in animals, he claims that it is futile to present them as causes . . .', he does not mean that such subjective phenomena may *not actually constitute* causal factors in behaviour, but only that it is useless to present them as such: 'since they cannot be observed by scientific methods.' This is really a mild Behaviourist position.

Tinbergen, however, seems to go much further than this and to hold that subjective phenomena *cannot*, in *fact*, be regarded as exercising any *causal* influence on behaviour. Pointing out that a mere *description* of the state of an animal (such as the statement that an animal is hungry) does not render further investigation into what is actually going on in the animal unnecessary (with which every one would agree), he then goes on to say: 'But when the conclusion that the animal hunts because it is hungry is taken literally, as a *causal* explanation, and when it is claimed that the subjective phenomenon of hunger is one of the causes of food-seeking behaviour, physiological and psychological thinking are confused.'

Now, whilst it is clear in this particular case that the mere statement that the animal was hungry would not suffice as a complete causal explanation of why the animal sought food, it is difficult to see why (on the grounds of some sort of *a priori* assertion) we should consider that the *experience* of hunger ought not to be allowed at all as at least one significant link in the causal chain of experience and behaviour. Tinbergen's statement, as it stands, seems to claim that *physiological* processes alone can be regarded as *causal* factors, and that *experiential* factors can never be held to exert any causal influence whatsoever upon behaviour.

This position, as an *a priori* assertion, is clearly untenable. There is much evidence to suggest that experiential features can have causal

[1]We shall later give reasons to uphold the view that this is not the case.

efficacy in modifying physiological and behavioural processes. Let us think of a case of human neurosis. Here, as in the case of animals, we are unable to observe directly the subjective phenomena themselves which are involved. But there is, nonetheless, much evidence to show that many of these 'functional' disorders are due to experiential and *not* organic causes. It seems, further, that certain of the hypotheses erected by psychologists to explain these disorders (hypotheses postulating certain kinds of *experiential conflict* and their effects) are approximating, at least, to a correct interpretation of the facts, since treatment on the basis of such an interpretation can lead to a curing of the disorder and an alleviation of the suffering. There is thus evidence that experiential elements are causally related and can have a positive effect upon physiological and behavioural processes.

Tinbergen could reply that he is speaking specifically of innate behaviour. But even here we see no reason why we should not suppose that certain experiential features are also innate, and may thus be important features in the causal relations existing between the several components of instinct. The reasons why we wish to maintain that the *subjective experience* of the animal has to be considered in any satisfying causal analysis of instinct will emerge as we discuss the ethological findings which Tinbergen describes as, for example, the fact that certain phases of instinctive behaviour are plastic, adaptable, and 'truly purposive'. But let us indicate, at this point, why we cannot accept Tinbergen's *a priori* postulate and its underlying assumptions.

Firstly, the *causes* of all the components of instinct are, strictly speaking, to be found in the process of evolution: in the process of genetic transmission, of mutation, and of natural selection. That is to say: all the components of instinctive activity (the specific mode of perception, the specific neuro-physiological process, the specific behavioural reactions) are the outcome of the hereditary process. An account of how these given components are co-ordinated in manifest behaviour during the growth and maturation of the individual is, strictly speaking, a *description* of the inter-connectedness of these components. One would not say that a certain secretion of hormones *caused* a certain perceptual mechanism in the nervous system. One would say that (*a*) a certain physiological process entailing the secretion of hormones, and (*b*) a certain perceptual mechanism in the central nervous system, were features of the hereditary endowment which, in the total functioning organism, *inter-acted* in particular ways and thus gave rise to a certain sequence of experience and behaviour. To select some of these inherited components, at the outset, as being *causally* important in this complex interconnection, and others as being insignificant in this way, seems quite an arbitrary procedure. It is true, we admit, that as far as inherited experiential features go—we can say that primary elements of *experience* are *dependent upon* physiological, structural, and environmental factors; but this is no reason to suppose that, as these experiential features emerge, they do not themselves constitute features of importance in the interrelations of the inherited components as a whole, and that they do not have functions of their own to perform which are necessary in the entire process. Thus, an innate 'instinct-interest' (as defined by the earlier writers) would give the element of 'directiveness' in perceptual experience, and would account for the observed 'purposiveness', 'plasticity', and 'adaptability' of some phases of instinctive activity. Though an *experiential* factor, it would be a necessary link in the interconnectedness of the various components of instinct, and a necessary postulate in any *causal* analysis of the observed facts. The causal analysis would be incomplete without it.

The fundamental fact which we wish to stress, is that *experiential* features, though depending upon bio-physiological conditions for their emergence, *cannot* be explained in terms of bio-physiological facts alone. Elements of *significance*, of *meaning* (even if only upon the plane of perceptual experience) enter with factors of experience; and an explanation in terms of structural and physiological conditions alone, becomes —at once—inadequate. This is a point which was emphasised time and time again by the earlier writers, but the confusion still persists, and seems to be a curious 'blindness' of the so-called 'natural' scientists. The unwillingness of the physiologist to regard an experiential feature as an efficacious link in any sequence of events seems to rest upon the notion that—since it is not a material object, and cannot be looked at, touched, smelled, heard, tasted, or put, like a drop of blood, on a microscope slide—it cannot possess unique qualities capable of influencing material processes. It is always at the back of the physiologist's mind, or so it appears, that *experiential* elements can ultimately be *reduced* to explanations in physiological terms. Somehow, experiential elements cannot be held to add anything qualitatively different to the organism, which can have some degree of determination upon its subsequent activity, but are regarded as ephemeral effects of structures and physiological process which are *alone* determining factors. They are interesting, perhaps—but causally negligible. They are never regarded as features *qualitatively different* from the physiological conditions which give rise to them, and as being themselves necessary features (as are the structural and physiological features also) in the fulfilment of biological functions. And this view, we maintain, is a fundamental fallacy; resting upon nothing more than an arbitrary assertion.

The truth seems to be what Drever insisted upon. In so far as we are giving a bio-physiological account of instinct, we must not confuse propositions referring to bio-physiological and behavioural features with those referring to psychological features. But when we are attempting a psychological account of instinct-experience, it is quite legitimate to conceive of experiential features (cravings, interests, perceptions, emotions, and the like) as being *causally* connected; especially when we come to attempt an account of subsequent learning processes, which stem from these elements of experience, and have a positive modifying effect upon patterns of behaviour.

Having pointed out the apparent ambiguity of Tinbergen's opinions on this point, and having stated the nature of our disagreement with him, it can be seen, nonetheless, that we can agree with his conclusion that the recognition of the distinction between the three studies—of the biological functions of innate behaviour (adaptation), of the psychology of instinct, and of the bio-physiological aspects of instinct—should be kept clearly in mind if confusion is to be avoided. We can then speak correctly about the degree of 'correlation' which obtains between the three aspects.

Tinbergen raises other interesting and important questions of method, but these are not essential to our purpose. Our main concern now, is to provide ourselves with an outline of the detailed causal analysis of innate behaviour which he offers.

(2) *The Causes of Innate Behaviour*. Tinbergen begins by pointing out that the old controversy as to whether behaviour was 'spontaneous' or 'reactive' is out-moded, since it is now known that both sides state part of the truth. 'Behaviour is reaction in so far as it is, to a certain extent, dependent on external stimulation. It is spontaneous in so far as it is also dependent on internal causal factors, or motivational factors, responsible for the activation of an urge or drive.'

His causal analysis is discussed under these two broad headings: (1) behaviour as a reaction to external stimuli, and (2) the spontaneity of behaviour, involving the study of internal causal factors. This detailed analysis is brought together in (3) an attempt at a synthesis; and the whole account is completed by (4) a section on the processes of growth and maturation. Chapters on the 'Adaptation' and the 'Evolution' of behaviour are also given, but we shall not concern ourselves with these. Tinbergen's whole account is liberally illustrated by experiments of great interest, but here we must confine ourselves to an elucidation of the main concepts used and of the chief findings, merely selecting one or two of the experiments to illustrate each point.

(A) *Behaviour as a Reaction to External Stimuli*

(i) *Each Animal has its own Perceptual World*. In the investigation of external stimuli, Tinbergen insists upon the necessity of discovering the *potential capacities* of the sense organs of the animal which is being studied. We must know, first of all, what stimuli the sense organs of the animal *can* receive. Much work has been done in this connection, and two facts of great importance have been established.

The first is that almost no two species have exactly the same sensory capacities. Each animal has its own 'perceptual world', and this perceptual world is different from the environment of the animal as we ourselves perceive it. This fact emphasises the importance of determining *objectively* the potential sensory capacities of each species.

The second fact of interest is that the animal does not react to *all* the changes in the environment which its sense organs are capable of receiving, but only to *particular features* of them.

(ii) *The Animal responds only to Special Features of its Perceptual World: Sign Stimuli*. This leads Tinbergen to point out the distinction between *actual* and *potential* stimuli.

'As a rule, an instinctive reaction responds to only very few stimuli, and the greater part of the environment has little or no influence, even though the animal may have the sensory equipment for receiving numerous details.' Such stimuli, found to be appropriate to the release of specific reactions, are termed *Sign Stimuli*. The occurrence of the 'errors' which are so common to instinctive behaviour are thus explained: 'by the fact that an animal responds "blindly" to only part of the total environmental situation and neglects other parts, although its sense organs are perfectly able to receive them (and probably do receive them), and although they may seem to be no less important, to the human observer, than the stimuli to which it does react.'

In order to illustrate this point, we might mention very briefly two of the experiments to which Tinbergen refers.

(*a*) The red throat and belly of the male stickleback is one of the most important stimuli releasing spring fighting. Models of sticklebacks were introduced to a number of males. Some of these models were very crude structural imitations but possessed the red belly. Others were very accurate structural imitations but lacked the red colouring. The live males attacked the crude models with the red marking much more vigorously than they attacked the accurate models which lacked the colouration. It was shown, therefore, that the fish reacted to the red colouring and neglected the other structural characteristics, although their eyes were perfectly capable of seeing them.

(*b*) When a domestic hen comes to the rescue of one of her chicks, it has been found that it is reacting to a 'distress-call' and not at all to any movements of the chick. When the chick is placed behind a screen, the hen will go to its rescue when she hears the call. But if the chick is placed under a glass dome so that the mother can see its struggling movements but cannot hear its call, the hen will ignore it.

(iii) *The Perceptual World of the Animal changes with the Activation of Different Instincts*. A further point of interest which is made here is that the animal's perceptual world is not the same at all times, but is perpetually changing as different instincts are activated.

(iv) *The Innate Releasing Mechanism*. Tinbergen then turns to a more detailed discussion of Sign Stimuli, and in so doing introduces the concept of the *Innate Releasing Mechanism*—which is the equivalent of what Lorenz termed the 'Receptory Correlate'. The Innate Releasing Mechanism is the term used to denote the 'special neuro-sensory mechanism that releases the reaction and is responsible for its selective susceptibility to such a very special combination of sign stimuli'. The existence of I.R.M.'s is suggested by the strict dependence of a reaction upon a specific set of sign stimuli.

(v) *The Combination of Sign Stimuli*. Here, Tinbergen points out that the 'sign stimulus' corresponding to a particular reaction is not a simple single stimulus, but a combination or configuration of single stimuli.

We have already seen that the red belly of the male stickleback is one of the most important stimuli in the release of spring fighting. This, however, is not the only stimulus involved. Other elements are discovered by investigating the 'optimal stimulus situation of a given reaction'. Besides the red belly, it has been shown that the 'threat posture' of the male (a peculiar vertical posture with the nose pointing downwards) is also a feature of the sign stimulus releasing the fighting reaction. Similarly, the courting behaviour of the male stickleback has been shown to be dependent on a combination of two sign stimuli: the swollen abdomen and the specific upward-tilted posture of the female. The female's reaction to the courting male, on the other hand, is a response to the red belly of the male and his peculiar zig-zag approach. It has been found, also, that the mating behaviour of the male grayling butterfly is released by (*a*) the typical fluttering flight of the female, (*b*) the degree of darkness of the female, and (*c*) the closeness of the female.

The stimulus of a reaction is thus shown to be a *combination* or a particular *configuration* of sign stimuli, about which more will be said presently.

(vi) *Differences in* (a) *The Intensity of Reactions, and* (b) *The Effectiveness of Sign Stimuli.* The same sign stimuli do not always call forth the same intensity or completeness of reaction. Sometimes, when the sign stimuli seem to be 'optimal', the animal will scarcely react at all, and, on the other hand, an intense reaction may be released by what appear to be very inadequate sign stimuli. This, Tinbergen tells us, is correlated with the internal state of the animal at the time. If the internal motivational factor is in a state of great tension, a small stimulus will be sufficient to release the reaction. If the motivational factor is low, an 'optimal' sign stimulus may result in only a very weak reaction, or even no reaction at all.

There is also evidence to suggest 'that there is no *absolute* distinction between effective sign stimuli and the non-effective properties of an object.' *Sometimes* a robin will posture to a specimen lacking a red breast, and *sometimes* a stickleback will attack a dummy lacking both the red colouring and the threat posture. This, Tinbergen says, means either (*a*) that the 'dependence on a sharply limited number of sign stimuli might represent an extreme case and is, perhaps, a specialization', or (*b*) 'that conditioning is responsible for the effectiveness of additional stimuli.' It is clear that further study is required for the solution of this problem.

(vii) *Each Reaction has its own particular Innate Releasing Mechanism.* As far as the available knowledge goes, it seems that each different reaction of the same animal has a different innate releasing mechanism. This fact is suggested most clearly when different reactions are made to the same object, and when the object has to furnish a different sign stimulus for each different reaction. This is illustrated by Tinbergen's analysis of the mating behaviour of the three-spined stickleback, which, it may be remembered, we used as an example of instinctive behaviour in our opening chapter. This whole sequence of behaviour seems to be *one* reaction, but Tinbergen shows that it is more correctly regarded as a *Reaction Chain* comprising a number of separate reactions each of which is released by specific sign stimuli.

In the first place, the female makes her appearance in the male's territory, The upward-tilted posture and the swollen abdomen are the sign stimuli releasing the 'zig-zag dance' reaction in the male. The male then turns sharply away and swims towards his nest. This movement causes the female to follow. If the female follows (if not in a state of full sexual motivation, she might not follow immediately), the male swims down to his nest and points inside the nest with his nose. The female then swims inside. This releases the quivering reaction in the male, which begins to thrust its snout at her rump with quick rhythmic movements. This induces spawning in the female. The presence of the fresh eggs in the nest then makes the male fertilize them.[1]

That this is a 'reaction chain' comprising several separate reactions is shown by the fact that the sequence of behaviour can be broken at any point. Thus, if—when the female has entered the nest—the male is removed and the trembling and prodding of the female's abdomen does not take place, the female will not spawn. If, however, the rump of the female is then prodded with the end of a glass rod, spawning occurs.

(viii) *Supernormal Sign Stimuli*. It is found, curiously, that the sign stimuli actually met with in nature are not necessarily the 'optimal' sign stimuli. Birds have been found to prefer clutches of eggs larger than their normal clutch, and to prefer eggs bigger than their own eggs. Such sign stimuli are referred to as 'Supernormal' sign stimuli, and the full significance of this phenomenon, we are told, is not yet clear.

(ix) *Ambivalent Behaviour*. Since each reaction has its own particular releasing mechanism, a state of conflict can exist when two sign stimuli, belonging to two different reactions, are present at the same time. Thus, (a) in the breeding season, a herring gull removes any red object from the nest, and (b) the reaction of sitting down on the nest to incubate is released by sign stimuli from the eggs, the most important of which is a visual stimulus. If, then, a *red egg* is placed in the nest, the gull finds itself in the situation of trying to remove the egg and to sit upon it at the same time. This conflict of two simultaneously released reactions is termed 'Ambivalent Behaviour'.

(x) *Social Releasers*. A social releaser is a sign stimulus or combination of sign stimuli *provided by a fellow member of the same species*, and which releases a particular reaction in an animal. It has been shown that the social relationships (as, above, in the reproductive behaviour of the stickleback) of some animals, 'are based upon the functioning of structural or behavioural elements releasing specific responses in fellow members of the same species.'

(xi) *Sign Stimuli: Complex and Configurational*. Later in his book, Tinbergen devotes more attention to the complex, 'configurational' nature of the combinations of sign stimuli to which an animal responds. The term stimulus, he tells us, is misleading, since a close study of the sign stimuli show that they are very complex and not easily measurable.

[1]See Fig. 48, p. 48 in Tinbergen's *The Study of Instinct*.

For example: newly hatched chicks of the herring gull beg for food by pecking at the tip of the parent's bill which is yellow and has a red spot at the end of the lower mandible. The parent then regurgitates food on to the ground, picks up a little in its beak, and presents it to the young. Experiments with various 'dummies' show that the chicks react especially to the red spot. Dummies were then presented on which the red spot was placed *unusually* on the head. This revealed the fact that the *location* of the red spot in relation to other parts of the head is of importance. The sign stimulus is not simply 'something red', Tinbergen says, but a 'red patch at the tip of the lower mandible.'[1]

Sometimes, too, *types-of-movement* act as a sign stimuli. In these cases it is clear that all the previous *elements* of the situation are in fact the same; only the *arrangement* of them has been changed.

Perhaps the clearest example of the configurational nature of sign stimuli is that of an experiment on the reactions of young gallinaceous birds to flying birds of prey. A model was prepared with a short protuberance on one side of the wings and a long one on the other. When the model was sailed in such a direction that it represented a long neck and a short tail it had no effect on the young birds. When it was sailed in order to represent a short neck and a long tail it elicited escape responses. The sign stimulus was therefore shown to be not only the *shape* of the bird of prey, but the *shape in relation to direction of movement*.[2]

The mere *recognition* of the 'gestalt' organisation of sign stimuli, however, does not satisfy Tinbergen. He regards it as a challenge to further investigation rather than as a solution, and goes on to indicate how the problem might be approached.

(xii) *The Phenomenon of Heterogeneous Summation*. We have already seen that the degree of accumulation of the reaction specific energy determines the degree of sensory stimulation necessary to release a reaction. Because of this mingling of internal and external factors reactions do not simply occur or not occur, but are manifested in different *intensities* and in different *states of completion*. Sometimes only a very slight response may be made—so slight that it may only be recognisable to the trained observer who has a detailed knowledge of the animal's whole behaviour. Such slight, incomplete movements are termed *Intention Movements*. Reactions, then, may vary from intention movements at the one end of the scale, through various degrees of incompletion, to the complete response at the other. There are reactions, however, where what Tinbergen calls 'the all-or-none law' holds. In such

[1] *The Study of Instinct*, Fig. 64.   [2] *Ibid.*, Fig. 65.

cases, incomplete external stimulation leads not to a decrease in the degree of intensity of the reaction, but to a decrease in the *number* of responses to repeated stimulation. Thus, the effects of incomplete external stimulation can be observed in the *degree of intensity* of the reaction, or the *frequency* of the reaction, or both.

The important point which emerges from the study of incomplete external stimulation is that, 'deficiencies in sign stimuli always have the same general effect on the reaction, regardless of which part of the stimulus situation is missing or incomplete. The form of the complete reaction is dependent not on *what part* of the stimulus situation is missing, but on *how much of it* is missing.'

An illustration is given from the behaviour of the grayling butterfly. We may recall that the sign stimuli which released the mating behaviour of the male were (1) the typical fluttering flight-movement of the female, (2) the degree of darkness of the female, and (3) the close proximity of the female. In spite of the fact, however, that dark models have a higher releasing value than light ones, a white model can release as many reactions as a dark one if it is sufficiently close. Or, if the dark model is moving smoothly, whereas the white model is moved with an accentuated fluttering motion, the latter will release as many reactions as the former. This experiment shows that inadequacies in any one of the sign stimuli can be compensated for by the others.

The conclusion drawn from this fact is that the influence of the sign stimuli (since it appears that they can compensate for each other in a *quantitative* way) is in some way 'added up' by the central nervous system. 'It is as if the "impulse flow" started by each sign stimulus, qualitatively different though it may be from the impulses arriving from other receptor fields, acts upon the motor centre in a purely quantitative way. In other words, either before they reach the motor centre or in the motor centre itself, the effects of the external stimuli are brought together and added.'

This additive combination of the sign stimuli is what Tinbergen calls the 'Phenomenon of Heterogeneous Summation'.

We shall see later that Tinbergen maintains that motor responses are also organised in a configurational or hierarchical way, but we might note in this place the importance which he attaches to this configurational character of both the afferent and the efferent sides of instinctive behaviour.

'These facts', he tells us, 'are highly significant in two respects. First, the additive co-operation of sign stimuli releasing a reaction as a whole indicates that the afferent impulses are collected into one single "container", which acts in a purely quantitative way on the motor centre.

Second, the configurational character of the motor response itself shows that the motor centre re-dispatches the stimuli and distributes them according to configurational principles. This "container" is, in the terms of neuro-physiology, a centre, or a system of centres.'

The full significance of these remarks will be seen when we consider Tinbergen's analysis of the internal causal factors of instinctive behaviour, and his 'attempt at a synthesis'.

(xiii) *Releasing and Directing Stimuli.* So far, Tinbergen has been discussing sensory stimuli with regard to their function of *releasing* reactions, but now he points out that many sensory stimuli *direct* reactions. For example, in some species of butterfly it has been shown that the visiting of flowers is *directed* by colours but *released* by odours. There are cases in which certain sign stimuli act as 'directing' stimuli whilst other, different sign stimuli, act as 'releasing' stimuli; but sometimes the same sign stimulus has the simultaneous effect of both directing and releasing.

(xiv) *The 'Fixed Pattern Reaction' and Taxes.* The distinction between releasing and directing stimuli corresponds with a similar distinction between two elements of the reaction itself. In the case of many oriented movements, two components can be distinguished.

Firstly, there is the *Fixed Pattern Reaction* (which depends upon certain external releasing stimuli and upon internal motivating factors) but which, once it has been released, is integrated by internal mechanisms only. Once the fixed pattern (which, in Lorenz's terms, constitutes the instinct proper) is released it runs its full course without any further external stimulus.

Secondly, there is the *Taxis* which comprises a series of reactions to external stimuli which results in a guiding or directing movement. The taxis is the component of behaviour resulting in orientation to certain objects of the environment, and the Fixed Pattern is the component of behaviour which is 'blindly' released.

To illustrate: the egg-retrieving response of the gray lag goose can be shown to comprise a fixed pattern reaction and a component which depends upon external stimulation encountered during the behaviour. The goose retrieves an egg by stretching out its neck, placing its bill behind the egg, and rolling it back into the nest. The reaction involves both the 'egg-rolling' movement and a side-to-side tapping, balancing movement of the bill. If the egg should happen to slip out of the bird's control, the 'egg-rolling' movement is not always broken off, but sometimes runs its full course. If this happens, the side-to-side balancing movements are absent. If, also, a cylindrical object is introduced to the bird, the 'egg-rolling' reaction will be manifested, but no side-to-side balancing movements will occur. This suggests that the 'egg-rolling' reaction is a fixed pattern, whereas the side-to-side balancing movement depends on the continual external (tactile) stimuli provided by the egg. The 'fixed pattern' character of the 'egg-rolling' response was demonstrated by introducing to the bird a very large egg. The goose could not adapt the response to this unusual situation, and 'got stuck half-way when the egg was pressed between the bill and the breast.'

Tinbergen goes on to discuss in detail various types of taxes, but these need not concern us here. It is sufficient for our purposes to note the distinction which is made between the 'fixed pattern' component and the 'taxis' component of an oriented reaction.

(B) The Spontaneity of Behaviour: Internal Causal Factors

In this section Tinbergen analyses the internal factors responsible for the element of 'spontaneity' in instinctive behaviour.

(1) Indirect Evidence for the Influence upon Behaviour of Internal Factors. The evidence for the effects upon behaviour of internal factors is grouped under two heads: indirect evidence, and direct evidence. As indirect evidence, three kinds of observation are cited.

Firstly, it is shown that, under *constant conditions*, there are variations in the intensity or frequency of an animal's reaction. Several examples are quoted, but here it will be sufficient to mention the intensity of the 'fanning' reaction of the male three-spined stickleback. After two or three clutches of eggs have been fertilised, the sex drive of the male begins to wane and the reaction known as the 'fanning' of the eggs begins. The time spent in fanning the eggs increases each day until the eggs hatch, when the reaction stops. This increase in the fanning response is partly due to an external chemical stimulus: the increased consumption of oxygen by the eggs. When the oxygen content of the water is reduced, fanning is increased. But if fresh eggs are put in place of partly developed eggs, the fanning does not decrease at all, but *continues* to increase until the original eggs, preserved in another tank, are hatched. A drop in the fanning then occurs, but this drop is not complete. The stimuli of the new eggs induce a second continual increase in the fanning reaction until this second clutch of eggs hatches. When this is repeated experimentally, keeping the external conditions constant, it is found that each successive 'peak' of the fanning reaction is lower than the previous one. This effect, it is proposed, must be due to an internal factor.

Secondly, it has been observed that the minimum stimulus required for the release of a reaction varies greatly. The 'threshold' for release varies in accordance with the intensity of the internal drive, or the accumulation of reaction specific energy. Tinbergen tells us, further, that a correlation exists between the intensity of the stimulus required to release a reaction and the length of time which has elapsed since the previous performance of the reaction. He points out that a drive may become so strong that the reaction may be forced out in the absence of any releasing stimulus, giving rise to the 'Vacuum Activity', of which we have noted an adequate account in our discussion of Lorenz.

Thirdly, besides studying the strength of stimuli necessary to release a reaction, it is possible to study the strength of an obstacle required to prevent or to inhibit the reaction. By testing the intensity of the obstacle necessary to block various drives, the relative strength of the drives can be measured.

To illustrate this third kind of indirect evidence, Tinbergen mentions an interesting experiment undertaken by Nice. The singing of male songbirds is a reproductive activity and can be inhibited by low temperatures. Having measured the temperatures which inhibited the singing of male sparrows during the early spring, Nice showed that the temperature inhibiting song became lower as the season advanced, indicating the growing influence of internal motivational factors.

(2) *Direct Evidence for the Influence upon Behaviour of Internal Factors*. The direct evidence for the influence on behaviour of internal factors is discussed under three heads.

(i) *Hormones*. The evidence of the effects upon behaviour of the injection of certain hormones is well known, and therefore only one or two examples need be given here.

(a) It has been shown in experiments on the domestic fowl that male chicks, when injected with testosterone proprionate, will manifest the sexual behaviour patterns of the adult cock—including crowing and complete copulatory behaviour.

(b) Growth in the testes of crows, and, in some cases, northward migration have been induced by subjecting them to artificially lengthened days in winter. This suggests that spring migration is activated by either pituitary or gonadal hormones.

Tinbergen quotes much evidence of this kind, but, for our purposes, these examples are sufficient.

(ii) *Internal Sensory Stimuli*. The example Tinbergen gives of internal sensory stimuli having an effect upon behaviour is that of the contractions of the muscles of the stomach walls which occur in rhythmic sequence and comprise at least one physiological feature of what we experience as 'hunger'. This is the only example given, but it suffices to illustrate this kind of internal factor.

(iii) *Intrinsic Central Nervous Factors.* In the case of hormones and internal sensory stimuli, Ethology has nothing really new to tell us. It is under this third category of intrinsic central nervous factors that the new concept of 'reaction specific energy' is introduced by Tinbergen.

There are some forms of spontaneous behaviour, he points out, which, as far as existing knowledge goes, cannot be adequately explained by the influences of either hormones or internal sensory stimuli. Thus, the hunting behaviour of dogs cannot always be suppressed by abundant feeding. Also, the fact that specific reactions fade in intensity or decrease in their frequency suggests that some kind of specific energy accumulates in connection with each reaction, and, once dissipated, requires a certain period of time for its restoration.

In discussing this point, Tinbergen considers various studies of the intrinsic activity of the central nervous system in relation to locomotion.

In particular, he mentions von Holst who considered that his work on the locomotion of fish indicated the automatic nature of the nervous mechanisms underlying locomotion. The evidence is to some extent conflicting, but it has at least been shown that whilst the initiation of the rhythmic movements of locomotion is not *completely* 'intrinsic' or automatic, nevertheless the external stimulus required to initiate them is very *slight* and unspecific. Experiments on the de-afferentation of various kinds of fish have shown that even when almost all the dorsal roots are severed (in one case only two were left intact), complete locomotory movements are manifested.

Another interesting experiment suggesting the intrinsic activity of the spinal cord was that carried out by P. Weiss on the axolotl.

A piece of embryonic spinal cord was implanted in the connective tissue of the dorsal trunk musculature of an intact axolotl. A fore limb was also implanted. It was found that the implanted spinal cord did not grow a connection with the central nervous system of the host, but grew both motor and sensory fibres towards the grafted limb. The motor neurones established connection with the muscles of the limb several weeks before the sensory fibres came into contact with the receptors. Yet as soon as the connection was made with the motor neurones, the limb began to carry out rhythmic movements. The implanted spinal cord was thus shown to be responsible for the production of impulses which were independent of external stimulation.

This evidence suggests, therefore, the intrinsic activity of the spinal cord. The conflicting evidence with regard to the *initiation* of these movements leads Tinbergen to suggest two possibilities. In the first place *some* external stimuli seem to be necessary to raise the general excitatory state; thereby bringing the intrinsic activity above 'threshold value'. In the second place, it seems that some of the external stimuli act in a way which can be conceived as the '*removal of a block* which is preventing the automatic impulses from expressing themselves in motion'. When this block is removed, the motor impulses are allowed a free passage from the automatic centres.

Tinbergen considers these facts to be of very great importance, since they indicate a close parallel between 'the mechanisms of the innate patterns as a whole and the locomotory patterns which are their constituent parts.' Both the study of instinctive behaviour, and the study of the neuro-physiology of locomotory patterns, point, therefore, to the importance of intrinsic internal factors and make necessary the rejection of any theory which attempts to explain manifest behaviour in terms of pure 'reaction' alone.

(3) *The Co-operation of the Internal Causal Factors.* The way in which internal and external causal factors are supposed to co-operate in instinctive behaviour is dealt with fully in Tinbergen's attempt at a synthesis, but two points of importance are briefly mentioned here.

Firstly, with regard to the co-operation of the internal factors, Tinbergen concludes that the hormones most probably act upon the central nervous system, thereby increasing the excitability of the sensorimotor mechanism specifically involved in any particular instinctive activity. The hormones cannot be said to exert their influence upon behaviour by (*a*) stimulating the growth of new nervous connections, or by (*b*) inducing changes in various organs, which then initiate sensory impulses which facilitate the special sensorimotor mechanisms, because it has been shown experimentally that animals show a very *quick* response to a change in hormone level. Neither can the hormones influence behaviour by increasing the *general* excitatory state. Tinbergen points out that the same muscles may be used in several instinctive reactions. In specific reactions, therefore, it is not *specific muscles* which are used, but specific *patterns* of muscular activity. Two reactions may utilise the same muscles; it is the muscles' *contractions* which are differently integrated. When hormones are shown to activate specific reactions, their influence, somehow, must therefore be upon the excitability of *specific* motor centres.

A second point is that there is a mutual relationship between the internal and external causal factors in the sense of an additive influence on the motor response. Though these various impulses are qualitatively different, they combine in a quantitative way in exerting their influence on the motor response. But this will be examined in more detail presently.

Concluding this section: Tinbergen shows how the close parallels between mechanisms underlying locomotion and those underlying an instinctive act as a whole; the fact that both are subject to internal factors and external stimuli; and the fact that both have the tendency to 'explode' in the absence of releasing stimuli, led Lorenz to formulate the hypothesis: 'that instinctive responses too are controlled by automatic centres that send out a continuous flow of impulses to central nervous motor mechanisms. Some kind of block prevents discharge into muscle action, which would lead to chaos. Discharge is brought about by adequate stimuli, namely, the combination of sign stimuli typical of each instinctive response. These sign stimuli act upon a reflex mechanism, which alone is able to remove the block, thus allowing the accumulated impulses to discharge themselves in muscle actions constituting the motor response.'

From this analysis, we can see how the breaking down of the earlier concept of instinct into these more precise factors has facilitated experimental work and, at the same time, shown how complex a matter the causation of behaviour is. Tinbergen states, with his characteristic care, that the present state of knowledge of this process of causation is very fragmentary indeed. With this qualification in mind, he attempts a tentative synthesis of the facts he has already outlined.

(C) A Synthesis

(1) *Hierarchical Organisation.* Tinbergen postulates that the mechanisms underlying behavioural reactions are organised in a hierarchical system. His illustration of this hierarchy of mechanisms is an analysis of the Reproductive Instinct of the male stickleback, and in the accompanying diagram we have brought together both the diagram and the explanation which Tinbergen gives.

A study of this schematic representation gives, very clearly, the nature of the hierarchical structure which is suggested.[1] It is important, too, to note that Tinbergen holds that this hierarchy comprises different *levels* of integration. This will be more fully appreciated when the present schema has been briefly described, and, especially, when we

[1]This may be compared with Thorpe's 'schema' of the concepts of Lorenz, p. 115.

come to see what Tinbergen has to say about the parallel neuro-physiological facts.

In the diagram it can be seen that the reproductive pattern as a whole, the activation of this 'major reproductive instinct', is brought about by the gradual increase in the length of day (when the male has migrated

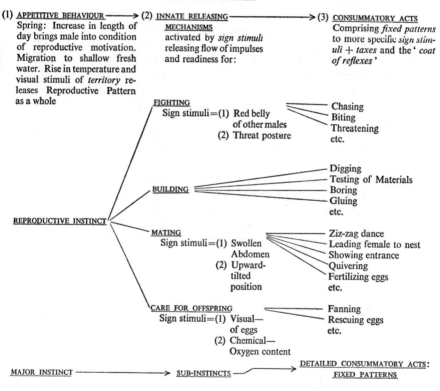

REPRODUCTIVE INSTINCT
STICKLEBACK

(1) APPETITIVE BEHAVIOUR ——→ (2) INNATE RELEASING ——————→ (3) CONSUMMATORY ACTS
Spring: Increase in length of   MECHANISMS   Comprising *fixed patterns*
day brings male into condition   activated by *sign stimuli*   to more specific *sign stim-*
of reproductive motivation.   releasing flow of impulses   *uli + taxes* and the ' *coat*
Migration to shallow fresh   and readiness for: *of reflexes* '
water. Rise in temperature and
visual stimuli of *territory* releases Reproductive Pattern
as a whole

FIGHTING   Chasing
Sign stimuli=(1) Red belly   Biting
                 of other males   Threatening
              (2) Threat posture   etc.

                                                          Digging
                                                          Testing of Materials
BUILDING   Boring
                                                          Gluing
                                                          etc.

REPRODUCTIVE INSTINCT

MATING   Ziz-zag dance
Sign stimuli=(1) Swollen   Leading female to nest
                 Abdomen   Showing entrance
              (2) Upward-   Quivering
                 tilted   Fertilizing eggs
                 position   etc.

CARE FOR OFFSPRING   Fanning
Sign stimuli=(1) Visual—   Rescuing eggs
                 of eggs   etc.
              (2) Chemical—
                 Oxygen content

                                          DETAILED CONSUMMATORY ACTS:
MAJOR INSTINCT ——————————→ SUB-INSTINCTS ——→   FIXED PATTERNS

into shallow water) the rise in temperature and the visual stimulus of a suitable territory. The reactions of 'fighting' and 'nest-building' are both dependent on this mian reproductive motivation, but both are also dependent for their release upon additional external sign stimuli, such as, in the case of fighting for example, the red belly of the male. Behavioural reactions at this level, then, will depend upon the sign stimuli encountered in the environment. But this is not the end of the story.

Whilst the sign stimuli at this level induce an appropriate reaction, the actual details of the final behaviour depend upon still more specific sign stimuli at the level of the 'consummatory act' (about which more will be said presently). The red belly of the male which intrudes into the territory will release attack and the readiness for fighting, but it does not determine which of the particular kinds of fighting will be manifested. 'When the stranger bites, the owner of the territory will bite in return; when the stranger threatens, the owner will threaten back; when the stranger flees, the owner will chase it; and so on.' There are thus certain levels of reaction, which are dependent upon the activation of the higher levels, but which also involve sign stimuli and mechanisms peculiar to themselves. 'They belong to different levels of integration and, moreover, they are organized in a hierarchical system, like the staff organization of an army or of other human organizations. The facts (1) that at each of the levels an external stimulus can have a specific releasing influence and (2) that each reaction has its own motor pattern, mean that there is a hierarchical system of I.R.M.s and of Motor Centres.'

More light is thrown on this question of levels of reaction by the distinction, within the chain of reactions, between 'Appetitive Behaviour' and the 'Consummatory Act'.

So far, the discussion of instinctive behaviour has been confined mainly, if not entirely, to the lowest level of reaction: the level of the consummatory act. The 'Consummatory Act' is the *end-response:* comprising the fixed pattern, the taxes, and the 'coat of reflexes'; and which (once released) seems to consume the reaction specific energy, resulting in a drop of motivation. This, it may be remembered, is what Lorenz called the Instinct proper, but Tinbergen, as we shall see, does not approve of this usage.

As can be seen from the above 'hierarchical organization', the consummatory acts come at the end of a long process of behaviour, and, whilst they are reactions to external stimuli, they are dependent also upon impulses proceeding from the higher levels. The activation of the higher levels results in behaviour which is quite different from that manifested in the consummatory acts. Partly, it results in a state of increased readiness to react to particular sign stimuli, but also it leads to behaviour which has been termed 'random', 'exploratory', 'seeking' behaviour. It is this random behaviour which brings the animal into those situations in which the specific sign stimuli will be encountered and the consummatory acts released. This random behaviour is termed 'Appetitive Behaviour' and is characterised *not* by any fixed, stereotyped motor patterns, but by its variability, plasticity, and purposiveness.

It is to be noted here that Tinbergen quite consciously and definitely uses the word 'purposive', but, as in the case of the 'gestalt' nature of the sign stimuli, he accepts it rather as a challenge to further inquiry than as a terminus of inquiry. This point of the plasticity and purposiveness of some phases of instinctive behaviour is important, and we must see what Tinbergen actually says about it.

'This distinction between appetitive behaviour and consummatory act separates the behaviour as a whole into two components of entirely different character. The consummatory act is relatively simple; at its most complex, it is a chain of reactions, each of which may be a simultaneous combination of a taxis and a fixed pattern. But appetitive behaviour is a true purposive activity, offering all the problems of plasticity, adaptiveness, and of complex integration that baffle the scientist in his study of behaviour as a whole. Appetitive behaviour is a conglomerate of many elements of very different order, of reflexes, of simple patterns like locomotion, of conditioned reactions, of "insight" behaviour, and so on. As a result it is a true challenge to objective science, and therefore the discrimination between appetitive behaviour and consummatory act is but a first step of our analysis.'

A further point is made here which is of importance.

Both Lorenz and Tinbergen maintain that purposiveness is typical only of appetitive behaviour and not of consummatory acts, and that 'the end of purposive behaviour is not the attainment of an object or a situation itself, but the performance of the consummatory action, which is attained as a consequence of the animal's arrival at an external situation which provides the special sign stimuli releasing the consummatory act.'

This statement clearly raises many problems.

If we are going to speak of *purposiveness* at all (and it seems that even the Ethologists, after the most objective study, find it indispensable) it is difficult to see why we should set against each other (*a*) the 'attainment of an object or a situation' and (*b*) 'the performance of the consummatory act'. Does not the performance of the consummatory act require the attainment of an object and a situation? And if an animal acts purposively with regard to the felt necessity of performing the consummatory acts, why may it not also act purposively with regard to the attainment of those objects and situations in the context of which the acts are performed? In a word, can there be any useful distinction here from the point of view of the experience of the animal? We may recall at this point the earlier *psychological* postulate of a primary 'instinct-interest' accompanying the activation of an instinct: the 'feeling of interest or worth-whileness' of the whole relation between (to use the new terms) the specific sign stimulus and the reaction specific energy; and the contention that, with the continual repetition of this whole situation in the animal's experience, there will develop a 'growing accustomed to' (or an increasing perceptual awareness of) the objects and related modes of behaviour involved in the particular situation. What we must insist upon is that—apart from some such awareness of the significance of certain sign stimuli in relation to a particular reaction specific energy, no matter how dim (i.e. even if it is only a *feeling* of interest confined purely to the level of perceptual experience)— behaviour can *never* be termed 'purposive' *at all* from the point of view of the experiencing and behaving animal, and *appetitive behaviour (if psychological postulates are to be completely discounted in causal analysis) must be regarded as being just as 'blind' as the consummatory act.*

The consummatory act seems to be dependent on the centres of the lowest level of instinctive behaviour. Appetitive behaviour, however, may be activated by centres of all levels above that of the consummatory act. There are, therefore, differing levels of appetitive behaviour. The initial 'random' behaviour is the most general; but when lower levels of reaction are brought into play—as, for example, when the male stickle-back reacts to the red belly of an intruder—more specific kinds of appetitive behaviour are released: in this case, the specific readiness to fight the intruder; the actual form of fighting being dependent upon more specific sign stimuli, and the taxes and fixed patterns then released. 'It seems, therefore', Tinbergen tells us, 'that the centres of each level of the hierarchical system control a type of appetitive behaviour.'

(2) *Neurophysiological Facts.* The suggested hierarchy of mechanisms underlying the reactions observed in the instinctive behaviour of an animal can best be appreciated by considering Tinbergen's hypothetical parallel hierarchy of neurophysiological centres.

It should be possible, Tinbergen says, if this notion of a hierarchy of 'collecting and re-dispatching centres' is correct, to trace these centres by neurophysiological methods. Evidence has already been cited to indicate the intrinsic central nervous factors which yield the rhythmic patterns of locomotion, but these facts refer to only the lowest level of instinctive activity. There is, however, evidence of centres which regulate behaviour at the higher levels of integration.

W. R. Hess discovered that, by probing the hypothalamic region of the brains of cats with minute electrodes, he could induce the complete behaviour patterns of fighting, eating, and sleeping. The behaviour patterns were not only present, but were performed in perfect co-ordination, and were initiated by genuine appetitive behaviour. Hess seems, therefore, to have found the anatomical basis of the centres controlling instinctive patterns as a whole, and seems to have shown that, whilst the spinal cord and the medulla seem to control certain components of the instinctive patterns, it is the hypothalamus which contains the highest centres concerned. Tinbergen expresses the belief that the continuation of such research will lead to the discovery of centres intermediate between these higher centres and the centres controlling the fixed patterns.

An interesting discussion of the work of Hess is to be found in the book, *General Theory of Neurosis* by Rudolf Brun. Commenting on Hess, Brun[1] shows how the pattern of sleep induced by electrical stimulation was completely 'natural'.

'Even animals, which immediately before the current was applied were still angrily spitting, now became suddenly gentle, crouched down, rolled themselves up, began to purr, and gradually fell asleep. In short, this artificially induced "electric" sleep showed all the characteristics of natural physiological sleep; even to the extent that the animal could at any time be awakened by sufficiently strong external stimuli.' Other tests in which other portions of the diencephalon and the hypothalamus were stimulated produced such definite visceral-nervous effects as 'sudden alteration of the blood pressure, inhibition of respiration, or the converse, forcible breathing, contraction or expansion of the pupils, activation or inhibition of the mobility of the stomach or the bowel, and finally, evacuation of the bladder and lower bowel. All these effects of stimulation occur infallibly and as often as required, whenever the relevant points are stimulated.' Brun continues:

'Particularly instructive, and of considerable importance as regards the problem of the instincts, were the experiments which induced the evacuation of the bowel. Here, as in the case of experimental sleep induced by stimulating the sleep-centre, it appeared once more that the act in question (defecation) did not result suddenly, convulsively, or in a disorderly and excited fashion, but only after adequate preparation, such as the assumption of the bodily posture characteristic of the action, and with the whole series of characteristic movements which are peculiar to this instinctive action. The same remarks apply to other effects which Hess was able to induce by stimulating other parts of the diencephalon; such as arching the back, spitting, leaping, and actual aggression; and, on the other hand, a comfortable purring, the attentive pricking of the ears, and, finally, the instinctive act of eating—and of attempting to eat even uneatable substances, such as wood—was

[1]*General Theory of Neurosis*, pp. 21-22.

involuntarily performed. According to Hess, even the instinctive direction of the attention and the preliminary turning of the head, and finally the whole body, toward a particular object seems to be localized in (or rather, can be actuated from) a perfectly definite locus of the dienceph-

TENTATIVE REPRESENTATION OF AN INSTINCTIVE 'CENTRE' OF AN INTERMEDIATE LEVEL

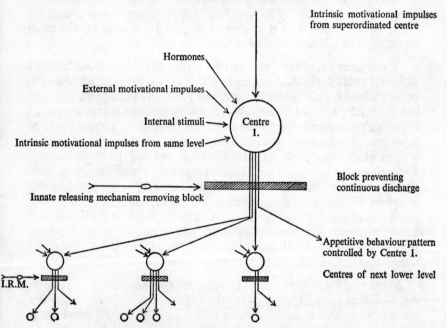

(Re-drawn from Tinbergen: 'Study of Instinct', p. 124)

alon, for after eliminating this "centre" by electro-coagulation of the point of stimulation in question the animal was no longer able to turn round towards the opposite side and an attempt to do so ended in falling over or spinning round and round. . . . Even more remarkable is the following observation: if an animal so treated is presented with a desirable object within the field of vision on the side toward which it could no longer turn, it no longer appeared to notice the object, so that one can speak of a unilateral "diencephalon psychic blindness".'

These findings are of the greatest interest.

We may turn now to the schematic representation of the hierarchy of neurophysiological centres which Tinbergen offers. But, whilst doing so, we must emphasise very strongly that Tinbergen puts his schema forward as a very tentative and hypothetical suggestion. 'These diagrams represent no more than a working hypothesis of a type that helps to put our thoughts in order.'

Firstly, Tinbergen describes one 'centre' of an intermediate level of instinctive activity. The diagram opposite, shows how various internal causal factors are operating on the centre. Outgoing impulses are prevented by a block which is removed when the appropriate sign stimuli act upon the I.R.M. The impulses are then released and can flow along a number of paths, all but one of which lead to the subordinate centres of the lower level. These subordinate centres, however, are still themselves blocked. Most of the released impulses therefore flow along the path leading to the nerve structures which control appetitive behaviour. This appetitive behaviour continues until one of the I.R.M.s of one of the lower centres is activated, thereby releasing the flow of impulses to the next lower centre, and so on to the final consummatory act.

Tinbergen then provides a diagram (see p. 140) to illustrate how these centres can be supposed to function in any particular major instinct. Here again, his illustration is that of the reproductive instinct of the male stickleback, and the first three levels of this hierarchy of neurophysiological centres can be compared with the diagram on p. 133 which showed the three main levels of reaction: the appetitive behaviour, the 'sub-instincts' or lower levels of appetitive behaviour, and the consummatory act.

The 'topcentre', Tinbergen suggests, can be called the 'migration' centre. Upon this is exerted a hormonal influence and also, probably, the increase in temperature, both of which cause the migration into shallow fresh water. This first centre is supposed to have no 'block'. No specific sign stimuli are necessary to release the migratory behaviour, which must therefore be the outcome of purely motivational factors. Sign stimuli of a territory then remove the first block, and the impulses flow through to the centres of the next lower level. Until specific sign stimuli (e.g. red belly of intruder; swollen abdomen of female, etc.) are encountered, no I.R.M. on this level is activated, and the animal is confined once again to a new level of appetitive behaviour: merely swimming round until it meets with appropriate sign stimuli. This releasing of the flow of impulses by the activation of I.R.M.s continues, down to the level of the consummatory acts.

The centres of different levels, Tinbergen holds, are not all organised in the same way. The highest centre has no block at all. The next higher

THE HIERARCHICAL SYSTEM OF 'CENTRES' UNDERLYING A MAJOR INSTINCT, viz. THE REPRODUCTIVE INSTINCT OF THE MALE THREE-SPINED STICKLEBACK

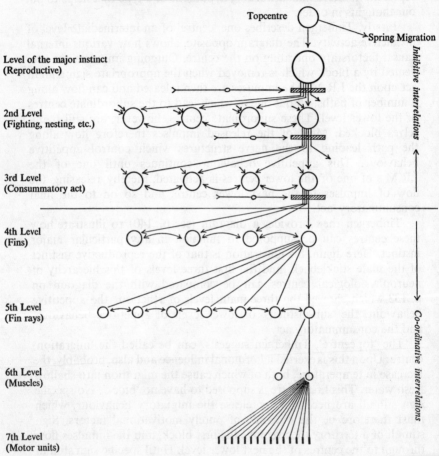

(Re-drawn from Tinbergen: 'Study of Instinct', p. 125)

centres respond to a greater number of motivational factors than do the lower centres, and, in general, 'the lower we go, the more pronounced the influence of external releasing stimuli becomes.'

In connection with the lack of any block where the highest centre of all is concerned, Tinbergen makes an interesting remark to which we shall call attention later.[1] 'If there were blocks at these very highest centres, the animal would have no means of "getting rid" of impulses at all, which, as far as we know, would lead to neurosis.'

This is a brief, but, for our purposes, adequate account of Tinbergen's hierarchy of neurophysiological centres.

Before we leave this question, however, we might take up a point which Rudolf Brun has to make in connection with the supposed 'centres' underlying instinctive activity.

A detailed anatomical examination of the brains of the cats on which Hess had operated, he tells us, was undertaken by Minkowski, and it was thereby established: 'that the instinctive actions which Hess aimed at producing were not dependent on an excitation of the ganglionic cells of the diencephalon, but on the stimulation of definite bundles of fibres which merely run through the hypothalamus. In fact, the nerves which are essentially in question are the neuronic paths descending from the cortex. . . .'

Following upon this, Brun says:

'On the basis of the pioneer researches of W. R. Hess it is often stated that: "the instinctive life has its seat in the diencephalon." However, serious objections against such formulation may be made on the basis of the data just cited: in the first place, it must be emphasised that we cannot speak of any localization of the instincts themselves in the diencephalon. For in the orderly actions which Hess was able to induce by the electrical stimulation of sharply circumscribed points, the instincts themselves were not in question, but merely the release of a few extremely primitive instinctive actions, corresponding with what Hess rightly assumed to be "structures directed towards functional purposes". And even these instinctive actions, according to Minkowski, did not have their "centres", in the sense of special cellular nuclei, in the medial sections of the diencephalon, which would bring about the integration of the motor mechanisms concerned; rather, the results of stimulation were due to the excitation of neuronic paths proceeding from the cortex. Normally, the impulse evoking an instinctive action proceeds either from the periphery (for example, defecation), or from the cortex, and especially from the forebrain. Ceni, for example, has demonstrated that in mammals after extirpation of the forebrain the maternal instinct is entirely absent; a female on whom this operation has been performed no longer cares for her young, and even manifests hostility towards them, driving them away and refusing to suckle them, etc. We see from this that the instincts or impulses cannot be localized in circumscribed

[1]See p. 275.

"centres", but that the relevant impulses and the constituent functional components obviously spread over wide sections of the central nervous system in the form of extensive arcs of excitation.'[1]

Again, Brun says when referring to the findings of Hess:

'. . . you must not forget that the sensitive points in the diencephalon from which such automatisms can be set in operation are by no means the "motor centre", the brain centre itself in which these compound kinetic trains are "localised" (they would be much too small for that); they are rather intercalary points through which—as at the throwing of a switch—the whole compound reflex chains comprising the palaeo-striatum, the between brain, the midbrain, the cerebellum, and finally, the spinal cord, are set to action, or through which—in the case of symptoms of defect, such as disorders of sensibility—they can be automatically cut out.'[2]

These comments of Brun are mentioned merely to indicate the differences of opinion which evidently exist upon this question of the 'centres' of the neurophysiological mechanisms underlying instinctive behaviour. It is clear that the problem awaits much further detailed work in neurophysiology.

On the other points Brun is in very close agreement with the Etho-logical school, and, whilst disagreeing with the view that the highest 'centres' of the instincts are to be found in the diencephalon, he none-theless stresses the importance of the diencephalon in connection with the 'affective moods' of the instincts. He says:

'On the other hand the affective mood which is the precondition of the release of an instinctive action is largely, if not entirely, dependent on the diencephalon. Today we have good grounds to assume that the diencephalon—as the seat of the nerve centres appertaining to the vegetative functions—acts like a sort of rheostat in respect of cortical activity. In accordance with the metabolic changes in the vegetative centres of the diencephalon . . . we find that these centres influence the activity of the cerebrum in different ways. These influences may have a damping or an amplifying effect. Thus, in a certain sense, the cerebrum is actually subservient to the diencephalon. This influence appears to extend to the affectivity, in particular, giving rise to what we describe as "mood". Thus, the instinctive impulses released in the cerebrum by way of the senses and the sensory regions are sometimes facilitated, some-times completely suppressed, according to the "mood" of the dien-cephalon. That hormonal influences are chiefly responsible is obvious. For example, the stag reacts to the hind with the most violent sexual

[1]*General Theory of Neurosis*, p. 23.   [2]*Ibid.*, p. 138.

desire only during the rutting season, and in the intervals does not even "recognize" her as a female; this is obviously due to the fact that his diencephalon—having been flooded with sexual hormones—is sexually attuned, and communicates its mood to the cerebrum only during the rutting season. But all other fundamental activities of the cortex, such as the general readiness to react and the promptness of reaction of the apparatus of perception and association, the primary intensity of attention, the perceptive faculty—in short, the "psychic elasticity"—are also largely influenced by the relevant processes in the diencephalon. . . .'

We shall return to some of the neurophysiological facts presented by Brun when we consider the ethological study of man, but the close approximation of his account to that of Tinbergen in describing how the internal factors give rise to 'appetitive behaviour' can be seen in the above quotation. It is also to be noted that the term 'mood', used by Brun, is also used by the Ethologists, but in an objective way and with an evident wish to minimise any imputation of subjective feeling. Thus, the term 'mood' is defined by them as: 'the preliminary state of "charge" or "readiness for action" necessary to the performance of a given course of instinctive behaviour.'[1] Tinbergen's system of levels of neurophysiological centres can also be described, therefore, as a 'hierarchy of moods'. Lorenz writes:

'It was a most decisive step forward in our understanding of innate behaviour when Baerends pointed out that appetitive behaviour by no means always leads immediately to the discharge of consummatory action. In the vast majority of cases, the appetitive behaviour with which an activity begins is of a much more *generalized* nature. The releasing situation attained by this first step of appetite and the innate releasing mechanism activated in this situation, do not lead to the discharge of the final consummatory act, but, as the next step, to another form of appetitive behaviour of a distinct and more *specialized* form, striving for another, also more specialized, releasing situation. A very general "mood", in the sense of a readiness to certain activities, as, for instance, the "reproductive mood" of a male stickleback, which comprises the several readinesses to a very considerable but finite number of consummatory acts, is, step by step, narrowed down to the discharge of one of these. There is, in other words, a hierarchical order of wider and narrower readinesses or moods. The action-specific appetite and the discharge of the consummatory action are the *lowest* rung in this ladder of superimposed commanding instances or "centres".'[2]

[1] 'The Definition of Some Terms Used in Animal Behaviour Studies', W. H. Thorpe, *Bulletin of Animal Behaviour*, No. 9, March 1951, pp. 34-40.
[2] K. Lorenz, *The Comparative Method in Studying Innate Behaviour Patterns*, pp. 122-268; Symposium: 'Physiological Mechanisms in Animal Behaviour.'

(3) *Displacement Activities*. The utility of this hypothetical hierarchy of neurophysiological centres can be seen in the explanation which it makes possible of Displacement Activities. Displacement movements (actions which sometimes occur during a particular sequence of instinctive activity, but which are peculiarly irrelevant in that they do not 'belong' to that particular instinctive activity) are always innate movements connected with the motor-patterns of other known instincts. Usually, they occur either when two strongly activated but antagonistic drives are in conflict, or when there is a strong motivation of a drive together with a lack of the sign stimuli necessary for the release of the appropriate consummatory act. In all cases, the flow of energy into the channel of the *appropriate* instinctive action is blocked; the normal discharge is prevented; and this energy, it is conceived, finds an outlet for discharge through the motor pattern, or through the 'centre' of another instinct. The energy is said to 'spark over' on to the neural paths, or centres, of another instinct. These facts appear to be successfully accounted for by Tinbergen's theory of the hierarchy of neurophysiological centres. The fact that displacement movements are usually (not always) incomplete, suggests, says Tinbergen, that the 'sparking over' meets with considerable resistance.

Displacement activities have been found to be of particular importance in the study of the *evolution* of behaviour patterns. It has been found that some displacement activities become adapted as Social Releasers. The process, by means of selection, whereby displacement activities become elements of those innate behaviour patterns which function as Social Releasers is termed 'ritualisation'. The complex behaviour patterns of courtship, for example, have been shown to involve elements of threat and escape behaviour. Tinbergen thinks this can be explained functionally since both the attack and the escape drives must be overcome before sexual relations can take place.

(*D*) *Growth, Maturation, and Learning Processes*

Tinbergen's analysis is completed by a study of the development of behaviour in the individual. A distinction is made between growth and maturation, and, finally, several modes of learning are discussed because of their intimate relationship with innate behaviour.

(1) *The Growth of Innate Motor Patterns*. Much of Tinbergen's discussion under this head refers to material which is widely known and which need not be reviewed in detail here.

The well-known work of Carmichael with tadpoles and salamanders in which, by keeping a control group and subjecting another group to anaesthesia, he has shown the development of locomotory patterns to be due to growth and not to learning, is mentioned; as also is the work of Coghill on the axolotl larva to which we have referred earlier, and which, it will be remembered, shows that the development of increasingly complicated behaviour patterns is closely correlated with the growth of the nervous system. An experiment by Grohmann is also mentioned which shows that the flight of birds is due largely to growth and not to learning. In this experiment, young pigeons were prevented from carrying out incipient flight movements by rearing them in narrow tubes which prevented the movement of their wings. When members of a control group were able to fly a certain distance, both groups were tested, and it was found that the achievements in flight of both groups were equal.

The conclusions drawn from these experiments are that the development of overt behaviour patterns is predominantly due to growth and not to learning; and, 'we may safely assume that development of overt behaviour usually is the result of growth processes in the nervous system and not of growth of muscles or receptor organs, which, as a general rule, are developed earlier.' 'From what we know of the order of appearance of reactions, it appears that each species has a fixed time pattern just as with growing morphological structures.'

Very little, however, is known about the actual processes of this growth and development of behaviour patterns, and Tinbergen mentions the findings of several workers to indicate how complicated a problem this is.

P. Weiss, who has experimented with nerve crossings, managed to establish the growth of connections between *flexor* nerve and *extensor* muscle in a limb, and vice versa. He then found that the nerve carried the impulse appropriate to the muscle which it now innervated. 'When the central nervous system sent out a "flexor call", the original extensor nerve carried the impulses to the flexor muscle, while the original flexor nerve did not transmit impulses.' It was shown, therefore, that 'the responsiveness of a motor nerve is not dependent on its localized connection with the centres but is, in some yet unknown way, conditioned to selective responsiveness by the muscle it innervates.' This makes evident the tentative nature of Tinbergen's theory of the hierarchy of neurophysiological centres, and Tinbergen himself readily admits this difficulty. 'These facts', he says, 'show that our picture of the localization of centres must not be too precise and formalistic. There is a gross anatomical localization of, for instance, locomotory centres in the spinal cord, and of higher centres in the hypothalamic regions,[1] but

[1]Compare the previously mentioned views of Brun.

the finer localization is of a physiological and topographically variable nature.'

A further complication which arises in the study of the ontogeny of behaviour is the fact that it does not seem possible to extend the conclusions of Coghill to the growth of all behaviour patterns. Coghill showed that the relative independence of certain behaviour mechanisms was the outcome of a process of differentiation within a whole rather than an addition of originally isolated parts. A study of the development of several behaviour patterns of the European cormorant by Kortlandt, however, points to just the opposite conclusions, namely, that the component parts of a behaviour pattern mature independently and 'are later combined into purposive patterns of a high order.' The complete behaviour pattern of nesting, for example, includes fetching twigs, pushing them into the nest, and fastening them by a typical quivering movement. Kortlandt found that the young began to show nesting behaviour at the age of two weeks. The quivering movement was performed, but inadequately, as the twigs were not fastened. At the age of four to five weeks, the quivering was continued until the twigs were caught in the nest. And still later they accepted twigs from the male, and fetched their own twigs to work into the nest. 'Our analysis of instinctive behaviour', Tinbergen says, 'allows us to describe this in more general terms: the lower units, of the level of the consummatory acts, appear first and the appetitive behaviour appears later.'

It is clear from these findings that nothing conclusive can be said about the ontogeny of instinctive behaviour at present, and that the problem requires further detailed study.

(2) *The Maturation of Innate Motor Patterns*. It is necessary, Tinbergen suggests, to distinguish the seasonal *maturation* of the reproductive patterns from the *growth* of neural motor patterns as described above. This is because, in the seasonal activations of these behaviour patterns, no new growth of neural mechanisms is involved. The neural paths and centres for this behaviour are there all the year round. This can be shown by two facts: (1) The reproductive patterns of behaviour can be induced out of season by the injection of sex hormones. (2) It is found that, even in periods of the year when the reproductive pattern is not activated, elements of this pattern appear as displacement activities in the behaviour-context of other instincts.

Though again Tinbergen stresses the very tentative and fragmentary nature of the work on this subject, the general conclusions he draws are in agreement with the findings of Kortlandt. Kortlandt shows that the growth of behaviour patterns in the young begins with the emergence of 'consummatory act' components and is followed later by the elements of the 'appetitive behaviour'. The growth of behaviour patterns is in the reverse order to their final performance. The *maturation* of behaviour patterns in the adult bird, however, is just the reverse of this. Here, appetitive behaviour appears first, and is gradually extended, through the lower levels of more specialised appetitive behaviour, to the consummatory act.

The hormone is thus held to act upon the higher instinctive centres (we may remember here Brun's remarks on the importance of the diencephalon in connection with the 'affective moods' of the instincts). Appetitive behaviour is then activated. As motivation increases, a definite sequence of behaviour patterns is manifested, and each of these behaviour patterns develops in a definite and gradual way. To take one example, the digging of a hole is activated in the stickleback before actual nest building. The complete digging response 'involves swimming towards the nesting site, pointing the head downward, thrusting the snout into the bottom, sucking up sand, swimming away with a mouthful, and spitting it out 10-20 cm. away.' Describing the actual course of development of this response, Tinbergen says: 'At the outset, when motivation is lowest, digging consists of a scarcely discernible downward bending of the head. The next stage consists of the actual boring of the snout into the soil without sucking up the sand. In the next stage the animal sucks sand and drops it on the spot. Then, with increasing intensity, the last component, that of carrying the sand away, is gradually added, the distance increasing from a few centimetres up to 20 and sometimes more. Thus the development of digging offers quite a clear picture: the first link of the chain of movements appears first in time and then the whole chain is gradually completed (1) by addition of subsequent elements, and (2) by intensification of each element, the earlier elements achieving their final form before the latter elements.'

(3) *Learning Processes.* There are several reasons, Tinbergen insists, why a study of learning processes cannot be ignored by the student of innate behaviour. Firstly, all learning effects a change in the innate functions. 'Learning is a phenomenon of ontogenetic growth of behaviour superimposed on the innate patterns and their mechanisms.'

Secondly, certain learning processes take place so early in the life of the individual that they often precede the complete development of innate patterns. And, thirdly, there is a very close relationship between the innate constitution of the individual and the learning processes which occur. By virtue of the innate constitution, an animal may inherit predispositions to learn *particular* things, whilst its capacity to learn in *other* directions may be extremely limited.

(i) *Localised Learning*. It has been found that some reactions of an animal can be changed considerably by learning, whilst other reactions remain fixed, and apparently unchanged by any process of learning. The animal learns some things more readily than others.

Herring gulls are very poor at distinguishing their own eggs from those of another gull. With regard to the recognition of their young, however, it is quite a different matter. Whilst the young of two nests can be inter-changed during the first few days after hatching without inducing any difference in the behaviour of the parent birds, when the young are five or more days old the parents become conditioned to their own individual young and will neglect or kill any other young which are forced upon them.

Similarly, after mating, the herring gull shows an amazing ability to distinguish its mate from other birds; to recognise it immediately when it is a member of a group of gulls thirty yards distant. 'The gull's ability to recognize its mate', Tinbergen tells us, 'is far superior to our powers of recognizing the gulls.'

A second example is: that although jackdaws show a poor learning ability with regard to their eggs and their young, Lorenz (in describing the order of social ranking which exists in their colonies) has been able to observe that when a 'low-ranking' female mates with a 'high-ranking' male, both she and all the other members of the colony immediately recognise her new ranking as being now on the same level as that of her mate.

Tinbergen concludes: 'As part of the innate equipment, such species have inherited certain strictly specific "dispositions to learn".'

(ii) *Preferential Learning*. Though two or more reactions of an animal may be subject to learning or conditioning, the perceptual elements in relation to which the conditioning takes place may differ in each case. As we have seen, the herring gull learns to recognise very accurately the individual differences among its own young (is able to distinguish them clearly from the young of other gulls). The reactions of the gull to its own eggs, however, are conditioned *not* to the qualitative characteristics of the eggs themselves, but to the *position* of the eggs in relation to the locality of the nest. If the eggs are removed a little way from the nest, the gull will retrieve them, or, alternatively, will sit on the empty nest (even though the eggs are in full view) because of the strong attachment to the original site. If the eggs are moved a little farther away, however, the gull will eat them. Thus, says Tinbergen: 'it seems to be a property of the innate disposition that it directs the conditioning to different parts of the receptual field.'

(iii) *Critical Periods of Learning.* The discovery that learning takes place at particular periods in the life history of the individual is known as the 'Critical Period Hypothesis'. It is of particular importance since it appears that the learning which takes place during these critical periods has a very great determining influence upon the subsequent experience and behaviour of the individual, and we shall consider the phenomenon again when we are discussing the ethological study of man and when we have considered the findings of Psycho-Analysis.

The most impressive description of this kind of learning is given by Lorenz in connection with the behaviour of very young geese. Young geese follow their parents soon after hatching. By removing the parents before the young had seen them, Lorenz was able to show that this initial reaction of the young geese is made towards the first large moving object that they see. A very rapid learning process then takes place (within a minute or so) which Lorenz has termed 'imprinting', whereby the detailed perception of the large moving object is established. Thereafter, the young goose attaches itself to this individual, even though the individual may not be a member of its own species. In this way, a goose may attach itself to a human being. Contrary to what one might expect, this attachment is by no means an ephemeral thing, but persists throughout the life-time of the animal, so that even later sexual display and other manifestations of adult behaviour will be directed to the human being and not to a member of its own species. Once the wrong object or individual has been accepted as the parent, it seems impossible to make the animal accept a member of its own species. The *critical period* is very brief; occurs at this very early stage; and, according to Lorenz, the process cannot occur later, and is irreversible.[1]

This is a very significant fact for our understanding of the early establishment of the 'social responses', and it is clear that if it could be shown that such critical periods occurred during the life-history of the human individual, this would constitute knowledge of the very greatest importance for social psychology and for educational theory. We shall have more to say on the possible application of this point to the problems of human development in our subsequent chapters.

[1]Subsequent evidence on the degree of permanence, and the degree of irreversibility, of 'imprinting' is conflicting; but it is not such as to discountenance this emphasis upon the importance of 'critical periods of learning'. See W. H. Thorpe, 'Learning and Instinct in Animals', 1956; especially p. 357 et seq.

For the present, we shall bring our account of Tinbergen's work to a close by quoting another interesting example of a critical period of learning which he gives.

'The Eskimo dogs of east Greenland live in packs of 5-10 individuals. The members of a pack defend their group territory against all other dogs. All dogs of an Eskimo settlement have an exact and detailed knowledge of the topography of the territories of other packs; they know where attacks from other packs must be feared. Immature dogs do not defend the territory. Moreover, they often roam through the whole settlement, very often trespassing into other territories, where they are promptly chased. In spite of these frequent attacks, during which they may be severely treated, they do not learn the territories' topography, and for the observer their stupidity in this respect is amazing. While the young dogs are growing sexually mature, however, they begin to learn the other territories and within a week their trespassing adventures are over. In two male dogs the first copulation, the first defence of territory, and the first avoidance of strange territory all occurred within one week.'

So far, our approach to Comparative Ethology has been, in the main, uncritical. We have concentrated upon the task of outlining the ethologists' conception of instinctive behaviour as clearly as possible, at the same time (by quoting selected examples) attempting to give some impression, at least, of the wide and detailed experimental work which is cited in support of their findings. Later, we shall indicate differences of opinion within the school itself.

Before leaving our present account, perhaps we should note briefly the definition of Instinct which is tentatively proposed by Tinbergen.

3. *The Definition of Instinct*

We have seen that Lorenz chose to restrict the concept of Instinct to the 'Fixed Pattern' component at the level of the consummatory act. His analysis, however, extended to the various levels of 'appetitive behaviour' which were then included under the broader term: 'instinctive behaviour'. Tinbergen disagrees with Lorenz on this question of definition. He does not wish to restrict the term 'Instinct' to the fixed pattern component of the whole sequence of activities, but thinks that it should refer to all the levels of such a particular sequence.

Tinbergen agrees with the method of classifying the instincts which was adopted by earlier writers, that is, in terms of the 'end-state' to which they appear to be directed, and on the attainment of which the activity ceases. But, he thinks, the neurophysiological basis of the instinct should also be taken into account. '. . . the purposiveness of any instinct is safeguarded by the fact that all the activities forming part of a purposive behaviour pattern aimed at the attainment of a certain goal depend on a common neurophysiological mechanism. Thus it is only natural that any definition of "an instinct" should include not only an indication of the objective aim or purpose it is serving, but also an indication of the neurophysiological mechanism.'

Emphasising that the tentative nature of his conception of the neurophysiological mechanisms necessarily makes his definition of an instinct also tentative, Tinbergen offers the following definition.

An instinct is: 'a hierarchical organised nervous mechanism which is susceptible to certain priming, releasing and directing impulses of internal as well as of external origin, and which responds to these impulses by co-ordinated movements that contribute to the maintenance of the individual and the species.'

It is of interest to compare this definition with those of William James (p. 30), Lloyd Morgan (p. 35), Hobhouse (pp. 42-43), McDougall (pp. 47-48), Drever (pp. 58-59), and Ginsberg (pp. 65-66). In so far as the bio-physiological aspects of instinct have been stressed in certain of these definitions, it can be seen that Tinbergen's definition adds little, if anything, to them. Particularly interesting is the 'biological' definition given by Drever, which can be seen to be practically identical with that of Tinbergen, but which is phrased perhaps more carefully, taking into account other but essential points.

We shall return to a comparison of the older work and this more recent work in a later chapter. For the present we must consider the observations which the Comparative Ethologists have had to make with regard to the study of human behaviour.

CHAPTER V

THE ETHOLOGICAL STUDY OF MAN

THE ethological study of man is in its infancy. One or two studies have been specifically directed towards an analysis of human responses. In the main, however, we shall have to confine ourselves to a brief survey of the more general comments on human experience and behaviour which have been thrown up during the course of ethological study, but which have not been followed by any thorough-going inquiry so far. At present, no writer of the ethological school would take it upon himself to classify and enumerate the instinctive tendencies of man. All are agreed that such a classification can emerge only from detailed future studies and that it would be unwise, at the moment, to pre-judge the issue. Nonetheless, many of the comments on human behaviour which are made are extremely interesting and suggestive, and lead us to anticipate significant findings when the concepts and methods of Comparative Ethology are applied to the field of human studies. The ethologists accept the continuity of animal and human development which is entailed in the theory of evolution and which we discussed in our opening chapter. The study of man is therefore within their field of investigation, and the various writers are agreed in believing that the development of their work will eventually throw a good deal of light upon the problems of human behaviour. In this chapter we shall bring together those comments of interest and value which are to be found widely scattered in the literature of Ethology.

1. *N. Tinbergen*

Tinbergen thinks it is too early to attempt an enumeration of the instincts to be found either in animals or in man. He believes, however, that 'it is possible to point out some inconsistencies in the present views on instincts.'

(1) *The Gregarious Instinct*. There is, he thinks, no 'Social Instinct' or 'Gregarious Instinct' in the sense in which it is usually found in psychological literature. Following his point that any instinct must have

an underlying neurophysiological basis, he holds that there is no such thing as the activation of a system of neurophysiological centres controlling social activities *in general*. 'There are no special activities to be called "social" that are not part of some instinct.' Certain instincts can be said to have their 'social aspect' when another member of the same species: 'is part of the adequate stimulus situation which the animal tries to find through its appetitive behaviour.' In other instincts, such as food-seeking, there may not be a social aspect. And the presence or absence of a social aspect in the manifestation of any instinctive activity may vary among species. Thus, whilst instincts may have their social aspects, differing among various species, there is no 'social' instinct in a general sense.

(2) *The Aggressive Instinct*. A second interesting conclusion that can be drawn from Tinbergen's many remarks on the subject is that there is no evidence of a general 'aggressive instinct' among animals. In the first place, Tinbergen stresses the fact that by far the greater proportion of fighting among animals does not take place between species, but between members of the same species and predominantly as a reaction involved in sexual rivalry.[1] Furthermore, the actual 'fighting' that occurs mainly consists of 'threatening or bluff', and does not often involve physical combat. 'Considering the fact that sexual fighting takes such an enormous amount of the time of so many species, it is certainly astonishing that real fighting, in the sense of a physical struggle, is so seldom observed.' This, Tinbergen says, is the outcome of natural selection. Sexual fighting between rivals is biologically advantageous in that it leads to a full exploitation of the territory available to a species. It would be disadvantageous, however, if it led to a large-scale destruction of adults. The compromise which has been effected is the development of conspicuous 'releasers' which *intimidate* without, as a rule, leading to actual physical combat and the causing of damage. We shall come to this question of the 'instinctive inhibition' of aggression again when we turn to observations made by Lorenz. For the moment, we may merely note that there is no one instinct of aggression even in animals.

The relevance of this point to the consideration of human behaviour will become clear when we discuss it together with the Psycho-Analytic notions concerning aggression in Chapter VII, but we may note here that it has a significant bearing on Freud's postulation of 'Death Instincts'.

[1]See (1) 'Fighting and Threat in Animals', *Penguin New Biology*, No. 14; (2) *The Study of Instinct*, p. 175; (3) 'The Social Life of Animals': Broadcast Talk, January 3rd, 1953, in which 95 per cent. of animal fighting was said to be spring fighting between rival males.

So much for general comments arising in Tinbergen's work.

In his section dealing specifically with the ethological study of man, Tinbergen indicates what kind of work has been done in this direction up to the present time. He reviews evidence which suggests that (1) *locomotion*, (2) *food-seeking*, (3) *sex*, (4) *sleep*, and (5) *care of the body-surface*, are instinctive in man.

It is demonstrable that these five areas of human experience and behaviour involve definite neurophysiological conditions, specific internal and external stimuli, specific identifiable feeling-states, and definite sequences of appetitive and consummatory behaviour. Certain of them—locomotion and sex are the most obvious examples—can also be definitely correlated with the processes of growth and maturation.

2. *K. Lorenz*

The work of Lorenz is full of allusions to human experience and behaviour, and it is clear that he is convinced of the usefulness of the ethological approach in the study of man. Indeed, he is convinced not only of its usefulness but also of its extreme urgency.

'We have particularly urgent reasons to want insight into the causal context of "instinct". With atomic bombs in its hands and with the endogenous aggressive drives of an irascible ape in its central nervous system, modern humanity . . . has got thoroughly out of balance. No teleological meditation will help us, we shall have to *do* something about it, and this implies the necessity of causal insight.'[1]

Later in the same paper, he advises: 'It is high time that the collective human intellect got some control on the necessary outlets for certain endogenously generated drives, for instance "aggression", and some knowledge of human innate releasing mechanisms, especially those activating aggression. Hitherto it is only demagogues who seem to have a certain working knowledge of these matters and who, by devising surprisingly simple "dummies", are able to elicit fighting responses in human beings with about the same predictability as Tinbergen does in sticklebacks.'

It is of interest to note that Lorenz does not adopt the extraordinarily strict view as to the relation between Ethology and Psychology which is maintained by Tinbergen. We shall return to his views on this topic in Chapter VII, but at this point we might mention the observations which he has to make about human experience and behaviour when he is considering the *psychological* aspects of Comparative Ethology. Surprisingly, we find that he adopts essentially the same position as does

[1]'The Comparative Method in Studying Innate Behaviour Patterns', *Physiological Mechanisms in Animal Behaviour*, 1950.

McDougall in regarding the 'conative-affective' feature of instinctive experience as being the most reliable criterion of instinct in man. 'I fully agree with McDougall in his fundamental assertion that man has just as many "instincts" as he has qualitatively distinguishable emotions.' And, again: 'We do not go far wrong if we suspect the existence of an innate releasing mechanism wherever we can introspectively ascertain a specific quality of sensual pleasure.' With regard to the use of introspection which is mentioned above, Lorenz says: 'To refrain from introspection in such cases would mean renouncing a superlatively valuable source of knowledge for purely dogmatic reasons which would be about the worst thing a natural scientist could do.' And, with further reference to the emotions of man, Lorenz says: 'I would stress the fact that the human expression of emotion is largely built up on exactly the same kind of intention movements as Charles Darwin knew long ago. In man, in whom innate behaviour patterns are, to a great degree, rudimentary, the study of these innate expressions of emotion may become a most valuable clue to the human "instincts".'

It can be seen from these remarks that Lorenz is very close to the position held by the earlier writers on instinct, though we have seen that they had good reasons for rejecting any simple identification of the instincts with the emotions.

We might turn now to some of the more general suggestions Lorenz makes as to the possible parallels between the instinctive behaviour of animals and some of the social responses in man. After this, we can describe one specific study Lorenz has undertaken on the nature of the 'innate releasing mechanism' in the human parental instinct.

It is when he is discussing Social Releasers in animal behaviour that Lorenz frequently suggests parallels in human social behaviour. Here, we shall give two or three instances which will serve to bring out the chief point which he has to make. Firstly, we may note the remarks which Lorenz makes when describing the 'male war-dance' of the Siamese fighting-fish.

On the approach of another of their own kind, these fish, which when alone are of a brown-grey colour, suddenly light up with brilliant incandescent colour and unfold their large fins. A highly ritualised (in the ethological sense of the word) dance follows. The sex of the other fish is recognised not only by seeing it, but by watching the way in which it responds to these ritualised dance movements. Commenting on 'the grandeur of the male war-dance', Lorenz says:

'When two males meet face to face, veritable orgies of mutual self-glorification take place. There is a striking similarity between the

war-dance of these fish and the corresponding ceremonial dances of
Javanese and other Indonesian peoples. In both man and fish the
minutest detail of every movement is laid down by immutable and
ancient laws, the slightest gesture has its own deeply symbolical
meaning. There is a close resemblance between man and fish in the style
and exotic grace of their movements of restrained passion. . . . The
beautifully refined form of the movements betrays the fact that they
have a long historical development behind them and that they owe their
elaborateness to an ancient ritual. It is, however, not so obvious that
though in man this ritual is a ceremony which has been handed down
from generation to generation by a thousand-year-old tradition, in the
fish it represents the result of an evolutionary development of innate
instinctive activities, at least a hundred times older.'

Now it is clear that an analysis of the development of ritual in any
human society would have to take into account far more than the
instinctive tendencies of man, and would have to include studies on a
strictly sociological level. Lorenz, therefore, would not wish to suggest
that there is a *strict* parallel between the instinctive ritualised responses
of animal behaviour and the detailed elements of ritual in a human
social tradition. His chief point in all remarks of this kind seems to be to
indicate the similarity between the ritualised Social Releasers in the
instinctive behaviour of animals—their *simplicity, conspicuousness,* and
specificity—and the symbols and symbolic actions which play such a
large part in the perpetuation of the social tradition in the history of any
human society. But before giving a further example of this, we might
note Lorenz's account of an actual social tradition in a colony of
jackdaws.

The only response to a particular sign stimulus which is innate in the
jackdaw, with regard to the recognition of an enemy, is that of furiously
attacking any living being that is carrying a 'black thing, dangling or
fluttering'. Lorenz found that the birds would attack and peck at his
hand when he held black paper strips or his black bathing trunks. Few
young jackdaws, however, first become aware of their enemies by this
means. The young are warned that a certain object is an 'enemy' by a
'rattling' call uttered by the older birds. Describing how this 'knowledge' of enemies is carried from generation to generation in the colony,
Lorenz tells us:

'Recognition of the enemy . . . must be learned personally by the
young jackdaws. Learned through their own experience? No, more
curious still: by actual tradition, by the handing-down of personal

these affective ties may (to some extent) permit of explanation in terms of the instinctive tendencies of man. In our final chapter we shall return to this question. For the present, it is enough merely to note the point which Lorenz makes, and to observe that, even though any strict parallel between animal and human 'tradition' must be treated with great care, the point is, nonetheless, highly suggestive for social psychology, and is worthy of further consideration.

In his description of the jackdaw colony, Lorenz comments on the 'order of ranking', the 'engagement' and 'marriage' behaviour, and so on, all the while pointing out the similarity between the behaviour of the jackdaws and that of human beings. To meet critics who might accuse him of anthropomorphism, Lorenz says: 'You think I humanize the animal? Perhaps you do not know that what we are wont to call 'human weakness' is, in reality, nearly always a pre-human factor and one which we have in common with the higher animals? Believe me, I am not mistakenly assigning human properties to animals: on the contrary, I am showing you what an enormous animal inheritance remains in man, to this day.' There is no doubt, in view of statements such as this, of the importance Lorenz attaches to the place of instinctive tendencies in the behaviour of human beings.

We have already seen that much of the 'fighting' among animals involves intimidation by means of certain conspicuous releasers, rather than actual physical combat, and we have mentioned the question of the 'instinctive inhibition' of the fighting response. We can now consider more detailed remarks on this point which Lorenz makes in his chapter on 'Morals and Weapons' in the book *King Solomon's Ring*.

Lorenz begins by telling us that our usual judgment that carnivorous animals are cruel and vicious compared with the herbivorous animals, which are harmless and peaceful, is quite mistaken. Doves or hares, when enclosed in a cage and given no opportunity to flee, are capable of the most horrible carnage, whereas the beasts of prey have certain instinctive inhibitory mechanisms which prevent carnage when one participant in a conflict submits to the victor. One of the examples which Lorenz gives of such an inhibitory mechanism is drawn from the behaviour of timber wolves.

'An enormous old timber wolf and a rather weaker, obviously younger one are the opposing champions and they are moving in circles round each other, exhibiting admirable "footwork". At the same time the bared fangs flash in such a rapid exchange of snaps that the eye can scarcely follow them. So far, nothing has really happened. The jaws of one wolf close on the gleaming white teeth of the other, who is on the

experience from one generation to the next![1] . . . On the appearanc
an enemy, as yet unknown to the young, an old guide jackdaw need
only one significant "rattle", and at once the young birds have for
a mental picture associating the warning with this particular enem
the natural life of jackdaws, I think it seldom happens that an inex
enced young bird first receives knowledge of the dangerous charact
an enemy by seeing him with a black dangling object in his clut
Jackdaws nearly always fly in a dense flock, in whose midst there
all probability, at least one bird which will begin to "rattle" a
merest sight of an enemy.

'How very human this is! On the other hand, how remarkably
and reflex-like is the innate perceptual pattern which in the inexperie
young jackdaws provokes a typical "rattling attack"! But have n
human beings also such blind, instinctive reactions? Do not v
peoples all too often react with a blind rage to a mere dummy pres
to them by the artifice of the demagogue? Is not this dummy in
cases just as far from being a real enemy as were my black ba
drawers to the jackdaw? And would there still be wars, if all this
not so?'

Here again, Lorenz is pointing out the similarity between the v
which knowledge is perpetuated by means of ritualised signals
tradition of this colony of jackdaws, and the way in which h
tradition also involves simple, conspicuous, easily recognisable syr
Elsewhere, Lorenz has pointed out the similarity between some
releasers, like the wing-specula of ducks, and the patterns of na
flags.[2]

This parallel between animal tradition and tradition in h
societies cannot be strictly maintained, as it is clear that many
symbols in human tradition are actually devised to commemora
to communicate events or ideas of significance for the society;
and ideas which are thus re-emphasised with each new observatic
ceremony. Some symbols, indeed, are especially intended to
definite events and principles of importance, as, for example, the
Jack'. Nonetheless, even though conscious device does go into th
duction of some human social symbols, and whilst the establisl
human attitudes to such symbols is greatly the outcome of teachi
learning, it remains true that the perpetuation of a social traditior
to require such simple, conspicuous, and specific symbols;
remains true that much of the attachment and devotion of humar
to these symbols is *affectively* rather than *rationally* establishe

[1] *King Solomon's Ring*, p. 140. But see the whole chapter: 'The Perennial Reta
[2] See Fig. 128, Tinbergen's *Study of Instinct*.

alert and wards off the attack. Only the lips have received one or two minor injuries. The younger wolf is gradually being forced backwards. It dawns upon us that the older one is purposely manoeuvring him towards the fence. We wait with breathless anticipation what will happen when he "goes to the wall". Now he strikes the wire netting, stumbles . . . and the old one is upon him. And now the incredible thing happens, just the opposite of what you would expect. The furious whirling of the grey bodies has come to a sudden standstill. Shoulder to shoulder they stand, pressed against each other in a stiff and strained attitude, both heads now facing in the same direction. Both wolves are growling angrily, the older in a deep bass, the younger in higher tones, suggestive of the fear that underlies his threat. But notice carefully the position of the two opponents; the older wolf has his muzzle close, very close against the neck of the younger, and the latter holds away his head, offering unprotected to his enemy the bend of his neck, the most vulnerable part of his whole body! Less than an inch from the tensed neck-muscles, where the jugular vein lies immediately beneath the skin, gleam the fangs of his antagonist from beneath the wickedly retracted lips. Whereas, during the thick of the fight, both wolves were intent on keeping only their teeth, the one invulnerable part of the body, in opposition to each other, it now appears that the discomfited fighter proffers intentionally that part of his anatomy to which a bite must assuredly prove fatal. . . . Every second you expect violence and await with bated breath the moment when the winner's teeth will rip the jugular vein of the loser. But your fears are groundless, for it will not happen. In this particular situation, the victor will definitely not close on his less fortunate rival. You can see that he would like to, but he just cannot! A dog or wolf that offers its neck to its adversary in this way will never be bitten seriously. The other growls and grumbles, snaps with his teeth in the empty air and even carries out, without delivering so much as a bite, the movement of shaking something to death in the empty air.'

Lorenz goes on to say that this inhibition persists only so long as the defeated animal continues to show this attitude of humility. If the victor withdraws, and the defeated animal attempts to escape, the victor will turn to him again in a flash, and again he will have to freeze into the same attitude of surrender. These instinctive inhibitions have been developed in the course of evolution, and have emerged side by side with the dangerous weapons of the beast of prey. Without such inhibitions, the birds and beasts of prey would soon exterminate themselves. The dove, on the other hand, does not need such inhibitions since it can only inflict a lesser degree of injury, and its ability to flee is sufficient to protect it even against enemies better equipped with weapons. The submissive attitudes involved in bringing about such inhibitions in fighting are all based on the same principle: 'The supplicant always offers to his adversary the most vulnerable part of his body, or, to be more exact, that part *against which every killing attack is inevitably directed!*'

Lorenz believes that man also possesses such inhibitory tendencies. 'What is a human appeal for mercy after all? Is it so very different from what we have just described? The Homeric warrior who wishes to yield and plead mercy, discards helmet and shield, falls on his knees and inclines his head, a set of actions which should make it easier for the enemy to kill, but, in reality, hinders him from doing so.... Even today, we have retained many symbols of such submissive attitudes in a number of our gestures of courtesy: bowing, removal of the hat, and presenting arms in military ceremonial.'

In spite of this, however, Lorenz concludes that man is the exception among animals in this respect.

'There is only one being in possession of weapons which do not grow on his body and of whose working plan, therefore, the instincts of his species know nothing and in the usage of which he has no correspondingly adequate inhibition. That being is man. With unarrested growth his weapons increase in monstrousness, multiplying horribly within a few decades. But innate impulses and inhibitions, like bodily structures, need time for their development, time on a scale in which geologists and astronomers are accustomed to calculate, and not historians. We did not receive our weapons from nature. We made them ourselves of our own free will. Which is going to be easier for us in the future, the production of weapons or the engendering of the feeling of responsibility that should go along with them, the inhibitions without which our race must perish by virtue of its own creations? We must build up these inhibitions purposefully, for we cannot rely upon our instincts.'

The remarks which Tinbergen makes on the same point are worth quoting:

'The same instinctive inhibition of the fighting-drive is found in man. One reason why wholesale slaughter in modern warfare is so relatively easily accomplished is to be found in the modern long-range arms that prevent one witnessing the action of lethal weapons. Our instinctive reluctance to kill is strengthened by the sight of a dying man in mutilated condition. Hence one is much less reluctant to direct artillery fire at a distant tower, thereby killing the enemy artillery observer, than to cut his throat in a man-to-man fight. Our instinctive disposition has not changed with the rapid development of mechanical long-range killing apparatus.'

Such observations give us a good deal to think about.

Finally, we might turn to the study of the parental instinct in man which Lorenz has undertaken.[1]

Lorenz suspects the existence of an innate releasing mechanism in man: 'wherever we can introspectively ascertain a specific quality of sensual pleasure.' A good example of this, he suggests, is the fact that: 'It is a distinct and indubitably sensuous pleasure to fondle a nice plump, appetising human baby.'[2] Furthermore, 'I can assert that my pleasurable sensations in fondling a sweet human child are of the same quality as those I experience in fondling a chow-puppy, or a baby lion.' Finding this distinct subjective quality of feeling towards young creatures, Lorenz elucidates the properties of the 'sign stimuli' which elicit this response.

Although no detailed experiments have been carried out, he points out that there are three sources of evidence which have the same value as experiments. (1) Dolls are designed to meet the demands of the innate releasing mechanism. (2) An 'optimal' baby has been developed by the Film Industry. (3) It is a well-known fact that childless women select substitutes for babies in their pets. A study of these three sources shows that the sign stimuli eliciting the human parental response can be distinguished as (a) a short face in relation to a large forehead, (b) protruding cheeks, and (c) maladjusted limb movements. Lorenz maintains also that these properties are 'additive' in their effect, and obey the law of heterogeneous summation.

Apart from this subjective reaction to these stimuli, however, Lorenz claims that the objective response which is activated can also be distinguished. 'A normal man—let alone a woman—will find it exceedingly difficult to leave to its fate even a puppy, after he or she has enjoyed fondling and petting it. A very distinct "mood", a readiness to take care of the object in a specific manner, is brought about with the predictability of an unconditioned response. Quite especially a strong inhibition to hurt or kill the "sweet" baby is activated by the innate releasing mechanism in question.'

This is one of the few ethological studies of human responses, but it suggests that the extension of these studies will yield interesting results.

[1]See Fig. 130, Tinbergen, *Study of Instinct*, p. 209.
[2]*Comparative Method in Studying Innate Behaviour Patterns*, p. 265.

3. *R. A. Spitz and K. M. Wolfe*

Spitz and Wolfe have investigated the smiling response in children; the specific aim of their study being to make a contribution to the 'onto-genesis of social relations'.[1]

The smile is the first strictly social response which the child makes, and it has been shown that this response becomes capable of activation at the age of about ten weeks. It is held that the innate releasing mechanism is activated by a very simple sign stimulus: a slowly moving object resembling a human face, with two eyes and a nose. Thus, the smile can be elicited between the ages of ten and twenty weeks by a mask suspended on the end of a broomstick which is slowly moved. After this age the baby begins to identify his own mother, and this simple sign stimulus will no longer do. Commenting on this study, John Bowlby says: 'It is possible that all I.R.M.s in man develop in this way, at first released by the elemental and biologically given sign stimulus and gradually, through a process of learning, being released only by a far more differentiated stimulus having the pattern of a complex gestalt. Such a learning process also commonly occurs in animals.'

4. *Rudolf Brun: Findings in Neurophysiology*

A full discussion of all the 'internal causal factors' which have a relevance for the study of instinct in man (entailing, as it would, a detailed review of endocrinology, neurophysiology, etc.) is clearly beyond our scope here. Since, however, we have mentioned the views of Tinbergen and Brun on the hierarchy of neurophysiological 'centres', and especially their remarks on the importance of the diencephalon, we might briefly consider two findings of importance in the field of neurophysiology which are not commonly mentioned, and which have a direct bearing on the neurophysiological basis of instinct in man. Both of these findings are presented by Rudolf Brun in his book, *General Theory of Neurosis*.

(1) *The Hemo-Encephalic Barrier*. During his discussion of the organic factors involved in the aetiology of the neuroses,[2] Brun outlines what is known about the hemo-encephalic barrier.

Having pointed out the importance of the hormones in the excitation of the instincts, Brun emphasises the fact that the endocrine glands are by no means independent, or autonomous, in their operation. 'On the

---

[1] 'The Smiling Response: A Contribution to the Ontogenesis of Social Relations', *Genetic Psychology Monographs*, No. 34 (1946), pp. 57-125.

[2] Lecture IV, p. 61, *General Theory of Neurosis*.

contrary, they themselves are first activated by the vegetative nervous system. And the vegetative nervous system, again, receives its stimuli in the first place from the brain, through the subcortical centres, and among these central excitations emotional impulses are by far the most important.' The point Brun wishes to stress here is that any disturbances in the equilibrium of the internal secretions are not necessarily *primary*, but may stem from some *psychic causation*.

It follows from the above-mentioned importance of the brain, Brun thinks, that the ultimate neurophysiological cause of nervous disorders should be sought in some derangement of the brain rather than in the sphere of the endocrine glands. Any disturbance in the 'harmoniously balanced central regulation of the total neuro-vegetative life' brought about by continued instinctual excitation, takes the path of a vicious circle. 'The flooding of the bloodstream with hormones which is thus provoked (through excitation of the vegetative nervous system by the affectivity, via the vegetative brain centres) has, in addition to the immediate effects on the neuro-vegetative end-apparatus of the periphery (enhancement of the relevant and distinctive reflexes), corresponding repercussions on the reactions of the brain, so that a vicious circle is brought into operation. We might compare these central hormonal effects with the effect of certain toxic substances—for example, the narcotic alkaloids, or alcohol.'

Under normal conditions, there are provisions ensuring that the functionally active tissues of the brain are not reached directly by the floods of toxic substances or hormones in the bloodstream. A process of filtering takes place, protecting the cerebral tissues from serious damage. Between the bloodstream and the cerebral tissues is a protective apparatus—*the hemo-encephalic barrier*—which holds back the flood of toxins or hormones, allowing them to reach the supersensitive nerve cells only in very minute quantities. In the simplest way, then, the hemo-encephalic barrier can be regarded as a chemical filter, protecting the cerebral tissues from the inundations of toxic substances or hormones in the bloodstream.[1]

Brun then reviews the evidence which supports this view of the function of the hemo-encephalic barrier, and we might mention one or two of his observations.

Firstly, it was found that guinea pigs and dogs could tolerate, without injurious effects, very large doses of poisonous dye-stuffs when these were injected into the bloodstream. When very small doses were injected directly into the subarachnoidal space, however, the animals soon died, 'with marked symptoms of cerebral irritation and paralysis.' It was also

[1] See.Plate (II), p. 74, *General Theory of Neurosis*.

found that when the dye-stuff was injected into the bloodstream the
brain was left uncoloured. All the dye-stuff was found to have been held
back by the plexus chorioidei, and was stored up in it.

Other observations are made whilst Brun is discussing the possible
ways in which lesions of the hemo-encephalic barrier might be produced.
Firstly, there may be a primary innate weakness of the barrier which
will constitute a definite physiological pre-disposition to neurosis. There
may, that is to say, be a congenital insufficiency of the hemo-encephalic
barrier to perform its protective function, and the brain will then be
subjected to unchecked inundations of hormones. Secondly, lesions of
the barrier could be brought about by direct physical injury of the skull
and brain, and, thirdly, by 'severe infectious maladies and intoxications'.
Fourthly, however, and it is upon this point that Brun lays most stress,
derangements of the filter may be the direct outcome of psychic conflict;
they may be due to *psychic causation*. Painful encroachments on instinctual interests are accompanied, Brun says, by 'affective storms'
which result from the sudden flushing of the brain with certain hormones. If such inundations (i.e. as occur in acute states of anxiety) were
to be continuous and successive, they might weaken the hemo-encephalic barrier, causing an increase in permeability, and, consequently,
the affective lability of the individual.

Several points supporting this view of the protective function of the
barrier are mentioned when Brun is insisting upon the psychic causation
of the neuroses. (1) It has been demonstrated that an increased permeability of the barrier occurs in women during menstruation, whereby
the chemical composition of the cerebral fluid undergoes modification.
This explains why the menstrual period, for many women, is a period of
'temporarily enhanced affective lability'. (2) In the study of psychoses,
von Monakow found: 'in a large quantity of dissection material . . .
distinct and often extreme pathologico-anatomical changes in the Plexus
chorioidei and the adjacent subependymal regions of the neuroglial
barrier—above all in cases of schizophrenia, which, as we know, are
distinguished by especially severe affective disturbances.' (3) An interesting piece of evidence derives from the examination 'of the brains of
two parrots, both of which, about six months before they were killed,
had suffered a severe fright with lasting anxiety affect. One of the birds,
in its owner's absence, had been chased about the room for hours on end
by a cat; the other, while crossing a lake, had fallen into the water, and
had only with difficulty been rescued from drowning. Both these parrots,
some time after the psychic trauma, developed severe organic cerebral
symptoms with progressive signs of paralysis and epileptic fits. Micro-
scopic examination revealed completely analogous conditions in both

cases; namely, severe degenerative changes in the protective filter apparatus of the brain; and again, the destruction was by far the most pronounced in the chorioid plexus and the periventricular regions of the brain, while in the direction of the cortex it was less and less perceptible.'

Though stressing these grounds for maintaining the psychic causation of the neuroses, Brun readily admits the possibility of some congenital predisposition to neurosis in the form of the constitutional deficiency of the hemo-encephalic barrier. Nonetheless, the existence of some congenital predisposition does not rule out the necessity of the 'psychogenic' approach. The 'content of the neurosis', and the 'choice of neurosis' (in Freud's words) cannot be elucidated by a knowledge of the physiological predisposition to psychic conflict. Brun holds, therefore, that both approaches are necessary. Whilst contending that von Monakow has given the conception of a 'constitutional predisposition' a solid anatomical and physiological basis, Brun argues that it remains impossible on this basis alone to explain why (given this predisposition) in one case a hysteria develops, or in another case an obsessional neurosis develops. For the elucidation of the latter problem, psychotherapy is necessary, based 'upon Freud's discoveries as to the definite connection between experience and symptom'.

These findings are of the greatest interest in a study of the neurophysiological basis of the instincts and of instinctual conflict in man. They have a direct bearing on the 'instinctual vicissitudes' discussed by Freud, and provide us with some knowledge of the neurophysiological concomitants of such psychic conflict and its attendant, continuing anxiety.

(2) *The Extra-Pyramidal Apparatus.* We mentioned in our last chapter Brun's claim that the diencephalon 'acts like a sort of rheostat in respect of the cortical activity', and that the particular points which were electrically stimulated by Hess could not be regarded as 'centres' in the sense of cellular nuclei, but that 'they are rather intercalary points through which—as at the throwing of a switch—the whole compound reflex chains comprising the palaeostriatum, the between-brain, the midbrain, the cerebellum, and finally, the spinal cord, are set to action, or through which—in the case of symptoms of defect, such as disorders of sensibility—they can be automatically cut out.'

It is in connection with this interaction between cortical and subcortical activity that Brun stresses the importance of the extra-pyramidal apparatus. In so far as we have mentioned it, Brun's discussion of this question has been chiefly to point out the extent to which the cortex is subject to subcortical processes. He has been concerned to show that the functional preparedness, the 'moods', the particular readinesses, of the cortex are dependent on the diencephalon. Later, however, he emphasises the danger of jumping to the conclusion that this is merely a one-way influence (e.g. on these grounds some have held that the psycho-neuroses are simply organic diseases of the diencephalon), and gives evidence to support the view that the cortex is constantly reacting on the between-brain: 'and is able to influence its functions in the most lasting fashion, and even, indeed, in certain circumstances, quite suddenly to modify them.' Brun wishes to maintain, therefore, that the influence of the cortical on the subcortical processes can be just as important as can the reverse influence in the bringing about of inhibitory mechanisms or psychic conflict, and here again he stresses the psychic aetiology of the neuroses.

Four points are given as evidence of the influence of cortical processes upon the lower brain processes. (1) The first is the evidence provided by the Conditioned Reflex, where it is shown that an often repeated perception (stimulus) closely associated with a certain reward, can, after a time, itself set a visceral-nervous process in motion. It may be remembered that Pavlov himself claimed that cortical activity was involved in the establishing of a conditioned reflex. (2) Brun refers to hypnotism in which the verbal suggestions of the physician, perceived by the auditory sphere of the cortex, are capable of provoking the modification of the function referred to in the suggestion. (3) In hysteria the converse process is observed. 'We see in hysteria the same between-brain symptoms as those which can be artificially evoked through hypnosis occurring spontaneously, and apparently in the same manner as the hypnotic phenomena, namely, through the shutting off (repression) of certain mnemic excitations from the apparatus of perception. . . . The hysterical barrage very probably depends on a partial functional isolation of the between-brain and the extra-pyramidal motor centres from the influence of the perceptual apparatus. On the other hand, the spontaneously arising hysterical symptoms can be made to disappear through hypnosis and other psycho-therapeutic methods—acting, once more, from the cerebral cortex; and in hypnosis they may disappear in a flash.' (4) Brun tells us that it has recently been possible to trace the paths by means of which the cerebral cortex exerts its influence over the between-brain and the extra-pyramidal apparatus.[1]

The extra-pyramidal apparatus (the brain centres and nervous circuits which lie outside the pyramidal circuit and its centres) is therefore conceived as being of great importance in connection with these reciprocal actions between the cerebrum and the between-brain. It seems

[1]See Plate (III), p. 142, *General Theory of Neurosis*.

that a 'psychic cleavage' can occur when these two normally interacting influences are functionally isolated. This is important, Brun points out, for the explanation of the 'physiological *modus operandi* of psychotherapy'. It shows how, by psycho-therapy, the connection between the now functionally isolated subcortical processes (which 'were established under the influence of unconscious impulses and the damming up of the critical function of the cerebrum') and the critical, analysing function of the cortex are restored.

Brun regards a congenital lability, weakness, or insufficiency of the vegetative midbrain apparatus, and above all of the extra-pyramidal system, as being of at least equal importance (as a factor predisposing an individual to neurosis) as a congenital insufficiency of the hemo-encephalic barrier. Here again, it is clear that these neurophysiological findings constitute an important contribution to our understanding of the nature of instinctual conflict in man.

*   *   *   *   *

It is abundantly clear from this brief survey that the ethological study of man is very much in its infancy and that what can be said with any certainty at the present time is very limited. Nonetheless, some of the comments we have discussed are highly suggestive for further inquiry. The study of specific innate releasing mechanisms and of Critical Periods of development in the human being has at least been commenced, showing that the ethological concepts and methods can be applied to the study of man, and that their further application may lead to significant results. Some headway has also been made in uncovering the neurophysiological basis of the instincts in man, and in the light of Tinbergen's hypothetical 'hierarchical organisation of centres', future neurophysiological research can be expected to throw still further light upon the internal causal factors of human behaviour.

We shall be comparing the findings of Comparative Ethology with the other contributions to the study of Instinct in a later chapter. For the present, it is sufficient to note that all the ethological writers are persuaded that instinctive tendencies do indeed exist in man, and that (although their study does not allow them to say a great deal conclusively at present) they are confident, in the light of what is already known, that these tendencies will be progressively clarified as their study proceeds and develops.

CHAPTER VI

INSTINCTS IN PSYCHO-ANALYSIS

In attempting a critical assessment of the account of Instinct given in Psycho-Analytic theory, we are met, at once, with many difficulties, some of which make necessary certain preliminary remarks.

The first difficulty is that the literature of Psycho-Analysis has by now assumed such vast proportions. In so far as the psycho-analytic theory of the *instincts* is concerned, however, it does not seem that any great changes have been made to the initial theory of Freud, and because of this we shall be content to examine the arguments of Freud alone. Freud's views on the subject of the instincts have been reviewed from time to time (for example, by T. W. Mitchell[1] and by Ernest Jones[2]) but it does not appear that they have anywhere been subjected to detailed criticism. In this chapter we shall undertake such a criticism, and here we shall slightly change our method of discussion. In treating Comparative Ethology, we minimised our criticism, aiming at a clear summary presentation of the ethological account, and leaving any critical remarks for a later chapter. In discussing the psycho-analytic account of instinct, it will be more convenient to state our criticisms as the argument proceeds. This procedure will avoid the difficulties which would be involved in first tracing the changing course of Freud's theory, and then, in another place, undertaking a parallel critical argument.

A second difficulty is the objection, sometimes encountered, that only those who have had actual experience of Psycho-Analysis are in a position to understand psycho-analytic theories. Criticisms offered by those without such experience may be completely misplaced. In the face of this 'hands off!' argument much could be said. It is sufficient, however, to point out that psycho-analytic speculations are open to at least two legitimate lines of criticism.

In the first place, the *logic* of such speculative lines of thought is open to criticism, and whilst such a criticism would not be injurious to the facts on which a particular speculation was based, it might be sufficient

[1] T. W. Mitchell, *Problems in Psychopathology*, Chapter V.
[2] Ernest Jones, 'Psycho-Analysis and the Instincts', *British Journal of Psychology*, January 1936, pp. 273-288.

to show that certain conclusions drawn from them were invalid. For example, Freud is very fond of the use of analogy, and if it were shown that a certain step in an argument rested upon a bad and incomplete analogy, such a criticism would have weight in pointing out the tentative nature of the conclusions arrived at. In the second place, a speculative line of thought might be extended beyond the bounds of psychology into other spheres of study—as, for example, biology. If so, this speculation would be open to criticism *in the light of established knowledge in that particular science.*

In these two ways, psycho-analytic theories are open to legitimate criticism from those who have no first-hand acquaintance with analysis, and we need have no qualms therefore in exercising these two modes of criticism as and when they seem to be appropriate.

A third difficulty which confronts us lies in the complexity of Freud's own work. We wish to adhere as closely as possible to what Freud has to say about *Instinct*, but it is impossible to do this without considering (to some extent, at least) the other concepts by means of which he depicts various features of the human personality and the conflicts to which they are subjected during the course of personality development. We shall have to include some discussion of unconscious mental processes, of the Ego and its functions, of the Super-Ego, and of the relations which these concepts bear to the nature and functionings of the instincts. A further difficulty is that Freud's theory of the instincts changed as his investigations proceeded. The changes can be described as three broad stages of development, as will be shown, but the changes are not simple —whereby new theories replace the old; rather each change of theory can be said to incorporate the previous theoretical position. We shall try, however, to present Freud's treatment clearly and methodically, and shall try to adhere as closely as possible to the specific subject of the instincts, venturing into wider aspects of psycho-analytic theory only where it appears to be necessary.

A further point which might be made at this stage is that, in the psycho-analytic account of instinct, we are faced with an approach to the subject of instinct which is the complete reverse of that which we have considered in our earlier chapters. Until now, we have been concerned with theories which were based predominantly on the comparative study of animal species, and which, from this position, sought to extend their methods to the study of human beings, wishing to discover to what extent elements of experience and behaviour described as instinctive were to be found in man. Psycho-Analysis, on the other hand, starts with the study of man, and of the nature of the instincts in man, and then, from this position, extends its generalisations to cover other animal species. We shall argue in this chapter that it is this naïve extension of generalisations from the field of human studies to the field of animal species at large which constitutes one of the chief weaknesses of the psycho-analytic theory of the instincts, and that some of the untenable extravagances of Freud's later speculations would have been avoided if he had paid at least some attention (he seems to have paid none!) to the opposite approach of Comparative Psychology. In these chapters, bringing together the findings both of Comparative Psychology and of Psycho-Analysis, we shall hope to be able to indicate in what ways the psycho-analytic account of instinct is in need of amendment, and what remains of significance and importance in its findings.

1. *The Importance for Psychology of a Theory of the Instincts*

In his earlier work Freud was predominantly concerned with the elucidation of the mental phenomena manifested in neurosis, and any study of the instincts was only incidental to this. As his investigations proceeded, however, it is clear that the subject of the instincts occupied his mind increasingly, and in his later work he turns specifically to the task of formulating a theory of the instincts. It is easy to see why this task was forced upon him, and why he came to regard it as having so great an importance.

All his earlier analytic work persuaded Freud that the psychoneuroses were the outcome of *conflict* in the personality and that this conflict was one between instinctual demands and the demands of the Ego. The neurosis, that is to say, constituted a pathological resolution of such conflicts. The evidence of this conviction is very widespread in the writings of Freud. We find him saying: 'Psycho-Analytic work has furnished us with the rule that people fall ill of a neurosis as a result of frustration. The frustration meant is that of satisfaction of their libidinal desires. . . . That is to say, for a neurosis to break out there must be a conflict between the libidinal desires of a person and that part of his being which we call his ego . . . which also contains his ideals of his own character.'[1] And again: 'All our analyses go to show that the transference neuroses originate from the ego's refusing to accept a powerful instinctual impulse existing in its id and denying it motor discharge, or disputing the object towards which it is aimed. The ego then defends itself against the impulse by the mechanism of repression; the repressed impulse struggles against this fate, and finds ways which the ego cannot control to create for itself substitutive gratification (a symptom), which is forced upon the ego in the form of a compromise; the ego finds its

[1]'Some Character Types Met With in Psycho-Analytic Work', *Collected Papers*, 1955, vol. iv, xviii.

unity menaced and injured by this interloper, pursues against the symptom the struggle it had formerly maintained against the original impulse, and all this together produces the clinical picture of a neurosis.'[1]

The theoretical work of Freud might be described as a continuing attempt to elucidate the important factors contributing to this conflict which resulted in mental illness. One of these factors comprises the instincts, and it is therefore quite clear why Freud was compelled to recognize the need for an adequate theory of the instincts, and to turn to the task of constructing such a theory for his own purposes.

A further feature of Freud's work which made the need for a theory of the instincts evident was his persuasion (whether right or wrong we need not inquire here) that the whole of human civilisation rested upon some degree of renunciation of the instincts. It is through suppression of the instincts, Freud believes, that instinctual energy becomes available for social feeling and social behaviour. In this way, there occur various modes of displacement and sublimation of instinctual energy which seek substitute-gratification in and through various social phenomena and social activities. Thus religion is analogously compared with a state of neurosis; art is described as an activity yielding substitute-gratification; and even the basis of social justice—the sense of equality (in Freud's terms)—is derived from the renunciation of a direct libidinal tie with the leader, and the simultaneous identification of the individual with the other members of society. (It is, that is to say, based on jealousy: 'If I cannot have this or that, it is not right that anyone else should have it!') 'Our civilization is, generally speaking, founded on the suppression of instincts. . . . From these sources the common stock of the material and ideal wealth of civilization has been accumulated.'[2]

Since the instincts are held to be such an important factor in the formation of civilisation, and such an important source of that energy whereby civilisation is maintained, it is clear why Freud was obliged to investigate the subject of the instincts as thoroughly as was possible and to erect the most satisfactory theory he could conceive.

It is not surprising, then, that Freud attached a very great importance for psychology to a satisfactory theory of the instincts, and that he was never really satisfied either with theories which existed at the time or with such theories as he himself was able to put forward. In his book, *An Autobiographical Study* (1927), he tells us: 'There is no more urgent need in psychology than for a securely founded theory of the instincts on which it might then be possible to build further. Nothing of the sort

---

[1] 'Neurosis and Psychosis', *Collected Papers*, 1924, vol. ii, XXI.
[2] ' "Civilized" Sexual Morality and Modern Nervousness', *Collected Papers*, 1908, vol. ii, VII.

exists, however, and psycho-analysis is driven to making tentative efforts towards some such theory.'

This conviction of the importance of the study of the instincts is also found in the work of Ernest Jones, a close follower of Freud, and we might note the interesting statement with which he opens his paper, 'Psycho-Analysis and the Instincts'.

'I have chosen the subject of the instincts for my lecture because it is in many ways the most interesting as well as the most fundamental, and the most difficult, one in all psychology. Increased knowledge in this field would perhaps more than any other bring psychology into closer relation to cognate mental disciplines, those of physiology, biology, sociology and philosophy. It has for some time now been apparent that mental and physical processes are more likely to become correlated by investigating the instincts, and their emotional expressions, than by the method that appeared so hopeful in the nineteenth century, of studying what may be called the higher phenomena of the mind and the cerebral cortex. The close connection between fear and anger, for instance, which has been established on psychological grounds, has been interestingly confirmed by Cannon and his pupils working on purely physiological lines. It is further evident that the study of the instincts, a field common to man and the lower animals, offers the most promising chance for getting psychology rightly placed in the hierarchy of science, namely, as one of the biological sciences. Then the same study brings us to the tremendous problem of evaluating the relative importance of inherited and acquired tendencies, a problem vital for all sociological aspects of psychology. Finally, any results obtained from this study should prove useful data for the most engrossing of philosophical speculations, that concerning the relation of body to mind. . . .'

After thus emphasising the importance of the subject, Jones voices his dissatisfaction with existing theories. 'Unfortunately, psychology has not as yet furnished conclusions in any way commensurate in importance to the high aims I have just indicated.'

2. *The Nature, and the Distinguishing Features of the Instincts*

In this section we shall discuss what Freud believes to be the main characteristics of an instinct. These considerations were outlined in the early paper, 'Instincts and their Vicissitudes', and were not subsequently changed, except in one point of emphasis which will be pointed out. We shall discuss these 'distinguishing features' of the instincts in some detail because, on the one hand, they reveal certain similarities to the criteria we have been considering in earlier chapters, and, on the other, we believe that they are insufficient in certain ways, and even incorrect in one respect, and we believe that it is this early inadequacy which probably led to what we can only regard as errors in Freud's later discussions.

Approaching the problem from the physiological point of view, Freud distinguishes first of all between a reflex and an instinct. Physiology 'has given us the concept of stimuli and the scheme of the reflex arc, according to which a stimulus applied *from the outer world* to living tissue (nervous substance) is discharged by action *towards the outer world*. The action answers the purpose of withdrawing the substance affected from the operation of the stimulus, removing it out of the range of the stimulus.' For the moment we shall not criticise this statement.[1] Freud then proceeds to inquire into the relation between 'instinct' and 'stimulus' and suggests that we might regard an instinct simply as a stimulus to the mind. This, he considers inadequate since there are other stimuli to the mind which are very similar to those externally applied stimuli which call forth a reflex action. Thus, a ray of light is a stimulus to the mind, but is not of instinctual origin. A stimulus to the mind which we *do* regard as being of instinctual origin is, say, the gnawing which makes itself felt in the stomach (hunger), or the sensation caused by the parching of the mucous membrane of the oesophagus (thirst). The first feature which distinguishes a stimulus of instinctual origin from the other stimuli which operate on our minds is then, 'that it does not arise in the outside world but from *within* the organism itself.' Because of this, an instinctual stimulus has a different mental effect from that of other stimuli, and different actions are necessary in order to remove it. An external stimulus acts as a single impact, whereas an instinct 'never acts as a momentary impact but always as a constant force'. Since the instinctual stimulus arises within the organism, 'it follows that no flight can avail against it'.

Summarising these considerations, the three main characteristics of an instinct which Freud puts forward are: (*a*) its origin lies in some source or sources of stimulation within the organism, (*b*) it appears as a constant, not a momentary force, and (*c*) no action of flight avails against it.

Before passing to the next step in Freud's argument, we must indicate the ways in which even these first points, whilst we can broadly agree with them, are not considered with sufficient care. There is, first of all, too sweeping a distinction between 'outer' and 'inner' sources of stimuli. This becomes evident when we consider such a reaction as fear,

[1]See later, pp. 174-175.

or (to be a little more precise in our example) the 'escape reactions' manifested, let us say, by young geese in the presence of certain birds of prey. In such an example it is clear that certain *external* stimuli are bound up with the excitation of the instinct and the release of the instinctive reaction. Furthermore, it cannot be said that 'fear' appears as a constant force, but that it is aroused only by certain external stimuli or situations. Finally, actions of flight *do* avail against it, and, in our example of 'escape reactions', the flight from predators would, in fact, be considered to be the instinctive reaction to this situation. All this is not to say that 'fear' does not have sources of stimulation within the organism, but merely that sources of stimulation *outside* the organism are also in some way connected with it. Freud does not notice the inadequacy of his criteria mainly because he never stops to consider the instincts in detail, nor does he refer to examples of instinctive behaviour in animals. It is clear that, in the face of responses such as 'escape reactions' and 'fear', Freud would either have to classify them as reflexes (reactions of flight from external stimuli) or would have to amend his criteria. A further point which we have mentioned but which we must emphasise, is that we cannot correctly speak of the instincts as *'constant'* forces, but rather as *'constantly recurring'* forces. Apart from these criticisms, it can be seen that Freud's notions of the instincts are generally in keeping with those of the earlier writers who held that the main instinctual elements in man took the form of inherited impulses.

Next, Freud states a 'necessary postulate', which, he tells us, will help 'to guide us in dealing with psychological phenomena'.

This postulate: 'is of a biological nature and makes use of the concept of "purpose" (one might say, of adaptation of the means to the end) and runs as follows: the nervous system is an apparatus having the function of abolishing stimuli which reach it, or of reducing excitation to the lowest possible level: an apparatus which would even, if this were feasible, maintain itself in an altogether unstimulated condition. Let us for the present not take exception to the indefiniteness of this idea and let us grant that the task of the nervous system is—broadly speaking —*to master stimuli.*'

In putting forward this postulate, Freud once again stresses rather too hard and fast a line between outer and inner stimuli. Thus, he suggests, the task of 'abolishing' stimuli is easy for the nervous system where external stimuli are concerned, since it merely requires withdrawal from them. Instinctual stimuli, however, coming from sources within the organism, provide a much more difficult task for the nervous system and lead it to complicated activities directed towards effecting those changes in the outer world which will satisfy the inner sources of stimulation. 'Instinctual stimuli oblige the nervous system to renounce its ideal intention of warding off stimuli, for they maintain an incessant and unavoidable afflux of stimulation.'

Now, whilst agreeing in general with the point Freud is making here as to the internal, recurring nature of the instincts, we must take exception at once to this so-called 'necessary postulate' concerning the 'task of the nervous system'. It is all very well for Freud to sweep forward with his speculations, asking us for the moment to overlook the inadequacy of some of his basic assumptions; but this simply cannot be done. If any of the basic premises of a line of reasoning are known from the outset to be erroneous, we must dispense with them at once. No doubt one can build up fascinating theories from any kind of premises, true or false, but this is not what we are looking for. We shall argue that it is this looseness in adopting vague and inadequate postulates, and in failing to return to them and examine them in detail after a certain speculation has been carried to its conclusion, that leads to the erroneous propositions of Freud's later theories. This initial 'necessary postulate', stating that the task of the nervous system is to 'abolish' stimuli and if possible 'to maintain itself in an altogether unstimulated condition', underlies all that Freud has to say later about the 'Nirvana Principle' and the 'Death Instinct'. But what evidence is there to suggest that this 'necessary postulate' is soundly based?

There are at least three points which show that it is, in fact, untenable. In the first place, we have seen that Freud conceives the nervous system as 'abolishing' *external* stimuli and maintaining itself in as low as possible a state of stimulation, by *withdrawing* from these stimuli. Reflex actions seem to be regarded, by Freud, as being always actions of *withdrawal* from stimuli. But this is not the case. Comparative Ethology has given us many examples of 'taxes', reflex-like directing movements, which activate the organism's behaviour *towards* external stimuli. Similarly, we have seen the part played in instinctive behaviour by the 'coat of reflexes'. Such reflexes have a definite and positive function, being activated by certain continuing stimuli during the performance of the 'consummatory act'. Thus, with regard to *external* stimuli, it cannot simply be said that the task of the nervous system is to 'abolish' them, or to 'ward them off'. *Some* reactions to external stimuli are movements of withdrawal, but others are functionally positive movements directed *towards* the stimuli.

Our argument that the nervous system must be regarded as having a more positive role, and cannot by any means be looked upon as some part of the organism wishing to escape stimulation (prodded into activity only in order to smother such stimulation as occurs) is given greater support from our second point, which has also been mentioned in our earlier chapters. This point is, that it is now established that the central nervous system is *active* before it is *reactive*. Furthermore, we have seen that the early growth of the nervous system is very closely correlated with the development of certain positive functions, such as locomotion. It has been shown that these movements of locomotion are the manifestations of more-or-less autonomous rhythms of the central nervous system, and that these rhythms can be fully initiated by only the very slightest external stimulation. In view of these considerations it is quite impossible to hold that the function of the nervous system is merely to maintain itself in as low a state of excitation as possible, and that its activities are directed to the warding off or the abolishing of stimuli.

A third, more general point, is that it seems a very doubtful procedure to assign particular functions to certain parts of the organism and then to conceive of other parts and processes as 'making demands' upon them. In the evolution of a particular species, various features of structure, physiological process, behaviour, and experience, have emerged in accordance with heredity, genetic variation, and natural selection, and are *co-ordinated* in the total functioning of the existing organism. To speak of the instincts *making demands* upon the nervous system is misleading, for, as we have seen in our study of Comparative Ethology, the various internal causal factors of instinct (*including* the intrinsic central nervous factors) are all co-ordinated to yield certain behaviour patterns directed towards (or away from) appropriate 'sign stimuli' in the environment. Freud's language is therefore very dubious in sentences such as the following: (1) 'Instinctual stimuli oblige the nervous system to renounce its ideal intention of warding off stimuli. . . .' or, (2) 'So we may probably conclude that instincts and not external stimuli are the true motive forces in the progress that has raised the nervous system, with all its incomparable efficiency, to its present high level of development.'[1]

In connection with this 'necessary postulate', Freud then puts forward a second postulate to the effect that the feelings of pleasure and pain 'reflect the manner in which the process of mastering stimuli takes place'. Painful feelings are held to be connected with an increase, and pleasurable feelings with a decrease, of stimulation. We shall return to this point later, but here it is sufficient to note that Freud's necessary

[1]Perhaps we should point out that, whilst holding that it is incorrect to conceive of the instinct *making demands* upon the central nervous system, we hold, nonetheless, that Freud's later proposition—that the instincts can be conceived as *making demands* upon the Ego of a human individual growing up in a certain physical and social environment—is quite intelligible.

postulate as to the task of the nervous system must be rejected in view of the considerations mentioned above.

Freud then points out that an 'instinct' is a border-land concept between the mental and the physical, and this corresponds with what was said by the earlier writers on instinct—to the effect that an instinct had its structural, physiological, and behavioural aspects *and* its *experiential* aspects. Following upon this, Freud describes the distinguishing features of instinct, and his remarks in this connection are of particular interest as we shall find that they are very similar to the conceptions of both the earlier writers and the ethologists.

A distinction is drawn between the impetus, the aim, the object, and the source of an instinct.

(1) *Impetus*. By the impetus of an instinct, Freud means 'the amount of force or the measure of the demand upon energy which it represents.' 'The characteristic of impulsion is common to all instincts, is in fact the very essence of them.'

This conception corresponds very closely with the 'reaction specific energy' of the ethologists, and with the element of 'conation' (resting upon certain physiological conditions) stressed by the earlier writers.

(2) *Aim*. 'The aim of an instinct is in every instance satisfaction, which can be obtained only by abolishing the condition of stimulation in the source of the instinct.' It is possible, Freud thinks, that—since there may be different ways of achieving the same goal—an instinct may have various intermediate aims.

This is very similar to the notion of various levels of 'appetitive behaviour', put forward by the ethologists, which leads the animal into the presence of those sign stimuli which are appropriate to its internal motivation and which release the consummatory act. We may remember that the ethologists stress the fact that the goal of appetitive behaviour is the performance of the consummatory act which releases the dammed up reaction specific energy and 'gives satisfaction' or eliminates the craving. Similar conceptions were put forward by the earlier writers. We may remember their emphasis upon the 'conative-affective' core of the instinct which led to persistent behaviour until the impulse or the craving was reduced.

(3) *Object*. 'The object of an instinct is that in or through which it can achieve its aim. It is the most variable thing about an instinct and is not originally connected with it, but becomes attached to it only in consequence of being peculiarly fitted to provide satisfaction. The object is not necessarily an extraneous one: it may be part of the subject's own

body. It may be changed any number of times in the course of the vicissitudes the instinct undergoes during life; a highly important part is played by this capacity for displacement in the instinct.'

It must be remembered throughout that Freud is considering the *human* instincts. What he says here with regard to the object of an instinct does not correspond very closely with the observations of the ethologists on the instincts of animals, where the 'sign stimuli' seem to be a fairly (though not entirely) invariable feature of particular instinctive reactions. Freud's remarks are in agreement, however, with the views of the earlier writers who maintained that the *perceptual* feature of instinct (whilst closely correlated with the other features in the case of animals) was highly variable and modifiable in man. Freud's conception of this feature compares well, therefore, with the earlier views we have considered, and only appears different from the views of the ethologists because they are concentrating, in the main, on the behaviour of animals, whereas Freud is concentrating on the study of man.

(4) *Source.* By the source of an instinct, Freud means 'that somatic process in an organ or part of the body from which there results a stimulus represented in mental life by an instinct. We do not know whether this process is regularly of a chemical nature or whether it may also correspond with the release of other, e.g. mechanical, forces.'

This, clearly, is the equivalent of the view of the earlier writers that certain physiological processes were the basis of the instinctual impulses, and also of the ethologists' view that 'internal factors' were largely responsible for instinctive behaviour. Freud does not go further into an analysis of these somatic sources as he thinks, rightly, that such a detailed study lies in the field of physiological investigation. We shall consider further comments which Freud makes on the sources of the instincts when we come to examine his method of classification, but here it is enough to note that, like all the earlier writers we have mentioned, he maintains that the felt impulses or cravings in instinct-experience are 'concomitant' with certain underlying somatic processes.

The final point we wish to consider in this section is that to which we referred in our opening paragraph, and with regard to which Freud explicitly changed his view during the course of his later work. This is the question as to whether the instincts are 'qualitatively' or 'quantitatively' distinguishable, and leads to a consideration of the emphasis which Freud lays upon what he calls the *economic* aspects of mental processes. In the early paper on 'Instincts and their Vicissitudes', Freud writes:[1]

[1]These remarks follow immediately upon Freud's discussion of the sources of the instincts.

'Are we to suppose that the different instincts which operate upon the mind but of which the origin is somatic are also distinguished by different qualities and act in the mental life in a manner qualitatively different? This supposition does not seem to be justified; we are much more likely to find the simpler assumption sufficient—namely, that the instincts are all qualitatively alike and owe the effect they produce only to the quantities of excitation accompanying them, or perhaps further to certain functions of this quantity. The difference in the mental effects produced by the different instincts may be traced to the differences in their sources. . . .'

This passage is confusing. It seems clear that Freud takes for granted the fact that the instinctive impulses are qualitatively different on the *experiential* side. Introspection convinces us of this. Our sexual impulses are a qualitatively different experience from the internal craving which we call hunger, and both of these experiences are qualitatively distinct from the feelings prompting us to seek rest and sleep. Freud accepts this, and holds that these differences of feeling can be traced to their different somatic sources. The organs, hormonal processes, and muscular activities involved in our sexual impulses and in the activity of copulation are different from those involved in hunger and food-seeking, or from those involved in resting and sleeping. Freud, however, evidently wishes to go beyond such qualitative distinctions and assume what we can only term some basic undifferentiated neuro-physiological energy. The qualitative distinctions in feeling arise from different somatic sources, but the energy arising from these sources and resulting in these differences of feeling has itself no qualitative distinction, but differs only in its *quantity*. All the energy arising from all the somatic sources is held to act in the mental life in the same way, the qualitative differences of feeling being due merely to the different quantities of this energy which is operative at different times. Now, whether this assumption is soundly based is clearly a question of extraordinary difficulty into which we cannot go here. We might, however, briefly indicate the place that the assumption holds in Freud's theory before going on to mention the change of view which he expresses later.

This assumption as to the differences in *quantities* of excitation (referred to as the *economic* aspect of mental processes) is of importance in connection with the functioning of the 'Pleasure Principle' and with Freud's whole theory of neurosis. At this stage, Freud regards Pleasure as being equivalent with a *decrease* of stimulation or tension, and Pain with an *increase* of stimulation or tension. Here we shall give two illustrations of the way in which he makes use of this notion of the equilibrium or disequilibrium of quantities of excitation, firstly in discussing repression, and secondly in discussing the relative importance of qualitative and quantitative factors in the development of a neurosis.

Freud maintains that repression itself is an outcome of the disequilibrium of quantities of excitation. The straight-forward gratification of an instinct (which would usually lead to pleasure—a reduction of tension) comes into conflict with other claims in the personality (say moral ideals), which means that the direct gratification of the impulse would cause heightened tension (pain) in the rest of the personality. The need to avoid this pain is greater than the pleasure of gratifying the impulse, and the impulse is therefore repressed (rejected and kept from consciousness). 'We . . . see that the satisfaction of an instinct under repression is quite possible; further, that in every instance such a satisfaction is pleasurable in itself, but is irreconcilable with other claims and purposes; it therefore causes pleasure in one part of the mind and "pain" in another. We see then that it is a condition of repression, that the element of avoiding "pain" shall have acquired more strength than the pleasure of gratification.'[1]

Perhaps a better example of the importance which he attaches to quantitative rather than qualitative factors in the development of neurosis can be seen in this second illustration.

In his paper on 'Certain Neurotic Mechanisms in Jealousy, Paranoia and Homosexuality',[2] Freud dwells at length on the fact that certain delusions can exist in the mind long before an actual neurosis breaks out. Certain qualitative features which are themselves considered to be neurotic formations may exist in the mind for a long time without being unduly troublesome. It is the quantitative factors which cause the disruption of the personality and bring about the neurosis proper.

Discussing Paranoia, Freud says:

'The new thing I learned . . . was that classical persecution ideas may be present without finding belief or acceptance. They flashed up occasionally during the analysis, but he (the patient) regarded them as unimportant and invariably scoffed at them. This may occur in many cases of paranoia; it may be that the delusions which we regard as new formations when the disease breaks out have already long been in existence.

'It seems to me that this is an important recognition—namely, that the qualitative factor, the presence of certain neurotic formations, has less practical significance than the quantitative factor, the degree of

[1]'Repression', *Collected Papers*, 1915, vol. iv, v.   [2]*Collected Papers*, 1922, vol. ii, xix.

attention, or more correctly, the measure of cathexis that these formations engage. Our consideration of the first case, the jealousy paranoia, led to a similar estimate of the importance of the quantitative factor, by showing that there also the abnormality essentially consisted in the hyper-cathexis of the interpretations of another's unconscious behaviour. We have long known of an analogous fact in the analysis of hysteria. The pathogenic phantasies, derivatives of repressed instinctual trends, are for a long time tolerated alongside the normal life of the mind, and have no pathogenic effect until by a revolution in the libidoeconomy they undergo hyper-cathexis; not till then does the conflict which leads to symptom-formation break out. Thus as our knowledge increases we are ever being impelled to bring the *economic* point of view into the foreground. I should like also to throw out the question whether this quantitative factor that I am now dwelling on does not suffice to cover the phenomena for which Bleuler and others have lately wished to introduce the term "switching". One need only assume that increased resistance in one direction of the psychical currents results in hypercathexis along some other path and thus causes the whole current to be switched into this path.'

These two illustrations indicate briefly the importance which Freud attaches to this notion of the quantitative aspects of the instinctual excitations, and at the end of the last passage we see a brief mention of what we shall discuss later under the heading of 'Displacement' (the ease with which an instinctual impulse, seeking discharge, can switch itself into other channels and direct itself towards other objects). It is interesting to note the obvious similarity between Freud's notion of quantities of energy capable of being switched into different channels in search of discharge when some resistance to the one outlet exists, and the notions put forward by the Ethologists. We may recall their concept of reaction specific energy, and their suggestion that, when discharge by means of the release of the appropriate reaction was prevented, this energy was dammed up and was either discharged 'pointlessly' in the absence of appropriate sign stimuli, or 'sparked over' on to the neural paths of another instinct, thus giving rise to 'displacement activities'. We shall be pointing out such interesting parallels between Ethological and Psycho-Analytic conceptions in our next chapter. For the present, we must indicate Freud's change of view as to the sufficiency of regarding the differences between the instincts as being purely quantitative in nature.

This change of view is expressed in a later paper—'The Economic Problem in Masochism'[1]—when Freud is distinguishing between the

[1]*Collected Papers*, 1924, vol. ii, XXII.

Nirvana Principle (based on the 'necessary postulate' we have mentioned) and the Pleasure Principle; and it amounts really to an expression of dissatisfaction with the previous quantitative distinctions between the different instincts. It is not, however, developed to the extent of presenting any alternative ideas.

So far, Pleasure has been equated with the decrease and 'Pain'[1] with the increase of instinctual stimulation. Freud decides, now, that this simple distinction is inadequate.

'It seems that we experience the ebb and flow of quantities of stimuli directly in perceptions of tension which form a series, and it cannot be doubted that there is such a thing as both pleasurable tension and "painful" lowering of tension. The condition of sexual excitement is the most striking example of a pleasurable increase in tension of this kind, but it is certainly not the only one. Pleasure and "pain" cannot, therefore, be referred to a quantitative increase or decrease of something which we call stimulus-tension, although they clearly have a great deal to do with this factor. It seems as though they do not depend on this quantitative factor, but on some peculiarity in it which we can only describe as qualitative. We should be much farther on with psychology if we knew what this qualitative peculiarity was. Perhaps it is something rhythmic, the periodical duration of the changes, the risings and fallings of the volume of stimuli; we do not know.'

This is a clear and decisive statement, and takes us back to Freud's first considerations as to the sources of the instincts and the nature of their difference. His final position is that the instincts are qualitatively different in experience, and that these differences of feeling are correlated with their different particular somatic sources. Beyond this, Freud does not go.

Let us briefly summarise this section.

It has been found necessary to take exception to the 'necessary postulate' as to the so-called 'task of the nervous system'. The full relevance of this criticism will be seen when we consider the several attempts at a classification of the instincts. The distinguishing features of the instincts, Freud suggests, are as follows. The instincts are qualitatively distinct impulses involving both experiential aspects of feeling and concomitant somatic processes. They are distinct from reflexes in that (a) their origin lies in some source of stimulation within the organism, (b) they appear as constant, not momentary forces, and (c) no action of flight avails against them, and the organism is prompted to

[1]It must be noted that Freud himself always writes 'pain' in inverted commas in this way, referring really to 'frustration', 'dissatisfaction', or 'increase of tension'.

undertake complicated activity directed towards the outer world in order to achieve satisfaction or the discharge of tension. Each instinct comprises certain closely related features: (*a*) the impetus: the specific energy or compulsion; (*b*) the aim: which is always satisfaction; the discharge of tension; (*c*) the object: which is that through which it can achieve its aim (and this, Freud holds, is not a feature rigidly established by heredity in human beings); and (*d*) the source: which is the concomitant somatic process.

With the several qualifications given above, we can broadly agree with Freud's presentation, and we can see that it is roughly in agreement with the views of the writers whom we have previously considered, though it is far from being as detailed and comprehensive. We should add, also, that (though it has not been mentioned here) Freud holds that the instincts are *inherited*; although, as we have seen in some of his comments as to the aim and the object of the instincts, he maintains that both the behavioural and the perceptual features are highly modifiable in human beings, and that the correlation of these features with the other features of the instincts is not closely and strictly established by heredity. This latter point, too, was made by the earlier writers.

So far we have met with nothing new. It must be remembered, however, that Freud is starting his inquiry from the nature of the instincts in *man*. All that he has to say about the human instincts cannot be set out concisely under the headings we have considered. We must turn now to a broader discussion of the 'nature of instinctual experience', in which we shall have to consider Freud's ideas as to the structure of the personality and the nature of the unconscious mental processes.

3. *The Nature of Instinctual Experience*

Before we can adequately discuss the nature and extent of instinctual experience in human life, it is necessary to give a brief account of the several sets of concepts by means of which Freud interprets the growth and development of the personality. First, we must see what Freud has to say about the Unconscious, Preconscious, and Conscious levels of mental processes. Secondly, we must outline the distinction which is made between the three main elements of the personality: the Id, the Ego, and the Super-Ego. Thirdly, it will be necessary to mention the three major 'principles' which are held to govern the complex functioning of mental processes: the Nirvana Principle, the Pleasure Principle, and the Reality Principle. In this connection we shall have, provisionally, to take for granted certain instincts which are held to be at work (the Life and Death Instincts) but we shall criticise these in detail in a later section when we consider Freud's classification of the instincts. Following upon this preliminary work, we shall be in a position to describe the nature and extent of instinctual experience in the human personality, and, in discussing the conflicts which arise in the personality, we shall have to describe the various 'mental mechanisms' which are brought into operation in order to deal with these conflicts. We shall suggest later that the elucidation of these mental mechanisms is of great importance for the question as to how far and in what ways the theory of the instincts can be of significance in social theory. Finally, we shall lay stress upon the outstanding aspects of his theory which Freud himself emphasises and which we consider to be of the very greatest importance. These are: the nature and importance of the sexual instinct in the individual and social life of man, and the nature and importance of the Super-Ego.

(1) *Unconscious, Preconscious, and Conscious Levels of Mental Processes.* The basic starting-point of psycho-analytic theory is its insistence on the predominating importance in the individual personality of dynamic unconscious mental processes. It is quite arbitrary and incorrect to equate 'psychic processes' with 'conscious mental processes'.[1] The area of consciousness is always extremely limited, and the greater bulk of human mental process takes place beneath the level of consciousness. This fact can readily be proved, Freud says, when we consider the content of our own consciousness at any moment compared with the whole range of remembered images, experiences, and propositions of which we are not conscious now, but which we can easily call back to consciousness whenever we feel inclined to do so. All that is comprised by what we call 'memory' evidently exists in our minds, is in some way retained by our minds, even though at any given moment we are not in the least conscious of it. But this is not all. There is a good deal of evidence, both in the material of psycho-analytic case-work and in the success of its therapeutic method, and also (perhaps most clearly and most convincingly of all) in the phenomena of post-hypnotic suggestion, to support the view that there is a realm of mental process of which we are completely unconscious; functioning on a level even below that which we have summed up as 'memory'; and that this com-

[1] In *The Ego and the Id*, 1923, p. 9, Freud says: 'The division of mental life into what is conscious and what is unconscious is the fundamental premise on which psycho-analysis is based; and this division alone makes it possible for it to understand pathological mental processes. . . . Stated once more in a different way: psycho-analysis cannot accept the view that consciousness is the essence of mental life, but is obliged to regard consciousness as one property of mental life, which may co-exist along with its other properties or may be absent.'

plex mental process possesses extraordinary power. Though its functioning is autonomous, as it were, from the small area of the Conscious, it nonetheless exerts a tremendous and far-reaching influence within the total personality. There is evidence, also, to suggest that the varied proliferations of unconscious mental activity are quite different from the conscious ideas and experiences of the individual; that, indeed, they often prove themselves to be intolerable when they attempt to force themselves into consciousness; and that, by a mechanism of adjustment known as 'Repression', they are actively rejected and kept out of consciousness. Freud insists that mental processes must be conceived as functioning on three levels: the Unconscious, the Preconscious, and the Conscious; and that the conscious level of the psyche is of relatively minor importance when compared with the complicated ramifications of those mental processes taking place at the level of the unconscious.

We must consider these three levels in greater detail.

In the first place, Freud regards the mental processes of the Unconscious level as being older, both phylogenetically and ontogenetically, than those of the Conscious. We might say, of the human mental processes, that those of the Unconscious approximate most closely to those of the higher animals, and are both primitive (phylogenetic) and infantile (ontogenetic). Thus, Freud tells us:[1] 'In Psycho-Analysis we are accustomed to taking as our starting point the unconscious mental processes. . . . These we consider to be the older, primary processes, the residues of a phase of development in which they were the only kind of mental processes.'

The unconscious mental processes may be said to be *perceptual* and *affective*, as contrasted with the conscious mental processes which are *verbal*, *conceptual*, and *logical*, though the word 'perceptual' will have to be qualified a little later to distinguish it from the perceptual activities of the Preconscious and the Conscious.

The nucleus of the Unconscious consists of the instincts. The Unconscious therefore comprises these instinctual impulses which are continually seeking gratification, and the mental processes stemming from them are governed completely by the Pleasure Principle; that is to say —they seek discharge and satisfaction (pleasure) and avoid the accumulation of tension (pain). 'The kernel of the system Ucs consists of instinct-presentations whose aim is to discharge their cathexis; that is to say, they are wish-impulses. . . .'[2] And again: 'The content of the Ucs may be compared with a primitive population in the mental kingdom.

[1] 'Formulations regarding the Two Principles in Mental Functioning', *Collected Papers*, 1911, vol. iv, I.
[2] 'The Unconscious', *Collected Papers*, 1915, vol. iv, VI, p. 118.

If inherited mental formations exist in the human being—something analogous to instinct in animals—these constitute the nucleus of the Ucs. Later there is added all that is discarded as useless during childhood development, and this need not differ in its nature from what is inherited.'[1] (Here again we see Freud's stress on the phylogenetic and ontogenetic primacy of the unconscious mental processes.) 'The sovereign tendency obeyed by these primary processes is . . . the pleasure principle. These processes strive towards gaining pleasure; from any operation which might arouse unpleasantness, mental activity draws back.'[2]

In turning to consider the way in which these impulses seek discharge or satisfaction at the level of the Unconscious, we must say a little more about the word 'perceptual' which was used above. It will be remembered that, when discussing the distinguishing features of the instincts, Freud maintains that the *object* is that through which the satisfaction of a particular instinct can be achieved. Now it seems that Freud holds that in the unconscious the link of cathexis between the instinctual impulse and its object is established in a purely perceptual way. When distinguishing between a conscious idea and an unconscious idea, Freud says: '. . . the conscious idea comprises the concrete idea plus the verbal idea corresponding to it, whilst the unconscious idea is that of the thing alone. The system Ucs contains the thing-cathexes of the objects, the first and true object-cathexes; the system Pcs originates in a hyper-cathexes of this concrete idea by a linking up of it with the verbal ideas of the words corresponding to it. It is such hyper-cathexes, we may suppose, that bring about higher organization in the mind and make it possible for the primary process to be succeeded by the secondary process which dominates Pcs.'[3] In the unconscious, then, the impulse seeks its object on the purely perceptual level.[4]

It is never altogether clear in Freud's writing, how this perception of the object in the unconscious is related to the perceptual activities of the

[1]'The Unconcious', *Collected Papers*, 1915, vol. iv, vi, p. 127.
[2]'Formulations Regarding the Two Principles in Mental Functioning', *Collected Papers*, 1911, vol. iv, i.
[3]'The Unconscious', *Collected Papers*, 1915, vol. iv, vi, p. 134.
[4]It will be of value throughout this discussion to bear in mind the views of the earlier writers on 'instinct-interest', and the distinction they made between perceptual experience and the conceptual and ideational level of intelligent control. Thus Freud's 'first and true object-cathexis' is the equivalent of the 'primary instinct-interest', and the distinction between the perceptual activities of Ucs and Pcs is very similar to the distinction between the perceptual level and the conceptual and ideational level. The question might be raised whether Freud is correct in terming this primary perceptual activity as being strictly *unconscious*, or whether it should more correctly be called 'perceptual consciousness'. In our final chapter, however, we shall suggest a reconsideration of our entire conception of the nature of 'perception'.

Conscious and Preconscious. At first glance, one would be inclined to suppose that all perceptions of objects would entail consciousness of them, but we come across statements such as the following which make the whole question difficult to disentangle. 'It is very remarkable', Freud says, 'that the Ucs of one human being can react upon that of another without the Cs being implicated at all.' However this may be, it is clear that Freud regards the unconscious ideas as being relations between appetitive urges and their concrete appropriate objects, perceived directly as sensory images and symbols, and quite distinct from any conceptual or logical knowledge about them.[1] Thus, Freud thinks that 'thinking in pictures' approximates more closely to the unconscious mental processes than 'thinking in words'. We are told: 'Thinking in pictures is, therefore, only a very incomplete form of becoming conscious. In some way, too, it approximates more closely to unconscious processes than does thinking in words, and it is unquestionably older than the latter both ontogenetically and phylogenetically.'[2]

These considerations lead us to other qualities of the unconscious.

The unconscious mental processes deriving from the fundamental instincts and their continuing search for gratification are not, Freud tells us, related to external reality. The complex fate of the unconscious processes depends entirely upon the strength of the instincts and the governing influence of the pleasure-pain principle. Out of touch with external reality, the unconscious processes are not regulated in accordance with its demands, and they are, in consequence, not subjected to conceptual, verbal, and logical control. They are completely *alogical*. 'In the Ucs there are only contents more or less strongly cathected.' Impulses towards certain objects, and achieved gratifications, which are utterly incompatible from the point of view of logic, can exist side by side in the unconscious.

'These instinctual impulses are co-ordinate with one another, exist independently side by side, and are exempt from mutual contradiction. When two wishes whose aims must appear to us incompatible become simultaneously active, the two impulses do not detract one from the other or cancel each other, but combine to form an intermediate aim, a compromise. . . . There is in this system no negation, no dubiety, no varying degree of certainty. . . .'[3]

In the same way as they are exempt from the demands of external reality and logical consistency, the unconscious processes are also held

---

[1] Here again, we see the similarity between this conception and that of the 'instinct-interest': a *feeling* of worthwhileness of the whole relation between impulse and object.
[2] *The Ego and the Id*, p. 23.
[3] 'The Unconscious', *Collected Papers*, 1915, vol. iv, vi, p. 119.

to be *timeless*. The continuing instinctual cravings for satisfaction bear
no relation to consciously conceived time, and consequently are not
ordered temporally.

Unaffected by these various external demands, and by the demand
for logical consistency, the unconscious mental processes enjoy a high
degree of mobility in their dynamic search for gratification. The several
instinctual tendencies do not seem bound to one mode of discharge only,
nor are they tied to very specific objects. On the contrary, when any
obstacle is encountered rendering discharge towards a certain object
'painful', the cathexis can easily be switched to other objects in connection with which alternative satisfaction can be achieved. Similarly,
by a process known as Condensation, one idea in the unconscious can
appropriate the cathexis directed to many other ideas. But we shall see
more of this when we come to consider the 'mental mechanisms'.

The sort of picture Freud has in mind when conceiving the proliferation of the unconscious mental processes in their search for gratification
can be seen in this passage from his paper on 'Repression':[1]

'. . . the instinct-presentation develops in a more unchecked and
luxuriant fashion if it is withdrawn by repression from conscious influence. It ramifies like a fungus, so to speak, in the dark and takes on
extreme forms of expression, which when translated and revealed to the
neurotic are bound not merely to seem alien to him, but to terrify him
by the way in which they reflect an extraordinary and dangerous strength
of instinct. This illusory strength of instinct is the result of an unin-
hibited development of it in phantasy and of the damming-up consequent on lack of real satisfaction.'

The mention of phantasy in this last passage leads to one or two
further characteristics of the Unconscious.

We have noted the importance of direct perceptual images (without
verbal, conceptual elements) in the unconscious mental processes, and
we have seen that there is an extraordinary degree of mobility of
cathexis towards these images or objects. The extreme mobility of the
unconscious mental processes is complicated still further by the construction of intricate 'phantasy-formations', which aim at the gratifications wished for, but which, again, have no relation to external reality.
And this consideration introduces a most important point, which is:
that—in the unconscious—'Psychic Reality' or 'the reality of the
thought-world' has great predominance as against the claims of external
reality. For the individual, this inner realm of experience *is real*. In the
normal development of the individual, this 'psychic reality' has gradually
to give way to the increasingly necessitous demands of the external

[1]*Collected Papers*, vol. iv, v, p. 87.

world as discovered through the activities of perceptual consciousness, but even so, this mode of experience, this fulfilment of wishes in phantasy, is not abandoned altogether. 'With the introduction of the reality-principle one mode of thought-activity was split off; it was kept free from reality testing and remained subordinate to the pleasure-principle alone. This is the act of "phantasy-making" which begins already in the games of children, and later, continued as "day-dreaming", abandons its dependence on real objects.'[1]

A further point is: that since the instinctual impulses strive only for gratification, the unconscious mental processes are, besides being alogical, also *amoral*.

A final characteristic of the unconscious which must be mentioned is that it comprises not only those mental processes and ideas which have never been conscious, but also those which *have* been conscious and which have been *repressed*.

In conclusion we must emphasise again that the unconscious mental processes are conceived as being intensely dynamic constituents of the mind; indeed, as being far more powerful, exerting a much more pervasive influence in the total personality, than the conscious mental processes. The great importance of the unconscious is that (quite without the awareness of the individual) it exerts a profound influence upon the conscious ideational life; and it is because of this, clearly, that a knowledge of the existence and nature of the unconscious is considered to be of so great an importance for the understanding of the human personality.

We must now consider briefly the other two levels of mental functioning postulated by Freud: the Preconscious and the Conscious. When Freud is discussing the growth of the individual and the development of perceptual consciousness, the two are very often treated as one, and we shall discuss them at first as though they were one process, and distinguish between them later.

As the individual grows, the necessitous demands of the external world (of the physical and social environment) are increasingly forced upon him. The 'psychic reality' of the unconscious becomes increasingly inadequate, and the individual finds that in order to attain instinctual satisfaction he has in some way to come to terms with the disquieting conditions of 'external reality'. This progressive 'becoming aware' of the external environment is called the development of perceptual consciousness. The domination of the pleasure principle in governing the impulses and their search for gratification has, now, to be modified in the light of

[1]Formulations regarding the Two Principles in Mental Functioning', *Collected Papers*, 1911, vol. iv, I.

the adaptations seen to be necessary in order to deal successfully with the external world. In short, the individual has to discover a mode of 'testing external reality', and Freud holds that a new principle comes into operation in governing the activities of perceptual consciousness: the Reality Principle. This new institution of the reality principle, however, does not mean that the pleasure principle is abandoned. On the contrary, the reality principle is a safeguard of the pleasure principle: coming into operation in order to deal effectively with those threats to pleasure which come from the outside world, and in order to learn how to manipulate the features of the outside world to ensure as full as possible a gratification of the impulses.

This development of perceptual consciousness is held to involve the following kinds of activity.

In the first place, the demands of the outside world lead to the heightened significance, for the individual, of the sense-organs directed towards the external world and of the consciousness attached to them. The individual now becomes increasingly aware of the *qualities of sense* in addition to the pleasure-pain qualities (internal appetites and their gratification) which have previously been his sole interest. In order to become familiar with the outer world and to know how to deal with it when any inner impulse arises, the individual develops the function of *attention*. The activity of perceptual consciousness, Freud says: 'meets sense impressions half-way instead of awaiting their appearance.' In order to retain the results of this 'periodical activity of consciousness', the individual develops a *system of notation* which leads to the establishment of *memories*. Repression (hitherto effective in keeping from consciousness those unconscious ideas, striving for expression, which are incompatible with, and therefore intolerable to, the conscious mind) is no longer of use in dealing with the discomforting demands of the outside world. In order to deal effectively with these objective external demands, the individual is bound to develop an *impartial passing of judgment*, which is the taking of decisions based upon those memory-traces of reality which are now established. *Action*, 'the appropriate alteration of reality', now becomes of importance to the individual in connection with motor-discharge, and, coupled with this, is the increasing importance of the *restraint* of motor-discharge which is achieved by the exercise of *thought*.

In connection with this whole change of orientation brought about by the necessary activities of perceptual consciousness in adapting the individual to the external world, Freud holds that (whereas in the unconscious cathexis is very free, changing its object or its symbol with great ease) 'free cathexis' has now to be converted into 'bound cathexis'.

By this, Freud means that the impulses are no longer allowed to seek freely their momentary and immediate gratification, and that the exercise of attention, thought, and judgment, brings with it a certain measure of control whereby the cathexis towards a certain object can be held in abeyance, or delayed for a time. As he puts it, thought 'makes it possible for the mental apparatus to support increased tension during a delay in the process of discharge'. As can be gathered from this statement, Freud holds that this ability to delay satisfaction (this 'binding' of cathexis) raises the degree of tension in the mind. Indeed, with the institution of thought and an experimental way of acting '... conversion of free cathexis into "bound" cathexis was imperative, and this was brought about by means of raising the level of the whole cathectic process.'

It will be seen that all these activities imply that perceptual consciousness becomes increasingly verbal, conceptual, ideational, and logical.

The distinction which Freud makes between the Preconscious and the Conscious, is really an 'ex post' rather than an 'ex ante' distinction. In describing the process of growth and development of the individual, Freud speaks, as above, of perceptual consciousness; speaking of conscious activities and the establishing of memories in the same breath.[1] The distinction he makes, however, has already been indicated in our remarks on the nature of the unconscious, and is this: *The Conscious* is simply the very limited momentary functioning of the mind of which the individual is aware at any given time. *The Preconscious* is all that can be summed up under the name 'memory'; of which the individual is not conscious at any given time but which he can readily call into consciousness should he be asked to do so.

We have, then, three levels of mental functioning: (1) the vast, archaic, dynamic region of the unconscious which is held to exert by far the most extensive and pervasive influence in the total personality, (2) the realm of memory, of which we are unconscious at any particular time, but of which we can become conscious in accordance with our inclination, and (3) the Conscious level which is very minute and momentary.

In concluding this outline of the three levels of mental functioning, it is important to emphasise that Freud does not by any means regard the personality as being literally split up into three completely discrete levels. Whilst he finds it necessary to insist upon these three levels, he

[1]For all the characteristics of 'perceptual consciousness' mentioned above, see, 'Formulations regarding the Two Principles in Mental Functioning', *Collected Papers*, 1911, vol. iv, I, pp. 14-16.

conceives of the mental processes as interacting in many and various ways.

'At the roots of instinctual activity the systems communicate with each other in the freest possible way; some of the processes here set in motion pass through the Ucs, as through a preparatory stage, and reach the highest mental development in the Cs, whilst some are retained as the Ucs. But the Ucs is also affected by experiences originating in outer perception. Normally all the paths from perception to the Ucs remain open; only those leading out from the Ucs are barred by repression.' Then again: 'The content of the system Pcs (or Cs) is derived partly from the instinctual life (through the medium of the Ucs), and partly from perception.' All these interrelations, we must emphasise, take place in the *normal* personality, and, Freud says: 'A complete divergence of their tendencies, a total dissociation of the two systems (i.e. Ucs/Cs), is a general characteristic of *disease*.'[1]

Freud believes that the influence of the Conscious on the Unconscious level is much smaller than the reverse influence of the unconscious on the conscious. Nonetheless, he says in·many places that ideas in the unconscious do permit of being brought into consciousness, and, indeed, '. . . Psycho-Analytic treatment is based upon influence by the Cs on the Ucs, and shows at any rate that, though laborious, this is not impossible.'

(2) *The Id, the Ego, and the Super-Ego.* When introducing this new set of concepts, Freud expressly tells us that it is not meant to supercede the concepts which we have just been considering. The distinction between unconscious, preconscious, and conscious levels of mental functioning is still considered correct and necessary for dealing with certain problems, but other problems arise which necessitate the use of these new concepts: the Id, Ego, and Super-Ego.

Through the activities of perceptual consciousness, described above, there develops in the individual a coherent organisation of mental processes involving the 'consciousness of Self'. This is termed the Ego. Psycho-Analytic experience shows that in many cases the Ego is not aware of those resistances (against concerning itself with the repressed) which must have emanated from *itself*. In a word, the Ego functions partly at the *unconscious* level, so that the concept of the Ego cannot be held to be synonymous with the concept of the Conscious, and the development of two sets of concepts is required to elucidate these newly discovered antitheses in the personality.

'We have come upon something in the Ego itself which is also uncon-

---

[1]'The Unconscious', *Collected Papers*, vol. iv, VI, p. 126.

scious, which behaves exactly like the repressed, that is, which produces powerful effects without itself being conscious and which requires special work before it can be made conscious. From the point of view of analytic practice, the consequence of this piece of observation is that we land in endless confusion and difficulty if we cling to our former way of expressing ourselves and try, for instance, to derive neuroses from a conflict between the conscious and the unconscious. We shall have to substitute for this antithesis another, taken from our understanding of the structural conditions of the mind, namely, the antithesis between the organized Ego and what is repressed and dissociated from it.'[1]

The concepts of Id, Ego, and Super-Ego are those developed to elucidate these 'structural conditions of the mind'.

The distinction between the Unconscious, Preconscious, and Conscious, on the one hand, and the Id, Ego, and Super-Ego, on the other, can thus be expressed as follows: the Unconscious, Preconscious, and Conscious are concepts representing *levels of mental functioning*, whereas the Id, Ego, and Super-Ego are concepts representing the *structural elements of the personality*. In this way, both sets of concepts can be seen to be necessary and complementary to each other.

Freud begins his analysis of these three new concepts by following up the suggestions of Georg Groddeck[2] to the effect that: 'the conduct through life of what we call our Ego is essentially passive, and that . . . we are "lived" by unknown and uncontrollable forces.' Mention of this is perhaps necessary to make quite clear the terminology used by Freud. Many readers turn away from Psycho-Analytic literature after a very short acquaintance because of the use of terms such as Id and Super-Ego which seem strange and unfamiliar, and because of a careless usage of these terms which gives the impression of certain discrete 'bits' of the personality doing things to one another. There is, however, nothing illegitimate about Freud's terms, though it is true that his writing does sometimes give the impression that he regards them as separate entities. No sympathetic and intelligent reader would accuse him of this fault. Freud's own terms were 'Das Ich und Das Es', and signify, really, '*I*' (the consciousness of 'self' which is now called the Ego), and '*It*' (the objective, impersonal appearance to the Ego of the instinctual demands; the compulsive nature of the internal urges). By thinking in terms of 'I' and 'It' it becomes quite clear what Freud means when he depicts the Ego as being confronted with the situation of (*a*) the demands of the external environment on the one hand, and (*b*) the demands of the inner instinctual appetites on the other. The compulsive urges of the instincts

[1] *The Ego and the Id*, 1923, pp. 16-17.
[2] *Das Buch vom Es*, G. Groddeck, Vienna, 1923. See *The Ego and the Id*, p. 27.

are thus treated as being as objective, impersonal, and unrelenting to the
Ego as are the necessitous conditions imposed by the outer world. In the
English translation of Freud's work, the Latin word 'Id' has been used
to denote this impersonal aspect of the instinctual demands, and the
term 'Ego' to denote the consciousness of self and the coherent mental
organisation arising out of the activities of perceptual consciousness.
There is thus no difficulty at all in understanding the reason for the use
of these terms, or in understanding their meaning.

The three concepts can best be described as the outcome of a *process
of differentiation* arising during the growth and development of the
individual personality, and we shall discuss them in this developmental
way, presenting them in order of temporal sequence.

In origin, the 'psyche' of the individual is regarded as an undifferentiated Id, functioning entirely in the unconscious. Though not identical
with the unconscious (we have already seen that the Ego, too, functions
partly in the unconscious, and we shall see later that this is also true of
the Super-Ego) the Id shares with it many of those characteristics which
we have already outlined. The Id is said to be the seat of the instincts
and the reservoir of instinctual energy. It consists chiefly of these compulsive appetites whose sole aim (under the governance of the pleasure
principle) is gratification or discharge and the avoidance of tension or
'pain'. In this search for gratification, the Id is completely amoral and
alogical, and cannot be said to have any unity or coherence of purpose
as this would be rationally conceived. The Id operates entirely in the
unconscious, and all the characteristics of the unconscious mental processes—the predominance of concrete perceptual images and direct ties
of cathexis with them; the proliferations of phantasy in accordance with
wish-impulses; the extreme degree of mobility of cathexis; can be
assigned to it. The Id is held to contain all such phylogenetic deposits as
exist in man. That which is repressed also merges with, and becomes
part of, the Id. Having no direct contact with the outer world and its
demands (a point which will be made clear when we discuss the Ego) the
Id has no such purpose as protecting itself from external dangers,
keeping itself alive, protecting itself from incompatibility by anxiety;
and, again, its search for gratification is completely timeless, bearing no
relation to the categories of time as perceived by the Ego.

The central importance of the Id (in that it sets all the major ends
of human activity with which reason has to concern itself) can be seen
in the following extract from Freud's book:

'The power of the Id expresses the true purpose of the individual
organism's life. This consists in the satisfaction of its innate needs. . . .'
And, 'The forces which we assume to exist behind the tensions caused

by the needs of the Id are called *Instincts*. They represent the somatic demands upon mental life.' Later in this same book, he tells us:

'The core of our being is formed by the obscure Id, which has no direct relations with the external world. . . . Within this Id the organic instincts operate, which are themselves composed of fusions of two primal forces (Eros and Destructiveness) in varying proportions and are differentiated from one another by their relation to organs or systems of organs. The one and only endeavour of these instincts is towards satisfaction, which it is hoped to obtain from certain modifications in the organs by the help of objects in the external world. But an immediate and regardless satisfaction of instinct, such as the Id demands, would often enough lead to perilous conflicts with the external world and to extinction. The Id knows no precautions to ensure survival and no anxiety; or it would perhaps be more correct to say that, though it can produce the sensory elements of anxiety, it cannot make use of them. The processes which are possible in and between the assumed mental elements in the Id (the primary processes) differ largely from those which are familiar to us by conscious perception in our intellectual and emotional life; nor are they subject to the critical restrictions of logic, which repudiates some of these processes as invalid and seeks to undo them.' . . . 'The Id, which is cut off from the external world, has its own world of perception. It detects with extraordinary clarity certain changes in its interior, especially oscillations in the tensions of its instinctual needs, oscillations which become conscious as feelings in the pleasure-unpleasure series. It is, to be sure, hard to say by what means and with the help of what sensory terminal organs these perceptions come about. But it remains certain that self-perceptions—conaesthetic feelings and feelings of pleasure-unpleasure—govern events in the Id with despotic force. The Id obeys the inexorable pleasure principle. But not the Id alone. It seems as though the activity of the other agencies of the mind is able to modify the pleasure principle but not to nullify it. . . .'[1]

In this passage, the Life and Death Instincts are mentioned. We shall leave any detailed discussion of these supposed instincts until we consider Freud's attempts at classification, but we must briefly mention them here as they constitute an important aspect of the Id as conceived by Freud. 'The Life and Death instincts struggle within it.' Quite apart from later conflicts between Id, Ego, Super-Ego, and External World—Freud holds that there is a fundamental instinctual conflict within the Id itself.

Freud believes that all organic life manifests a conflict between two fundamental tendencies: one towards disintegration and death and to

[1] *An Outline of Psycho-Analysis*, 1940, p. 67.

the reinstatement of the earlier condition of inorganic existence, and the other towards ever-increasing unities and the maintenance and the furtherance of life. Even the single cell is held to be invested with these two tendencies. Thus, every cell in the organism's body is endowed with these two opposed tendencies. In the Id, the death instincts exert their influence towards disintegration and death but are countered by the exertions of the life instincts. The life instincts to a great extent master the death instincts in this struggle, whereupon much of the initial tendency of self-destruction is diverted towards the outer world and manifests itself as outwardly directed aggression. Later, as a result of the condemnation of such aggression by the parents and, thereafter, the Super-Ego, this aggression is again turned inwards and directed against the individual, which accounts (so it is held) for the extreme intensity and harshness of the Super-Ego.

This account of the operations of the life and death instincts in the Id is brief, but sufficient for our present purpose of outlining the characteristics of the Id. A more detailed and critical account will be given later.[1]

We have described how, as the individual grows, he becomes increasingly aware of the necessitous demands of the external world, and how the activities of perceptual consciousness gradually establish a coherent organization of mental processes and a consciousness of self. 'We shall . . . look upon the mind of an individual', Freud now tells us, 'as an unknown and unconscious Id, upon whose surface rests the Ego, developed from its nucleus the Pcpt-system.' The Ego is a differentiation of the Id brought about by the activities of perceptual consciousness. Bearing in mind what we have already said about these activities, we can turn to the following exposition of what is comprised by the concept of the Ego.

'It is easy to see that the Ego is that part of the Id which has been modified by the direct influence of the external world acting through the Pcpt-Cs: in a sense it is an extension of the surface-differentiation. Moreover, the Ego has the task of bringing the influence of the external world to bear upon the Id and its tendencies, and endeavours to substitute the reality-principle for the pleasure-principle which reigns supreme in the Id. In the Ego perception plays the part which in the Id devolves upon instinct. The Ego represents what we call reason and sanity, in contrast to the Id which contains the passions. . . .' 'The functional importance of the Ego is manifested in the fact that normally control over the approaches to motility devolves upon it. Thus in its relation to the Id it is like a man on horseback, who has to hold in check the superior strength of the horse; with this difference, that the rider seeks to do so with his own strength while the Ego uses borrowed forces. The illustration can be carried further. Often a rider, if he is not to be parted from his horse, is obliged to guide it where it wants to go; so in the same way the Ego constantly carries into action the wishes of the Id as if they were its own.'[1]

In general, Freud regards the Ego as being as weak and passive an agent as his original remarks on the suggestions of Groddeck imply. At various points he insists that we should not under-estimate the capacity of the Ego, and it is clear that the success of psycho-analytic work depends entirely on whether the Ego can be helped to such a position of strength that it can then and thereafter deal adequately with the conflicts to which it is a prey. Nonetheless, in the main Freud stresses the weakness and passivity of the Ego, and we shall return to illustrate this point presently.

The Ego, then, perceives the outer world, builds up a knowledge of it, guards itself against its dangers, and learns how to manipulate it in order to satisfy the appetites emanating from the Id. Also, the Ego perceives, and then tries to control, the instincts, or, as Freud says, proceeds 'from obeying instincts to curbing them' in accordance with the temporal and spatial demands of the external world. The Id and the external world are not the only problematic factors, however, with which the Ego is faced, and in order to complete our sketch of the characteristics of the Ego we shall have to mention here one or two points in anticipation of what will be said a little later with regard to the Super-Ego.

Firstly, the Ego 'withdraws libido from the Id and transforms the object-cathexes of the Id into Ego-constructions.' The character of the Ego, that is to say, consists largely of Id-abandoned object-choices. Secondly, the Ego strives to be moral in accordance with the demands of the Super-Ego, and it is this striving which constitutes the source of its repressions of the appetites emanating from the Id.

Finally, two further features of the Ego must be mentioned. Freud suggests that the Ego, besides representing the limited conscious functionings of the mental apparatus, must also be conceived as a mental projection of the body-surface. 'The Ego is first and foremost a body-ego; it is not merely a surface entity, but is itself the projection of a surface.' In this point we can see how closely Freud conceives the association between the activities of perceptual consciousness and the nature of the Ego. Secondly, we must emphasise that only a part of the

[1] *The Ego and the Id*, 1923, pp. 29-30.

Ego is held to be conscious. The Ego is not a separate, altogether conscious entity, but extends into the unconscious, and into the massive Id of which it is a surface-differentiation.

The Ego, then, is conceived as being faced with three masters, none of which can be ignored since they all make continuous and grave demands upon it. The perpetual task of the Ego is to resolve the conflicts which arise between the demands of these three masters. And here, finally, we might turn again to see how Freud's portrayal of the Ego and its task suggests that its character is, in the main, negative and passive.

'Like the dweller in a borderland that it is the Ego tries to mediate between the world and the Id, to make the Id comply with the world's demands and, by means of muscular activity, to accommodate the world to the Id's desires. In point of fact it behaves like the physician during treatment by analysis; it offers itself to the Id as a libidinal object in view of its power of adaptation to the real world, and aims at attaching the Id's libido to itself. It is not only the ally of the Id; it is also a submissive slave who courts the love of his master. Whenever possible, it tries to remain on good terms with the Id; it draws the veil of its Pcs rationalizations over the Id's Ucs demands; it pretends that the Id is showing obedience to the mandates of reality, even when in fact it is remaining obdurate and immovable; it throws a disguise over the Id's conflicts with reality, and, if possible, over its conflicts with the Super-Ego too. Its position midway between the Id and reality tempts it only too often to become sycophantic, opportunist and false, like a politician who sees the truth but wants to keep his place in popular favour.'[1]

In view of this complex and continuing three-sided conflict, Freud concludes, 'The Ego is the true abode of anxiety'.

It is interesting to see how closely this view of Freud approximates to the views of much earlier thinkers—the view, that is to say, that the ends of human life are set by the impulses or the passions, and that reason functions almost entirely in their service. To quote but two well-known examples, Thomas Hobbes tells us that '. . . the Thoughts, are to the Desires, as Scouts, and Spies, to range abroad, and find the way to the things Desired'.[2] And David Hume holds that 'Reason is, and ought only to be, the slave of the passions'.[3]

But we must turn, now, to the concept of the Super-Ego.

Just as the Ego is conceived to be a differentiation of the Id, emerging

---

[1] *The Ego and the Id*, 1923, p. 83.
[2] *Leviathan*, Thomas Hobbes, Everyman's Edition, p. 35.
[3] *Treatise of Human Nature*, David Hume, Book II, Part III, Section III.

during the process of growth and adaptation to the environment, so the Super-Ego is held to be a later differentiation of the Ego itself and can be said to be the outcome of the Ego's need to accommodate itself to its earliest *social* environment: the family situation. It is the outcome of the Ego's need to accommodate itself to the commands and corrections of the parents: not only to the environment as a set of objects, but also to what is *permitted* in the environment. We shall take the view that this concept of the Super-Ego is of the very greatest importance, and consequently, we shall devote a separate section to a thorough discussion of it after having considered Freud's account of the Sexual Instinct. At this point we shall give only a general and more or less dogmatic description of the Super-Ego for the purpose of our present discussion.

As the individual grows, not only do the *physical necessities* of the environment force themselves increasingly upon his attention, but he finds more and more that he has to *conform* to the *corrections* and *commands* of his parents, which, like the demands of the physical environment, come to him from outside. Some kinds of behaviour are *permitted*; some are *forbidden*; and the child has to accommodate himself to this fact. Until the age of about five years, the ties of the child to his parents are of a libidinal nature, and during this period the Oedipus-Complex develops. At this age, because of a collocation of factors which we shall elucidate later, the Oedipus-Complex has to be overcome, and the relations of the parents to the child (as conceived in the child's mind) have to be 'de-sexualised'. This is accomplished by a process which Freud calls 'Introjection'. The ideal represented by the moral precepts of the parents, together with the child's love of the parents, is incorporated into the child's own Ego, and thus becomes the 'Ego-Ideal' in the child's own nature. In common language, this process would be called the formation of the Conscience. After this Conscience has been established, its demands upon the Ego no longer come from *outside* but from *within* the individual's own personality. After this process of introjection, it is as though, Freud says, one element in the personality, the Super-Ego, continually 'watches over' the activities of the Ego, harshly reprimanding it and giving rise to feelings of guilt when, in accordance with the promptings of the Id, any of its precepts are broken. The chief functions of the Super-Ego are therefore to inhibit certain actions undertaken by the Ego in the service of the Id (though we shall qualify this statement, as indeed most of the statements given here, later). Bearing in mind what we have said earlier as to the course followed by the Death Instinct, it is held that the aggression directed towards the outer world by the Ego, is now, because of condemnation, turned inward again, against the Ego itself. This is said to intensify the harshness

of the Super-Ego in its criticism of the Ego; and the Super-Ego is conceived as being much more tyrannical and compulsive than the simple
introjection of the precepts of, and the love for, the parents would lead
us to expect. Whilst the later influence of teachers and other individuals
in the environment may reinforce the Super-Ego, Freud holds that its
most powerful and permanent character is established by this first introjection of the parental influence. One reason for this is that the results
of this earliest introjection operate largely in the unconscious. The
Super-Ego extends farther into the unconscious than does the Ego, and
is therefore to a large extent inaccessible to the Ego. Because of this
deeper extension into the unconscious and also because of the libidinal
nature of the id-abandoned object-choice which was introjected (this
will be clarified in our later section), there is held to be a close contact
with the Id, and a free communication between the Id and the Super-
Ego. The Super-Ego is said to know more about the unconscious Id
than does the Ego.

Freud also suggests, in ways which we shall discuss later, and with
which we shall disagree, that the Super-Ego is to some extent phylogenetically determined. And (a final point which must be mentioned)
Freud tells us that the Ego, in its state of weakness, by introjecting the
precepts of the parents and their forcefulness, 'borrows', or incorporates
into itself, the strength of the father in order to succeed in the repression
of the Oedipus-Complex. One aspect of the Super-Ego, then, is that it
represents the moral forcefulness of the father which is set up as an
element in the individual's own personality to aid the Ego in its task of
overcoming the Oedipus Complex.

Described baldly in this way, the concept of the Super-Ego may not
seem particularly impressive, but later we shall discuss Freud's treatment of the concept more fully, when it will be seen to be much more
convincing. For the present, we merely wish to complete our sketch of
the Id, Ego, and Super-Ego with reasonable adequacy so that we can go
on to indicate the extent and importance of instinctual experience in the
psycho-analytic account of the human personality. For this purpose,
this brief description of the Super-Ego will suffice.

Perhaps the chief point to comment on at the moment is the over-
whelming importance of the part played by instinctual experience in
human life as revealed by this brief discussion of Id, Ego, and Super-
Ego. The massive Id is held to comprise the instincts and their continual
compulsive striving for gratification. The Ego is largely the servant of
the Id, acting in relation to the outer world in order to secure gratification. Finally, even the moral ideals, the conscience of the individual, are
held to be derived from basic instinctual impulses and the suppression

of them. But we can turn to a full discussion of this when we have considered one further set of concepts: the three so-called 'Principles' which govern the functioning of human mental processes.

(3) *The Nirvana Principle, the Pleasure Principle, and the Reality Principle.* The clearest statement of the relations between these three principles is given in Freud's paper on 'The Economic Problem in Masochism'. In the passage which follows, the Life and Death Instincts are again involved, but our detailed consideration of this question must be left until later. For the present we must accept what Freud says concerning the Life and Death Instincts, but only to see clearly the significance he attaches to each of the three principles we are now considering. In this passage, too, we shall repeat to some extent what has been said earlier on the 'quantitative' and the 'qualitative' distinction between the feelings accompanying instinctive excitations, but this is necessary in this context.

Freud says (i.e. in *Beyond the Pleasure Principle*):
'As will be remembered, we have conceived the principle which governs all mental processes as a special case of Fechner's *tendency to stability*, and consequently have ascribed to the mental apparatus the aim of extinguishing, or at least of maintaining at as low a level as possible, the quantities of excitation flowing into it. For this tendency that has been presumed by us Barbara Low has suggested the name *Nirvana Principle*, which we accept. But we have unquestioningly identified the pleasure-pain-principle with this Nirvana-Principle. From this it would follow that every "pain" coincides with a heightening, every pleasure with a lowering, of the stimulus-tension existing in the mind; the Nirvana-Principle (and the Pleasure-Principle which is assumed to be identical with it) would be entirely in the service of the death-instincts (the aim of which is to lead our throbbing existence into the stability of an inorganic state) and would have the function of warning us against the claims of the life-instincts, of the libido, which tries to disturb the course life endeavours to take. Unfortunately, this view cannot be correct. It seems that we experience the ebb and flow of quantities of stimuli directly in perceptions of tension which form a series, and it cannot be doubted that there is such a thing as both pleasurable tension and "painful" lowering of tension. The condition of sexual excitement is the most striking example of a pleasurable increase in tension of this kind, but it is certainly not the only one. Pleasure and "pain" cannot, therefore, be referred to a quantitative increase or decrease of something which we call stimulus-tension, although they

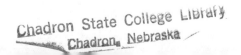

clearly have a great deal to do with this factor. It seems as though they do not depend on this quantitative factor, but on some peculiarity in it which we can only describe as qualitative. We should be much farther on with psychology if we knew what this qualitative peculiarity was. Perhaps it is something rhythmic, the periodical duration of the changes, the risings and fallings of the volume of stimuli; we do not know.

'Whatever it is, we must perceive that the Nirvana-Principle, which belongs to the death-instincts, underwent a modification in the living organism through which it became the Pleasure-Principle, and henceforth we shall avoid regarding the two principles as one. It is not difficult to infer what force it was that effected this modification, that is, if one has any interest at all in following this argument.[1] It can only be the life-instinct, the libido, which has thus wrested a place for itself alongside the death-instinct in regulating the processes of life. In this way we obtain a series, a small but an interesting one: the *Nirvana-Principle* expresses the tendency of the death-instincts, the *Pleasure-Principle* represents the claims of the libido and that modification of it, the *Reality-Principle*, the influence of the outer world.

'None of these three principles can actually be put out of action by another. As a rule they know how to tolerate one another, although conflicts must occasionally arise from the various aims towards which each strives—a quantitative reduction of the stimulus-pressure on one side, on another side some qualitative feature in it, and lastly a postponement of the discharge of tension and a temporary acquiescence in "painful" tension.'

From this passage we can summarise what is comprised by each of the three principles.

The Nirvana Principle, is that principle governing mental processes which stems from the operation of the death-instincts. In accordance with Freud's 'necessary postulate', with which we disagreed, this principle tends towards the reduction and if possible the complete extinction of quantities of excitation, aiming at disintegration and death. The struggle between the death-instincts, manifesting the Nirvana-Principle, and the life-instincts, manifesting the Pleasure-Principle, takes place in the Id and at the level of the unconscious.

[1]Note the curious way in which Freud argues here. It is as though he was aware that his line of reasoning at this point was very speculative and very flimsy. We shall see later that he admits openly that he has no idea whatsoever as to how this 'wresting of a place alongside the death-instincts' by the life-instincts takes place. It can be seen, too, in his next sentence above, that in some way the life-instinct is held to exert itself after, or later than, the death-instincts, which would seem to be absurd, since—if the death-instincts alone 'regulated the processes of life' before the life-instincts came into operation, it is difficult to see how they would ever have come into being at all! But it can be seen from this brief query that the whole idea very quickly becomes smothered in terminological absurdities.

The Pleasure Principle, is that principle governing mental processes which stems from the operation of the life-instincts. This is manifested as the tendency in mental life to seek the gratification of qualitatively distinct impulses, the satisfactory discharge of tension (Pleasure); and, on the other hand, to avoid frustration or the accumulation of tension ('pain'). As distinct from the Nirvana-Principle which seeks the reduction of *quantities* of excitation, the Pleasure-Principle involves *qualitative* feelings attendant upon the satisfaction or the dissatisfaction of impulses. The life-instincts establish the operation of the Pleasure-Principle in their conflict with the death-instincts, which takes place in the Id and the unconscious, and this 'victory' is regarded as a modification of the Nirvana-Principle, won by the life-instincts in the course of this struggle. Whilst operating 'with despotic force' in the Id and at the level of the unconscious, the Pleasure-Principle is also held to exert a governing influence in the activities of the Ego, and can be said to extend into the Reality-Principle and into the sphere of conscious activity.

The Reality-Principle, is that principle governing mental processes which arises from the demands of the external world and from the need, on the part of the individual, to accommodate himself successfully to these demands. It is manifested as the tendency in the individual to control the instincts and to order his mental life and his behaviour in accordance with the demands of external necessity. Whilst it is 'secondary' upon the Pleasure-Principle (acting in its service), it nonetheless mitigates the free operation of the Pleasure-Principle by enforcing a 'postponement of the discharge of tension and a temporary acquiescence in "painful" tension' when circumstances in the external world require it. The Reality-Principle is introduced by the activities of perceptual consciousness, and is therefore a principle governing the mental processes of the Ego at the level of the Conscious and Preconscious (i.e. in present activity, and in the established memories of external reality).

None of these principles is held to supersede the governing influences of the others. All are held to be operative simultaneously in their respective spheres, and to interact in the ways we have indicated.

(4) *The Nature, Extent, and Importance of Instinctual Experience in the Human Personality.* We have now investigated Freud's view of the personality and its complex functionings sufficiently to discuss the general nature of instinctual experience and the extent and importance which is attributed to this experience in the Freudian system. Nothing at this stage, however, can be said about the particular instincts which are at work. As we shall see, Freud treats only the sexual instinct in detail, and we shall claim when we come to his classifications of the

instincts that his work fails to give an adequate enumeration of the human instincts, though it could have been expected to succeed in this task. Here we must concentrate on the general considerations as to the nature and extent of instinctual experience which emerge from Freud's work.

The instincts are held to be (1) innate compulsive appetites or urges, arising internally and therefore comprising necessitous demands upon the organism, (2) qualitatively distinct in feeling, (3) aiming at satisfaction by means of certain objects in the outer world, (4) involving a specific energy (the impetus), and (5) being directly correlated with specific somatic processes or organic sources. The Id, comprising all these instinctual strivings, is by far the most massive element of the human 'psyche', and the mental processes stemming from these strivings are held to occur primarily at the level of the unconscious. In the Id and at the unconscious level of mental functioning, the instinctual striving for satisfaction is supreme and is governed entirely by (a) the Nirvana-Principle—the aim of reducing and, if possible, extinguishing tension and excitation, and (b) the Pleasure-Principle—the aim of achieving satisfaction and avoiding frustration. Governed by these two principles, there is a free proliferation of mental processes involving direct cathexis with concrete perceptual images; a cathexis which is easily and freely displaced and directed to other objects when any obstacle to the former object is encountered, and involving symbolisation and the formation of phantasies in accordance with the striving of the wish-impulses. In man, two major points help to account for this freedom of cathexis and this 'wild' proliferation of phantasy life and substitute gratification. In the first place, the human child is *completely* dependent upon its parents for the satisfaction of its needs during a long period of infancy, and this dependence gives rise to a strong love-relationship (which we shall discuss in detail later). In the second place, Freud holds that neither the *objects* nor the *behavioural-mechanisms* appropriate to the instinctual urges are established by heredity as 'automatisms' in man (in contrast with the lower animals). Thus, in the realm of early 'psychic reality' there is a relatively free cathexis in the Id and in the unconscious towards any object, symbol, or phantasy which appears to offer instinctual gratification. On the other hand, the way in which the instincts can achieve real gratification in relation to actual objects in the external world (by means of appropriate behaviour towards these objects) has to be painfully learned by the emerging Ego, which, in view of external circumstances, has to exert some measure of control over the discharge of the instincts; holding them at bay, and, in extreme situations, repressing them and thereby giving rise to anxiety.

The Ego has to *learn* how to react satisfactorily to the many features of the external world in order to achieve instinctual gratification. This learning, however, is not a simple cognitive process but a complex process of accommodation which takes place very largely upon the unconscious and perceptual levels and mainly involves *affective* processes, as contrasted with the *conceptual-ideational* learning process (involving the logical ordering of knowledge, etc.) which takes place later and which is of relatively minor importance. This is a point of the utmost importance which we shall elaborate presently.

The Id, then, is the most massive element of the human psyche, and is dominated by the instinctual strivings and the mental processes stemming from them at the unconscious level. But this is not all. Freud holds that the instinctual tendencies of the Id set all the major ends of human activity, and that even such activities as are involved in Religion, and Art, can be considered as 'substitute-gratifications' following upon the part-suppression of the instincts. Thus, even the Ego (whose activities comprise reason and the more conscious aspects of learning) is largely dominated by the task of serving the instinctual demands, by learning to deal adequately with the complex features of the physical and cultural environment. Further than this, in Freud's view, the whole fabric of human civilisation (physical, artistic, religious, moral)—one might even say the very *existence* of *social* life—is based upon the part-suppression of the instincts; and its *continued* existence rests upon such suppression and the energy which is thereby released for these various 'sublimated' activities. Even the moral element in human society, in the parent, and thence in the personality of the child (the Super-Ego), is held to be the outcome of suppressing those instinctual tendencies which give rise to the Oedipus Complex; and its chief function always remains the inhibition of instinctual tendencies and gratifications. The formation of individual character, too (e.g. the introjection into the Ego of id-abandoned object-choices) is held to be the outcome of instinctual impulses and their vicissitudes.

According to Psycho-Analytic theory, then, the instincts play a very far-reaching and overwhelmingly important part in human life: both in the development of the individual personality and in the many manifestations of social life. A vast area of experience, the basic ends of activity, the shaping of individual character, the nature of moral conflict and moral striving, the nature of social ties and social feeling, and the energy which supports and makes possible the continuity of social life: all these features of human nature are held to be closely and significantly related to the instincts.

Before leaving this discussion of the nature and extent of instinctual experience in man, we must elaborate the point we raised earlier concerning the ways in which the individual accommodates himself, especially during the earliest years of his life, to the features of the physical and social environment.

According to Freud, this early process of adaptation to the demands of things, people, and permitted behaviour, in the environment in order to secure a modicum of actual instinctual gratification, involves the operation of 'mechanisms' which are not *themselves* learned. They are better described as 'mechanisms of adjustment to stress' and are the outcome, fundamentally, of *affective* conflicts. In a word, Freud's treatment emphasises the utmost importance of the *affective* aspects of human experience for our understanding of the process of *learning*.

It is of great interest to recall what the earlier writers had to say on their concept of 'instinct-meaning' or 'instinct-interest', and their view that, following upon such primary instinct-interests, learning on the perceptual level took place essentially in the sphere of practical activity in accordance with feelings of satisfaction or dissatisfaction (the 'psychological values'). At this level the accommodation of the individual to situations in the environment was achieved not by the formation of conceptual inferences or of conscious 'apprehensions' of the relation between himself and the separate features of the situations encountered, but by the formation of habitual reactions and sentiments which were established in accordance with satisfying or unsatisfying feeling-states. Lloyd Morgan, Hobhouse, and Drever explicitly held that much of human learning took place upon this level, and their comments on this whole question are highly relevant to our present discussion.[1]

One of the greatest contributions of Freud is that he has given us a detailed account of how this perceptual affective process of learning, of accommodation to the environment, takes place in the human individual. He has given us a different and far more elaborate account of this non-ideational process of accommodation—which the earlier writers had treated in their own way. Having provided a description of the instinctual experience of man, and having stressed its far-reaching influence and importance in the personality, Freud then provides us with this *Learning Theory* (though it has not been called such) which describes those mechanisms—themselves unlearned—by means of which the vicissitudes encountered by the instincts are resolved; which describes the ways in which the human individual, with all his persistent, inescapable instinctual cravings, adjusts himself to the demands of the physical and social environment.

Our account of the nature and extent of instinctual experience in man

[1]Lloyd Morgan, pp. 37-39; James Drever, p. 59.

must include at least some mention of these mechanisms, which are so closely related to the strivings of the instincts. It must be emphasised that whilst these mechanisms are held to operate throughout the lifetime of the individual, the more important vicissitudes of the instincts and the most fundamental accommodations thus rendered necessary occur in the earliest years of life. This early period, the conflicts then encountered, and the 'mechanisms' then called into play, are therefore held to be of the very greatest importance as comprising the basic formative situation in the development of the personality. The pattern of mental adjustment established during this period constitutes the main determining influence upon later personality trends, and, indeed, on the later more rational processes of the mind. Here again, we cannot but be impressed by the tremendous importance which is attributed to the instincts and their vicissitudes in the Freudian theory of the human personality.

Firstly, we might deal with those mechanisms stemming directly from the striving for gratification of the instincts.

Displacement, refers to the free 'switching'.of the instincts from one pathway of discharge to another, and to the way in which the cathexis directed towards one object can, when any obstacle to gratification arises, be easily diverted to another object.

Transference is a similar mechanism, but involves the Ego more, and refers to the way in which the out-flowing of narcissistic libido towards an object (e.g. falling in love) can be transferred to another object.[1] By and large, Freud uses this concept with reference to the analytic situation, when, during the course of analysis, the patient comes to transfer to the analyst the love or hatred which had been directed to the actual loved or hated objects of his infantile conflict-situation. Some degree of, or capacity for, displacement and transference is considered to be necessary for mental health, and the mechanism which might be said to be the opposite of these is:

Fixation: 'a close attachment of the instinct to its object', or the inability to give up a particular object in connection with which an early gratification has been achieved. Such early 'points of fixation' are held to be of importance in establishing personality-traits, and are also of importance in understanding symptom-formation in the neuroses (the 'choice of neurosis').

Regression is the tendency, in the face of a severe conflict-situation, to fly back to an earlier constellation of feelings; some earlier condition of satisfaction; that is to say—to one of the 'fixation-points' mentioned

---

[1]Using the terms of the earlier writers, we might say that 'Displacement' refers to the 'Impulse', and 'Transference' to the 'Sentiment'.

above. Such regression is *forced upon* neurotics (i.e. it is pathological), and it is in this connection that a knowledge of the 'fixation-points' is of use in understanding the causation of the particular neurosis.

Symbolisation is that process of association in the unconscious whereby one object comes to represent another, or other objects, and therefore serves as a 'symbol' towards which several instinctual tendencies, through displacement, can be directed in seeking gratification. It is emphasised that, in the unconscious, the similarities between objects thus yielding a symbol which can gratify many wish-impulses are not such as would be recognised by the conscious ideational processes of the Ego. A closely related mechanism is:

Condensation: a process whereby one such symbol or idea can sum up several other ideas, and thus attract to itself the cathexes previously directed towards these separate ideas.

Unconscious Phantasy can, very briefly, be said to be the proliferation of the unconscious mental processes, taking place in the realm of inner 'psychic reality', and employing the various mechanisms which have been mentioned so far, in accordance with the wish-impulses stemming from the instincts. A similar mechanism is the:

Dream-Work, which also makes use of displacement, symbolisation, condensation, phantasy, and so on. When the Ego has relaxed its control over the instincts (in sleep), the cravings of the Id for satisfaction, for 'wish-fulfilment', are manifested in dreams, which involve symbolic, condensed, pictorial representations of objects and situations and sequences of 'dramatic scenes'. The Ego, however, does not withdraw control altogether, and is still held to exercise some degree of censorship even in sleep.

All the above mechanisms are the outcome of the striving for direct, or substitute, gratification on the part of the instincts. There are other mechanisms which represent the Ego's 'modes of defence' in dealing with its three-fold task.

We have mentioned Freud's view that the organism distinguishes between 'outer' and 'inner' stimuli. Outer stimuli can be escaped, or dealt with by learning how to manipulate them, whereas, in the case of inner stimuli, 'no action of flight avails against them'.

Projection is the mechanism whereby whatever is found to be troublesome or disquieting *within* is projected *outwards* and is then perceived as pertaining to things or people in the external environment. When the elements of conflict are perceived as 'coming from outside', the Ego then feels better able to deal with them since it is accustomed to dealing with external conditions. It is now the people outside who are blameworthy for harbouring these disquieting instinctual tendencies, not the Ego itself, so that any element of guilt is also escaped by attributing the 'fault' to others. The converse, one might say, of projection is:

Introjection: and this is the process whereby the Ego incorporates into itself those loved object-choices which, because of some obstacle or circumstance, have to be abandoned. Freud speaks of this process as though, when gratification in connection with a certain object proves to be impossible (when the object is 'lost' as far as the possibility of gratification is concerned) the Ego sets itself up as this object, or sets the object up as part of itself, and in this way attracts the libidinal cathexis to itself. It is in this way that Freud speaks of the Ego's character as consisting of 'id-abandoned object-choices'; and in this way that he conceives the setting up of the Ego-Ideal or Super-Ego—as the outcome of the introjection of the earliest object-choice: the parents.

Repression is the mechanism whereby the Ego rejects and keeps from consciousness any *idea* or *affect* against which it must protect itself in the face of the demands of the external world and the Super-Ego. Freud says in his earlier work that the Ego must keep certain instinctual manifestations from consciousness in view of (a) the strength of the instinct, and (b) its own weakness in the dangerous context of the outer world. Later, he stresses more and more that the chief cause of repression is the Super-Ego and the harsh criticism which it continually directs towards the Ego. These two sources of repression are brought together, however, by Freud's generalisation that repression occurs when 'the element of avoiding "pain" (increase of tension and mental conflict) shall have acquired more strength than the pleasure of gratification.' Freud thinks there are two aspects of repression. Firstly, the *idea*, or 'instinct-presentation', of an underlying instinctual impulse may be repressed. This may only constitute a partial or inadequate repression, as, driven into the unconscious, the instinctual tendency—employing the various mechanisms we have mentioned—will seek gratification by attaching itself to other (perhaps remotely-associated) ideas which will be continually striving to penetrate into consciousness. Secondly, the repression may be a repression of *affect*, and though it is difficult to follow Freud's suggestions as to the fate of the repressed affect, it seems that he holds this repression to be the chief cause of anxiety. One of the outcomes of repression, and the consequent conflict and anxiety in the personality is:

Conversion: the mechanism whereby the 'psychic content' of the repression is converted into physical or bodily manifestations. This mechanism is typical of hysteria, and, much more than the other mechanisms we have mentioned, is strictly pathological, and is therefore of minor interest to us here. A mechanism by means of which the Ego attempts to achieve something even more radical than repression is:

Undoing: which consists of the unconscious attempt to eliminate from the mind completely a past experience which has been intolerably 'painful' to the Ego; to 'blot it out of existence'. A similar mechanism is that of:

Isolation: whereby the memories of past conflict-experiences are deprived of their 'affective' (painful) aspects; leaving in the memory only ideas stripped of their emotional significance.

Reaction-Formation is the mechanism whereby the Ego attempts to reverse emotional attitudes and tendencies which persist in the unconscious. To give an example, a persisting infantile attitude of hatred and hostility towards a parent (say the father) may manifest itself as an excessive anxiety about him or an attitude of excessive devotion. Reaction-formations, however, are only 'appearances', and the actual impulses persist beneath these surface attitudes. A reaction-formation, might be regarded as a process of conveniently 'camouflaging' the true underlying motives.

Rationalisation is the outcome of the Ego's need to harmonise or integrate its activities on both the unconscious and conscious levels. In view of all that has been said with regard to the extraordinary ramifications of the unconscious mental processes, it is clear that the Ego cannot be aware of all the motives, with their manifold connections, which have provoked it to undertake certain activities; and indeed, many of these motives will have been repressed into the unconscious because of their incompatibility with the claims of the outside world and the Super-Ego. At the unconscious level of the Ego, then, the promptings to activity are non-rational and amoral. At the conscious level of activity, however, the Ego employs a body of ordered knowledge about the world and about its own place in the world, and insists upon rational consistency in establishing and practising this knowledge. Much of the activity of the Ego prompted by motives at the level of the unconscious will therefore conflict with the rational consistency demanded on the level of its conscious activity. Its actual behaviour will not always permit of an easy and evident rational explanation. Rationalisation is the name given to that process whereby the Ego *smoothes over*, or *evades* the irrationality and inconsistency of its *actual* motivation and behaviour (stemming from impulses and ideas at the level of the unconscious) by arriving at, or constructing, a tolerably coherent explanation to satisfy its conscious rational tendencies and to fit in with its conscious moral proprieties. We might say, simply, that Rationalisation is the way in which the Ego explains and justifies its own motives and activities satisfactorily to itself.

INSTINCTS IN PSYCHO-ANALYSIS 211

Finally, we can turn to three further mechanisms which are, perhaps, more important for our purposes: Idealisation, Sublimation, and Identification. As far as one can gather from Freud's writing:[1]

Idealisation stems fundamentally from primary narcissism. From the beginning, there is a core of self-love in the individual, from which centre, love later flows out towards object-choices. In Freud's terms: 'Thus we form a conception of an original libidinal cathexis of the Ego, part of which cathexis is later yielded up to objects, but which fundamentally persists and is related to the object-cathexes much as the body of a protoplasmic animalcule is related to the pseudopodia which it puts out.' When love flows out towards an object in an object-cathexis, the primary narcissism is to some extent impoverished, but an element of this narcissism is now transferred to the object and takes the form of 'over-estimation' of the qualities of character of the object. It is this over-estimation of the object which is given the name 'Idealization'. '. . . marked sexual over-estimation . . . is doubtless derived from the original narcissism of the child, now transferred to the sexual object. This sexual over-estimation is the origin of the peculiar state of being in love, a state suggestive of a neurotic compulsion, which is thus traceable to an impoverishment of the Ego in respect of libido in favour of the love-object.'[2] And again: 'Idealization is a process that concerns the *object*; by it that object, without any alteration in its nature, is aggrandized and exalted in the mind. . . . For example, the sexual over-estimation of an object is an idealization of it.'[3] Idealisation is also involved, however, in the process of introjection and the formation of the Ego-Ideal or Super-Ego. As the individual grows, his primary narcissism suffers a good many blows from the admonitions and corrections of others. We have seen how the earlier object-choices of the child, including these moral precepts and this 'over-estimation', are introjected and incorporated as part of the Ego. The child, therefore, now loves himself not 'as he actually is' but as 'what he ought to be'. 'To this ideal Ego', Freud says,[4] 'is now directed the self-love which the real Ego enjoyed in childhood. The narcissism seems to be now displaced on to this new ideal Ego, which, like the infantile Ego, deems itself the possessor of all perfections. As always where the libido is concerned, here again man has shown himself incapable of giving up a gratification he has once enjoyed. He is not willing to forgo his narcissistic perfection in his childhood; and if, as he develops, he is disturbed by the admonitions of others and his own critical judgment is awakened, he seeks to recover the early perfection, thus wrested from him, in the new form of

[1]'On Narcissism: an Introduction', *Collected Papers*, 1914, vol. iv, III.
[2]*Ibid.* p. 45.   [3]*Ibid.* p. 51.   [4]*Ibid.* p. 51.

an Ego-Ideal. That which he projects ahead of him as his ideal is merely his substitute for the lost narcissism of his childhood—the time when he was his own ideal.'

Freud distinguishes clearly between Idealisation and Sublimation. Sublimation is a process that concerns the *instinct*, whereas, in the way we have outlined, Idealisation is a process that concerns the *object*. The formation of the Ego-Ideal should not therefore be confounded, Freud emphasises, with Sublimation. The setting up of the Ego-Ideal *requires* sublimation, but cannot *enforce* it, and much conflict results from the incompatibility between the Ego-Ideal on the one hand and the capacity for sublimation on the other.

Sublimation is defined, 'as a process that concerns the object-libido and consists in the instinct's directing itself towards an aim other than, and remote from, that of sexual gratification; in this process the accent falls upon the deflection from the sexual aim.'[1] The sexual instinct is held to be extremely important in human life because of its 'capacity for sublimation'. The end achieved by the mechanism of sublimation, then, is that of deflecting an instinct from its appropriate aim, and it is often described as a process of 'de-sexualisation' or ' aim-inhibition'. When frustration results from the fact that the discharge of an instinct is prevented by some obstacle, this tension is reduced by the process of sublimation, whereby the instinctual tendency achieves gratification in connection with another, and perhaps remote, aim.

Identification is mentioned as a distinguishable mechanism by Freud, bnt it seems to overlap considerably with what we have described as Idealisation and Introjection. Whilst stating that Identification is, 'the earliest expression of an emotional tie with another person', and illustrating it as the boy's special interest in his father (his wish to be like his father) as distinct from the 'true object-cathexis' which is developed towards his mother, Freud says, 'We may say simply that he takes his father as his ideal.' In view of what has been said earlier as to the origin of idealisation (the over-estimation resulting from the narcissistic component in the object-choice) Freud now seems to hold that, in this process of Identification, there is a more simple and direct setting up of an ideal. Similarly, Freud speaks of Identification, in another sense, in precisely the same way as he speaks of the 'introjection into the Ego of object-choices'. And, thirdly, he suggests that identification can be established when a common quality is perceived to be shared by the individual and some other person or persons. In this latter sense, children will identify themselves with each other in respect of their common position with regard to the parents; and members of an adult group will

[1] 'On Narcissism: an Introduction', *Collected Papers*, 1914, vol. iv, III, p. 51.

identify themselves with each other in respect of their common relation to the leader of the group.

'What we have learned from these three sources may be summarised as follows', Freud says. 'First, identification is the original form of emotional tie with an object; secondly, in a regressive way it becomes a substitute for a libidinal object tie, as it were by means of the introjection of the object into the Ego; and thirdly, it may arise with every new perception of a common quality shared with some other person who is not an object of the sexual instinct. The more important this common quality is, the more successful may this partial identification become, and it may thus represent the beginning of a new tie.'

It is clear from this, that Identification cannot be strictly separated from other mechanisms we have described. Essentially, however, according to Freud, Identification is the name given to that process whereby a person attempts to mould his own Ego, 'after the fashion of one that has been taken as a "model".'[1]

In concluding this account of the 'mental mechanisms', it must be emphasised that, as presented above, these mechanisms are not intended as *explanations* of the process whereby the individual accommodates himself to the demands of the environment, but are simply *descriptive concepts* indicating the particular ways in which this process of accommodation takes place. The *explanation* of the mechanisms and their operation lies in the detailed consideration of the nature of the personality (the Unconscious, Preconscious, and Conscious; the Id, Ego, and Super-Ego; the Nirvana-Principle, Pleasure-Principle, and Reality-Principle) and the demands of the external environment in the context of which the individual has to seek a balanced and satisfactory continuity of experience and behaviour.

(5) *The Nature and Importance of the Sexual Instinct.* Most of the evidence which Freud brings up in support of his account of instinctual experience is in connection with the sexual instinct alone. Indeed, although Freud often speaks about the 'Ego-Instincts' as opposed to the sexual instincts, and of the 'Life-Instincts' as including instincts of self-preservation, he does not, at any point, attempt a detailed account of these other instincts. We shall turn to this inadequacy of Freud's treatment later. Meanwhile, we must note that Freud laid emphasis upon the sexual instinct quite consciously and purposefully. Always aware of the existence of other instinctual tendencies, he did not undertake a detailed account of them for the simple reason that Psycho-Analysis had not succeeded in establishing any far-reaching knowledge of them, whereas,

[1]Chapter VII on 'Identification' in *Group Psychology and the Analysis of the Ego*, 1921.

in the case of the sexual instinct, Psycho-Analytic work had revealed a good deal which Freud considered to be of great importance. Moreover, his psycho-analytic experience had led Freud to the conviction that a knowledge of the sexual instinct was of the utmost importance for an understanding of the aetiology of the neuroses.

'The development of this line of investigation, however (the psycho-analytic investigation of mental disturbances), has necessarily produced hitherto information of a more or less definite nature only in regard to the sexual instincts, for it is this group in particular which can be observed in isolation, as it were, in the psycho-neuroses.'[1] 'The greater part of what we know about Eros (the Life-Instincts)—that is, about its exponent, the libido—has been gained from the study of the sexual function. . . .'[2]

Before describing the development of the sexual instinct, it is important that we should be clear as to what is implied in the word 'sexual' in the Freudian account. Freud himself provides us with a perfectly clear and explicit statement:

'The nature of my extension of the concept of sexuality . . . is of a two-fold kind. (1) Sexuality is divorced from its too close connection with the genitals, and is regarded as a more comprehensive bodily function having pleasure as its goal and only secondarily coming to serve the ends of reproduction. (2) The sexual impulses are regarded as including all those merely affectionate and friendly impulses to which usage applies the exceedingly ambiguous word "Love".'[3]

Sexuality is extended to embrace not only what is involved in adult sexual intercourse, but also certain infantile impulses seeking the pleasurable stimulation of particular erotogenic zones. Tender feelings, feelings of affection, and all that is popularly implied by the word 'love', are also sexual for Freud since he believes that these affectionate impulses derive from original erotic impulses. It is important to bear this extension closely in mind throughout our description of the development of the sexual instinct, for (simply because of the customary ways in which we use the words 'sex' and 'love') many of the points which Freud makes can often be better understood if we think in terms of profound love-attachments or love-relationships rather than 'object-cathexes' in connection with 'sexual gratification'.

Two further points in connection with this extension of the term 'sexuality' require elaboration here.

Firstly, Freud insists that we must recognise the existence of *infantile*

[1] *Instincts and their Vicissitudes.*
[2] *An Outline of Psycho-Analysis.*   [3] *An Autobiographical Study.*

sexuality. In infancy, sexual excitation is not closely correlated at the outset with the genitals, but with other erotogenic zones of the body—the lips and mouth, the anal zone, and only later the genitals. The impulses aiming at pleasure through the stimulation of these erotogenic zones (impulses, incidentally, which Freud conceives as single and independent impulses in the early stages of infancy, coming into operation with the basic instincts upon which they rest: sucking (feeding), defecation, etc.) are termed '*component instincts*', and we shall enumerate these presently.

The second point of importance Freud stresses is the fact that the sexual instinct of man develops in two 'waves' or 'thrusts', with an interval of relative inactivity between them. The first period is that of infantile sexuality which comes to an end in the fourth or fifth year of the child's life. This is followed by a period of relative quiescence, called 'The Latency Period', which lasts until the onset of puberty and during which reaction-formations to the infantile sexual tendencies are set up. The second 'wave' of the sexual instinct is manifested in puberty, and it is at this stage that the adult sexual impulse proper, and the full distinction between male and female, is established. Freud maintains that the earlier experiences of the individual re-emerge in this later stage, and exert a determining influence upon the course of adult sexual life and upon the choice of a sexual object. The earlier infantile impulses and love-relationships are re-awakened, and a conflict ensues between these and the Super-Ego and those inhibitions which have been established during the Latency Period.

Perhaps we should mention, before going on to describe the development of the sexual instinct, that—in connection with this point—both Freud and Ernest Jones seem to attach some importance to a biological hypothesis, '. . . that man is descended from a mammal which reached sexual maturity at the age of five, but that some great external influence was brought to bear upon the species and interrupted the straight line of development of sexuality. This may also have been related to some other transformations in the sexual life of man as compared with that of animals, such as the suppression of the periodicity of the libido and the exploitation of the part played by menstruation in the relation between the sexes.'[1]

A brief and clear account of the development of infantile sexuality is given by Freud:

'The sexual function . . . is in existence from the very beginning of the individual's life, though at first it is assimilated to the other vital functions and does not become independent of them until later; it has

[1] *An Outline of Psycho-Analysis*, p. 11.

to pass through a long and complicated process of development before it becomes what we are familiar with as the normal sexual life of the adult. It begins by manifesting itself in the activity of a whole number of *component instincts*. These are dependent upon *erotogenic zones* in the body; some of them make their appearance in pairs of opposite impulses (such as sadism and masochism or the impulse to look and to be looked at); *they operate independently of one another* in their search for pleasure, and they find their object for the most part in the subject's own body. (Elsewhere—in the paper, 'Instincts and their Vicissitudes', Freud tells us, 'the aim which each strives to attain is "organ-pleasure".') 'Thus to begin with they are non-centralised and predominantly *auto-erotic*. Later they begin to be *co-ordinated*: a first step of organization is reached under the dominance of the *oral* components, an *anal-sadistic* stage follows, and it is only after the third stage has at last been reached that the primacy of the *genitals* is established and that the sexual function begins to serve the ends of reproduction.'[1]

Earlier, in 'Instincts and their Vicissitudes', Freud holds that these component instincts are supported 'upon the instincts of self-preservation, from which they only gradually detach themselves. . . .' It appears, then, that there is an erotic component attached to the original activities of sucking and defecation (which are 'self-preservative' instincts in Freud's terms) and that these erotic excitations, involved in the functionings of these instincts, become detached from them (i.e. are subsequently sought for 'organ-pleasure' alone), and become components of the sexual instinct.

Similarly, Freud holds that the earliest object-choices (love-attachments) of the infant are directed towards the person—usually the mother—in relationship with whom these self-preservative instincts and their erotic components are satisfied. 'The first auto-erotic sexual gratifications are experienced in connection with vital functions in the service of self-preservation. The sexual instincts are at the outset supported upon the ego-instincts; only later do they become independent of these, and even then we have an indication of that original dependence in the fact that those persons who have to do with the feeding, care, and protection of the child become his earliest sexual objects: that is to say, in the first instance the mother or her substitute.'[2]

The description of the organisation of the infantile component instincts given above requires further qualification. It is not enough to

---

[1] *An Autobiographical Study*, p. 62.
[2] 'On Narcissism: an Introduction', *Collected Papers*, 1914, vol. iv, iii. Freud terms this kind of object-choice, the 'Anaclitic Type' (the 'leaning-up-against' type).

say that the final organisation of infantile sexuality centres about the primacy of the genitals.

In his paper on 'the Infantile Genital Organization of the Libido', Freud comments as follows:

'The approximation of childhood-sexuality to that of the adult . . . is not limited solely to the establishment of the object-attachment. Even if perfect concentration of the component-impulses under the primacy of the genitals is not attained, at any rate at the height of the development of childhood-sexuality the functioning of the genitals and the interest in them reaches predominant significance, which comes little short of that reached in maturity. The *difference* between the two—the "infantile-genital-organization" and the final genital organization of the adult—constitutes at the same time the main characteristic of the infantile form, namely, that for both sexes in childhood only one kind of genital organ comes into account—the male. The primacy reached is, therefore, not a primacy of the *genital*, but of the *phallus*.'[1]

This primacy of the phallus is of great significance, Freud holds, for understanding the Castration Complex and the passing of the Oedipus Complex—to which we shall refer presently. At this point, it is of interest to note the 'polarities' which are involved in the development of the sexual instinct according to Freud. In the first place we have seen that the early auto-erotic state of the child gives way to later object-choices, which gives the polarity, *Subject-Object*. In the anal-sadistic stage there is still no distinction between maleness and femaleness, and the polarity is that of *Activity-Passivity*. In the infantile genital stage, 'maleness has come to life, but no femaleness. The antithesis runs: *a male genital organ or a castrated condition*.' It is not until puberty, the stage of the complete development of the sexual instinct, that the polarity of sexuality coincides with *male and female*.

The central phenomenon of the sexual period of early childhood is the Oedipus Complex, and this must be understood not simply because it *is* the central phenomenon, but also because of its importance in tracing and understanding the formation of the Super-Ego. The earliest emotional ties of the child comprise an object-cathexis towards the mother (a direct love-attachment) and an identification with the father. The earliest object-choice of the child, Freud tells us, is an 'incestuous' one. As the child grows, the father, with his admonitions and prohibitions, becomes, more and more, an obstacle standing between himself and his mother. Hence develops the ambivalence of feeling (of love and of hatred) towards the father. At the age of four or five, at the

[1]'The Infantile Genital Organization of the Libido' (A Supplement to the Theory of Sexuality), *Collected Papers*, 1923, vol. ii, xx.

infantile-genital stage—the Phallic stage—the emotional ties of the child
are complicated by the emergence of the Castration Complex. With the
primacy of the phallus, in various direct and indirect ways, threats of
castration arise. The child's final belief in his fear of the loss of his penis
is, Freud thinks, the sight of the female genitalia. We must remember
that there is no full distinction between male and female at this stage,
only the antithesis between the possession of a male genital organ or a
castrated condition. The gratification of the child's love now appears to
him to involve the danger of castration, and this constitutes the chief
factor in the passing of the Oedipus Complex. 'If the gratification
desired in consequence of the love is to cost the child his penis, a conflict
must arise between the narcissistic interest in this part of the body and
the libidinal cathexis of the parent-objects. Normally, in this conflict the
first of these forces triumphs; the child's ego turns away from the
Oedipus Complex.'[1]

The way in which the Oedipus Complex is overcome involves the
setting up of the Super-Ego, and it is of interest to note Freud's description at this point of his speculation as he makes clear the part played by
the Castration Complex and the relation of the whole process to the
Latency Period.

'I have described elsewhere the way by which this aversion is accomplished. The object-cathexes are given up and replaced by identification.
The authority of the father or the parents is introjected into the Ego and
there forms the kernel of the Super-Ego, which takes its severity from
the father, perpetuates his prohibition against incest, and so insures the
ego against a recurrence of the libidinal object-cathexes. The libidinal
trends belonging to the Oedipus Complex are in part de-sexualised and
sublimated, which probably happens with every transformation into
identification; in part they are inhibited in their aim and changed into
affectionate feelings. The whole process, on the one hand, preserves
the genital organ, wards off the danger of losing it; on the other hand,
it paralyses it, takes away its function from it. This process introduces
the latency period which now interrupts the child's sexual development.'[2]

At the end of the period of infantile sexuality, then, there is a close
relationship between several factors: the primacy of the phallus in the
infantile sexual organisation, the Oedipus Complex, the threat of
Castration, the formation of the Super-Ego, and the beginning of the
Latency Period.

[1]'The Passing of the Oedipus Complex', *Collected Papers*, 1924, vol. ii, XXIII.
[2]*Ibid.*

It should be mentioned here, in order to do full justice to Freud's view, that the development and the passing of the Oedipus Complex are regarded as being much more complicated than the simple description we have given. The Oedipus Complex as we have described it (an ambivalent attitude to the father and an object-relation of a purely affectionate kind to the mother) is, Freud tells us, the most simple example of the Oedipus Complex. As a rule, the development of the complex is complicated by the degree of bisexuality of each individual. The relative strength of the masculine and feminine sexual dispositions in the individual determines whether—on the passing of the Oedipus Complex —the predominant identification will be with the father or with the mother. 'Closer study usually discloses the more complete Oedipus Complex, which is twofold, positive and negative, and is due to the bisexuality originally present in children: that is to say, a boy has not merely an ambivalent attitude towards his father and an affectionate object-relation towards his mother, but at the same time he also behaves like a girl and displays an affectionate feminine attitude to his father and a corresponding hostility and jealousy towards his mother. It is this complicating element introduced by bisexuality that makes it so difficult to obtain a clear view of the facts in connection with the earliest object-choices and identifications, and still more difficult to describe them intelligibly. . . .'[1] 'As the Oedipus Complex dissolves, the four trends of which it consists will group themselves in such a way as to produce a father-identification and a mother-identification. . . . The relative intensity of the two identifications in any individual will reflect the preponderance in him of one or other of the two sexual predispositions.' Concluding these remarks, Freud says: 'The broad general outcome of the sexual phase governed by the Oedipus Complex may, therefore, be taken to be the forming of a precipitate in the Ego, consisting of these two identifications in some way combined together. This modification of the Ego retains its special position; it stands in contrast to the other constituents of the Ego in the form of an Ego-Ideal or Super-Ego.'

During the latency period reaction-formations are established as the individual encounters social attitudes and the process of education. With the onset of puberty comes the completion of the development of the sexual instinct with the emergence of the adult sexual impulse proper and the full sexual discrimination between male and female, though, even during this period, complications arise because of the re-activation of the infantile impulses and object-relationships and the conflicts which ensue between these and the dogmas of the Super-Ego and the subsequently established reaction-formations.

[1] For these quotations see *The Ego and the Id*, 1923, pp. 40-44.

The functioning of the mental mechanisms which we described earlier relates predominantly to this development of the sexual instinct (including the component-instincts) and the vicissitudes which it undergoes. We need not repeat what we have had to say about these mechanisms, but we might illustrate their relevance to the sexual instinct in particular by emphasising one instance—the close relationship between *phantasy* and the development of the sexual instinct as described above.

In the development of the personality, the Reality Principle begins to exert a governing influence on the mental processes (largely in defence of the Pleasure Principle) as the necessitous demands of the external world are encountered. Because of its peculiar long-drawn-out and delayed development, the sexual instinct is, in this connection, something of an exception to the rule. The demands of external reality do not act so forcefully upon it until a relatively late stage, and it is therefore peculiarly susceptible to extensive and continued phantasy formation. In 'Formulations Regarding the Two Principles in Mental Functioning', Freud writes as follows:

'The supersession of the Pleasure Principle by the Reality Principle with all the mental consequences of this . . . is not in reality accomplished all at once; nor does it take place simultaneously along the whole line. For while this development is going on in the ego-instincts, the sexual instincts become detached from them in very significant ways. The sexual instincts at first behave auto-erotically; they find their satisfaction in the child's own body and therefore do not come into the situation of frustration which enforces the installation of the reality principle. Then when later on they begin to find an object, this development undergoes a long interruption in the latency period, which postpones sexual development until puberty. These two factors—auto-eroticism and latency period—bring about the result that the mental development of the sexual instincts is delayed and remains far longer under the supremacy of the pleasure principle, from which in many people it is never able to withdraw itself at all. . . . In consequence of these conditions there arises a closer connection, on the one hand, between the sexual instincts and phantasy, and, on the other hand, between the ego-instincts and the activities of consciousness. . . . The perpetuated activity of auto-eroticism makes possible a long retention of the easier momentary and phantastic satisfaction in regard to the sexual object, in place of real satisfaction in regard to it, the latter requiring effort and delay. In the realm of phantasy, repression remains all-powerful; it brings about the inhibition of ideas "in statu nascendi" before they can be consciously noticed, should cathexis of them be likely to occasion the release of "pain". This is the weak place of our mental organization, which can be utilized to bring back under the supremacy of the pleasure principle thought-processes which had already become rational. An essential part of the mental predisposition to neurosis thus lies in the delayed training of the sexual instincts in the observation of reality and, further, in the conditions which make this delay possible.'

All that we have said earlier as to the proliferation of unconscious mental processes (phantasy-formation, symbolisation, condensation, displacement, transference, fixation, regression—and even such pro- cesses as idealisation, identification, and sublimation, and the setting up of the Super-Ego) can be seen to refer predominantly to the complex development of the sexual instinct. Indeed, it is not too much to say that, according to the Freudian system, it is the peculiar nature and develop- ment of the sexual instinct in man, which, coupled with the long period of utter dependence of the human child, gives rise to such an extra- ordinary capacity for profound love-attachments and varied sublimated love-tendencies, and which forms the fundamental basis of all the varieties of social feeling to be observed in human life.

This emphasis on the importance in human life of the sexual instinct, and this elucidation of the ways in which the deep-rooted love-tendencies of the human individual can be deflected into so many and various affective manifestations, is perhaps one of the most important findings which emerges from the work of Psycho-Analysis. In concluding our account of the sexual instinct, therefore, we must indicate the degree of importance which Freud himself attributes to it.

Freud has often been adversely criticised because of his insistence on the basic importance of the sexual instinct, and has been charged with ignoring more obvious social factors in the causation of 'modern nervousness'. These charges are not well founded. In his paper on ' "Civilized" Sexual Morality and Modern Nervousness', Freud mentions many attempts to explain modern nervousness in terms of the complicated changes in the social fabric of modern society, and perhaps the most revealing passage is his quotation from the work of W. Erb.

'. . . the extraordinary achievements of modern times, the discoveries and inventions in every field, the maintenance of progress in the face of increasing competition, have been gained and can be held only by great mental effort. The demands on the ability of the individual in the struggle for existence have enormously increased, and he can meet them only by putting forward all his mental powers; at the same time the needs of the individual, and the demand for enjoyment have increased in all circles;

unprecedented luxury is displayed by classes hitherto wholly unaccustomed to any such thing; irreligion, discontent, and covetousness are spreading widely through every degree of society. The illimitable expansion of communication brought about by means of the network of telegraphs and telephones encircling the world has completely altered the conditions of business and travel. All is hurry and agitation: night is used for travel, day for business; even "holiday" trips keep the nervous system on the rack; important political, industrial, financial crises carry excitement into far wider circles than formerly; participation in political life has become quite general; political, religious, and social struggles, party-interests, electioneering, endless associations of every kind heat the imagination and force the mind to ever greater effort, encroaching on the hours for recreation, sleep and rest; life in large cities is constantly becoming more elaborate and more restless. The exhausted nerves seek recuperation in increased stimulation, in highly-seasoned pleasures only thereby to become more exhausted than before; modern literature is concerned predominantly with the most questionable problems, those which stir all the passions—sensuality and the craving for pleasure, contempt of every fundamental ethical principle and every ideal demand; it brings pathological types, together with sexual psychopathic, revolutionary and other problems, before the mind of the reader. Our ears are excited and over-stimulated by large doses of insistent and noisy music. The theatres captivate all the senses with their exciting modes of presentation; the creative arts turn also by preference to the repellent, ugly, and suggestive, and do not hesitate to set before us in revolting realism the ugliest aspect offered by actuality.'[1]

Written in 1893, this highly coloured passage could hardly contain more observations, on the sociological level, as to the complicated nature of modern social life. It is also highly applicable to contemporary conditions, and might have been written yesterday.

The important point for us, is that Freud never suggests that such observations of modern society are in any sense fallacious. All he maintains is that they are not, in themselves, adequate to explain the facts of neurotic disturbance.

'Of these and many other similarly-worded opinions I have to observe, not that they are erroneous, but that they show themselves insufficient to explain in detail the manifestations of nervous disturbance, and that they leave out of account the most important aetiological factor. If one passes over the less definite forms of "nervousness" and considers the actual forms of nervous disease, the injurious influence of

[1]'Civilized Sexual Morality and Modern Nervousness', *Collected Papers*, 1908, vol. ii, VII.

culture reduces itself in all essentials to the undue suppression of the sexual life in civilized peoples (or classes) as a result of the"civilized" sexual morality which prevails among them.' And it is emphasised again that the psychoneuroses, 'originate in the sexual needs of unsatisfied people, and represent a kind of substitute for gratification of them.'

When outlining the nature and importance of the sexual instinct, Freud suggests that it is probably more strongly developed in man than in most of the higher animals, and that, 'it is certainly more constant, since it has almost entirely overcome the periodicity belonging to it in animals.' Furthermore, 'It places an extraordinary amount of energy at the disposal of "cultural" activities; and this because of a particularly marked characteristic that it possesses, namely, the ability to displace its aim without materially losing in intensity.' In discussing the process of sublimation, Freud makes the point that—when the sexual instinct matures in the stage of puberty—many of the earlier auto-erotic (self-obtained) sexual gratifications are subordinated and checked as being useless for the reproductive functions, and 'in favourable cases' may thereafter be diverted to sublimation. 'The energies available for "cultural" development are thus in great part won through suppression of the so-called perverse elements of sexual excitation.'

We need not dwell further upon the fact that the sexual instinct is the source of sublimated social feelings. Briefly, however, we might show how important a factor it is considered to be as a determining influence in the formation of personality as a whole.

To take the simplest case first, Freud maintains that a *fixation* at any stage in the development of the sexual instinct has an important determining influence on the later development of the personality, and his chief example is that of a fixation at the stage of anal-erotism which gives rise to the three character-traits of orderliness, parsimony, and obstinacy in the later personality. Freud thinks that further investigation might reveal other connections between early fixations and later character-traits. 'One ought to consider whether other types of character do not also show a connection with the excitability of particular erotogenic zones. As yet I am aware only of the intense, "burning" ambition of those who formerly suffered from enuresis. At any rate, one can give a formula for the formation of the ultimate character from the constituent character-traits: the permanent character-traits are either unchanged perpetuations of the original impulses, sublimations of them, or reaction-formulations against them.'[1]

Elsewhere,[2] Freud stresses the fact that the repression of the sexual

[1]'Character and Anal Erotism', *Collected Papers*, vol. ii, IV.
[2]'Civilized Sexual Morality and Modern Nervousness', *Collected Papers*, 1908, vol. ii, VII.

instinct is not simply a 'once-for-all' accomplishment, but that the resistance involved necessitates a continuous expenditure of energy which impoverishes the individual for social and cultural activity. Intense repression 'inwardly stunts and outwardly cripples' the individual, and this tension is aggravated by the fact that, '. . . in the great majority of cases the fight against sexuality absorbs the available energy of the character, and this at the very time when the young man is in need of all his powers to gain his share of worldly goods and his position in the community'. The way in which an individual faces and deals with these complications arising in sexual matters, is often 'a prototype for the whole of his other modes of reaction to life. A man who has shown determination in possessing himself of his love-object has our confidence in his success in regard to other aims as well. On the other hand, a man who abstains, for whatever reasons, from satisfying his strong sexual instinct, will also assume a conciliatory and resigned attitude in other paths of life, rather than a powerfully active one.'

A further illustration of the way in which a mode of dealing with the sexual instinct may extend as a mode of reaction in other spheres of behaviour is that in which sexual abstinence is maintained by the employment of auto-erotic activities, as, for example, masturbation. 'The character is undermined in more ways than one by this indulgence', says Freud, 'first because it shows the way to attain important aims in an otiose manner, instead of by energetic effort, in line with the view that the attitude to sex is the prototype of the attitude to life; and, secondly, because in the phantasies accompanying this gratification, the sexual object is exalted to a degree which is seldom to be reproduced in reality. A witty writer (K. Kraus) has, as it were, expressed this truth paradoxically in the cynical saying: "Coitus is merely an unsatisfactory substitute for onanism!" '[1]

Enough has been said to show the importance attributed to the sexual instinct, both as the source of the varieties of social feeling, and as a far-reaching determining influence in the formation of individual character. Psycho-Analysis provides us with detailed knowledge of the sexual instinct alone, but this knowledge is of the greatest importance.

We might summarise as follows.

The human infant, for a considerable period (a longer period than is the case in any other animal species) is utterly dependent upon his parents for the satisfaction of all his instinctual tendencies with their erotic components. In the absence of automatic behavioural mechan-

---

[1]Recalling the concepts of Ethology, we might note in this connection a remark by Konrad Lorenz to the effect that much so-called human 'vice' consists of the search for 'Super-Normal Sign-Stimuli'.

isms established by heredity, modes of behaviour appropriate to the satisfaction of the instincts have to be gradually and tentatively learned by the Ego—that is to say, they have to be learned as the consciousness of self emerges during the process of growth, maturation, and accommodation to the environment. The sexual instinct develops over a long period in three more or less well-defined stages: firstly, the period of infantile sexuality up to the age of four or five, during which the gratification of the component-instincts is auto-erotic; secondly, the latency period; and thirdly, the final period of puberty during which the sexual instinct reaches maturity.

The long period of utter dependence, the early auto-eroticism, the lack of inherited behaviour-mechanisms, the latency period, and the delay in the necessity of coming to terms with the conditions of external reality, lead to at least three important consequences: (1) the pleasure principle continues to hold predominating sway over the desires for erotic gratification until a relatively late stage of development, giving rise to elaborate phantasy-formation and modes of substitute gratification which have a far-reaching influence upon the later, adult personality; (2) the individual develops the need for profound and satisfying love-attachments to such an extent that the history of this need for love and of the vicissitudes experienced in relation to the love-objects, can be regarded as the central phenomenon of his personality development, exerting an influence upon all other and later aspects of his activity; and (3) this need for love, strong as it is, when encountering obstacles and suffering repressions can be diverted towards other aims which may appear to be quite remote: for example, in the devotion to God and a religious cause, or to absorption in the creative process of painting or music. By means of sublimation, the love-tendencies of man can be transformed into affective social ties and related social activities; can be deflected towards various symbols in the individual's social environment: the King, Queen, or Royal Family (Patriotism and the service of one's country); the Cross of Christ (Religious faith and devotion to the Christian cause); or the Hammer and Sickle (Family and Class Loyalty and devotion to the ultimate attainment of the new society and the betterment of the lot of humanity). The sexual instinct and its derivatives are therefore of the utmost importance in human life.

In his account of the sexual instinct, Freud gives a most interesting explanation of the process whereby the instinctual vicissitudes lead to the establishment within the personality of *secondary impulses*, which, though *not* instincts proper, are yet derived from the instinctual demands and the conflicts which they encounter, and thereafter operate *as if they were* of an instinctive nature. To the personality they are, like the instincts themselves, compulsive demands arising (after introjection) internally, and constituting necessitous demands upon the Ego. Freud's elucidation of this process provides us with a most important account of the means whereby the socialisation of individuals and the continuity of the social tradition in any society is achieved.

(6) *The Nature and Importance of the Super-Ego.* The concept of the Super-Ego, describing the development of the 'secondary impulses' in the human personality, is of the very greatest importance for Social Psychology, and in this section we shall make qualifications and additions to what has been said earlier. But it is important, first of all, simply to emphasise this fact: that, born with certain instinctual tendencies, and encountering in the early family situation the value judgments of a particular society, the human personality develops within its own individual constitution 'secondary impulses' which are derived from and related to the social tradition of that society, which are largely the outcome of unconscious mental processes and experience on the perceptual plane, and which are compulsive and affective in nature rather than being consciously and rationally acquired.

In what follows, three points will be discussed. (1) We shall emphasise the fact that Freud conceived the commands and corrections of the parents as being to a large extent representative of the wider social tradition. (2) We shall show that Freud regarded the Super-Ego not entirely as a feared, harsh, and oppressive agent, but also as a source of positive aspiration on the part of the Ego, and, to some extent, a source of positive desire on the part of the Id. (3) We shall argue against Freud's view that the *content* of the Super-Ego can be said to be individually inherited, and we shall put forward the view that it can be accounted for more legitimately and more fruitfully in terms of the continuity of Social Tradition.

(1) Whilst Freud never attempts to trace the full sociological implications of the Super-Ego (i.e. he never investigates in detail the relations between the prohibitions and values of the parents and the wider complex of the social tradition) many of his remarks make it clear that he was aware of these implications. In his paper on 'The Economic Problem in Masochism', he tells us, 'These same persons, however (the parents), whose effect persists as the power of conscience after they have ceased to be objects of libidinal impulses in the Id, belong also to the real outer world. This is where they came from; their power, *behind which lie concealed all the influences of the past and of tradition*, was one of the most acutely-felt manifestations of reality.' And again, in the same paper, whilst stressing the fundamental importance of the earliest

content of the Super-Ego (the parents) Freud maintains that the later influences of the wider society also have their effect. 'In the course of development through childhood which brings an ever-increasing severance from the parents, their personal significance for the Super-Ego recedes. To the images they leave behind *are then linked on the influences of teachers, authorities, of self-chosen models and heroes venerated by society. . . .*'[1] Then again, in his paper on 'Narcissism', we find Freud saying, 'The ego-ideal is of great importance for the understanding of group psychology. Besides its individual side, this ideal has a social side; *it is also the common ideal of a family, a class or a nation.*'[2]

These remarks will suffice for the point we wish to make, but we shall comment upon them further in our final chapter.

(2) The Super-Ego is often represented solely as a harsh, tyrannical, inhibiting agent towards which the Ego reacts with fear, submission, and guilt, in an entirely negative way. This view is an over-emphasis of one side of Freud's teaching only, and, as such, is a definite misrepresentation. An analysis of the Super-Ego reveals the fact that it contains elements involving positive desire and positive aspiration on the part of the Ego, and several of Freud's comments make it perfectly clear that he held this view.

The setting up of the Super-Ego occurs with the passing of the Oedipus Complex, and, indeed, it is by this introjection and de-sexualisation of the parent object-choices that the Oedipus Complex is overcome. There are then, *two* aspects to the Super-Ego: on the one hand the love-objects themselves (which have been the objects of the Id's desire) and, on the other hand, the *commands* and *prohibitions* of these love-objects. In consequence, the Super-Ego is not only forbidding and inhibitory, but also contains, firstly, elements which are objects of love and desire on the part of the Id (the abandoned libidinal object-choice), and, secondly, 'ideal' elements which are positively desired by the Ego— towards the attainment of which the Ego positively aspires (the narcissistic attachment to the Ego-Ideal). When Freud calls this establishment of the secondary impulses the '*Super*-Ego', he does not mean that they comprise an element of the personality which is harsh, tyrannical, bigger and more powerful than the Ego in a dictatorial way alone. He means also that they comprise something *greater* than the Ego in the fullest sense of the word; something towards which the Ego aspires; something, the attainment of which the Ego positively desires; a goal, an ideal resolution of the Ego's entire task, upon the attainment of

---

[1]'The Economic Problem in Masochism', *Collected Papers*, vol. ii, XXII.
[2]'On Narcissism: an Introduction', *Collected Papers*, 1914, vol. iv, III, p. 59.

which the Ego feels that it would achieve complete fulfilment and aesthetic satisfaction.

Perhaps it should be mentioned at this stage that, when Freud is emphasising the harshness and tyranny of the Super-Ego in pathological cases, he calls in the directing inwards of the aggression stemming from the Death Instinct as an explanation. Later, we shall give reasons which make it necessary to reject the postulation of a Death Instinct. But all we are concerned to point out here is that the general emphasis upon the harsh, prohibitive aspects of the Super-Ego often leads to a neglect of the fact that Freud postulated other aspects also, and that these other aspects are of great importance.

Let us note briefly some of the remarks which Freud made in this connection. In his paper on 'Neurosis and Psychosis', after discussing the relations between the Id, the Ego, and the Outer World, Freud continues: 'In this apparently simple situation, a complication is introduced by the existence of the Super-Ego, which, in some connection not yet clear to us, combines in itself influences from the Id as well as from the outer world, and is to some extent *an ideal prototype of that state towards which all the Ego's endeavours are bending, a reconciliation of its manifold allegiances.*' The same point is made in 'The Economic Problem in Masochism' where Freud says, 'We have said that the function of the Ego consists in uniting with one another the claims of the three powers it serves, in reconciling them; and we can add that *it has in the Super-Ego a model for this which it can strive to emulate.*' And again, in the same paper, Freud speaks of the Super-Ego as, '*a model for the Ego's endeavours*'.

The Super-Ego, then, contains *Ideal* elements in the fullest sense of the word, besides harsh inhibitory dogmas; and comprises an ideal solution of the tasks with which the Ego is faced. It must be emphasised, too, that this 'Ideal' state includes a certain satisfaction for the instinctual strivings; and it is clear that Freud provides a psychological support here for the arguments of many moral philosophers that the 'Ideal' is not only right and good, but also *desirable*. It is something which we feel would give us complete satisfaction and fulfilment in all respects if only we could achieve it. Similarly, Freud gives psychological support to the recognition on the part of many philosophers of the element of the *beautiful* in the good; of the *aesthetic* element in moral striving. And with these considerations, we can see that Freud's moral psychology brings him completely into line with the main tradition of moral philosophy. If we recall Plato's analysis of human nature (into the desiring element, the spirited element, and the rational element) and his subsequent teaching that 'righteousness' is best defined in terms of 'functional excellence', which involves that ordering of the parts of the soul which will give each part its proper work and satisfaction with due regard to the harmony of the whole, and which involves, consequently, the rational elucidation of moral ideals (the clarification of the 'ideal constitution of the soul') and a striving towards them—we can see how similar Freud's psychological analysis is. Many examples could be given from the literature of moral philosophy, but it is not within the scope of our present task to trace such parallels in detail. It is clear, however, that Freud's moral psychology gives us an excellent starting point for moral philosophy. The moral precepts comprised by the Super-Ego are not themselves rationally discovered by the individual; they are simply the introjection of a particular constellation of values peculiar to that Social Tradition into which the individual happens to be born. Rational investigation can, however, then proceed with a critique of these given moral ideals; clarifying them, uncovering their presuppositions, discovering and resolving incompatibilities, and so on. It has often been stressed that one of Freud's slogans has been, 'Where the Id is—there shall Ego be!' Now it seems that another slogan is also appropriate, 'Where the Super-Ego is—there also shall Ego be!'

It should be emphasised here, in view of the confusion that can arise in connection with the relation between the psychology of morals and moral philosophy, that Freud does not, and indeed could not—at his own level of investigation—put forward any ethical theory. All we are saying here is that his analysis is very similar to that upon which many moral philosophers have based their theories; that his work sheds light upon some of the propositions of moral philosophy; and that it provides an extremely interesting starting point for ethical inquiry. The kind of inquiry we have in mind, undertaken upon the basis of the Freudian system, would stem a great deal from Plato himself, and (to mention but two present-day writers) Professor G. C. Field, who stresses the notion of the Ideal as being central for ethics in his book *Moral Theory*, and Professor M. Ginsberg, whose paper 'Basic Needs and Moral Ideals' is the most suggestive and stimulating work pointing to the direction of positive and fruitful future inquiry that has appeared during recent years.[1]

(3) We come now to the question as to whether the Super-Ego can be said to be inherited.

---

[1]'Basic Needs and Moral Ideals', M. Ginsberg, *Proceedings of the Aristotelian Society*, 1947. I say that this paper indicates the direction of 'positive and fruitful' future inquiry in that it gets to grips with the complex data of morals, as distinct from most contemporary moral philosophy which is still predominantly under the influence of Logical Positivism and employs the method of linguistic analysis. Other valuable suggestions are made by Professor Ginsberg in *The Idea of Progress*, 1953, and the 1953 Huxley Memorial Lecture: 'On the Diversity of Morals'.

In *The Ego and the Id*, Freud writes:

'. . . we . . . perceive it (the Super-Ego) to be the outcome of two highly important factors, one of them biological and the other historical: namely, the lengthy duration in man of the helplessness and dependence belonging to childhood, and the fact of his Oedipus Complex, the repression of which we have shown to be connected with the interruption of libidinal development by the latency period and so with the twofold onset of activity characteristic of man's sexual life. According to the view of one psycho-analyst, the last-mentioned phenomenon, which seems to be peculiar to man, is a heritage of the cultural development necessitated by the glacial epoch. We see, then, that the differentiation of the Super-Ego from the Ego is no matter of chance; it stands as the representative of the most important events in the development both of the individual and the race; indeed, by giving permanent expression to the influence of the parents it perpetuates the existence of the factors to which it owes its origin.'

There are two points in this statement with which we can agree, and a third with which we must disagree. In the first place we can agree that both the long period of dependence of the human child and the twofold onset of the sexual life of human beings are inherited features of the human species; they are established *phylogenetically* in the species and manifest themselves in a definite course of development *ontogenetically* in each individual. We can also agree that the Oedipus Complex and, indeed, the propensity of the human being to form strong love-attachments, is a resultant of these two hereditary features—coupled with, we might add, a third phylogenetic feature: the *lack* of automatic behaviour-mechanisms closely correlated with the instinctual demands, and the consequent need of the human being to *learn* appropriate modes of behaviour. So that when Freud tells us that the Oedipus Complex and the setting up of the Super-Ego have a *historical* aspect, we can agree in two ways.

Firstly, we can agree that this process is an ontogenetic development in the life-history of each individual (though, of course, Freud does not hold that its development is completely *typical* in each individual case). This falls in completely with our previous phylogenetic-ontogenetic statement. Secondly, we can agree that any particular human society manifests a complex Social Tradition which has been historically fashioned, and that, therefore, the *content* of the Super-Ego in the individuals of this society will have its historical aspects, and may well be similar in many respects in the individuals of many generations. In this latter sense, we have long been accustomed to speak of our 'Social

Heritage' as distinct from our 'Biological Inheritance'. In this sense, then, we can agree with Freud when he tells us that, 'the differentiation of the Super-Ego from the Ego is no matter of chance; it stands as the representative of the most important events in the development both of the individual and the race. . . .'

The various conditions of the ontogenetic growth and development of individual human beings, laid down phylogenetically, give the biological and psychological predispositions and capacities for the formation of deep-rooted and important love-attachments—together with all the manifold ways of dealing with them, and with the vicissitudes to which they are subjected, which we have described. The social tradition, appearing first of all to the child in the form of the values and commands encountered in the early family situation, provides the actual *content* with which the affective tendencies of the child will concern themselves; the actual content about which the personality will mould itself during the course of its growth and development. At this point we receive a hint of the importance of the concept of the Super-Ego for Social Psychology, for we see now the intimate relation between the symbols of the social tradition (whether in the form of language or of pictorial and auditory symbols such as King, Queen, Dictator, Cross of Christ, National Flag, National Anthem, etc.) and the actual content of the individual personality; between the formation and change of the social structure and the formation and change of individual personality.

Freud goes much further than this, however, in discussing the way in which the Super-Ego can be said to be inherited, and it is on this final point that we disagree. When maintaining that the Oedipus Complex and the content of the Super-Ego have historical as well as biological aspects, Freud seems to hold definitely to the view that they originated in a certain historical-cultural event, and that, thereafter, they have been *phylogenetically* transmitted from generation to generation of the human species. This view (concerning the supposed banding together of the brothers to kill the tyrannical father of the primal horde) is put forward in 'Totem and Taboo', and though Freud seems, later, to be content to regard his hypothesis as a 'just-so story', in *The Ego and the Id* he nonetheless continues to adhere to his view that the basic content of the Super-Ego is 'phylogenetically acquired'. Thus he tells us: 'Religion, morality, and a social sense—the chief elements of what is highest in men—were originally one and the same thing. According to the hypothesis which I have put forward in Totem and Taboo they were acquired phylogenetically out of the father-complex: religion and moral restraint by the actual process of mastering the Oedipus Complex itself, and social feeling from the necessity for overcoming the rivalry that then remained between the members of the younger generation.'[1] Freud then inquires as to whether it is the Ego or the Id which can be said to have inherited these elements, and having pointed out that no external vicissitudes can be experienced or undergone by the Id, except by way of the Ego, he says:

'. . . one must not take the difference between Ego and Id in too hard-and-fast a sense, nor forget that the Ego is a part of the Id which has been specially modified. The experiences undergone by the Ego seem at first sight to be lost to posterity; but, when they have been repeated often enough and with sufficient intensity in the successive individuals of many generations, they transform themselves, so to say, into experiences of the Id, the impress of which is preserved by inheritance. Thus, in the Id, which is capable of being inherited, are stored up vestiges of the existences led by countless former Egos; and, when the Ego forms its Super-Ego out of the Id, it may perhaps only be reviving images of Egos that have passed away and be securing them a resurrection.'[2]

It is this view of Freud's with which we must disagree, and for two reasons.

In the first place, it clearly involves a Lamarckian view as to the possibility of the inheritance of acquired characteristics which does not find support in the modern science of Genetics. Thus, to refer to only one contemporary geneticist, we find the following view expressed. 'Mutation—that is, the alteration of a gene—does not seem to be directly influenced by the environment, so the old ideas of direct genetical adaptation, which are now usually described as Lamarckian, are not supported by genetical evidence, and evolution seems to work by a system of trial and error in which the mutation of the genes provides Darwin's inherited variation, and the environmental factors select the organisms carrying favourable gene combinations.'[3] Again: 'The belief in the inheritance of acquired characters, which is often called Lamarckism . . . has now been given up by most biologists. . . . Genes do not often mutate, but rather go on producing genes of the same constitution, and, if they do change, the direction of their mutation does not seem to be correlated with any special requirements of their environment and is more frequently harmful than advantageous. There-fore most biologists are inclined to regard evolution as an adaptive process composed essentially of two elements, both of them being subject to selection by the environment: variability, caused by the

---

[1] In order to be perfectly clear, we must emphasise that it is not the question of whether such an event actually happened that we wish to dispute, but that its effects could be *phylogenetically* acquired and transmitted.

[2] *The Ego and the Id*, 1923, p. 52.   [3] H. Kalmus, *Genetics*, p. 11.

mutation of individual genes, and fresh re-combinations of genes.'[1] In the light of such findings, Freud's view as to the phylogenetic continuity of the *content* of the Super-Ego is not tenable.

There is a further reason why we disagree with Freud, and this rests upon considerations of a sociological nature. The social traditions manifested by the many human communities in the world (and, even within the bounds of any one community, by the various social classes and other forms of social grouping within that community) are exceedingly complex, and change during the course of history: sometimes very slightly over long periods, but sometimes very rapidly during what we may call 'revolutionary' periods. It is clear, therefore, that the *content* of the Super-Ego in any society, or in any social grouping within that society, is by no means a simple matter, and requires, for a complete understanding, a detailed inquiry on the sociological level: taking into account, for example, such factors as changes in the size and composition of the population, the nature and influence of contacts with other societies, the changes in the class-structure of the society, the changes in the dominant ideologies of the society, and so on. This recalls all that was said earlier by Lloyd Morgan, Hobhouse, and Ginsberg, to the effect that a full investigation of the *development of the human mind* required the study of *social development* as well as the clarification of man's given biological and psychological endowment.

The view, therefore, which we propose to adopt is that (accepting the importance and utility of Freud's concept of the Super-Ego) it is more correct, and certainly more useful from the point of view of prospective work in Social Psychology, to reject the idea that the *content* of the Super-Ego is established phylogenetically, and to hold that this *content* can best be explained in terms of the *social tradition* of any particular human group. The content of the Super-Ego certainly has a degree of continuity (varying in accordance with the degree of magnitude and rapidity of social change which we have mentioned above) but this continuity is the outcome of *social* cohesion and *social* processes, rather than being due to biological heredity alone. We then have, as firm points for any inquiry, on the one hand the inherited biological and psychological endowment of man—inclusive of all that Freud has taught us with regard to the instincts, their vicissitudes, and the modes and tendencies of personality-development; and, on the other hand, a sociological analysis of the social tradition, the complex framework of the social structure. This social tradition will have, however, its subjective, symbolic, dynamic side, in the sense that its various elements will not appear to individual members of the community in the form of a

[1]H. Kalmus, *Genetics*, p. 122.

structural sociological analysis, as it appears to the objective sociologist, but will be *experienced* during the context of day-to-day life as a complex of symbols—linguistic, visual, auditory, and so on. These symbols, first encountered through the influence of the parents in the early family situation, will form the 'objects' (in the Freudian sense) to which the earliest affective tendencies of the child will react, and will thereafter comprise, in varying combinations, the *content* of the Super-Ego; the *content* about which the personality and character will be moulded. In these brief considerations we can recognise the great suggestiveness and utility of the concept of the Super-Ego for Social Psychology.

We have now seen how important and extensive a place instinctual experience is given in Freud's account of human psychology, and how the predominance and urgency of the instincts are held to constitute one of the greatest continuing demands upon the activities of the Ego, and are held to be of the utmost importance in the setting up within the personality of the 'moral impulses'.

So far, however, although Freud's earlier analysis of the distinguishing features of the instincts (object, aim, impetus, and source) might have led us to expect a treatment of various instincts, we have been able to give a detailed account of the sexual instinct alone. We come to this question of the number of instincts at work in human nature as we turn to consider Freud's several attempts at a classification of the instincts.

4. *The Classification of the Instincts*

Freud made three attempts to achieve a satisfactory classification of the instincts, but, before examining these, we must consider one or two preliminary points which emerged during the course of his work on this question.

Firstly, it is interesting to note Freud's remarks with regard to the supposed 'gregarious instinct' in man. Tinbergen, we have already seen, maintains that there is no 'gregarious instinct' as such, but that social activities are invariably aspects of other particular instincts: as in the case of the reproductive instinct, or the parental sub-instinct. Freud, we find, is in agreement with Tinbergen on this point. He argues against the view maintained by Trotter that the Herd Instinct is irreducible, and gives his own account of the origin of 'social feeling'.[1] This account stresses in the first place the libidinal tie between the child and the parent in the case of the family, and between group-members and the group-leader in the case of the group, and, in the second place, the identification of the children or of the group members, respectively, with each other. In a word, for Freud, social feeling is born of jealousy. In the first

[1] *Group Psychology and the Analysis of the Ego*, Chapter IX.

instance the children of the family, or the members of the group, are jealous of each other (in connection with the shared libidinal object-choice) and harbour hostile wishes against each other. They cannot, however, maintain this attitude of hostility without danger to themselves (from the other children or from the other group members) and they are therefore forced into identifying themselves with their fellows. This gives rise to the vehement demand for equality of treatment and consideration. 'This demand for equality is the root of social conscience and the sense of duty.' There grows up, among the members of a group, a 'social feeling' which '. . . is based upon the reversal of what was first a hostile feeling into a positively-toned tie. . . .' Whether this constitutes an adequate account of the basis[1] of social justice we shall not inquire here. Our chief point is to emphasise that Freud, during his psycho-analytic investigation of human nature, finds no evidence to support the postulation of an irreducible 'gregarious instinct', and that his conclusion is in agreement with that of Tinbergen, which is drawn from the ethological study of other animal species.

A second point is the particular nature of Freud's approach to the whole problem of classification. This can best be indicated by considering one basis of classification which is evident in his work, but which he neglects altogether. We may recall that, when investigating the distinguishing features of the instincts, Freud mentions the *sources* and the *aims* of the instincts. At this point it will be of value to mention some of the comments he has to make in this connection in the paper 'Instincts and their Vicissitudes', keeping in mind the problem of classification.

Thus Freud tells us: 'The study of the sources of instinct is outside the scope of psychology; although its source in the body is what gives the instinct its distinct and essential character, yet in mental life we know it merely by its aims. A more exact knowledge of the sources of instincts is not strictly necessary for purposes of psychological investigation; often the source may be with certainty inferred from the aims.' Then again: 'I am altogether doubtful whether work upon psychological material will afford any decisive indication for the distinction and classification of instincts. Rather it would seem necessary to apply to this material certain definite assumptions in order to work upon it, and we could wish that these assumptions might be taken from some other branch of knowledge and transferred to psychology.'

Now there is some inconsistency in these two statements; for if the aims of the instincts are closely correlated with their sources, there is at least (in an analysis of these aims) some psychological basis for the classification of the instincts. But, leaving this aside for the moment, it

[1] I.e. the fundamental feeling upon which social justice is erected.

is surely the case that if 'the source in the body is what gives the instinct its distinct and essential character', and if 'often the source may be with certainty inferred from the aims', we are here provided with the basis for an adequate classification? After investigation, our classification would comprise a number of instincts denoted by, on the one hand, their aims (the 'end-states' on the attainment of which the behavioural sequences ceased and satisfaction was achieved) and, on the other hand, those sources (neuro-physiological processes) which were closely correlated with these aims. Indeed, these two features of the instincts are the basis of classification put forward by both the earlier writers and by the ethologists; and we have seen that Tinbergen, whilst accepting the principle of classifying the instincts according to their aims or 'end-states', also expressly states that the neurophysiological basis of the instincts should be taken into account. Freud, of course, was writing before the formulation of the ethological concepts, but even a little attention to the earlier writers would have shown him that their mode of classification corresponded with the one he suggested. Quite wrongly, however, Freud assumed that all these earlier classifications were of an altogether arbitrary nature. We find him saying: 'No knowledge would have been more valuable as a foundation for true psychological knowledge than an appropriate grasp of the common characteristics and possible distinctive features of the instincts. But in no region of psychology were we groping more in the dark. Everyone assumed the existence of as many instincts or 'basic instincts' as he chose, and juggled with them like the ancient Greek natural philosophers with their four elements—earth, air, fire and water.'[1] This statement is simply absurd, and shows that Freud paid scant attention to the earlier literature on the subject and must have completely overlooked or ignored the efforts that were being made in Comparative Psychology. This was unfortunate, since the classification which emerged from the work of this early group of writers (as represented by the classification put forward by Drever) is much more satisfactory than the one at which Freud himself ultimately arrived, and was based upon a mode of classification which Freud himself recognised, but which he neglected to pursue.

Elsewhere, to return to the paper 'Instincts and their Vicissitudes', Freud is not so polemical against previous classifications, but even here he stresses the *sources* of the instincts as the basis of classification. 'Now what instincts and how many should be postulated?' he asks. 'There is obviously a great opportunity here for arbitrary choice. No objection can be made to anyone's employing the concept of an instinct of play or of destruction, or that of a social instinct, when the subject demands it,

[1] *Beyond the Pleasure Principle*, p. 69.

and the limitations of psychological analysis allow of it. Nevertheless, we should not neglect to ask whether such instinctual motives, which are in one direction so highly specialised, do not admit of further analysis in respect of their sources, so that only those primal instincts which are not to be resolved further could really lay claim to the name.' Here again, we are led to expect a classification of the instincts based upon their bodily sources, but Freud completely neglects this method in his own speculations. The question arises: why did Freud abandon this mode of classification which he had stated so clearly?

The truth seems to be that Freud's approach was determined by the consideration which was uppermost in his mind: the facts of instinctual *conflict*. In all the three classifications which he suggests we find a confessedly *dualistic* analysis—in which two groups of instincts are conceived as being in opposition to each other. In trying to provide an instinctual basis for the fundamental cleavages which he found in human personalities, Freud dispenses with the relatively straight-forward method of classifying the instincts according to their aims and sources, and enters upon much more obscure and less reliable lines of speculation which lead him to no satisfactory outcome.

The three classifications which Freud offers, each framed in terms of two opposing groups of instincts, are as follows: (1) The Ego-Instincts (self-preservative) and the Sexual Instincts (race-preservative), (2) Narcissistic Libido and Object Libido (Self-love and Object-love), and (3) The Life Instincts (Eros) and the Death Instincts (Thanatos).

We shall discuss them in the order given here, which is the chronological order in which they emerged during the course of Freud's speculations.

Throughout the early work of Freud the existence of two opposed groups of instincts is assumed: the *Ego-Instincts* and the *Sexual Instincts*, and this classification is formulated chiefly in the paper 'The Instincts and their Vicissitudes'. The occasion for this classification arose, Freud tells us, 'in the course of the evolution of psycho-analysis, which was first employed upon the psycho-neuroses, actually upon the group designated transference neuroses (hysteria and obsessional neurosis); through them it became plain that at the root of all such affections there lies a conflict between the claims of sexuality and those of the Ego.' Though this distinction is made on psychological grounds, Freud thinks that it receives support from Biology. 'The contribution of biology on this point does not run counter to the distinction between sexual and ego-instincts. Biology teaches that sexuality is not on a level with the other functions of the individual, for its "purposes" go beyond the individual, their content being the production of new individuals and the preservation of the species. It shows, further, that the relation existing between the Ego and sexuality may be conceived of in two ways, apparently equally well justified: in the one, the individual is regarded as of prime importance, sexuality as one of his activities and sexual satisfaction as one of his needs; while in the other the individual organism is looked upon as a transitory and perishable appendage to the quasi-immortal germ-plasm bequeathed to him by the race.'

Whilst it is true, as Freud says, that the relation between the Ego and sexuality can be *conceived of* in two ways, it is difficult to see that there is, in the actual natural situation, any radical dichotomy between 'the preservation of the individual' and 'the preservation of the race', since it is clear that the successful transmission of the germ-plasm and hence the continuity of the species depends upon the survival of individuals. In the case of the lower animal species, as the work of Comparative Ethology has shown, the sexual instinct in its periodical recurrence is as well adapted to the ecological situation (including other individuals with their appropriate sign-stimuli) and is as adequately provided by heredity with appropriate behavioural mechanisms as is any other instinct, and there is no evidence to suggest that the sexual instinct is in any sense opposed, in its operation, to the other instincts. Though, therefore, Freud's suggested distinction may be of use in psycho-analytic practice, and though it may point to a particular source of conflict in the human personality, it does not appear to be a satisfactory basis for the classification of the instincts. Quite apart from these considerations, it is unsatisfactory from the further point of view that Freud never, in fact, attempts to complete the classification in detail. Whilst he gives us a detailed account of the sexual instinct in the human species, he nowhere attempts to clarify what is comprised by the term 'Ego-Instincts', although it is at least clear from his remarks that hunger (and the initial sucking of the child) and defecation would come under this head.

This first classification had to be augmented (but not abandoned) to take into account Freud's further concept of 'primary narcissism', discussed in his paper 'On Narcissism—an Introduction'. In this paper, Freud maintains that before the libido of the child becomes attached to, or flows out towards, objects, there is an earlier stage in which the libido fills the child's own Ego, or has the child's own Ego for its object. This is the state of primary narcissism or self-love, and Freud holds that it never completely ceases. 'All through the subject's life his ego remains the great reservoir of his libido, from which the attachments to objects (object-cathexes) radiate out, and into which the libido can stream back again from the objects. The narcissistic libido is constantly being converted into object-libido, and vice-versa.'[1] This view complicates the previous distinction between Ego-instincts and Sexual or Libidinal instincts, since it now appears that *all* the object-attachments of the Ego are of a libidinal nature. The new antithesis set up by Freud is therefore that of *Self-Love* as against *Object-Love*. 'It had been said that repression was set in action by the instincts of self-preservation operating in the Ego (the Ego-instincts) and that it was brought to bear upon the libidinal instincts. But since the instincts of self-preservation were now recognized as also being of a libidinal nature, as being narcissistic libido, the process of repression was seen to be a process occurring within the libido itself; *narcissistic-libido was opposed to object-libido*, the interests of self-preservation defended themselves against the demands of object-love, that is, against the demands of sexuality in the narrower sense.'[2] Here again we must say that whilst the distinction between self-love and object-love might be useful in psycho-analytic practice and point to a source of conflict in the human personality, it does not prove to be a satisfactory classification of the instincts, for, again, Freud does not go on to give us a clear analysis of the instincts which are involved. Indeed, as Ernest Jones suggests,[3] it is difficult to see what distinction is really made as far as the instincts are concerned; conflict seems now to be attributed not to the opposition between two groups of instincts, but to the opposition between two aspects of the same group of instincts— the libidinal instincts. Freud claims, however, that this classification is not intended to supersede the previous one, and that his earlier distinction between Ego-Instincts and Sexual Instincts still holds good. Evidently, then, there are at least *some* Ego-instincts which are not of a libidinal nature, but Freud nowhere enlightens us as to what these are.

Freud himself was evidently dissatisfied with this classification, and he tells us, 'This was clearly not the last word on the subject; biological considerations seemed to make it impossible to remain content with assuming the existence of only a single class of instincts.'[4] It seems clear from this statement that, in this second classification, Freud did think that *all* the instincts were of a libidinal nature, and that, dissatisfied with this position, he was still looking for an essentially *dualistic* basis of classification.

The line of speculation which leads Freud, finally, to adopt the classification of the instincts into two groups—the Life and the Death instincts—is to be found in his book *Beyond the Pleasure Principle*. Of all Freud's speculations this is the most tentative, and the one most removed from facts. Indeed, Freud himself tells us that he undertakes

---

[1]*An Autobiographical Study*, p. 101.   [2]*Ibid.*
[3]Ernest Jones, *Psycho-Analysis and the Instincts.*   [4]*An Autobiographical Study*, p. 104.

it merely as an interesting line of thought which he wishes to pursue to its logical conclusion, largely as a matter of intellectual curiosity; and at the end of the book he tells us that he is not at all convinced by the conclusion he has reached, though he believes that his argument merits consideration. Nonetheless, in his later writings, Freud speaks as though he does in fact seriously accept his conclusion in this argument, and he does utilise it in his interpretations of sadism and masochism, of the harshness of the Super-Ego, and so on. The view we shall adopt, for reasons given below, is that Freud's argument is totally invalid and that the classification he arrives at is quite untenable. We shall show that there is no evidence whatsoever to support the postulate of Death Instincts in all animal species (for Freud extends his generalisation to the entire organic world) and we shall mention evidence which constitutes a positive and complete refutation. This is not to say, it must be noted, that the tendencies in the *human* personality[1] which Freud seeks to explain by the Life and Death instincts do not exist; and we shall argue that one of the mistakes which Freud makes is to generalise too widely from manifestations of experience and behaviour which are probably peculiar to human beings (and possibly the higher mammals) alone.

Freud begins his argument by emphasising the 'necessary postulate' as to the function of the nervous system which we discussed and with which we disagreed earlier.[2] Since this is one of the basic points of his argument we must consider it a little further. Freud attaches importance to the views of Fechner on the question of pleasure and unpleasure, and the quotation he takes from Fechner's work is as follows: 'In so far as *conscious* impulses always have some relation to pleasure or unpleasure, pleasure and unpleasure too can be regarded as having a psychophysical relation to conditions of stability and instability. This provides a

[1]In our own attempt at classification, we shall treat these tendencies as 'General Instinctive Tendencies' and not as 'Instincts Proper', and we shall refer to them as 'Positive and Negative Ego-Tendencies'. In so doing we shall be following suggestions thrown out by Freud himself on the nature of hatred and the impulses to destruction, as may be seen in the following quotations from *Instincts and their Vicissitudes* (pp. 80-81). 'We might at a pinch say of an instinct that it "loves" the objects after which it strives for purposes of satisfaction, but to say that it "hates" an object strikes us as odd; so we become aware that the attitudes of love and hate cannot be said to characterize the relations of instincts to their objects, but are reserved for the relations of the Ego as a whole to objects.' And, 'It is noteworthy that in the use of the word "hate" no such intimate relation to sexual pleasure and the sexual function appears: on the contrary, the painful character of the relation seems to be the sole decisive feature. The Ego hates, abhors, and pursues with intent to destroy all objects which are for it a source of painful feelings, without taking into account whether they mean to it frustration of sexual satisfaction or of gratification of the needs of self-preservation. Indeed, it may be asserted that the true prototypes of the hate-relation are derived not from sexual life, but from the struggle of the Ego for self-preservation and self-maintenance.'   [2]See pp. 174-176.

basis for a hypothesis into which I propose to enter in greater detail elsewhere. According to this hypothesis, every psycho-physical movement *crossing the threshold of consciousness* is attended by pleasure in proportion as, beyond a certain limit, it approximates to complete stability, and is attended by unpleasure in proportion as, beyond a certain limit, it deviates from complete stability; while between the two limits, which may be described as qualitative thresholds of pleasure and unpleasure, there is a certain margin of aesthetic indifference. . . .'[1] Freud suggests that his own postulate with regard to the function of the nervous system is a special case of Fechner's 'tendency towards stability'.

The points of emphasis in the above quotation are our own, and we wish to suggest that there is a great distance between Fechner's hypothesis that qualitatively distinct impulses *consciously experienced* tend towards a certain state of balance, stability, or equilibrium; and the hypothesis of Freud that 'the nervous system is an apparatus having the function of abolishing stimuli which reach it, or of reducing excitation to the lowest possible level: an apparatus which would even, if this were feasible, maintain itself in an altogether unstimulated condition'. The two hypotheses do not entail each other, and are not necessarily connected. Thus, the individual—conscious of certain impulses which yield a feeling of dis-equilibrium or unpleasure (in Fechner's sense)— will tend towards behaviour which will satisfy these impulses and thereby lead to a pleasurable state of equilibrium or stability; but the nervous system, it must be noted, will have been involved in *all* these processes! It will have been involved in those particular neuro-physiological processes which constitute the source of the impulses, as, also, it will have been involved in the motor-activity leading to the satisfaction or the quiescence of the impulses. In this example, which would satisfy Fechner's hypothesis, it is far from being self-evident that Freud's hypothesis (that the function of the nervous system is to 'extinguish' or 'abolish' stimuli) is also true. Indeed, it does not seem to be feasible, since the nervous system is one of those factors *giving rise to the impulse* as well as one of the factors employed in gratifying it through appropriate behaviour. We have, however, given reasons for disagreeing with Freud's 'necessary postulate' earlier, and here it is only necessary to point out that Freud seems too hasty in concluding that his own hypothesis receives support from that of Fechner, and that he does not adequately establish his suggestion that his own hypothesis is a special case of the latter. What we wish to emphasise is that whereas Fechner's view supports that of Freud with regard to the operation of the Pleasure Principle, it by no means supports Freud's more radical statement that

[1]Quoted, with source, in *Beyond the Pleasure Principle*, p. 3.

the function of the nervous system is to seek a completely unstimulated condition, or to seek the complete extinction of stimuli.[1]

The second step in Freud's argument is the description of certain phenomena which seem to contradict his hypothesis as to the operation of the Pleasure Principle. Four examples are given. Firstly, Freud refers to the dreams occurring in traumatic neuroses (he mentions, in particular, the war neuroses) which 'have the characteristic of repeatedly bringing the patient back into the situation of his accident, a situation from which he wakes up in another fright.' Secondly, Freud mentions one instance of childhood play, in which the painful departure of the mother was, repeatedly, the centre of the child's games. In these cases, Freud points out that what is repeated cannot possibly have constituted, in the original situation, a source of pleasure; rather the reverse! How, then, can these facts be made compatible with the supposed dominance of the Pleasure Principle? Only by assuming, Freud concludes, that there is a principle of mental functioning which is more primitive than that of the Pleasure Principle, and that this compulsive repetition of a painful situation is undertaken not primarily because of the desire for pleasure or gratification, but because of the need to *master* the situation.[2] Brief mention is then made, thirdly, of the tragic and painful situations which often form the content of artistic and dramatic entertainment for adult audiences. And, fourthly and finally, Freud refers to the actual analytic situation, in which the patient is 'obliged to *repeat* the repressed material as a contemporary experience, instead of, as the physician would prefer to see, *remembering* it as something belonging to the past'.

[1] Perhaps we should mention at this point that, in *Beyond the Pleasure Principle*, Freud is equating what—in his paper, 'The Economic Problem in Masochism'—he later distinguishes as, on the one hand, the 'Nirvana-Principle', and, on the other, the 'Pleasure-Principle'. Our criticism above suggests that whereas Fechner's hypothesis supports Freud's view of the Pleasure-Principle, it does not support that of the Nirvana-Principle.

[2] There is a definite inconsistency here. Freud previously argues that the necessity of 'binding the instinctual excitations' in the face of difficult external situations occurs only when the Pleasure-Principle is threatened by the conditions of the outer world. The Pleasure-Principle is therefore primary. If it is *not*, then all that Freud says in connection with the primary unconscious mental processes, the early state of 'psychic reality', and the free mobile cathexis of this early mental state, falls to the ground. Furthermore, if the pleasure-principle is not primary, there seems to be no reason *why* mastery should be sought. The examples which Freud gives above do not seem to make necessary any change in his earlier hypothesis: i.e. that the task of 'binding the instinctual excitations' takes place in the service of the Pleasure-Principle. Thus, with regard to the four examples above, we should hold that—even though the compulsion to repeat aimed at retrospective mastery of painful situations—this mastery would be sought in the service of the Pleasure-Principle. The repetition of the painful experience would not be for its own sake; nor would the 'mastery' over the experience be sought for its own sake; but in order to attain once more the pleasurable state which had existed before the severe disruption of the painful situation. There seems to be no reason, then, why Freud should abandon his earlier hypothesis, and turn to this new one.

Here again, Freud holds that the repetition is necessary for the mastery of the situation.

On the basis of these examples, Freud postulates a *compulsion to repeat* which, he says, must be ascribed to the unconscious repressed, and which is 'something that seems more primitive, more elementary, more instinctual than the Pleasure-Principle which it now sets aside'.

It is important for our argument (and this point must be emphasised) to bear in mind that these examples, for the interpretation of which Freud postulates his 'compulsion to repeat', are *all* examples of *human beings* who have suffered various kinds of severe *conflict-situations*; and that the 'compulsion to repeat' is held to be a function of the *unconscious repressed* which seeks, retrospectively, the mastery over the conflict to which it has been subjected.

'What follows', Freud continues, 'is speculation, often far-fetched speculation, which the reader will consider or dismiss according to his individual predilection. It is further an attempt to follow out an idea consistently, out of curiosity to see where it will lead.' The argument from this point onward can be divided into two main parts: the first, in which he gives reasons to support his suggestion that the function of the compulsion to repeat is to achieve the mastery over situations or stimuli, and the second (with which we shall be mainly concerned) in which he discusses at length the 'instinctual' aspects of the compulsion to repeat.

In the first part of the argument, whilst discussing the system Pcpt.-Cs, Freud presents us with a brief sketch of the supposed course of development of the living organism. The outer surface of the organism, it is suggested, is developed as a protective shield against stimuli coming from the external world. The central nervous system originates (in the embryo) from the ectoderm, but is later withdrawn into the depths of the body, leaving only portions on the surface—the Sense Organs—which deal with small quantities of external stimulation only. The effect on the organism of the hostile external stimuli is reduced by the development of this protective surface-shield. On the other hand, no such shield is formed to protect the sensitive cortex from the excitations arising from sources *within* the body—i.e. from the instinctual excitations. As we have seen before, Freud holds that instinctual excitations are mobile processes pressing towards discharge, and he now suggests that the earliest task of the higher strata of the mental apparatus is to *bind* the instinctual excitation reaching the primary process in order to facilitate successful discharge. Only after this process of binding has been accomplished can the Pleasure-Principle govern without hindrance. In this early process, then, the task of binding or mastering excitations has precedence.[1] At this stage, Projection is held to be an extremely important mechanism since any instinctual excitations which are particularly troublesome to the individual are thereby treated as though they were coming not from within, but from outside, and in this way the individual feels that the outer protective shield will be of some defence, and can be employed against them. The traumatic neurosis, Freud concludes, can be regarded as the outcome of a breach in this protective shield against stimuli; it is caused by the absence of any preparedness for anxiety, and it follows that the 'compulsion to repeat' can be regarded as a persisting effort to gain mastery over this breach which has occurred. Thus, says Freud, when referring to the dreams occurring in the traumatic neuroses, 'These dreams are endeavouring to master the stimulus retrospectively, by developing the anxiety whose omission was the cause of the traumatic neurosis'. Throughout this discussion it will be seen that, though Freud begins with reference to neurotic conditions, he conceives the 'compulsion to repeat' as a normal principle governing the earliest mental processes of the child. It is important to stress this fact (that Freud regards the binding or mastering of instinctual excitations as being a normal process preceding the governance of the pleasure-principle) since it is because of this that he speaks of this process as being 'Beyond the Pleasure-Principle' and as being of an 'instinctual' character.

It is at this point that Freud enters upon an elaborate discussion of the 'instinctual' aspects of the compulsion to repeat, and this is a fundamental turning point in the whole of the argument. What follows from this point is only very tenuously connected with what has been put forward before, and it is from here onwards that Freud makes analogies and generalisations which are quite unwarranted.

Let us remember that what has been presented so far is, (a) the necessary postulate that the nervous system aims at the complete extinction of stimuli, (b) the postulate of a 'compulsion to repeat', in order to account for certain manifestations in the experience of human beings which seem to contradict the governance of the pleasure-principle, and (c) the view that this 'compulsion to repeat' is a principle governing the earliest processes of mental life, and that its function is the *mastery* of excitations.

Now, Freud asks the question: 'How is the predicate of being "instinctual" related to the Compulsion to Repeat?'

His answer is as follows.

Firstly, he voices his suspicion that, in this 'compulsion to repeat' he may have discovered a *universal attribute* of the instincts and perhaps of

[1]See the previous footnote.

organic life in general. 'It seems', he says, 'that an instinct is a compulsion inherent in organic life to restore an earlier state of things which the living entity has been obliged to abandon under the pressure of external disturbing forces; that is, it is a kind of organic elasticity, or, to put it another way, the expression of the inertia inherent in organic life.'

Now it can be seen at the outset that nothing Freud has previously said justifies this sweeping generalisation with reference to the instincts of all animal species, and, indeed, to the processes of organic life in general. Even if we assume that Freud is correct in suggesting that, in the human species, individuals are confronted with the early task of mastering instinctual excitations; that this gives rise to the compulsion to repeat; and that this process can be observed, pathologically enhanced, in the traumatic neuroses—this gives us no ground whatsoever for supposing that the instincts of all other animal species possess the same attribute. On the contrary, from what we know of animal behaviour, we would be led to think that this necessity of binding or mastering instinctual excitations was probably peculiar only to man and, possibly, the higher mammals, since in all the lower species appropriate behavioural mechanisms are established by heredity, and the task of 'binding excitations' would not seem to arise. Furthermore, it is one thing to speak of a 'compulsion to repeat' with reference to human mental processes when, as Freud suggests, individuals are seeking the mastery over some severe conflict-situation which drove them into neurosis; or, on the other hand, when the emerging Ego of the human individual has to control the instinctual demands in accordance with the conditions of the outer world; and quite another thing to speak of a 'compulsion to repeat' with reference to the life-history of an organism which follows the pattern of its genetic constitution during the process of its growth. The first refers to an event or situation in an individual's own experience arising from 'external disturbing forces', and which—assuming Freud is right—the individual is compelled to repeat in an effort to achieve mastery over it. The second, however, refers to the organism's growth in accordance with that genetic constitution which has been established by heredity; and it is to be noted in this connection that the evolutionary chain of mutations which has led to the existing genetic constitution of the species *cannot* be regarded as the outcome of 'external disturbing forces'![1] The mutations are *spontaneous variations* of the genetic constitution, and it is the *survival* of the resulting individual or species which depends upon external forces, in accordance with the principle of natural selection.

[1]See our quotation from Kalmus, p. 232.

It is quite false, therefore, to speak as though each evolutionary change in the many animal species has been brought about by external disturbing forces, and that the fact that each individual organism grows in accordance with its existing genetic constitution means that the organism is 'seeking to restore an earlier state'. Freud completely confuses in this discussion, the phenomena of the mental experience of human individuals and the phenomena of genetics and heredity. These phenomena are not on the same level, are not even homologous, and the most that can be said is that an analogy might be drawn between the two. As we have seen, however, this would be an extremely bad analogy as there seem to be scarcely any points of similarity.

The utter weakness of Freud's reasoning here can also be seen in such mention as he makes of animal instincts, supposedly in support of his thesis. One would have thought that, when making broad generalisations of this kind, the first thing which Freud would have done would have been to examine in detail what was known of the instincts of animals, to see whether or not such knowledge supported his generalisations. In fact, however, Freud all but ignores this sphere of investigation, and the remarks he does make with regard to the instincts of animals would have been better not made at all. Thus, to support his view that the instincts aim at restoring an earlier state of things, he tells us, '. . . we soon call to mind examples from animal life which seem to confirm the view that instincts are historically determined. Certain fishes, for instance, undertake laborious migrations at spawning-time in order to deposit their spawn in particular waters far removed from their customary haunts. In the opinion of many biologists what they are doing is merely to seek out the localities in which their species formerly resided but which in the course of time they have exchanged for others. The same explanation is believed to apply to the migratory flights of birds of passage. . . .'

And this, incredibly, is all that Freud finds it necessary to say on the subject of animal instincts!

'We are quickly relieved of the necessity for seeking for further examples', he goes on to say, 'by the reflection that the most impressive proofs of there being an organic compulsion to repeat lie in the phenomena of heredity and the facts of embryology.' In these quotations we see how confusedly Freud lumps together all these various phenomena: human mental experience, animal behaviour, and the facts of heredity and embryology. It must be pointed out, too, that in the above illustration Freud uses the term 'historically determined' in a literal sense. In connection with the spawning-migration of the fish, he definitely means that the species used to frequent a certain area; that, at a certain historical point, they were compelled to move elsewhere; and that since that time they have had the impulse to return to an earlier state of things, and have therefore returned to the home of their fathers to spawn. Fish, it appears, are perpetually homesick. For Freud, then, historically determined does not mean 'genetically determined' as we now understand the phrase; and it is clear that, if instincts are held to be genetically determined (as we ourselves in fact hold) then to speak of an individual organism which is the outcome of a new mutation as, 'seeking the state which existed before the mutation took place' is simply absurd.

One further point must also be made here. In discussing the compulsion to repeat with reference to human mental processes, Freud holds that its function is to attain mastery over the instinctual excitations or over conflict-situations. But what is the mastery which is being sought by the so-called conservative nature of the instincts of animals or of 'organic life'? Freud's answer to this rests upon his fundamental error with regard to genetics. For him, all modifications of the living organism are conceived as being imposed by external disturbing forces, and consequently the earlier state that the instincts of the animals are seeking to restore is that state which existed before such disturbances were imposed. This, it must be emphasised, is a fundamental mistake; for according to modern genetics, mutations are *not* imposed or even brought about by external forces, but are spontaneous variations of the genetic constitution of the germ-plasm, and the external forces merely determine whether or not the new individuals shall survive. In view of this, Freud's whole case falls to the ground. All that we can say as far as the evolutionary process is concerned is that mutations occur, and that, if the new individuals and species survive, then their life-history, as individuals, will develop in accordance with their new genetic constitution. There is no reason to suppose that these individuals are in any sense seeking the state which existed before the mutations occurred.

Mixing up psychological phenomena with the phenomena of heredity and embryology, Freud speaks of them all in much the same terms, and thus seems guilty of the most gross errors of anthropomorphism. We find him saying, 'The elementary living entity would from its very beginning *have had no wish to change*; if conditions remained the same, it would do no more than constantly repeat the same course of life'. Well, we might say, we should be surprised to find that an elementary living organism had any wishes at all! Then again, Freud tells us that the instincts are '. . . *seeking to reach an ancient goal* by paths alike old and new'. It is, indeed, by speaking in this way (i.e. as though all living organisms, even the most elementary, were actually seeking or desiring an earlier state of affairs, and were positively seeking to avoid the problem of coming to terms with external circumstances) and by regarding all evolutionary modifications as being unwanted disturbances imposed upon unwilling, conservative organisms by external forces, that Freud comes to the conclusion that all life is seeking that state which existed before there were any disturbances at all—death, or inanimate, inorganic existence. 'The goal of all life', Freud tells us majestically, 'is death.'

At this point, however, Freud pauses for reflection and decides that the conclusion at which he has arrived cannot be wholly true because of the existence of the Sexual Instincts which, far from leading to death, actually bring about the reproduction and the continuation of the processes of life. '. . . and this fact', says Freud, 'indicates that there is an opposition between them and the other instincts. . . .'

But let us stop for a moment and inquire a little further into this notion of *opposition* between the two sets of instincts. How does Freud come to this idea of a fundamental dualism between the two groups of instincts? We must note very clearly that this opposition does *not* rest on the view that one group of instincts is any less conservative than the other. The sexual instincts are just as conservative as the 'Death Instincts' and seek, just as strongly, 'to bring back earlier states of living substance', and, indeed, Freud holds that, 'they are conservative to a higher degree in that they are peculiarly resistant to external influences'.[1] The truth is that this supposed opposition between the two groups of instincts is simply an outcome of Freud's speculation, and is nothing more than a verbal antithesis. His argument so far has led him to suggest that all instincts seek an earlier state of things, and are conservative. The ultimate 'earlier state of things' which the instincts seek is the state of *death*. Here, however, are instincts (the sexual instincts) which result in the perpetuation of *life*. They must, therefore, work in *opposition* to those instincts which seek death.

Now it can be seen in this argument that *all* the instincts, including the sexual instincts, are conceived by Freud as being equally conservative; *all* the instincts 'seek' to repeat an earlier state of things. It simply happens that Freud has speculatively asserted that there must be some instincts which seek *death*, and consequently, when he reconsiders his position and finds that there are at least some which perpetuate *life*, he at once takes it for granted (since Life and Death are opposite ideas) that the two groups are diametrically opposed to each other in their operation. But, of course, apart from Freud's verbal exercises, there is no reason whatsoever to suppose this.

[1] *Beyond the Pleasure Principle*, p. 53.

We can admit that all instincts are a repetition of an earlier state of things in so far as they are genetically determined and that, therefore, the offspring of a species repeat the structural, behavioural, and experiential pattern of life transmitted in their genetic constitution. But to say this is not to say at all that the instincts are in any sense *seeking* a state of affairs which existed before the present genetic constitution of the organism was established; and it is certainly not to say that they can be divided into two groups, one of which aims at the disintegration and death of the individual and the other at the perpetuation of the species, and that these two groups are in conflict with each other within the individual.[1] It must also be mentioned, as Freud himself maintains in other contexts, that—because the reproduction of life is the *result* of the operation of the sexual instincts it cannot be held to follow that the sexual instincts *aim* at reproduction and the perpetuation of life; and it is therefore altogether misleading when Freud speaks of the *aim* of the Life Instincts (Eros) as being the establishment and the preservation of ever greater unities, and the *aim* of the Death Instincts (Thanatos) as being the undoing of connections and the destruction of things.[2] As we have said before, the investigation of the instincts of any animal species does not suggest any grounds for such a dualistic classification, and certainly does not justify the marking out of the sexual instinct as being in any sense opposed to the other instinctual tendencies. But perhaps we should be careful on this point, since Freud, in this particular argument, embraces a good deal by his term the Sexual Instincts or the Life Instincts.

Indeed, the odd thing is that under the heading of the Life Instincts, Freud includes *all* the instincts, and does not seem to have any example of a Death Instinct at all—in spite of the desperate conflict which is supposed to result between the two groups! Here again, Freud maintains that his new classification by no means supersedes the earlier ones, but includes them. In the early pages of *An Outline of Psycho-Analysis*, he tells us, 'The contrast between the instincts of self-preservation (Ego-Instincts) and of the preservation of the species (Sexual Instincts), as well as the contrast between ego-love and object-love, fall within the bounds of Eros'. We might well ask, then: what remains on the side of

[1] When Freud asks, then, 'Let us consider whether there is any basis at all for these speculations. Is it really the case that, apart from the sexual instincts, there are no instincts that do not seek to restore an earlier state of things? that there are none that aim at a state of things which has never yet been attained? I know of no certain example from the organic world that would contradict the characterization I have thus proposed.' (*Beyond the Pleasure Principle*, p. 54.) he is completely missing the point, since the proof that instincts are genetically determined is no proof whatever of his thesis.

[2] The impression thus given is that the whole of organic nature is the manifestation of two fundamental forces, both of which are teleologically striving in opposite directions.

the Death Instincts? Can any one example of a Death Instinct be provided?

Freud does, in fact, do his best to cite one example by trying to relate two polarities: (1) between the Life and Death Instincts, and (2) between Love (or affection) and Hate (or aggressiveness). This develops into a discussion of Sadism. How, Freud asks, can the sadistic component in the sexual instinct be derived from 'Eros, the preserver of life'—when its aim is to injure the love-object?[1] It is more plausible, he suggests, to suppose 'that this sadism is in fact a death instinct which, under the influence of the narcissistic libido, has been forced out of the Ego and has consequently emerged in relation to the object'. In his discussion of Sadism, Freud suggests he has met the demand that he should produce an example of a death instinct, 'though', he says, 'it is true that our example is a displaced one'.

Freud's final position on this point, as expressed in *The Economic Problem in Masochism*, seems to be that there is a primary masochism in the multicellular organism which is the self-destructive impulse of the death instincts. This primary self-destructive impulse is opposed by the libido (the energy of the life instincts) and is thereby diverted outwards towards the external world, when it becomes, or can be called, the instinct of destruction or aggressiveness. This sadism is repressed at the command of the Super-Ego and is then re-directed towards the self, thus accounting for the extreme harshness of the Super-Ego. We see, then, that the primary death instincts, under the influence of the life instincts, are directed outwards and that they then manifest themselves as an urge towards the destruction of objects in the outer world. Freud goes so far as to say that the musculature is the 'special organic system' which is employed for this destructive purpose.

Two points of criticism arise here. In the first place, though this is the only example of a death instinct which he gives, Freud admits that he has no knowledge at all as to how this conflict between the death instinct and the life instincts takes place. In *The Economic Problem in Masochism* he tells us, 'We are entirely without any understanding of the physiological ways and means by which this subjugation of the death-instinct by the libido can be achieved'. We can only conclude that this is a very lame ending to a very lengthy, though equally lame, argument. The second point we have to make is that there is no evidence whatsoever among the observed instincts of animal species to support Freud's postulate of the existence of the death instincts throughout

[1]With reference to this question, see our quotations on the nature of love and hatred in the footnote on p. 240.

'organic life in general'. Freud might well argue, as indeed he does, that the death instincts work in silence and unobserved, but we must insist that it follows from his own argument that—even though the death instincts themselves cannot be observed—there should be, in all animal species which survive (since, if they survive, the life instincts must have successfully combated and overcome the death instincts) the manifestation of a positive urge of aggressiveness or destruction, representing the death instincts which have now been directed outwards towards the external world. As a matter of fact, there is no evidence at all of such a generalised aggressive urge in any animal species which has so far been studied. Tinbergen stresses this point particularly. There is, he tells us, no evidence of a general 'aggressive instinct'. In his short article on 'Fighting and Threat in animals',[1] Tinbergen writes as follows: 'The expression "they live like cat and dog" occurs in more than one language. Somehow this relationship between two different species is considered to be a model of hostile relationship. This is surprising, since in nature fighting between animals of different species is relatively rare. The great majority of fights we can witness in nature involve individuals belonging to the same species. Usually, the fighting animals are of the same sex; as a rule they are males. This intraspecies fighting occurs mainly during the breeding season; outside the breeding season, the members of many species live peacefully together. . . .' And, later in the same article, we are told, 'So far I have used the word fighting to denote all types of hostility. However, actual fighting is relatively rare; in most clashes the opponents do not really come to grips with each other. Instead they display "threat ceremonies".' This evidence of the lack of any general aggressive urge in animals seems to positively and completely refute Freud's generalisation.

Incidentally (although we cannot elaborate upon the point here) it may be that an explanation of the sadistic element in the sexual instinct can be derived satisfactorily from the analysis of Courtship put forward by the Ethologists. The behaviour patterns of the courtship of some animals are shown to be a complex of ritualised threat, escape, and appeasement reactions. If sexual intercourse is to take place, the ethologists suggest, both the threat and the escape reactions have to be overcome, and this might be the function of sexual display and courtship. Whether the facts of sadism might be explained by the presence of these conflicting components (i.e. sexual desire on the one hand, and other conflicting ego-considerations on the other) and their pathological enhancement, we cannot here decide; but it is a consideration of interest, and in the case of human beings, of course, such an account would not

[1] *Fighting and Threat in Animals*, Penguin, 'New Biology', 14, p. 9.

be in terms of inherited 'ritualized' mechanisms, but would require an analysis of conflicting ego-tendencies.

However this may be, it is certain that there is no evidence to support the general existence of death instincts or derived instincts of destruction as postulated by Freud. In addition to his mention of sadism, Freud again refers to his original 'necessary postulate' in connection with the function of the nervous system, leading to his concept of the Nirvana Principle, and, he tells us, 'Our recognition of that fact is one of our strongest reasons for believing in the existence of death instincts'. We have already given reasons to show, however, that this 'necessary postulate' is quite untenable.

In bringing his remarks to a conclusion, Freud stresses that his 'assertion of the regressive character of instincts' rests upon observed material, 'namely, on the facts of the compulsion to repeat'. But, he concludes, 'It may be that I have over-estimated their significance'.

In connection with this point, we must emphasise again that, although Freud starts out from four observed examples of what he calls the compulsion to repeat, these examples are all cases of *mental conflict in the personal experience of human beings*, and the compulsion to repeat is held to be a function of the *unconscious repressed*. In the entire argument which follows these examples, Freud utterly confuses these questions relating to human psychology with other questions relating to genetics, embryology, and the mechanisms of organic evolution. At the best, his speculation rests on analogies, and the analogies are bad. In no place, then, does Freud present the slightest legitimate grounds for extending his generalisation from the realm of human experience to the rest of the organic world.

As a final point of criticism, we might ask: what has now become of those distinguishing features of the instincts which Freud outlined in his earlier work? How would Freud now apply his criteria—source, impetus, aim, and object—to the death instincts? We need not dwell on this point, but it is clear that Freud's latest speculation took him well away from the earlier points upon which he insisted.

Our conclusion in this section is, then, that none of the attempts which Freud made at a classification of the instincts proved to be satisfactory. The only basis for classification which appears in his work which would have been sound (classification in accordance with sources and aims) he neglected to pursue. The most outstanding factor in each of Freud's three attempts is his preoccupation with the necessity of establishing a fundamental *dualistic* basis for classification. All his efforts seem to have been dominated by this need to provide a conceptual basis for the interpretation of *instinctual conflict*. It is difficult to see why, in the light of his later work, this need persisted. Conflicts between various instinctual demands could have been readily admitted without the necessity of postulating some *fundamental cleavage* between *two basic groups* of instincts, and, in any case, it would seem that the intense conflicts in the personality could now have been explained adequately in terms of tensions between the Id, Ego, and Super-Ego, without the necessity of postulating some irreconcilable conflict at the instinctual level.

5. *Conclusions: The Contribution of Psycho-Analysis to the Study of Instinct*

Our discussion has made it clear that what Psycho-Analysis has to say of importance on the subject of Instinct is solely with reference to the part played by Instinct in *human* life. Those generalisations which are made with regard to instinct in animals, or in organic life in general, are practically worthless. We have tried to show that these generalizations are erected upon the basis of extremely unreliable, and, in many places, totally invalid lines of speculative thought. In bringing our discussion of Psycho-Analysis to a close, we might mention in the first place those features of Freud's work on Instinct which are of little use, and then, secondly, those other features which represent a positive and extremely valuable contribution to the subject.

On the negative side there are only two points, and only one of these is really important. The first is—that Freud's attempts at a *classification* of the instincts are quite inadequate and are of no help to us. In particular, the speculation leading to the classification of the Life and Death Instincts does not stand the test of the two kinds of criticism which we mentioned in our opening section. The *logic* of the argument is seen to be weak and faulty in several respects, so that the argument is proved to be *invalid*, and secondly, the evidence of the independent sciences into which Freud extends his generalisations (Biology and Comparative Ethology) is seen to refute the generalisations which are made, so that the conclusions of the speculation are shown to be *false*.

The second point on the negative side is that, whilst we can broadly agree with Freud's account of the *distinguishing features of instinct* (source, impetus, aim, and object), it is clear that nothing new is said in this respect. Nonetheless, Freud's views lend support to what had been maintained previously by the early writers on Instinct, and what is now being taught by the Ethologists. In our introductory chapter[1] we

[1]See p. 25.

mentioned the fact that there appeared to be a curious gap between instincts as discussed by Psycho-Analysis and instincts as discussed by the other theorists. We can now see that—when the Life and Death Instincts are discarded—there is no such gap at all. We have seen, too, that in his discussion of the sources and aims of the instincts, Freud put forward the same basis of classification as was suggested by the other theorists we have considered, even though he did not apply this principle consistently in his own work.

On the positive side there is more to be said. In the first place, the whole of Freud's theory lays great emphasis upon the existence, the extent, and the importance of instinctual experience in the development of human personality and in the complex activities of social life, and—following from this—upon the importance for Psychology of achieving a satisfactory theory of the instincts.

Secondly, Freud's account of instinctual experience in man (and its relation to the more conscious and rational elements of experience) is far more elaborate than anything put forward by previous psychologists, and, during the course of his investigations, Freud developed a set of completely fresh concepts which prove to be extremely useful in the task of interpreting the complexities of the human personality. In this way Psycho-Analysis represents a most important addition to, and extension of, the work of the earlier writers in that it provides a much more detailed and satisfactory analysis of what they referred to in such terms as 'instinct-interest', 'experience on the perceptual plane', and the like (and in respect of which they, too, stressed the importance of conative and affective elements).

Thirdly, during his investigation of instinctual experience in general, Freud has revealed, clarified, and stressed the great importance of the Sexual Instinct in particular (with its various components of eroticism) in the individual and social life of man.

Closely coupled with this account of the sexual instinct, Freud has given us, fourthly, an account of the establishment in the personality of the Super-Ego. In his discussion of this concept, Freud has provided a most interesting Moral Psychology; an explanation of the way in which the primary impulses (the instincts proper) give rise—during the course of the individual's accommodation to the social environment—to secondary impulses which operate in the individual personality after the manner of instincts: compulsively, and making themselves felt internally; although their function, as opposed to the tendencies of the instincts proper, is in the main inhibitory. Thus, we have a system of primary impulses, affective ties and vicissitudes, and secondary impulses, in the establishment of which (in the individual) critical reason has played an almost negligible part (though, of course, Freud believes that reason can subsequently influence, and can effectively extend its influence, over these non-rational and irrational elements).

Fifthly, Psycho-Analysis constitutes a contribution of the utmost importance to Social Psychology.

Freud himself considers the application of his work to Social Psychology when he turns to the analysis of the Ego. This discussion takes place in *Group Psychology and the Analysis of the Ego*, but interesting observations are also made in two other books which are sociologically inclined: *Civilization and its Discontents*, and *The Future of an Illusion*. Throughout his discussion, Freud is considering mainly the 'crowd', or the 'face-to-face' group, and those groups which have noticeable leaders, as, for example, the Church and the Army. The suggestiveness of his approach, and the use he makes of his concept of the Super-Ego can be seen in the following diagram by means of which he illustrates his 'formula' for the libidinal constitution of groups (which have leaders). The formula is phrased as follows: 'A primary group of this kind is a number of individuals who have substituted one and the same object for their ego ideal and have consequently identified themselves with one another in their Ego.'[1]

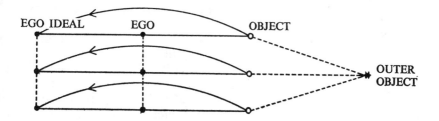

It is clear that Freud's treatment would permit of a much more detailed application than this. Thus we might assume that the affective ties for individuals will involve not only *leaders*, nor indeed only *persons*, but also all kinds of social *symbols* which have been associated with the parents and the influential persons of the individual's early experience. These symbols, like the loved and admired persons with whom they are associated, will constitute the *contents* about which the formation of the personality will take place; the objects in connection with which affective sentiments and attitudes will crystallise. Here we are back to the concept of the 'Sentiment' as formulated by Shand and adopted by

[1]*Group Psychology and The Analysis of the Ego*, Chapter VIII, p. 80.

McDougall, and we can see that this concept is still of use in Social Psychology, even within the context of the Freudian system of ideas. Freud's analysis, in particular his elaboration of the various 'mental mechanisms', may well provide us with a more detailed explanation of how these relatively stable sentiments come to be established. In a word, Freud's system may well comprise a better 'Learning Theory' for the purposes of Social Psychology, than any of the orthodox learning theories in Psychology. Sublimation, Idealisation, Identification have an obvious bearing on the way in which the individual accommodates himself to the social and cultural environment; the way in which his personality is shaped in relation to the complex of social symbols. Even such mechanisms as Symbolisation and Condensation, however, might prove to have an extremely important bearing on the investigation of the relations between the social structure and the formation of personality. Thus, Freud's analysis leads to the conclusion that the earliest and most fundamental 'learning processes' of the human individual (the earliest and most important ways in which he accommodates himself to the complex social environment) are predominantly *affective* in nature, and occur during a *critical period* of development: during the first four or five years of the child's life, and in the context of the early family situation. All that Freud has to say about the nature of the unconscious mental processes and the operation of the various mental mechanisms has particular force with reference to these earliest processes; and the early, basic core or foundation of the individual's personality will comprise a certain constellation of affectively tinged social symbols, including the first persons (in the vast majority of cases the parents) through which primary affective tie the associated symbols have been perceived. The 'secondary impulses' constituting the Super-Ego will also be compulsive impulses of inhibition and aspiration related in definite ways to this earliest constellation of social symbols. Freud's description of instinctual experience thus points to the fact that men, by and large, will tend to perceive the fabric of their social and cultural environment *affectively*, *selectively*, and *symbolically*, and not in the form of a rationally considered system as, for example, the trained sociologist might conceive it.

It is clear that this human disposition has long been known to governments and propagandists of various complexions, as well as to commercial advertisers, and all others who wish to exert a maximum influence upon the tastes, opinions, and loyalties of the members of a community. Simply and conspicuously designed symbols and slogans are always sought and employed by those who wish to promote uniformities of attitude and social cohesion. National Flags and other emblems; National Anthems which are played before or after every public ceremony or concert; Slogans ('Workers of the world unite!' 'Liberty, Equality, Fraternity!'); the constantly repeated portrait of the recognised head of the State—King, Queen, and Royal Family in practically every issue of the daily papers and weekly magazines, or the immense pictures of Stalin or Malenkov or Krushchev on every street corner hoarding or on every building of note—all these illustrate the forcefulness of simple, conspicuous, specific symbols in engendering shared affective ties and shared identifications among widely distributed groups of people. Similarly, many affective ties may be 'condensed', in the Freudian sense, into one major symbol as in the case of a national symbol of the kind mentioned above. The hearing of 'God Save the Queen' or 'Land of Hope and Glory' may arouse in an English citizen not merely the feeling of loyalty to his leader, but also the whole complex of his affective ties to his home, his parents, his wife, his children, his locality, the physical landscape to which he has grown accustomed, the football team he goes to watch on Saturdays, the Silver Prize Band in which he plays on Sundays, and the whole mode of life, feeling, and thought, which has taken shape within him.

All this is very reminiscent of the work of Graham Wallas in his wonderfully suggestive and entertaining book, *Human Nature in Politics*, in which such a psychological analysis of political behaviour is undertaken. Graham Wallas, however, begins his work on the basis of an unsatisfactory and rather arbitrary list of some half-dozen instincts, and the material he presents during the course of his discussion is almost entirely of an anecdotal nature; although, of course, this is of the greatest interest in view of his wide experience of political life. The work of Graham Wallas might be regarded as an important starting point in Social Psychology which has not yet been adequately exploited; and our point here is that, with a sound theory of the instinctual tendencies of man, and a detailed knowledge of the mental mechanisms (the 'learning theory') with which Freud has provided us, such an investigation could now be undertaken on a much sounder basis. It is clear that the possibility of such an inquiry cannot be pursued here, but we can at least see from this very brief discussion how important a contribution Freud has made to the development of Social Psychology, and how stimulating and suggestive a starting point his concepts provide for the study of the relations between the structure of social institutions and associations on the one hand, and the formation of individual personality on the other.

Our conclusion is that the Psycho-Analytic account of Instinct (apart from Freud's attempted classification) constitutes a most valuable contribution. Though inadequate in some respects, it lends support to the findings of both the early 'Doctrine of Instincts' and Comparative Ethology. It also makes a positive addition to the findings of these other spheres of inquiry in so far as it gives us an elaborate account of the nature, extent, and importance of instinctual experience in *man*; emphasising in particular the importance of the Sexual Instinct, and the closely related development of the Super-Ego and the 'secondary impulses'. Finally—in providing an account of the process whereby individuals accommodate themselves to the various features of their social and cultural environment—Psycho-Analysis makes an extremely valuable and suggestive contribution to the development of Social Psychology.

PART THREE

_____

THE CONTEMPORARY THEORY OF INSTINCTS

CHAPTER VII

SOME COMMENTS ON THE ETHOLOGICAL
ACCOUNT, THE PSYCHO-ANALYTIC ACCOUNT,
AND THE EARLY DOCTRINE OF INSTINCTS

WE have now completed our review of the three main bodies of work on the subject of Instinct which we set out to investigate. In the next chapter we shall bring the various threads of our discussion together in an attempt to achieve a satisfactory synthesis. Before doing this, however, it will be of use to spend a little time in considering certain points of interest which have emerged from our discussion so far, and in making a few further points of criticism which it did not seem expedient (for purposes of clear exposition) to make earlier. This chapter therefore comprises a few after-thoughts on our previous discussion, a sorting out of some of the more significant points which have emerged, and a preparatory discussion for the synthesis of the next chapter.

Some Criticisms of Comparative Ethology

Our comments in this section fall into two groups. Firstly, it is necessary to mention certain differences of opinion among the ethologists themselves, and secondly, we must return to a brief reconsideration of the relation between Ethology and Psychology which we mentioned whilst discussing the work of Tinbergen and Lorenz.

1. *Differences of Opinion with regard to certain Ethological Concepts*

It must be pointed out that certain of the concepts which are used quite confidently by Tinbergen and Lorenz are not yet accepted by all other contributors to the Ethological school. Brief mention might be made of some of these critical attitudes.

Whereas Tinbergen is prepared to postulate the importance of 'Intrinsic Central Nervous Factors' in the causation of innate behaviour and tends to emphasise the central control of patterns and rhythms of locomotion (though he does this guardedly, after a careful review of the evidence), we find that J. Gray doubts the correctness of introducing the conception of central control. In his paper, 'The Role of Peripheral Sense Organs During Locomotion in the Vertebrates', after reporting detailed experimental investigation of the locomotory patterns of Amphibia (the experiments were performed with toads), Gray concludes:

'To my mind, the role of the proprioceptors in amphibian ambulation seems to be sufficiently clear to doubt the necessity of introducing conceptions of central control for which there is at present no direct experimental evidence. How far we are justified in attempting to extend this picture to mammals is more doubtful. For present purposes, however, the main conclusion must be that the existence of centrally controlled patterns of locomotion should be regarded as non-proven. So far as the reflex picture is concerned, the data derived from a study of the Amphibia indicate that the pattern of peripheral excitation arising in a single limb does not necessarily result in a fixed or predetermined pattern of muscular response in any of the others, it only contributes to a general pattern of excitation coming from sense organs located throughout all the rest of the ambulatory musculature and elsewhere. . . . This integrated pattern of stimulation elicits a pattern of response from the musculature as a whole. An application of these principles to wider fields of animal behaviour suggests that particular patterns of behaviour are not so much due to the activity of specific sense organs or to the intrinsic properties of the central nervous system, but to the whole pattern of peripheral stimulation and to the ability of the central nervous system to direct this excitation along pathways which involve the whole of the animal's musculature.'[1]

We have already seen that Rudolf Brun disagrees with the hypothetical postulate of 'neurophysiological centres' in the diencephalon such as Tinbergen puts forward, and we have considered sufficiently the evidence he presents in support of his view.[2]

Differences of opinion with regard to other important ethological concepts are expressed by Edward A. Armstrong in his paper, 'The Nature and Function of Displacement Activities'. In our previous outline of Tinbergen's work it was held, with only slight qualification, that a specific 'Sign Stimulus' was very closely correlated with a particular 'Reaction Specific Energy', and was responsible for releasing this energy and the appropriate fixed pattern reaction. Armstrong criticises this point. Having given many instances in which particular instinctive behaviour patterns were elicited by 'an incongruous object or cognitive situation', he goes on to say: 'The inference is that drive and the releaser

[1] See *Physiological Mechanisms in Animal Behaviour*.   [2] See pp. 141-142.

of the behaviour-pattern associated with it are not always as rigidly connected as might at first appear to be the case. These instances show that while in what we may define as normal behaviour the adequate object or stereotyped releaser is essential to the evocation of the behaviour-pattern, there are other types of behaviour in which the specific characteristics of the object which acts as "catalyst" for a movement-pattern or other item of behaviour have minimal significance. The situation may be compared with that in which machinery begins to move irrespective of whose finger presses the switch. . . .' Armstrong then mentions examples of behaviour-patterns which are manifested during sleep, as though indicative of 'dreaming', and tells us: 'Whether or not we regard such forms of behaviour as suggesting that an image of an object, or something akin to an image, can exist in an animal's mind, they indicate that in a wide variety of organisms[1] drive and exteroceptive object may become to a large extent, or even entirely, divorced. . . . It is thus evident that in animal behaviour the correlation between behaviour-pattern and releaser is not necessarily rigid. It is possible for the behaviour-pattern to achieve a large measure of independence of its "traditional" releaser.'

Armstrong also finds himself unable to accept without qualification the concept of Reaction Specific Energy. In discussing this, he is critical of concepts such as 'Vacuum Activity' and the 'exhaustibility of specific instinctive acts' from which the notion of reaction specific energy is inferred. It is on the question of 'exhaustibility' that his criticism seems to be most potent. Both Lorenz and Tinbergen, we may remember, maintained that a particular instinctive behaviour pattern gradually diminished both in the number of performances and in the intensity of performance when the animal was induced to repeat the action many times, and, since the animal as a whole was far from being exhausted, they postulated the exhaustion of a *specific* energy appropriate to this particular fixed pattern reaction. Armstrong emphasises the view that this apparent exhaustion in connection with the repetition of particular actions may be due to *habituation*, and not to any 'draining away' of some specific store of energy, and he gives observations of his own to suggest that this 'exhaustion' does not, in fact, always occur. 'He (Lorenz)', says Armstrong, 'cites as evidence injury-simulation by a bird which on successive occasions decreased in vehemence. But this single instance does not provide a sound basis for generalisation. Again and again, for hours at a time on successive days, I induced a ringed plover to simulate injury without there being any noticeable diminution in the

[1] *Physiological Mechanisms in Animal Behaviour*, p. 364. Armstrong mentions: the short-tailed shrew, the dog, the black-headed gull, the robin, and the toad.

vigour of the performance, which, indeed, increased when the birds were hatching. I have noticed almost equally persistent injury-simulation by a little ringed plover. . . . The behaviour of the bird commented upon by Lorenz may be attributed to habituation. He has himself drawn attention to the fact that the owner of a tame bird is unable to elicit injury-simulation because he is an insufficiently terrifying object.' 'We must conclude that in so far as the concept of reaction specific energy is dependent on the evidence of "Leerlaufreaktion" (i.e. "Vacuum Activity") and "specific exhaustibility" being valid concepts, it is unproven.'[1]

We are not competent to decide upon one or other of these opinions, but it is clear that much further investigation lies ahead of the ethologists themselves before these disagreements can be resolved. We have mentioned them simply to show that disagreement does in fact exist among the ethologists, and in order to dispel any impression of undue simplicity which might have been received from our condensed presentation of the ideas of Lorenz and Tinbergen.

2. *The Relation between Ethology and Psychology*

We turn now to our second point: the question of the relation between Ethology and Psychology, and here again we do not find a clear unity of opinion among the Ethologists. We may firstly remind ourselves of the emphatic stand taken by Tinbergen on this question. On the one hand, he approximates to the Behaviourist point of view, as when he says: 'Because subjective phenomena cannot be observed objectively in animals, it is idle either to claim or to deny their existence.' On the other hand, he maintains that subjective phenomena cannot be regarded as *causal* agents in behaviour at all. 'When it is claimed that the subjective phenomenon of hunger is one of the causes of food-seeking behaviour, physiological and psychological thinking are confused . . .' and: 'Hunger, like anger, fear, and so forth, is a phenomenon that can be known only by introspection. When applied to another subject, especially one belonging to another species, it is merely a guess about the possible nature of the animal's subjective state. By presenting such a guess as a causal explanation, the psychologist trespasses on the domain of physiology.' Again, Tinbergen says: 'The study of directiveness, the study of subjective phenomena, and the study of causation are three ways of thinking about behaviour, each of which is consistent in the application of its own methods. However, when they trespass into each other's fields, confusion results.'

It is clear from these statements that, in the study of behaviour,

[1] *Physiological Mechanisms in Animal Behaviour*, p. 366.

Tinbergen equates the *study of causation* with the *study of the physiological aspects of behaviour*. Subjective phenomena may be studied, but such a study can never hope to throw light upon the *causation* of behaviour, and if it does attempt to do this, then it is charged with trespassing upon the territory of physiology. Now physiology is an important study, but it is most certainly not in the position of being able to exalt itself to the status of the sole study of the causation of behaviour. Let us see what can be said against Tinbergen's view.

In the first place there is ample evidence to support the view that subjective, or experiential factors enter into the causation of behaviour, and, indeed, that some sequences of behaviour cannot be causally accounted for without reference to experiential factors. Psycho-Analysis has shown that physiological conditions (as in conversion), as well as behavioural reactions, can be the outcome of severe experiential conflict. Similarly, the phenomena of post-hypnotic suggestion surely prove that a mental factor—a suggestion—can cause a subsequent manifestation of behaviour. But there is a multitude of everyday examples of behaviour in human beings which cannot possibly be explained without reference to experiential factors. Let us ask for a physiological explanation (since psychology cannot contribute to a causal analysis) of why the editor of a Communist newspaper resigns his post, enters the Catholic Church, and writes an article in a liberal paper giving the reasons for his decision; of why this person prefers the music of Beethoven to that of Grieg and attends some concerts rather than others; of why this thirty-five year old spinster commits suicide after a broken engagement of marriage? But of course it is ludicrous to go on with such a list, since it is quite evident that in providing a causal explanation of the detailed experience and behaviour of men and women, psychology and sociology can give us a much more satisfactory analysis than can physiology. Even if we take the simplest kind of case—let us say that of pain—we can see that physiology alone cannot give a complete causal account. Thus we know that many persons do not go to the dentist even though they are well aware that one of their teeth is in a state of decay and needs attention. They finally visit the dentist when the *pain* from the decayed tooth is so severe as to outweigh their dread of sitting in the dentist's chair and having the tooth extracted. In this example, it is clear that the severity of pain, the subjective experience, is at least one of the necessary factors in any causal explanation of the behaviour of these individuals in attending the dentist's surgery. It is clear that experiential factors must be regarded as contributing causes to at least *some* manifestations of behaviour.

We might go further, however, and say that it is extremely doubtful whether physiological detail will ever be able to throw light upon such psychological phenomena as *meaning, significance, interests, attitudes*, and the like, which, as we have seen, are causal factors in some sequences of behaviour. This is not to say that there is not a physiological side to all our experience; clearly there is. But it is by no means evident that each subtlety of our mental experience has its own peculiar concomitant physiological process; or that the pointing out of any such peculiar physiological process would constitute an explanation of the experiential subtlety. Thus, if I am sitting at my desk with paper and pencil, I may (*a*) try to write down a particular tune I heard yesterday and which I liked, (*b*) try to analyse, in syllogistic form, an argument which I had heard made by a politician and which appealed to me, though I felt that it was not altogether valid, or (*c*) check my bank account in the light of a statement which I have just received. Now these three activities, though embodying very similar overt behaviour (sitting at a desk and writing on paper with a pencil) are quite distinct from each other in terms of experience: aesthetically, for example, or in terms of meaning, interest, and so on. But why should we suppose that each subtle discrimination of meaning or interest has a distinct and peculiar physiological process? And, even if it has, why should we suppose that the pointing out of the latter is a causal explanation of the former, rather than vice versa? What we wish to emphasise here is that there are causal factors of behaviour on the level of interest, meaning, significance, and the like, which cannot be *explained* by physiological investigation at all, even though the latter may add to our knowledge by describing the physiological concomitants of these features.

But in all this, it may be replied, you are talking about the intricacies of *human* experience, whereas Tinbergen's comments are with reference to the study of animal behaviour. True—but our point so far has been simply to show that *subjective* phenomena cannot be ruled out of the picture as *causal* factors in any analysis of behaviour. Now, returning to the question of animal behaviour, we must at least admit that subjective phenomena *may* be causal elements. The possibility cannot be simply ruled out on the grounds of an *a priori* dogma. And several points arise in this connection.

In the first place we must note that Tinbergen himself is compelled to introduce terms referring to subjective phenomena, even though he regards them analytically and objectively. Thus, he speaks of the 'perceptual world' of the animal, and of the 'true purposive activity' of the animal in the 'appetitive' phase of instinctive behaviour. In this connection we might refer to the views of E. S. Russell whose work we have mentioned earlier.

COMMENTS ON THE ETHOLOGICAL ACCOUNT

In his review of Tinbergen's book, *The Study of Instinct*, Russell writes:

'One of the most interesting points which has been established in recent years is that many animals respond not to all the sensory impressions they receive but only to a limited number of rather simple "sign-stimuli"; experiments show, for example, that the essential stimulus which incites a male stickleback to attack an intruding male is the red colour on the belly of the intruder, and that its other visible characteristics are disregarded. Here arises a fundamental question. Is it sufficient to speak of stimuli, or of stimulation, meaning by that a purely physiological process? Or is there not involved the psychological function of perception, an active selective activity, having, no doubt, a physiological basis or background, but different in nature from purely physiological activity? Tinbergen seems to accept the view that each animal has its own perceptual world (p. 16), and he does in practice assume that animals see, hear, smell, taste, and experience tactile sensations. If this be so, then there is a limit to a purely causal interpretation. We must accept perception as a function of the animal organism, but it can never be explained in purely physiological terms, though its physiological conditions may, of course, be studied with profit. Tinbergen recognises also that on the executive side instinctive behaviour shows clear signs of striving to attain an end, at least in its first phase of "appetitive" behaviour. The "consummatory act" in which it culminates "is relatively simple; at its most complex, it is a chain of reactions, each of which may be a simultaneous combination of a taxis and a fixed pattern. But appetitive behaviour is a true purposive activity, offering all the problems of plasticity, adaptiveness, and of complex integration that baffle the scientist in his study of behaviour as a whole" (p. 106). . . . It does not seem possible to study behaviour adequately without taking into account such psychological functions as perception and directive striving, and they do not fit in to the "causal structure". That is the difficulty which confronts the student of animal behaviour.'[1]

Whilst agreeing with this criticism of Tinbergen's view, we must also add, to qualify Russell's statement, that these psychological features 'do not fit into the "causal structure" ' only because the 'causal' analysis is limited—in our view arbitrarily—to the sphere of physiological investigation. If psychological concepts and hypotheses are also utilised in the causal explanation, then there is no reason why these features should not be taken into account. If besides the concept of 'reaction specific energy' we use also the concept of 'conation' (the

[1]*Nature*, vol. 169, No. 4310, June 7th, 1952, p. 940.

experiential concomitant); and if, besides the concept of a closely correlated 'sign-stimulus' and 'innate releasing mechanism', we use the concept of a subjective 'perception' appropriate to the felt 'conation', and the concept of a primary 'instinct-interest' uniting these various features in a whole feeling of worth-whileness, then we can quite well take such features as directive striving into account—and this, within the 'causal structure'. This, the earlier writers on instinct did, and in this connection we must recommend once more the extraordinarily clear statement of James Drever. It might be argued that such concepts as 'instinct-interest' or 'instinct-meaning' savour too much of a projection of human, rational features into the experience and behaviour of animals, but we have seen earlier that this is not so, and writers such as Lloyd Morgan and Drever speak of this concept quite legitimately, referring entirely to the level of perceptual and conative-affective experience. We have also seen in our last chapter that what is, in effect, the same concept is utilised by Freud in his description of human instinctual experience, when he speaks of 'object-cathexis'; and he does in fact give us an elaborate account of 'instinct-interest' and the 'perceptual and conative-affective' aspects of experience in man.

This question of the validity of introducing psychological concepts and hypotheses into the study of the causation of animal behaviour raises another point on which Tinbergen—along with many others who favour the physiological approach—is guilty of inconsistency.

As we have seen, Tinbergen holds that hunger, anger, fear, and so on, can only be known introspectively, and that when we apply such terms to the interpretation of behaviour (especially when the behaviour is that of another species) we are simply making *guesses* 'about the possible nature of the animal's subjective state'. But let us consider: is this so? It is true that, for each of us, the content of the words 'fear', 'hunger', etc., depends upon what we ourselves have experienced. But these experiences are usually accompanied by involuntary overt gestures, facial expressions, and movements of other kinds, which make our recognition of these experiences in others quite reliable. If it were not so, human sympathy would have no basis, and literature and the dramatic presentation of human situations would be impossible. We are never really in doubt that a child who shrieks uncontrollably when he spills boiling water over his leg is suffering excruciating pain; nor do we doubt that a dog is also suffering pain when boiling water is spilled over his back and he yelps and bolts away from the spot—although in neither case can we be certain that the experience of these two subjects is *precisely* the same as the past experience of our own. Similarly, we know well enough when a person is terrified, when he is angry, and so on. The question is: even supposing we can attain a reasonably satisfactory knowledge of subjective phenomena in human beings, how can we possibly infer that animals also have subjective experience and that this is in any way similar to ours? And this brings us to the point on which, we believe, inconsistency arises.

When Tinbergen, and others, are claiming that their findings with regard to animal behaviour can legitimately be extended to the study of man, they argue as follows:

'Man is an animal. He is a remarkable and in many respects unique species, but he is an animal nevertheless. In structure and functions of the heart, blood, intestine, kidneys, and so on, man closely resembles other animals, especially other vertebrates. Palaeontology as well as comparative anatomy and embryology do not leave the least doubt that this resemblance is based on true evolutionary relationships. Man and the present-day primates have only recently diverged from a common primate stock. This is why comparative anatomy and comparative physiology have yielded such important results for human biology. It is only natural, therefore, that the zoologist should be inclined to extend his ethological studies beyond the animals to man himself.'

These are Tinbergen's own words, and again, after telling us that the ethological study of man has not yet advanced very far, he says: 'One of the main reasons for this is the almost universal misconception that the causes of man's behaviour are qualitatively different from the causes of animal behaviour.'[1]

In order to show the legitimate extension of their own study of animal species to the study of man, Tinbergen and others quite rightly stress the likeness, indeed the kinship, of man to the animals, and emphasise the similarities in anatomy and in physiological processes between man and other animal species.

Why, then, we ask in astonishment, are such writers so opposed to the converse of this line of reasoning?—to the suggestion that, since these structural, physiological, and behavioural processes are accompanied by certain subjective phenomena in man, the probability is that they are also accompanied by subjective phenomena of a similar kind in many animal species? It seems that the observed similarity, in a multitude of respects, between man and the animals can be quite happily called in to support the extension of generalisations from the animals to man, but not, conversely, from man to the animals. This is a real inconsistency. If this similarity exists, and if, as Tinbergen so

[1]*The Study of Instinct*, p. 205.

rigorously maintains, 'the causes of man's behaviour are qualitatively the same as the causes of animal behaviour', then this is a ground which will justify our tentative hypothetical approach to the study of the psychology of animals, just as it will justify the extension of hypotheses from the behaviour of animals to that of man. Darwin, of course, was quite ready to accept this two-fold implication of man's kinship with the animals, and, as we have pointed out in our introductory chapter, his work in *The Descent of Man*, and in the *Expression of the Emotions in Man and Animals*, provides a great number of fascinating observations on the external behavioural signs whereby the emotions of various animals can be recognised.

However, we do not wish to suggest that the study of subjective experience, whether in man or in animals, is an easy or straightforward matter. Obviously it is not.

All we wish to insist upon is that, on the basis of (*a*) the similarities between man and other animal species, (*b*) the facts of our own subjective experience, and (*c*) the observed behaviour (including postures, gestures, facial expressions, and calls) of animals, such postulates as 'perception', 'conation', 'instinct-interest', and 'emotion', are, far from being extravagant, quite legitimate, and prove to be indispensable in any full account of behaviour, and especially of such aspects of behaviour as the phenomena of learning. After the treatment of Freud, it can be seen that these concepts prove to be applicable to the study of man also, and they are consequently extremely useful concepts for Comparative Psychology.

Having said all this, we must emphasise that we are not by any means arguing against the study of the physiological causes of behaviour. We are simply objecting to the *a priori* supposition that subjective phenomena cannot be regarded as causal factors in behaviour, and that psychology cannot therefore contribute to a causal analysis of behaviour. We maintain, as the earlier writers did, that the study of instinct has its bio-physiological and behavioural aspects *and* its experiential aspects, and that a knowledge of *both* is required for a complete causal explanation.

A further point which must be mentioned here is, that both Tinbergen and Lorenz sometimes write as though they believed that, because the *data* of a science are *subjective* (i.e. experiential: impulses, emotions, thoughts, dreams, learning processes, etc.) then that science must be a *subjective* science; and that a science is *objective* only if it deals with so-called concrete data which can be directly observed. Tinbergen says: 'while the phenomena studied in this book are for the most part the same as those studied in psychology, the type of approach will be physiological or objective.' We wish simply to make the point that one can conduct an *objective* study of *subjective* phenomena. Thus, we have seen how Freud went to great pains to formulate concepts whereby he could interpret and explain the many facts of experiential conflict as he observed then in his many case studies. It is perfectly true that the study of *experiential* phenomena is hedged round with extraordinary difficulties, but this, surely, is not the point. As Tinbergen himself maintains in another context, Science must not proceed, and cannot expand, by ruling out of court such material as it cannot adequately deal with by means of its present method and techniques—but must rather change and extend its methods and techniques in order to investigate material which, though intractable, our experience shows us to be both existent and important.

Other Ethologists, whilst adopting as 'objectivist' a viewpoint as Tinbergen, are not so emphatic or final in their views on Psychology. W. H. Thorpe holds that the new conceptual scheme of Ethology does not eliminate the psychological approach 'but makes it clear where it is useful, indeed essential', as, for example, in the 'purposive, highly plastic phases of the appetitive and goal (releaser) behaviour'. Lorenz, whilst holding that a 'real "psychology" of animals is on principle impossible', nonetheless stresses the importance, for comparative studies, of cases where *both* the physiological *and* the psychological aspects permit of investigation. 'In my opinion, every physiological process which can . . . be approached simultaneously from the objective and from the subjective side is of paramount theoretical and practical importance. The cardinal problem of psychology, the question of the interdependence of body and mind, cannot be inductively approached in any other way than by studying those not too common cases, in which the intrinsic unit of one of these highest life processes *can* be studied from the objective, physiological side as well as from the subjective, psychological one. To refrain from introspection in such cases would mean renouncing a superlatively valuable source of knowledge for purely dogmatic reasons which would be about the worst thing a natural scientist could do.'[1]

The most satisfactory position still appears to be that adopted by the earlier writers, namely, that both aspects of the experience and behaviour of living organisms must be viewed as being 'concomitant' with, or closely correlated with, each other. This seems the best view to hold, although, especially after the work of Freud, we now know that experiential features can be as causally efficacious in bringing about certain sequences of behaviour as can bio-physiological features alone.

[1]*Physiological Mechanisms in Animal Behaviour*, p. 266.

Some Significant Parallels between Comparative Ethology and Psycho-Analysis

It will have been noticed, during the course of our discussion, that several similarities have emerged between the concepts of Comparative Ethology and those of Psycho-Analysis. These appear to be more than mere analogies, and we shall devote this section to the task of elaborating them in some detail.

Some of these parallels have already been mentioned by certain writers. In his paper 'Critical Phases in the Development of Social Responses in Men and Other Animals',[1] John Bowlby gives the following list:

(*a*) 'Many of the most important social responses can be understood as the result of an inner drive (instinct) seeking discharge in a consummatory act. This consummatory act commonly has survival value, but it is the release of tension not the fulfilment of a biologically useful act which brings action to an end.

(*b*) 'The drive to make a love relationship with a parent-figure is innate (in mammals and some species of birds).

(*c*) 'The selection of a love object in adult life may be strongly influenced by the character of the individual's early love object—a process which may be carried to the point of a fixation.[2]

(*d*) 'Adult social responses, especially sexual responses, often utilise in new configurations social responses of childhood, especially child-parent responses. . . .[3]

(*e*) 'Instinctual responses go through critical phases of development with special reference both to the nature of the object selected and the precise motor pattern adopted.

(*f*) 'Instinctual energy can be discharged by "sparking over" to find

[1] *Prospects in Psychiatric Research*, Ed. J. M. Tanner (Oxford, Basil Blackwell, Autumn, 1952).

[2] We may remember Lorenz's example of 'imprinting' in the case of the young geese which became attached to the first large moving objects they saw (a human being) and, in later life, directed their adult responses towards this object.

[3] An interesting example of this is given by Lorenz in his study of jackdaws which, it appears, utilise infantile sounds in their adult mating relationships. Lorenz writes: 'it is really touching to see how affectionate these two wild creatures are with each other. Every delicacy that the male finds is given to his bride and she accepts it with the plaintive begging gestures and notes otherwise typical of baby birds. In fact, the love-whispers of the couple consist chiefly of infantile sounds, reserved for adult jackdaws for these occasions. Again, how strangely human! With us too, all forms of demonstrative affection have an undeniable childlike tendency—or have you never noticed that all the nicknames we invent, as terms of endearment for each other, are nearly always diminutives?' (*King Solomon's Ring* p. 158).

expression in behaviour patterns belonging to a quite different instinct —a process of displacement.'

'Enough has been said', Bowlby concludes, 'to suggest that the time is already ripe for a unification of psycho-analytic concepts with those of ethology, and to pursue the rich vein of research which this unification suggests.'

In what follows, we shall comment upon those parallels between the two fields of work which appear the most striking and the most important.

1. *Displacement*

Before turning specifically to the concept of displacement, we might remind ourselves that for Freud, as for the Ethologists, features of experience and behaviour are dependent to a great extent upon 'internal causal factors'. 'There can be no question', says Freud, 'that the libido has somatic sources, that it streams into the Ego from various organs and parts of the body. . . .' Or, again: 'The phenomena with which we have to deal do not belong only to psychology; they have also an organic and biological aspect. . . .'

With this psycho-biological approach of Freud in mind, it can be seen that the concept of Displacement in Psycho-Analysis is extremely similar to that in Ethology, if it is not, in fact, identical. In the first place, let us recall Tinbergen's hypothetical 'Hierarchical System of Neuro-physiological Levels and Centres'. According to this system, a displacement reaction occurs when the release of a certain reaction specific energy is blocked, and it is therefore deflected through the 'centre' of another instinct, thus stimulating the motor pattern of this other instinct into activity; and this process is termed the 'sparking over' of the instinctual energy on to the neural paths of another instinct. Now, secondly, let us recall Freud's discussion of the 'quantitative' aspects of instinctual excitation. 'I should like to throw out the question', he says, 'whether this quantitative factor that I am now dwelling on does not suffice to cover the phenomena for which Bleuler and others have lately wished to introduce the term "switching". One need only assume that increased resistance in one direction of the psychical currents result in hyper-cathexis along some other path and thus causes the whole current to be switched into this path.'

The use of the concept of Displacement in the two spheres of investigation seems to be identical and not simply analogous.

E. A. Armstrong mentions this parallel, but is chary about making too close a comparison between the usage of the concept in Ethology and Psycho-Analysis. He seems, however, to be unnecessarily dubious. In the first place, what he takes to be Displacement in the Freudian sense is what Freud would actually term 'Transference'; 'the transference of emotion from one object to another.'[1] In the second place, it is true that Displacement as conceived by Freud refers to the very mobile cathexis of the unconscious mental processes by means of which an instinctual impulse can derive satisfaction by finding an outlet in connection with other objects when satisfaction in connection with the original object is blocked, whereas, in Ethology, the concept refers to a deflection of energy which results in the release of a definite 'out-of-context' motor-mechanism. This, however, does not seem a great difficulty. It is what we would expect if we assume that, in the lower species, a relatively hard-and-fast correlation between internal causal factors, sign-stimuli, and fixed behavioural automatisms is established by heredity, whereas, in the case of man, this correlation is not rigidly established by heredity, and satisfactory behaviour (linking the internal instinctual excitation with the external object which yields satisfaction) is only gradually established as an outcome of individual experience. In the lower species, since the fixed pattern reactions are so closely correlated with their reaction specific energy, any deflection of energy on to other neural paths may be expected to result in the manifestation of some other behavioural automatism. In man, however, since this connection between the two features is not so rigidly established phylogenetically, we may expect that the mobile cathexis of the instinctual excitations can exist and take place (as Freud describes in his account of the unconscious mental processes) without any close tie with particular behaviour mechanisms. As Drever suggests, and as Freud confirms, we would expect this mobility of excitation and this lack of inherited behavioural automatisms to be accompanied by an increasing dominance of the *emotional* factor in the instinctual experience and behaviour of man. We may remember, in this connection, what Freud has to say about the human individual's task of 'binding instinctual excitations', and his claim that this task can only be accomplished by 'raising the level of the whole cathectic process' and by achieving what he terms 'a preparedness for anxiety'.

It seems, then, that both Psycho-Analysis and Comparative Ethology, working on quite different levels and with different techniques, have arrived at this same concept of 'Displacement'. The concept is essentially the same in the two spheres of investigation, and is applicable both to the study of animal behaviour and to the study of man.

[1] *Physiological Mechanisms in Animal Behaviour*, p. 361, n.

2. *There is no Social Instinct*

Little need be said here on this point as we have already examined the views of both Freud and Tinbergen on the subject. We can merely note, however, that Psycho-Analysis and Ethology are agreed in their teaching that there is no evidence of a social instinct proper, and that all social activities and social feelings are either aspects of particular instincts, or are derived from such instincts.

3. *The Hierarchy of Neurophysiological Levels and Psychic Inhibition*

An interesting point is made by Tinbergen when putting forward his hypothetical 'Hierarchy of Neurophysiological Levels and Centres' which is worthy of mention here. He maintains that the highest centre of the hierarchy—the 'topcentre'—has no block.[1] The appetitive behaviour which is the outcome of the activity of this highest centre does not require any specific sign-stimuli for its release, but is dependent upon 'purely motivational' or predominantly internal causal factors. The levels of the hierarchy are graded in this way: the higher centres being activated mainly by *internal* causal factors, and the lower centres being (increasingly, the lower we descend) activated by *external* releasing stimuli. Having described this hierarchy, Tinbergen tells us: 'If there were blocks at these very highest centres, the animal would have no means of "getting rid" of impulses at all, which, as far as we know, would lead to neurosis.'

This idea links up admirably with the Freudian system. For, in giving his account of the human instincts and their vicissitudes, Freud describes the 'blocks' which are preventing the direct discharge of the impulses of these highest centres as 'psychic inhibitions'. In the setting up of the Super-Ego (the establishing of the 'secondary impulses', whose influence is chiefly inhibitory) we are provided with these 'blocks' which lead to the repression of the instinctual demands, and, consequently, to mental and even physical disorders, and to various degrees of 'dissociation' of the personality.[2]

This point, too, is one of the reasons for our inclusion of the findings in neurophysiology mentioned by Rudolf Brun; for his description of the centres and neural paths of the Diencephalon and his account of their functioning (as a kind of 'rheostat circuit') gives a further suggestion as to the neurophysiological means whereby the process of inhibition and dissociation is effected.

[1] See pp. 139-141.
[2] It may be, too, that the hypothetical scheme of Tinbergen's coupled with the observations of Brun, could be of use in investigating the detailed processes of 'conversion'.

4. *The Similarity of the Concepts Denoting the Distinguishing Features of Instinct*

This point requires only brief mention. But it is worth while to note that the concepts which Freud adopts to indicate the distinguishing features of instinct are very similar to those adopted by the Ethologists. Freud's concept of the 'source' of an instinct can be equated with the Ethologists' concept of 'internal causal factors'. The 'impetus' can be equated with the 'reaction-specific energy'. The 'object' can be equated with the appropriate 'sign-stimulus' or 'releaser'. And the 'aim'—which, for Freud, was 'in every case satisfaction' or the reduction of tension— can be equated with the Ethologists' conception of the release of the 'fixed pattern reaction' or the performance of the 'consummatory act'. It is to be noted that, in both cases, in connection with this latter point, the 'aim' is held to be the release of tension, the actual performance of the instinctual action, and not the purposive striving for a biologically useful end.

5. *Ambivalent Behaviour: Instinctual Conflict*

In Comparative Ethology, 'ambivalent behaviour' is the outcome of the fact that each reaction has its own releasing mechanism and appropriate sign-stimuli, and occurs when two sign-stimuli, belonging to different reactions, are present at the same time. The illustration given by Tinbergen was that of the herring gull which tried both to remove the red egg from its nest and to sit upon it at the same time. Freud, too, uses the concept of 'ambivalence', but with reference to the simultaneous presence of feelings of love and hatred in a relationship with a love-object. Although both concepts of 'ambivalence' can therefore be brought under the heading of 'Instinctual Conflict', they are not identical.

On the other hand, their similarity may be greater than appears to be the case. We may remember how the presence of elements of the escape-reaction and of the aggressive-reaction in patterns of courtship behaviour leads Tinbergen to suggest that the function of Courtship may be to overcome these two reactions so that intimate sexual relations can take place. In a similar way, it may be that in the mating behaviour of human beings, the ambivalent feelings of love and sadism discussed by Freud can be explained in terms of simultaneously operative instinctual tendencies. Thus, it is possible that this notion of 'ambivalence' also will prove to be more similar in the two fields of study than appears at first sight.

6. Social Releasers and Social Symbols

When pointing out the parallels which Lorenz makes between animal and human 'tradition' during his discussion of some 'Social Releasers',[1] we were careful to emphasise that these parallels could not be held too strictly, since the Social Releasers of animal species are established by heredity, whereas the Social Symbols of human societies are often purposefully designed. This point still holds good. Nonetheless, after Freud's description of the unconscious mental processes of human individuals—in which he lays stress upon the predominance of 'pictorial' and 'symbolical' thinking, and the 'affective' aspects of the process of accommodation to the social and cultural environment—we cannot help thinking that there is something to be said for such parallels, if held with care, after all. Individuals approach the many features of their social context through the channels, as it were, of affectively-charged sentiments and attitudes towards persons, localities, institutions, and associations, and it does appear to be true that very simple, conspicuous, well-designed symbols arise, and are necessary, for the effective continuity of a social tradition: whether these symbols are visual (in the form of flags, badges, uniforms, portraits), verbal (in the form of slogans and catch-phrases, or even in the form of ordinary words which carry certain complexes of status with them: such as mother, father, priest, policeman, state, etc.), or auditory (in the form of national anthems and popular tunes). Whilst rejecting, therefore, the notion of any strict parallel between the Social Releasers of animals and the Social Symbols of human societies, we feel that the similarity is, nonetheless, worth keeping in mind, and it has been suggested elsewhere how it might prove to be of use in our approach to Social Psychology.

7. The Instincts: The Learning Processes: The Critical Period Hypothesis

In both Comparative Ethology and Psycho-Analysis we find the conclusion that the learning processes of the individual are not to be conceived as separate cognitive processes in isolation from the instincts, but, on the contrary, that they are very intimately related to the activation of the instincts, and that they are closely related to definite and critical periods of instinctual development.

In Comparative Ethology, the critical period hypothesis points to the fact that certain important kinds of learning process and certain important periods of learning coincide with critical periods in the growth

[1]See pp. 155-158.

and maturation of the individual. It is interesting, too, to note that many of the illustrations given by the ethologists are connected with the parent-offspring relationship and the process of sexual development. We have the example of 'imprinting' in the case of young geese, which was mentioned earlier in this section. Similarly, we have the example from Tinbergen of the Eskimo dogs which learn the territories of the other dogs in the settlement very quickly as they become sexually mature.

Freud, too, emphasises the importance of certain critical periods in the development of the human individual. The affective relationships established during the first four or five years (the period of infantile sexuality) together with the formation and the content of the Super-Ego established towards the end of this period, are held to be of the utmost importance in the actual formation of the personality, and as a determining influence upon the later life of the individual. A relatively quiescent period follows (the Latency Period) but this is also of importance since it is during this period that the attitudes and conventions of the wider social environment are encountered and consequent reaction-formations are set up: especially, it seems, against the infantile components of eroticism. Then comes the critical period of puberty with its re-activation of infantile trends and influences, and its difficulties of adjustment between the awakening demand of adult sexuality and the demands of the Super-Ego and the established reaction-formations of the Latency Period. In all this, we must note that the so-called 'Learning' of the individual (the process of accommodation to the material and cultural environment) is far from being a simple, conscious, rational matter of a purely cognitive nature; but is a predominantly *affective* process, intimately related to instinctual excitations and the vicissitudes they encounter, and taking place largely on the level of perceptual and unconscious mental process, and employing various mental mechanisms which are themselves not learned.

It is clear that Psycho-Analysis and Comparative Ethology are agreed upon the intimate relation between the instincts and the nature of the learning processes, and, also, of the importance of the Critical Period Hypothesis, and we can see that these conceptions are applicable and useful in the study of both animals and man.

We have concentrated so far upon the similarities between Comparative Ethology and Psycho-Analysis, since some of the parallels which have emerged in these two spheres of study are particularly striking. It will have been noticed, however, that some of these similarities also confirm and supplement the theory of instincts put forward by the earlier writers, and we must now trace the agreements or disagreements which are to be found among all the three bodies of work.

The Early Doctrine of Instincts, Comparative Ethology and Psycho-Analysis

It was fairly evident as our outline of the recent ethological work proceeded, that the early 'Doctrine of Instincts' was receiving experimental confirmation and support at every step. After our discussion of the Psycho-Analytic account of Instinct, we come to the very satisfying conclusion that the three groups of findings we have considered are not in any way opposed to each other, but, on the contrary, that they support and supplement each other in such a way as to provide a fairly rounded and conclusive theory of the instincts.

Comparative Ethology gives a detailed account of the bio-physiological and behavioural aspects of instinct in animals, and extends its findings to the study of man. The early Doctrine of Instincts, whose postulates have received confirmation in this recent work, also provides a parallel account of instinct-experience (of the experiential aspects of instinct in animals and in man) which supplements the Ethological account and merges into the strictly psychological account of human instinctual experience put forward by Freud. Psycho-Analysis, starting out from the attempt to provide an account of the instincts which would prove satisfactory for the explanation of psychic conflict in human individuals, is found, (a) to agree with and to elaborate considerably the concepts put forward by the early Doctrine of Instincts to describe the instinctual experience of man, (b) to agree with the concepts put forward by the Ethologists in their bio-physiological account of instinct, and (c) to contain valuable suggestions as to how our knowledge of the instinctual experience of man can be related to wider social theory. The three bodies of theory fit together very satisfactorily.

The chief contribution of Ethology seems to have been the 'taking-to-pieces' of the earlier concept of instinct, and, by so doing, to have arrived at more particulate concepts which permitted of detailed experimental investigation. Ethology has also actually undertaken this experimental investigation, and has finally placed the study of instinct upon a recognised scientific basis. Nonetheless, it would be a mistake to think that, because of this 'dissection', the concept of instinct has in any way radically changed from that put forward by the earlier writers. They too recognised that instinctive experience and behaviour as a whole had particular features (internal physiological factors, reflexes, sensorimotor actions, particular perceptions, and the like) but they maintained that these several features were all closely correlated into one experiential and behavioural process, and that this correlation (which comprised the concept of 'an instinct') was established by heredity.

Particular instincts were then classified in accordance with their 'aims' or 'end-states'. Similarly, though Lorenz began by using the term 'Instinct' to refer to the inherited behavioural automatism, this practice was subsequently dropped, and Tinbergen and Ethologists generally have now adopted the practice of conceiving a particular instinct as a whole sequence of behaviour—from the internal condition and the appetitive behaviour down to the final performance of the particular consummatory act—and such particular instincts are classified according to both their 'end-states' and their neuro-physiological bases, or, as Freud would say: their 'sources'. The concept of instinct remains unchanged even though it has been subjected to detailed analysis and experimental investigation.

To add emphasis to this point, we might see what Lorenz himself has to say about it.

'It is in the very nature of analysis that it leads to a progressive narrowing in of formerly wider and more general conceptions. What formerly was very simply conceived of as "an instinct" is shown by the advance of analysis to be a very complex mechanism of very distinct and very different constituents, such as endogenous automatisms, releasing mechanisms, taxes, kineses and, maybe, quite a number of further as yet unrecognized particulate functions. For this we have been reproached by many psychologists, all of them more or less under the influence of vitalistic and finalistic preconceptions.[1] We were accused of pulling to pieces what really was a whole. . . . I would emphatically deny this charge. When we distinguish independent and particulate constituent functions of innate behaviour, we are just as much justified in doing this as the physiological anatomist is justified in distinguishing between the bones, joints, muscles and nerves of, let us say, a human arm or leg. The conceptional distinction of constituent parts and of their particular qualities does not in any way preclude the fullest cognizance of the general mutual interdependence of interaction of these parts. . . .'[2]

The chief contribution of Psycho-Analysis (in so far as the study of instinct is concerned) is that it enables us to assess the extent and importance of instinctual experience in man, and gives us an elaborate description and interpretation of this experience and of its far-reaching influence upon the more conscious and rational activities of the personality. In doing this, it provides us with a most useful approach to the study of the 'socialisation' of the individual, and to the whole field of Social Psychology. Also, Freud's psycho-biological approach links his account of the experiential aspects of instinct very significantly with the bio-physiological aspects investigated by the Ethologists.

[1] It would be interesting to know to which psychologists Lorenz was referring here.
[2] *Physiological Mechanisms in Animal Behaviour*, p. 261.

In the next chapter we shall attempt a synthetic statement of the contemporary theory of the instincts, taking these three bodies of work into account. In preparation for this, we might take particular points put forward in the early Doctrine of Instincts and briefly discuss them in turn, with the object of tracing their relationship with points of theory put forward by the Ethologists and by Freud.

1. *The Instincts are Established by Heredity*

The early Doctrine of Instincts maintained that the instincts were inherited; that the close correlation of the several features of instinct was phylogenetically established. Both Comparative Ethology and Psycho-Analysis support this view, although the Ethologists refer mainly to the physiological and *behavioural* features of instinct in animals, whereas Freud refers mainly to physiological and *experiential* features in man. Freud, too, seems to favour a Lamarckian view of heredity which the Ethologists and the early writers reject. He argues that the *content* of the Super-Ego may be phylogenetically established—which would lead to the view that the 'secondary impulses' were themselves also of an instinctive nature. We have rejected this view, though still holding to the opinion that the 'secondary impulses' can be regarded as operating '*as if*' they were instinctive; possessing certain likenesses to instinctual impulses owing to their close relation to the instincts and the way in which they become established. A second point closely attendant upon the fact that the instincts are phylogenetically established is that, among the earlier writers, they are held to be common to members of the same species. This view also receives confirmation from the Ethologists, who regard the automatic core of the instinct (the fixed pattern reaction) as being 'as characteristic of the species or group as are structural features'.

2. *The Physiological Components of Instinct*

It was held by the early writers that an instinct had its underlying physiological aspects, and that these comprised complex internal physiological processes (nervous, visceral, chemical, muscular) though, at the time, little could be said about them. We have mentioned the postulates which McDougall and Drever put forward concerning the neurological basis of the instincts.[1] This point too, has been confirmed and supplemented by Comparative Ethology and Psycho-Analysis. The Ethologists have analysed the 'internal causal factors' into (*a*) Hormones, (*b*) Internal Sensory Stimuli, and (*c*) Intrinsic Central Nervous factors, and have discussed the way in which they are co-ordinated in any instinctive

[1]See McDougall, p. 52-53, and Drever, p. 58.

action, at the same time emphasising the need for much more work in this direction. Freud, too, has emphasised the importance of the 'somatic sources' of the instincts. The early hypotheses as to the underlying nature and functioning of the central nervous system in instinctive behaviour are paralleled by Tinbergen's account of the 'hierarchy of neurophysiological levels and centres'.[1]

3. *The Behavioural Components of Instinct*

The early Doctrine of Instincts maintained that the sequences of behaviour observed to be common to animals of the same species, and which occurred before there had been any opportunity for learning, could only be explained by assuming that certain *behavioural* mechanisms were also inherited. They referred to these mechanisms as the 'functional correlates' of inherited structures, and distinguished, at least, between reflexes and sensori-motor actions within the context of the instinctive act as a whole. Comparative Ethology has confirmed this view and has provided a great deal of evidence in support of it, though its analysis of the behavioural mechanisms involved is slightly different, and includes (*a*) appetitive behaviour (random, searching, exploratory behaviour) and (*b*) consummatory acts, including fixed pattern reactions, taxes, and the 'coat of reflexes'. Psycho-Analysis does not deal specifically with this point since it is dealing with man, and, as both Ethologists and earlier writers agree: 'in man, innate behaviour patterns are, to a great degree, rudimentary. . . .'[2]

4. *The Perceptual Components of Instinct*

A further point maintained by the earlier writers was that *appropriate perceptions* were closely correlated with particular instinctive actions, and that these too were established by heredity. This point again has been confirmed and considerably supplemented by Comparative Ethology. Each species has its own 'perceptual world' which changes with the activation of the instincts; and each instinctive action has its own 'innate releasing mechanism' which is activated by a specific 'sign-stimulus' or 'releaser'. Sign-stimuli have been subjected to detailed experimental analysis, and their mode of operation has led to the postulation of the 'law of heterogeneous summation'. These releasers, however, have been shown to be not so rigidly correlated with specific actions as appears at first sight. (*a*) Other stimuli can call forth *some* reactions at least, (*b*) other stimuli can become associated with the

[1] It might be remarked that the position of Tinbergen is scarcely less tentative and hypothetical than that of the earlier writers.　　[2] A remark made by Lorenz.

initial releaser and can thereafter have a releasing function, and (c) some stimuli ('super-normal sign-stimuli') have a greater releasing value than the releasers encountered in the normal environment. All this suggests that the Ethologists would agree with the point made by the earlier writers: that the 'perceptual feature' of an instinct is highly modifiable; more so in the higher than in the lower species. In the Freudian account, this feature of instinctual experience is termed the 'object', and we may recall that it is held to be *not* rigidly correlated with the other instinctual features. '. . . it is', Freud says, 'the most variable thing about an instinct.'

5. *Instinct-Experience*

Before considering the concepts introduced by the earlier writers in order to describe and interpret instinctual *experience*, we might first point out that the supposition that the features of instinctive behaviour *have* subjective aspects, receives support from both Psycho-Analysis and Comparative Ethology. Thus, both Freud and Ernest Jones regard the concept of Instinct as a 'border-land' concept, having *both* bio-physiological and behavioural aspects, *and* concomitant experiential aspects. Freud's account of instinct is, indeed, couched mainly in experiential terms. That the Ethologists agree with this view may be seen from the following remarks of Lorenz.

'Though comparative ethology is resolutely and exclusively concerned with an *objectivistic* study of behaviour, as long as it is concerned with animals, we do not, by any means, shut our eyes to one important fact: just those particular physiological processes that are the main object of our investigations, undoubtedly belong to the kind which *does have a correlated psychological side to it*.[1] This is true of all the three most important elementary processes of innate behaviour, of endo-genous-automatic activities as well as of innate releasing mechanisms and of taxes. . . . There cannot be the least doubt that the discharge of accumulated specific energy is accompanied by very intense and very specific subjective phenomena. I fully agree with W. McDougall in his fundamental assertion that man has just as many "instincts" as he has qualitatively distinguishable emotions. Jan Verwey, an indubitably objectivistic student of animal behaviour, is evidently of the same opinion when, in his famous paper on the grey heron (1930), he writes: "Where reflexes and instincts can be distinguished from each other at all, there the reflex is functioning mechanically, whilst instinctive activities are accompanied by subjective phenomena." . . .'

[1] Lorenz's own emphasis. *Physiological Mechanisms in Animal Behaviour*, p. 263.

Lorenz goes to some length to stress this conviction, and we might note a few more of his remarks before leaving the point. Later in the same paper, he tells us:

'The psychological aspect of innate releasing mechanisms presents some parallels to that of endogenous activities. We know for a certainty that the attainment of the releasing stimulus situation represents the end or goal to which appetitive behaviour is directed. We can give an exact and purely objective definition of this kind of directedness or purpose. In all human behaviour, which also objectively fits this definition, we furthermore know for certain that the organism, as an experiencing subject, is striving for certain pleasurable subjective phenomena accompanying as well the perception of the releasing stimulus situation as the discharge of the accumulated endogenous activity. I do not think that any observer really familiar with appetitive behaviour in higher animals will ever doubt the fact that the animal as a subject also experiences intense sensual pleasure as the subjective correlate of attaining the releasing stimulus situation.'

This is a position identical with that of the earlier writers. In view of this acceptance of the fact that subjective experience is concomitant with the behavioural and bio-physiological aspects of instinct, and in view of Freud's agreement with this position, no objection can possibly be raised to the attempt made by the earlier writers to introduce psychological concepts in order to describe and interpret this experience.

6. Some Experiential Aspects of Instinct

The proposition of the earlier writers, then, that certain primary experiential features are involved in instinct, receives support both from Ethology and Psycho-Analysis. The concept of 'persistently recurring appetites or cravings' is parallel with the recurring 'motivational conditions' of the internal causal factors as described by the Ethologists, and with their concept of 'appetitive behaviour'. The concept of 'conation' is the subjective parallel of 'reaction-specific energy'—which accumulates until the appropriate instinctive activity is released, and which therefore gives the objective basis of the element of 'persistence' or 'striving' in instinctual experience towards the appropriate object and mode of activity which brings the satisfying release of tension, or 'gratification'. These ideas are also equivalent with Freud's concept of the 'impetus' of the instinct: which has both its physiological side (the 'quantitative' aspect of the instinctual excitation, deriving from its 'somatic source') and its experiential side (the 'qualitative' aspect of the instinctual impulse which can be distinguished subjectively). Freud also gives support to the earlier writers' contention that, in man, the perceptual and behavioural features of the instincts are rudimentary, and that the essential distinguishing feature of instinct in man is the 'conative-affective core'. The instincts in man, that is to say, are of the nature (as Drever clearly stated) of *inherited impulses*. It is in view of this emphasis that the absurdity of rejecting the concept of instinct and of adopting the concept of drive in its place becomes so apparent. It is clear that this change of *names* does not represent a change of *concept* at all.

7. *Instinct-Interest and Emotion*

Closely related to the concepts of 'perception', 'conation', and the 'conative-affective core' of instinctual experience, are the concepts of 'instinct-interest' and 'emotion'. The earlier writers held (*a*) that, especially in the lower species, the activation of an instinct was not necessarily attended by emotion if the 'instinct-interest' was immediately attained and the performance of the instinctive action was not obstructed or frustrated in any way. The 'instinct-interest' (the whole feeling of worthwhileness embracing impulse and appropriate object) was thus held to be the *primary* affective element in instinctual experience, and emotion might or might not enter in accordance with circumstances. (*b*) Emotion occurred if and when the performance of the instinctive act was obstructed or thwarted; and the function of the emotion was that of increasing the persistence of behaviour and the variability of responses. (*c*) Emotion could reach such a pitch of intensity as to render behaviour completely maladaptive. (*d*) Emotion was not aroused by the thwarting of instinct alone, but also by the sudden presentation of a situation for which the animal was not prepared, or for which no appropriate automatic behavioural mechanisms were provided by heredity. In this case, the emotion first passed through a 'shock-phase'[1] from which the animal might or might not recover in time to deal effectively with the situation. (*e*) Emotion played a comparatively minor part among the lower animal species (in which automatic behavioural mechanisms are established by heredity) but an increasingly noticeable and important part in instinctual experience among the higher species in accordance with the degree to which behavioural mechanisms are *not* phylogenetically laid down. This was in accordance with the fact that, from the evolutionary point of view, it was biologically advantageous to be capable of adaptation to unusual environmental conditions, and not to be confined to one narrow ecological

---

[1]Ginsberg, *Emotion and Instinct*.

niche. (*f*) Perhaps we should add that some of the earlier writers held that emotion was not exhaustively accounted for by an account of its relation to instinct.[1]

These propositions appear to be supported by Ethology and Psycho-Analysis. Ethology tells us that, in the absence of the appropriate releaser, and with the consequent thwarting of the instinctual activity, reaction-specific energy accumulates, resulting in a lowering of the threshold for release, and even to vacuum activity: when the energy and the behavioural mechanism is forced out in the complete absence of stimuli. Similarly, increasing tension resulting from the obstruction of one instinct may result in 'sparking over', and the manifestation of 'out-of-context' instinctive behaviour. Such observations lend support to the view that increased tension (subjectively: emotion) is an outcome of obstruction and thwarting, and that it has the function of releasing reactions other than those typical of the instinct, thus contributing to an increased variability of response. Freud's account of instinct definitely accords with these various points of view. His discussion of the 'impetus', 'object', and 'aim' of the instincts, and his emphasis upon the central importance of 'object-cathexes' in primary mental experience, established or avoided in accordance with feelings of satisfaction or dissatisfaction, is clearly identical with the earlier concept of 'instinct-interest'—conceived as an essentially *affective* element of primary experience and taking place upon the perceptual plane. Freud also lends support to the view of Drever (and McDougall) that emotion plays a dominant part in the instinctual life of man. In this connection, Freud's work tends to confirm Drever's hypothesis that the degree of importance of *emotion* in the experience of a member of a species is directly proportional to the *lack* of behavioural automatisms established by heredity. Thus, Freud attributes the 'raising of the level of the whole cathectic process' to the *absence* of inherited behavioural automatisms and the consequent task of the emerging Ego to 'bind' cathexis; to exercise and establish some measure of control over instinctual excitations until satisfactory behaviour in relation to the demands of the external world is learned.

Here again, we find that the three bodies of theory support each other; each emphasising different aspects of the same points.

8. *Instinct in Man*

A further point of comparison is that Freud's analysis of human mental processes reveals complete agreement with the view expressed by both earlier writers and Ethologists: that—although man does not

[1]Ginsberg, *Emotion and Instinct.*

inherit fixed motor mechanisms to any important extent, and though he is more capable of adapting his behaviour effectively on the basis of individual experience than are any of the other animal species—nonetheless, instinctual experience, mainly in the form of ineradicable inherited impulses, comprises an extremely important and extensive part of his mental life; setting the major ends of activity, and exerting a powerful and far-reaching influence upon the more conscious and rational aspects of individual and social life.

9. *The Critical Period Hypothesis*

A final point is that the Critical Period Hypothesis, supported by both Psycho-Analysis and Comparative Ethology, was put forward quite clearly and explicitly by William James.[1] With regard to this concept also, we find firm agreement between the three 'schools of thought'.

[1]See p. 34.

CHAPTER VIII

THE CONTEMPORARY THEORY OF INSTINCTS

WE are now in a position to attempt a clear synthetic statement. Since the Early Doctrine of Instincts requires only amendment and addition as a result of the subsequent work we have considered, and does not require radical change in its formulation, we can retain the method of statement adopted towards the end of Chapter II, where we were concerned with summarising the work of the earlier writers.[1] That is to say: we can still formulate our conclusions as an answer to two questions; and the findings of Comparative Ethology and Psycho-Analysis which we shall be able to introduce as additions to our earlier statement will bring together all those propositions concerning the subject of Instinct upon which there is agreement at the present time. It will lead us to the formulation of what can be called 'The Contemporary Theory of Instincts'. It is impossible, however, to condense every detail of our earlier discussion into the compass of a few pages, so that our statement must inevitably be compact and summary in form.

Let us begin with the questions which we posed at the beginning of our investigation.

(A) Among animals, especially among those species low in the evolutionary scale but also among the higher species, which, in processes of learning do not seem to manifest a very high degree of intelligence, we find numerous examples of complicated trains of behaviour which seem well adapted to those situations which are normally encountered in the 'ecological niche' of the species, which seem to be periodically and recurrently directed towards specific features of the environment and towards the attainment of a certain 'end-state', and which, though they may be modified to some extent in the light of subsequent experience, are performed with a surprising degree of perfection without previous experience; without any previous possibility of learning on the part of the individual. Such trains of unlearned behaviour and the particular acts which they comprise are very similar, if not identical, in all members of the same species, at least, of the same sex. How are we to account for such behaviour?

[1]See p. 67.

(B) In view of the evolutionary hypothesis which views human experience and behaviour as being to some degree continuous with animal experience and behaviour: to what extent are the features of such behaviour discernible and of importance in the nature of man?

Taking all our points from the writers whose work we have considered, we may frame the answers which the Contemporary Theory of Instincts gives to these questions in the following manner:

In reply to question (A):

1. *Those Features Established by Heredity*

The theory of evolution postulates that the structural characteristics of existing species have been brought into being by a long process of heredity and hereditary change, depending upon (*a*) the transmission of genes from parent to offspring, (*b*) mutations, or 'spontaneous variations' in the transmitted genetic constitution, and (*c*) the process of natural selection. It is now held that, not only the structural characteristics of species, but also:

(1) the complex *internal processes* (nervous, visceral, chemical, muscular), of the organism, which are classified as (i) Hormonal processes, (ii) Internal Sensory Stimuli, and (iii) Intrinsic Central Nervous Factors, and which are co-ordinated in any manifestation of instinctive experience and behaviour; in connection with which the central nervous system is conceived as an organised hierarchy of neurophysiological levels and centres on both its afferent and efferent sides;

(2) certain uniform, automatic behavioural mechanisms called *Reflex Actions*, *Taxes*, and *Kinesis*;

(3) certain behavioural mechanisms which, whilst uniform and automatic, are more dependent for the intensity and frequency of their activation upon internal motivational conditions and combinations of external sign-stimuli, called *Fixed Pattern Reactions*;

(4) certain sequences of random, exploratory behaviour which are not so uniform or automatic but which, nonetheless, are dependent for their activation upon internal and external causal factors, and which are regarded as differing levels of '*Appetitive Behaviour*';

(5) certain specific features of experience, accompanying and arising from the complex internal processes, and having, moreover, their specific concomitant neurophysiological basis—the 'Reaction-Specific Energy'—called *Persistent and Recurring Impulses*, or *Cravings*; and also less specific feelings of uneasiness and restlessness, called *Appetites*; both of which persist in the organism and lead to the utilisation, in a certain behavioural sequence (Appetitive

Behaviour first, leading to the release of the Fixed Pattern Reaction with its associated Taxes and its Coat of Reflexes) of the above-mentioned types of action, until a certain 'end-state' is attained and the craving relieved;

(6) certain other features of experience called *Emotions* which (i) follow upon the frustration of the above impulses and sequences of behaviour and the consequent accumulation of reaction-specific energy, or (ii) follow upon the sudden presentation of an unusual situation for which the animal is either unprepared or in connection with which it is not adequately equipped with behavioural automatisms; and which appear to function as a reinforcement of impulses and as a means whereby a greater variation of behavioural responses is brought about;

(7) certain features of perceptual experience—specific and selective *'modes of perception'* (called *'Innate Releasing Mechanisms'*)—which are intimately related to the accumulation of a particular reaction-specific energy, and which are closely adapted to particular sensory features of certain objects in the normal environment (called *'Sign-Stimuli'* or *'Releasers'*) in the presence of which the appropriate behavioural mechanism is released, the reaction-specific energy is discharged, and the impulse is gratified; and which are held to operate in accordance with the 'Law of Heterogeneous Summation';

(8) a certain feature of experience called *'Instinct-Interest'* or *'Instinct-Meaning'*, which is conceived as the feeling of the whole relation between felt impulse, appropriate object, and behavioural means (i.e. a primary feeling of significance or worthwhileness), and which is held to be of the nature of an elementary 'cognition'; and

(9) certain *capacities* for subsequent *intelligent control*

—are brought into being by heredity, and by the same process of evolution.

These internal neurophysiological conditions; these various kinds of behavioural mechanism—which may be regarded as 'functional correlates' of structures and neurophysiological processes; and these various features of experience—perceptual and cognitive, conative and affective; are also (as is the inherited structure of the organism) held to be common among the members of a species, at least, of the same sex.

2. *The Concept of Instinct*

The trains of unlearned behaviour which we find among animals are therefore accounted for as being the manifestations of these inherited features of structure, neurophysiological process, behaviour, and experience, which are activated in a co-ordinated manner when the animal encounters the various situations of its environment; and the concept which is used to describe the way in which these features are related in any such manifestation of experience and behaviour is the Instinct. The Instinct is simply a concept used to denote a certain correlation of these various features; a correlation which, though well-adapted in all its aspects to the normal situations of the environment, is established by heredity, and which can therefore account for the trains of unlearned behaviour which we observe in animals without entailing assumptions of individual experience and consequent learning.

The term 'Instinct' is thus a descriptive concept which can itself be analysed into various component features and causal factors. But the fact that it can be dissected into particulate features does not alter the fact that the instinct is a distinguishable unity, a definite and recognisable correlation of these features. The instincts of any particular species are, therefore, those correlations of the various features which have been mentioned, which can be distinguished from each other and classified in accordance with (*a*) the 'end-state' at which the sequence of behaviour terminates, (*b*) the actual behavioural mechanisms and the sequence of actions which are performed, and (*c*) the underlying neurophysiological basis of the particular sequence of experience and behaviour.

In an effort to be perfectly clear, we might enumerate the features of the instinct precisely, as follows. The Instinct—that correlation of structural, physiological, behavioural, and experiential features established by heredity—is held to comprise:

(1) *Internal Neurophysiological Features.* These are the internal neurophysiological conditions which form the basis of the behavioural and experiential features. They consist of (i) Hormonal processes, (ii) Internal Sensory Stimuli, (iii) Intrinsic Central Nervous Factors, and (iv) the co-ordination of all these factors, producing 'motivational conditions' (i.e. objectivistically conceived) on various levels of the hierarchy of neurophysiological centres; thus forming the basis of the 'spontaneous' elements in behaviour.

(2) *Behavioural Features.* (i) A sequence of actions—sometimes of long duration—which leads to a specific end (i.e. sexual courtship and mating, nest-building, migration) and which, whilst comprising certain behavioural automatisms, shows a unity and complication and a degree of prospective reference which cannot be accounted for in terms of an associative 'addition' of these automatic type-reactions alone. Such a sequence of behaviour comprises: (*a*) Appetitive behaviour, manifested

at different levels, and leading the animal to the situation necessary for the release of (*b*) Consummatory Acts, which themselves comprise Fixed Pattern Reactions with their associated Taxes and Reflexes.

(ii) A persistence of such behaviour, and, further, an increase in the intensity, complexity and variability of such behaviour, including the manifestation of displacement reactions (and even, on occasions, the performance of the behaviour in the complete absence of normal sign-stimuli—'Vacuum Activity') when the animal encounters any unusual obstacle which prevents it from attaining that 'end-state' to which its activity appears to be directed (i.e. the performance of that consummatory act which releases the accumulated reaction-specific energy, thus yielding satisfaction).

(iii) A cessation of such behaviour when this 'end-state' is attained.

(3) *Experiential Features.* (i) A perceptual feature of experience which indicates a sensitivity to *specific* elements of the environment. This perception appears to be *selective*: appropriate to the instinctual experience of the moment and rendering the animal relatively insensitive to other features of its perceptual world even though, in fact, it is capable of perceiving them. Aspects of this 'mode of perception' can be studied objectively. The 'appropriate elements of the environment' (Sign-Stimuli or Releasers) can be experimentally determined, and since —when some sensory components of these releasers are varied—the same releasing effect can be achieved by accentuating the remaining components, thus 'compensating' for the inadequacies of the former group, these sensory components are regarded as operating upon the perceptual mechanism in an 'additive' way in accordance with the Law of Heterogeneous Summation. Since the Fixed Pattern Reaction seems to be released automatically (as though by a 'trigger' action) when the animal encounters the appropriate releaser, a very specific perceptual mechanism is postulated as the basis of such perceptual experience: the 'Innate Releasing Mechanism'. The degree of rigidity or specificity of this perceptual mechanism, is still not established with certainty. Coupled with the persistently recurring impulse and the 'instinct-interest' mentioned below, this selective perception gives the appearance, in the animal's behaviour, of 'concentration' or the 'narrowing of attention' to certain objects in the environment.

(ii) A conative feature of experience: a craving or persistently recurring impulse, which is the experiential concomitant of a particular Reaction-Specific Energy, and which continues until a specific 'end-state' (which releases the energy and gratifies the impulse) is attained in the performance of appropriate behaviour.

(iii) A feeling of the significance of the whole relation between specific craving and specific perception which is termed the 'instinct-interest', and which can best be described as a feeling of worth-while-ness. This is an elementary 'cognitive' feature, even though it is an element of feeling, and it is relevant to what we shall have to say later on the importance of the affective aspects of the learning processes. This postulate adds a psychological side to the observed 'concentration of attention' upon a particular object, the apparent absorption in the particular sequence of behaviour, and the relative insensitivity of the animal to other features of the environment during the performance of this behaviour.

(iv) A feeling of heightened tension, termed Emotion, which is not a necessary affective element in instinct-experience, but which arises when normal instinctual activity is obstructed, and which reinforces the specific impulse (at the same time 'lowering the threshold for release') and leads the animal to increase its efforts to carry out this behaviour successfully, leading to an increased variability of responses by en-gendering the employment of other elements of its equipment of behavioural reactions; but which may, in its most excessive form (as, also, in the 'shock-phase', when a completely unusual and unexpected situation is suddenly encountered) render the experience and behaviour of the animal completely diffuse, incoherent, undirected, and ill-adapted to the situation.

3. *The Degree of Rigidity of the Instinctual Mechanisms and the Place of Emotion in Instinct-Experience*

It is held that, among the simplest animals, the correlation of these several features is very closely and rigidly established by heredity, and that by far the greater part of their behaviour can be explained in terms of the instincts. Among these species the instincts are very specific, comprising rigid and definite behavioural mechanisms closely correlated with the instinctual impulse and the appropriate perception, and in the situations encountered in the normal 'ecological niche', they are usually well-adapted. Because of their highly invariable nature, they tend to become maladaptive when there are unusual changes in these situations, and they are consequently regarded as being relatively 'blind', leading often to error. Among these lower species, emotion is held to play a very small part, and among the lowest, a negligible part in instinctive experience and behaviour. As we come to the study of animal species higher in the evolutionary scale, however, it is held that, (*a*) behavioural mechanisms and perceptions are less closely and rigidly correlated with the specific impulses by heredity, and (b) that, correspondingly, the emotional element of the affective experience becomes more prominent, as some delay of discharge or of gratification of the impulses occurs whilst appropriate behaviour is learned. Emotion now has a more positive biological function to serve, and is of greater importance in leading the animal to persist in and vary the behaviour necessary to reach the appropriate 'end-state'. This is a broad generalisation, and requires further detailed investigation of particular species.

4. *The Conative Element: The Chief Distinguishing Feature of Instinct*

In view of the above points, and because of our knowledge of the modifiability of the perceptual and the behavioural elements, *it is the conative-affective element of instinctive experience and behaviour, together with its underlying neurophysiological conditions, which must be regarded as the most central distinguishing feature of Instinct*. It is this feature which, throughout the whole range of species, gives unity and persistence to the features of behaviour which, whether rigidly correlated by heredity, or to some extent variously selected in the light of individual experience, are utilised in attaining the appropriate 'end-state'.

5. *Instinct and Intelligence*

It is held that the capacity for intelligent control, inherited in varying degrees by various species, comes into play in connection with the experience and activity of the instincts. Among the lower species intelligence may be almost negligible; capable of only very minor adjustments in connection with the reactions involved in immediate activity; but among the higher species, intelligence becomes capable of grasping the relations between impulses, ends, and behavioural means, on the perceptual level, and finally, in the case of man, achieves a much more refined knowledge of these relations on the conceptual and ideational level. Instinct and intelligence are therefore not regarded as being separate and distinct from each other, but as mingling modes of correlation, the one determined by heredity, and the other coming into play, within this given context, during the course of individual experience. All experience involves instinctual and intelligent elements, mingled in various degrees. Perhaps it should be added that intelligent control is conceived as developing from the primary 'instinct-interest' in the light of 'feelings of satisfaction or dissatisfaction' encountered during the course of individual experience.

6. Habit and Sentiment Formation, and the Learning Processes

Besides maintaining that behaviour may be modified by means of intelligent control, it is also held that instinctive experience and behaviour is conditioned by habit-formation and by sentiment-formation, thus centring the instinctive activity of the animal, and the human being, about certain objects, and rendering it relatively insensitive to other objects of the same kind. Experiment has shown that certain modes of learning are closely related to the earliest activations of the instincts, and that these learning processes are responsible for the very rapid establishment of the intimate and relatively permanent attachments to particular objects mentioned above. Even in the case of man, learning is not a purely cognitive, rational, consciously controlled process, but is very largely of an *affective* nature; and on the basis of fundamental affective tendencies, the accommodation of the entire personality to the complex fabric of the material and social environment is accomplished by the employment of a variety of 'mental mechanisms' which are themselves not learned.

7. Maturation and the Critical Period Hypothesis

It is held that, though innate, the instincts are by no means present, in the sense of being mature, at birth, but that they emerge with the growth and maturation of the individual, so that certain instincts are important, even predominant, at one stage of growth and not at another; though some instincts are held to persist throughout the lifetime of the individual. Such stages of growth, during which particular constellations of instinctive tendencies are predominant, are termed 'Critical Periods', and certain extremely important processes of learning, of accommodation to objects in the environment, are held to take place during these periods. It is held, therefore, that—even though some instincts 'fade away' after their period of particular importance—they exercise, nonetheless, an important and extensive influence upon the subsequent experience and behaviour of the individual.

8. The Instincts and the Organism as a Whole

Whilst the instincts of an animal are held to be specific (i.e. they are distinguishable as particulate correlations of a specific craving, a specific appropriate perception, a specific behavioural sequence, and a specific set of neurophysiological conditions) it is not held that the individual can be regarded as a mere 'aggregate' of them. The individual organism is regarded as a unity, a whole, with a complex experience and a detailed continuity of behaviour, the elements of which have some kind of central order, or integration, which is furthered by intelligent control. Nonetheless, the instincts remain distinguishable and specific within the integrated complex of individual experience and behaviour. They exert a determining influence upon behaviour, and, when activating the individual, they tend to bring the attention and efforts of the individual as a whole to bear upon that behaviour which is necessary to gratify them.

In reply to question (B):

1. *Instinct in Man*

It is held that instinctual experience and behaviour *is* discernible, and *is* of the utmost importance in the nature of man.

2. *Certain Features of Instinct are Rudimentary in Man, and are not rigidly established by Heredity*

It is held that, in this instinctual experience and behaviour, two of the previously mentioned features of instinct—the perceptual feature, and the equipment of behavioural automatisms—are not rigidly established by heredity; nor are they closely correlated wth the specific cravings by heredity. (Much more work is required before the *extent* of hereditary determination can be delineated with certainty.) Both these features are held to be highly modifiable and dependent to a great extent upon experience and learning. At the same time, it is held (1) that there are at least some simpler instincts which appear to comprise well-defined motor-responses, and (2) that even in the more intricate behavioural sequences which are the outcome of experience and learning, there are at least some behavioural responses which are specifically related to certain 'cravings' and which are not wholly learned.

3. *The Conative and Affective Elements of Instinctual Experience are of central Importance in the Nature of Man*

It is the conative-affective feature of instinctual experience and behaviour, with its underlying neurophysiological conditions, which is held to be of basic importance in the nature of man. Certain distinguishable cravings; periodically recurring and relatively persistent impulses; prompting behaviour and the exercise of intelligence towards the attainment of specific and appropriate ends, are certainly inherited by man, and emerge in each individual during the course of growth and maturation. These inherited impulses are common to all members of the human species, at least, of the same sex.

4. *The Lack of Inherited Behavioural Automatisms and the Task of the Human Ego*

Since automatic behavioural mechanisms are not established by heredity in man, the sequences of behaviour employed by the human individual in gratifying his instinctual cravings are noted for their plasticity, and (1) are largely dependent upon processes of learning which take place during the period of infancy and youth, and (2) permit of great modification by the individual himself in accordance with the circumstances and situations peculiar to his own experience. The important point is that the growing individual has no automatic inbuilt solution to the instinctual demands which he experiences, and the emerging Ego has to learn how to control these demands and how to endure a measure of dissatisfaction and tension in the face of the necessitous requirements of the external world; and has to learn, often with difficulty, the modes of behaviour by means of which these inner demands can be satisfied. This situation is further complicated by the fact that the expression of certain of these instinctual demands, and of some behavioural means of satisfying them, may be forbidden by the parents of the individual, and by the conventions of the wider society.

5. *Emotion plays a comparatively large part in the Instinctual Experience of Man*

In accordance with the hypothesis that it is of biological advantage to possess the capacity of adaptation to varied environmental changes, rather than to be rigidly dependent upon a narrow 'ecological niche'; in view of the highly modifiable nature of certain features of human experience and behaviour as mentioned above; in view of the longer period of infancy and utter dependence upon the parents of the human offspring; and in view of the lack of automatic and well-adapted behavioural responses in the innate endowment of man—it is held that the element of emotion plays a comparatively greater part in the instinctual experience of man than it does in that of other animal species.

Firstly, tension or emotion arises because the instinctual impulses are experienced, with all their forcefulness, in the absence of automatic, appropriate motor-responses, and a measure of delay and suppression is involved whilst the behaviour which will give gratification is learned. The Ego is faced with the task of mastering the instinctual excitations, of so controlling them that he can tolerate delay in their discharge, and of learning the appropriate behaviour to achieve satisfaction which is permissible in his environment. This mastery and capacity for delay is achieved by 'raising the level of the whole cathectic process', and involves a 'preparedness for anxiety' in the individual.

Secondly, there are certain instincts in man of which the emotion is the dominant element, as, for example, in fear. In such cases, an instinctual tendency involves multiple responses, and it has been suggested that the emotion, here, *is* so dominant and important *because* of the multiplicity of possible responses and the fact that none of them are automatic, thus rendering a certain degree of selection necessary in relation to the particular situation. The less rigid the correlations of various innate features established by heredity, and the greater the capacity for variability of response and for intelligent control in a species —the greater, it seems, is the emotional tension involved in the experience of the individual, and the more prominent and extensive is the part played by emotion in instinctual experience.

Thirdly, emotion may arise as a severe and diffuse disturbance—as in the 'shock-phase' when the individual suddenly encounters a completely unexpected and unusual situation for which he is altogether unprepared. In this stage, the emotion may be extremely diffuse and may lead to behaviour which is completely incoherent and maladaptive. The diffuseness may then gradually diminish, the emotion developing into a definite, recognisable form—such as fear or anger—which will thereafter act as a reinforcement of the particular effort and mode of behaviour which is required to deal adequately with the situation.

Fourthly, emotion also arises in man, as in animals, when the normal activity undertaken in the service of an instinctual impulse is obstructed or thwarted. In this case, the emotion functions as a reinforcement of the impulse, leading to a more intense exertion of effort and to a greater variability of behavioural responses.

6. *The Nature of Instinctual Experience: The Importance of the Sexual Instinct: The Early Formation of Profound Affective Attachments*

The fact that no rigid correlation is established by heredity between instinctual impulses, perceptions, and behavioural automatisms, together with the fact that the child spends a long period of infancy in utter dependence upon its parents for the satisfaction of all its impulses with their erotic components (thus enjoying a measure of delay in coming to terms with the necessitous demands of the environment) has extremely important corollaries.

In the first place, the unconscious mental processes (which are the earliest mental processes, and which, of all features of human experience, are those nearest in nature to the mental processes of the higher animals) are characterised by an extreme mobility of cathexis; an exceedingly mobile proliferation of excitations seeking gratification by attachment to concrete perceptual images or symbols, capable of easy displacement and substitute gratification, and accompanied by extensive phantasy-formation. At this earliest level of mental functioning, these psychic processes *are reality* for the individual, and are completely under the sway of the pleasure principle.

In the second place, the development of the Sexual Instinct becomes of the utmost importance in human life. The early instincts of hunger, thirst, and defecation have erotic components which become separated from these specific activities, and become sources of excitation in their own right, being subsequently involved in the further development of the sexual instinct and in the development of love-attachments. The infantile period is thus one of 'auto-eroticism' in which organ-pleasure is derived through the stimulation of certain erotogenic zones of the subject's own body. After passing through a stage of phallic orientation towards the end of the period of infantile sexuality, and through the subsequent and relatively quiescent latency period, the sexual instinct achieves full adult genital orientation only at the stage of puberty. During this long period of development of the sexual instinct, the individual enjoys an almost complete dependence upon his parents, and, in consequence, is not brought up forcefully against the demands of the real world. Beginning with auto-eroticism, and passing through the relative quiescence of the latency period, the sexual instinct remains for a long time under the supremacy of the Pleasure Principle, and is thus peculiarly prone to the continuity and proliferation of phantasy-life and to a mobile deflection of its aim: permitting of diverse forms of substitute-gratification and sublimation.

In the third place, during this long period of dependence, and bearing a close relation to the critical periods of development of the sexual instinct, the human individual forms profound affective attachments (makes important object-choices) which are of the utmost importance for the very structure of his personality; which actually lay down the content, the foundations of his personality; and which thus exert an important determining influence upon his subsequent development.

7. *The Affective Aspects of the Human Learning Processes*

From what has been said, it is clear that the earliest processes of human learning (those processes of accommodation to the material and social environment which occur during the first critical period of the individual's development) take place almost entirely upon the perceptual level of experience, in relation to primary 'instinct-interests', in accordance with feelings of satisfaction and dissatisfaction, and through the employment of various 'mental-mechanisms' of adjustment to stress which are themselves not consciously learned. In a word, these early learning processes are predominantly *affective* in nature.[1]

8. *The Super-Ego and The Secondary Impulses*

It can be said, further, that this process of accommodation to the various features of the physical and cultural environment is intimately related to those affective attachments of the individual which are established in the early family situation. These affective attachments give the first and most important tinge to the spectacles through which the individual then and subsequently views his world.

By far the most important aspect of this process is the setting up of the Super-Ego; the introjection of the earliest love-objects together with their associated moral precepts; which involves the setting up within the personality of 'secondary impulses' which are, in the main, inhibitory. The earliest moral impulses are thus not the result of considered rational thought, but the direct outcome of the relation between the instinctual impulses and the earliest affective attachments formed by the individual, together with the kind and degree of control over the instincts exercised by the objects of these earliest attachments. The secondary impulses, however, are not entirely inhibitory in nature. The ideality of the content of the Super-Ego, and its element of desirability, gives rise to secondary impulses of positive aspiration. The relation between the secondary impulses and the primary impulses is not one of harsh condemnation and inhibition alone; it involves also elements of positive ordering in the light of some desired ideality. The inhibition of the primary impulses has therefore something positively creative about it; there is a noticeable aesthetic element in it; the Ego is positively striving to *become* something better and more desirable. We might say that the struggle and degree of achievement of the Ego in this task of aspiration is accompanied by its own, qualitatively new, sublimated feeling-tones; and in this we can see the attraction of the ascetic religious life for some individuals. As with the inhibitory moral impulses—so with the experiences of positive and creative aspiration: the spiritual goals and strivings of men appear to be established primarily on the level of early affective and perceptual experience, though they may subsequently be subjected to various degrees of rational criticism.

[1]We are aware that no clear-cut line of demarcation can be drawn between the 'tendency towards harmony and integration' existing among the *feelings*, and that manifested in conscious reason. All we wish to emphasise above is that at this early stage, this tendency manifests itself predominantly in the *affective* elements of experience, and at the *perceptual* level.

9. Sublimation, and the Detailed Process of Accommodation to the Social Structure

Encountering various vicissitudes, and bringing into operation mental mechanisms which we have described earlier, the instinctual impulses of man follow a complex and tortuous course of development. A point of the utmost importance is that: partially suppressed from following their direct aims (and this point refers mainly to the sexual instinct and the components of eroticism which it comprises) they permit of an extensive degree of deflection to aims other than, and even remote from, those of direct gratification in connection with their initial appropriate objects. They are capable of *sublimation*, and consequently, though the instinctual energy of man may be partially and even severely suppressed in some ways, it can find certain outlets in relation to various kinds of social phenomena and in associated forms of social activity.

The earliest constellation of affective and attitudinal relations with objects and symbols established in the early family situation, can thus be seen to extend outwards towards the much wider sphere of social symbols and institutions as the individual grows and encounters (during the course of his activity) the wider and more detailed social environment. During this later development, the individual may increasingly employ critical reason in considering his relations with the things, people, and institutions he encounters, and he may go to great pains to establish a body of objectively verifiable knowledge (on the conceptual and ideational plane) about these manifold and complicated features of his experience. In all cases, however, such rational processes do not 'start from scratch', but emerge within an existing and deeply-rooted body of sentiments and attitudes already established on the perceptual and affective level of experience.

10. The Importance of Social Facts

In view of the last two or three points we have made, and because human individuals always live within particular social contexts, and are from the beginning of their lives subjected to many and varied social influences; in view, too, of the modifiability of human behaviour and the capacity for intelligent control which has been mentioned earlier; it must be held that the total structure of social facts into which individuals are born is a factor of the utmost importance in shaping the patterns of their behavioural responses and moulding their emotional attachments and their attitudes to various features of personal and social life. Though the instinctual endowment of man is held to be common to all members of the species, setting the major common ends of all human activity, it is also held that the manifest details of individual and social behaviour will differ from society to society, or from social group to social group. This point has, really, two aspects.

Firstly, though our theory of the instincts and our theory of personality-development deriving from it, tell us what the chief components of the human personality will be in the context of *any* society, and how these components will be linked with each other in the process of development, we cannot tell from this theory alone what the empirical *content* of the personality will be. It is the actual structure of social facts constituting a particular society to which we must go for this empirical knowledge. It is the total structure of things, symbols, institutions, etc., which form the Social Tradition as a whole which comprise the potential *content* of the individual personality—that complex of phenomena in connection with which, selectively, the individual personality is moulded. We say 'selectively' here, because whilst there will be a total objective 'Social Structure' in any community; each individual will experience, subjectively, different constellations of these social facts in accordance with his geographical situation, the nature of his locality, his family, his social class, and so on.[1]

Secondly, the social facts to which we are referring, whilst exerting a constraining influence upon individual personalities, cannot themselves be adequately explained in terms of being 'derived from' individual personalities.[2] Whilst having their psychological effect, social facts cannot wholly be explained in psychological terms, and require a different kind of investigation at the sociological level. We wish to emphasise, then, that—whilst maintaining the theory of instincts as set out above—we do not by any means hold that this theory is all that is required for an explanation of all the complexities of human individual and social life. On the contrary, we insist that much more than this is required. This statement is necessary only in view of those critics who believe, without justification, that those who maintain the correctness of the theory of instincts automatically maintain, also, that this theory can, of itself, explain everything.

At the same time, this statement is far from constituting an admission that the theory of the instincts is negligible in the part it can play in any explanation of human experience and behaviour, and, indeed, of social processes. The part played by instinct in human experience is very

---

[1]In accordance, too, with his own unique genetic constitution; a factor we should not neglect.

[2]This is the view of Emile Durkheim, with which we are largely in agreement. We would, however, in view of the nature of the interaction between individual personality and social facts as stated in our theory, retain Psychology and Social Psychology within our total scheme of social explanation to a much greater degree than he is prepared to do.

extensive indeed, and we shall indicate some of its important implications for various aspects of social theory in our final chapter.

11. *The Instincts and the Ends of Human Activity*

It is held that the instincts (the distinguishable inherited impulses or cravings, with their physiological concomitants) lay down the basic and permanent ends of human activity, and that the extension of rational direction and control, emerging from an already established body of sentiments and attitudes, is employed predominantly in the continuing task of so ordering behaviour as to achieve the satisfactory attainment of these ends. This is not to say that *all* the ends of human activity are *derived* from the instincts. Even though instinctual energy may be deflected into the desire to attain a certain end (let us say: the attainment of objective truth in scientific inquiry) this is not to say that this end is itself derived from the instincts. There are some ends which do not appear to be simply derived from the instincts. On the other hand, after considering the work of Freud, we must hold that it would seem to be extremely doubtful whether any human activity (no matter to what end it may be directed) can wholly escape the influence of deep-rooted instinctual experience, with all its ramifications in the unconscious mental processes, and with the importance of the part it plays in laying the very foundations of the individual personality and in establishing the fundamental moral impulses of inhibition and aspiration. The theory of the instincts must conclude that the major ends of human activity are rooted in the instincts, and that instinctual experience is, indeed, an extremely extensive and important feature of human nature, exerting a far-reaching influence upon conscious and rational activity in both individual and social life.

It follows that a knowledge of the human instincts is of great importance for both Psychology and Sociology. We are confronted, therefore, with the question which Freud posed so concisely: 'Now what instincts and how many should be postulated?'

A Classification of the Human Instincts

In view of the extreme reluctance of the Ethologists to attempt, at the present stage of investigation, an exhaustive enumeration of the instincts in any one animal species, let alone an enumeration of the instincts in man; and in view of the unsatisfactory nature of the three attempts at classification made by Freud; it is doubtful whether we should attempt such a classification at this stage. On the other hand, if our basis of classification is clearly stated, and if the obviously tentative nature of our approach is emphasised and continually borne in mind, there can be no harm in such an attempt. Indeed, our investigation would be unsatisfyingly incomplete if such an attempt were not made. Perhaps the best excuse for our efforts in this direction is that put forward by a London Psychiatrist during a seminar at the London School of Economics: 'We *must* generalize—otherwise we get no satisfaction from our work!'

To a large extent, we are in agreement with the classification offered by Drever, which represents a refinement upon McDougall's earlier classification. We shall, however, base our own attempt upon the criteria which, after our discussion of the three bodies of work on the subject, appear to be the most reliable; but a comparison of Drever's scheme and our own will show how we have incorporated his earlier suggestions into the new framework of presentation, and which elements of his classification we have left out because of uncertainty on our part. We must also point out that we cannot, in this place, undertake a detailed parallel schema of the human emotions. This is an extremely intricate subject, and would require a separate piece of work.

In presenting this new classification we do not pretend to completeness, nor to certainty. We are trying, simply, to enumerate those features of human experience and behaviour which, in our view, can reliably be said to have a definite inherited neurophysiological basis, together with a subjectively distinguishable appetitive or conative element, neither of which is learned, but which are closely correlated with each other and with a certain sequence of activity terminating in definite consummatory behaviour and a definite end-state. It must be noted that (in accordance with our earlier discussion on this point) the fact that learning enters into such activity does not in the least invalidate our classificatory scheme, since we do, in fact, maintain (a) that the perceptual and behavioural elements of human experience and behaviour are, to a large extent (though we do not know definitely to *what* extent) rudimentary in the hereditary endowment of man, (b) that they are highly modifiable in relation to the circumstances of individual experience, (c) that intelligent control arises in the service of, or in the ordering of, the instinctual strivings, and (d) that the sequences of behaviour manifested in the service of these cravings will be closely dependent upon the structure of social facts within which the individual is born, grows, and develops. The neurophysiological sources and the correlated conative experiences of the instincts proper, however, are (we claim) definite and ineradicable features of the human hereditary endowment.

In our classification, we shall give the instincts the simple names of the activities in which they are manifested, but these names will refer to certain correlations of neurophysiological, experiential, and behavioural features which will be outlined within the framework of the Ethological concepts. This may seem too precise a method considering the inadequacy of the data at our disposal, but it will have the advantage of analysing fairly precisely the various components we conceive to be of importance; and the classification (whether complete or not) will thus be framed within conceptual categories which are quite clear, which can be examined in detail by subsequent research, and which, consequently, will permit of reliable amendment and supplementation as this research proceeds. A full knowledge of the physiological basis of the instincts is, of course, not yet available; and even such knowledge as exists is of too intricate a nature to permit of adequate summary within a schematic classification of this kind. Furthermore, it is beyond our province. There seems to be no doubt, however, that all the instincts we postulate have a definite and distinguishable concomitant physiological process, and, for the sake of completeness, we shall indicate this in the very simplest of terms. Also, because of what we have said in our earlier pages—to the effect that, in our view, at least *some* of the behavioural responses of man may be established by heredity, and appear to be necessarily involved in the satisfaction of instinctual excitations—we shall try to indicate, under the heading of 'Consummatory Behaviour', what these innate features of behaviour might be. Here again we do not wish to profess certainty, but are merely concerned to make feasible suggestions which we believe to be probably true. The degree to which such behavioural responses can be said to be innately established must depend upon further Ethological study.

Whilst setting out our classification of the instincts in accordance with the Ethological concepts, however, we find that these concepts do not strictly apply to all the instinctive tendencies of man, and we shall also take into account suggestions which have arisen from our discussion of the work of Freud. All the instincts to which we have been referring so far will be presented under the heading of the *Instincts Proper*; and we conceive all of these to be definite primary instincts resting upon a definite neurophysiological basis and having a primary unlearned conative element of experience. Collectively, they comprise the fundamental urges of the Id. They are fundamental correlations of structures, neurophysiological processes, and subjectively experienced excitations, phylogenetically laid down in the innate constitution of man. The innate constitution of man, however, when coming to terms with its environment during the process of growth, is such as to give rise to the emergence of the Ego-element in individual experience. And in connection with this emergence of the Ego, certain *General Instinctive Tendencies* can be distinguished. These may be termed *Ego-Tendencies*, but we must be careful to note two points: (*a*) They are not peculiar to the *conscious* Ego alone, but are extensions into the Ego of tendencies arising from the total functioning of the instincts proper, at the level of the unconscious, and in relation to the pressing demands which they make during the development of perceptual consciousness. (*b*) Though the Ego may, at a later stage, subject these tendencies to radical conscious and rational criticism, they themselves are tendencies set up and developed in the Ego on the perceptual level of experience in the service of the instincts proper, in relation to their vicissitudes; and are established in connection with the predominating *affective* elements of experience, long before conscious rational processes occur. The subsequent extension of intelligent control arises within this already established body of general instinctive tendencies. Indeed, we tend towards the view that, in the vast majority of human individuals, intelligent control itself is always extended in the service of these general instinctive tendencies, and takes place within the accepted bounds, and upon the accepted assumptions, which these tendencies set. According to this view, it is only very rarely the case that the individual extends his power of rational criticism radically to the questioning of the fundamental basis of feeling and thinking of his own social group. These general instinctive tendencies, and the social content which form the substance of them in any particular society, carry a certain authority of feeling with them; the contents about which they are moulded are felt, somehow, to be fundamentally *true*; established elements in the nature of things; and to question them radically and objectively is felt to be rather pointless and ridiculous, and also irreverent and undesirable. Indeed, in any community or in any particular social group, the objective detachment of a member will always bring upon him the suspicion and distrust of others, and any really radical criticism of these fundamental tendencies and the social contents about which they are moulded is frequently met with general hostility and is often regarded as a form of fundamental disloyalty, even of treachery. Men and women (though they themselves like to be considered rational and objective) rarely like or trust an individual who appears to be *too* rationally and objectively critical of these general instinctive tendencies, and who does not share the same deep ties of feeling towards some social content. Thus, in time of war, a man who questions objectively the justifiability of his own country, is invariably branded either as a coward or a traitor; and much war-time literature (radio-plays, films, and novels) is directed towards a deprecation of such objectivity, pouring social disapproval upon it.[1]

Thirdly, in accordance with the importance which we attach to Freud's explanation of the formation of the Super-Ego, we shall take account of the *Secondary Impulses* in our classification. These are intimately related to the instincts and the vicissitudes they encounter, and (though *not* instincts proper, nor general instinctive tendencies) because of their origin in, and their development from, the instincts, they do operate *in the manner* of instincts: being compulsive elements of experience arising internally and being concerned with the inhibition and ordering of the instincts proper. Nothing can be said as to the empirical content of these secondary impulses without detailed studies of particular societies; but something of importance can be said about their nature from our theoretical basis alone.

A few final comments on our classification should be made. It might be said that BREATHING is a relatively automatic process, and should not be included in a classification of instinctive experience and behaviour. Our treatment, however, should make it clear that we *do* regard the functioning of respiration (in the normal course of events) as a relatively automatic process. We have included it because, when normal respiration is severely interrupted, the behavioural reactions are far more complicated than simple reflex activity, and involve the concentrated behaviour of the organism as a whole. At the same time, these behavioural responses seem to be common to members of the human species, and do not appear to be learned.

It will be seen, too, that we have followed the practice of Tinbergen in conceiving some correlations of experience and behaviour as 'sub-instincts' of a major instinctive activity. Thus, Play, Curiosity, and Hunting, probably crystallise out of general vital activity when certain perceptual features in the environment are encountered. Similarly, erotic 'courtship', jealousy and sexual fighting, parental experience and activity, and home-making, can all be considered parts of sexual and reproductive activity as a whole, which come into being in a certain sequence, and, again, in relation to different perceptual elements.

Finally, it must be insisted that the 'General Instinctive Tendencies' are, in fact, conceived as *tendencies*, so that we do not regard the three tendencies we have postulated as definite entities in any particular personality. This point must be made especially in connection with the third general instinctive tendency: Positive and Negative Ego-Tendencies. We do not hold that, in any particular personality, *either* the

---

[1]The same applies to loyalty in political parties, or loyalty to religious causes, or, indeed, the deep and shared attachments of feeling which bind together any human group.

positive *or* the negative tendency will be manifested. We conceive of any human Ego as manifesting these two tendencies in varying proportions; fluctuating to some degree, between one and the other. In some personalities, one or the other may have a greater dominance. But we maintain that both tendencies are there to some degree; so that all human beings will experience a fluctuation from one tendency to the other to some extent. It may be the relative dominance of one tendency over the other in particular personalities which has led to the attempt to classify personalities into two types: Intraverts and Extraverts.

Our classification is tentative; does not pretend to finality or completeness; and is offered as openly and clearly as possible for the explicit purpose of amendment and criticism in the light of subsequent research. Nonetheless, such propositions as are presented within our framework of classification do appear to be reliably based.

The Instincts Proper have a definite inherited neurophysiological basis which can be objectively investigated. The degree to which perceptual and behavioural features are established by heredity can also be clarified by subsequent research. These instincts are common to all members of the human species by virtue of their hereditary endowment, and they set the basic and unalterable ends of human activity, about which by far the greater part of complicated social behaviour and social organisation is centred. *The General Instinctive Tendencies* are also common to all members of the human species. The task of the human Ego is everywhere related to the same internal constitutional (instinctual) factors, and can find satisfaction for these ineradicable cravings only by means of successful accommodation to some definite set of material and social environmental factors. The basic features of *the Secondary Impulses*, too (the elements of *Inhibition* and *Aspiration*), are common to all human beings (though in differing combinations and in differing degrees), since all human individuals—having the same inherited endowment, and having the same task of the Ego before them—are born into family units set within a wider social system, and, through their affective experience in this early primary group, have to accommodate themselves successfully to the wider structure of their society.

With this attempt at a reliable classification of the instincts in man, we bring our statement of the Contemporary Theory of Instincts to a close.

(1) THE INSTINCTS PROPER (PRIMARY IMPULSES)

Physiological 'Sources'	Instinct	Appetitive Experience	Appetitive Behaviour	Sign Stimuli	Consummatory Behaviour
Physiology of respiration.	(1) BREATHING	(Normally—no experience) but discomfort, choking, laboured breathing when encountering:		Stifling, humid, suffocating atmosphere: e.g. gas, smoke, etc.	In stifling, humid atmosphere: fanning hands near mouth; breathing consciously, deeply, laboriously; blowing forcefully through lips. In smoke, gas, etc.: attempting to hold breath; placing hands tightly over mouth and nose; gasping, gulping, coughing; violently attempting to escape from situation. Afterwards: relaxing, gulping in fresh air.
Contraction of stomach walls. Centre in Hypothalamus?	(2) EATING	Hunger	Searching for food, water, etc.	Not specific.	Sucking (in child), salivation, licking lips, taking food to mouth in hands, biting and mastication; tearing with teeth and gulping when hunger intense; swallowing, wiping mouth with hands.*
Parching of Membranes of throat, etc.	(3) DRINKING	Thirst	Hunting, food-gathering storing food and water.	Not specific.	Sucking (in child), sipping, drinking, gulping when thirst intense, wiping mouth with hands.*
Physiology of maintenance of body temperature.	(4) MAINTAINING COMFORTABLE TEMPERATURE (a) Keeping Warm	Uncomfortable coldness, and desire to seek warmth.	Shivering, seeking shelter, clothing, proximity of other people, etc.	Sunny places shelter, clothes and furs, smoke and fire, sight of other people.	Beating hands together and on body; flapping arms about violently; stamping feet to the ground; maximising activity and exercise; putting on clothing—or more clothing than usual; huddling together with others; living inside heated shelters; drinking and eating hot substances.
	(b) Keeping Cool	Uncomfortable heat, and desire to seek coolness.	Perspiring, Seeking:	Shaded places, cool water. Perhaps sound of running water?	Reclining and resting; minimising activity and exercise; bathing in cool water; fanning face and body; resting in cool air currents; discarding clothing; living outside enclosed shelters; finding or erecting cool shelters.
Physiology of fatigue. Centre in Hypothalamus?	(5) SLEEPING &	Tiredness, lassitude.	Escaping stimuli; seeking comfortable, undisturbed place for sleep.	Not specific. Dependent largely upon internal causal factors? But, perhaps darkness, warmth, comfort after exertion, or after eating	Yawning, stretching limbs, lying down, relaxing body, curling up (viz. Freud's remarks, somewhere, about the foetal position assumed in sleep), covering body for warmth, closing eyes, easy regular breathing, over-all slowing of physiological processes.

* Perhaps an innate Nausea and Disgust at the taste and the sensation of swallowing certain unpleasant foods and liquids?

(1) THE INSTINCTS PROPER (PRIMARY IMPULSES)—Continued

Physiological 'Sources'	Instinct	Appetitive Experience	Appetitive Behaviour	Sign Stimuli	Consummatory Behaviour
Centre in Hypothalamus?	WAKING	Becoming conscious; feeling refreshed and vigorous.	Seeking stimulus and normal activities.	Not specific, but perhaps light? disturbing sounds?	Opening eyes, gradually arousing, stretching, flexing limbs and hands and feet, rubbing eyes, getting up, resuming normal bodily activities.
The tactile sensitivity of the body-surface; but more complicated than a simple reflex.	(6) CARING FOR COMFORT OF BODY-SURFACE	Feeling of bodily comfort, and hyper-sensitivity to any stimulus of the skin; feeling of disgust and revulsion at the sight and touch of small crawling insects.	Seeking bodily comfort in general: body-coverings, cleanliness, etc. Also: avoidance of small, creeping, crawling forms of life: insects, worms, snails, etc.	Sensation of insect crawling on skin; any irritation or movement sensed next to skin—especially on unseen part of body (e.g. in hair or under clothing). Even the sight of crawling insects.	Violent throwing-off movement of limbs; 'brushing-away' movements. Convulsive movements of the whole body. Shuddering movement—either when insect is found and removed, or, even, at the prospect of insects crawling on the body. Scratching. Tidying of the hair. Wiping the lips after eating and drinking, with fingers, with back of hand, or with knuckle of the wrist.
Increase in heart-beat; increasing activity of sweat-glands; inhibition of digestion; adrenal activity, flow of blood to large muscles, etc.?	(7) FEARING	(a) Arrested tension and concentration of senses; followed by: (b) Perplexity, continued tension and caution (if no development of situation). (c) Panic Terror if development of situation is altogether unfamiliar or overwhelming in its power, or (d) desperate effort to grapple with situation; intense exertion and concentration.	Avoiding the dark when alone; avoiding isolated places, the unfamiliar; seeking the familiar; seeking the company and response and mutual help of fellow creatures.	Darkness itself. Sounds and movements in the darkness, especially unfamiliar and unexpected ones. Any sudden, startling event. Unfamiliar, inexplicable occurrences.	'Freezing'; standing in an arrested, completely still, silent, rigid posture; hardly breathing; waiting to see 'what it is'. Complete inhibition of uttering sounds, or screaming. Cautious movements. Sometimes noisy and over-emphasised movements of 'bravado'. Flight, escape—accompanied by panic-terror. Perhaps screaming. Fighting or grappling with the situation: (a) desperate, abandoned exertion, or covering face and eyes with hands or arms, if situation is completely overwhelming. (b) Intense, positive, concentrated effort (gradually changing into anger) if 'enemy' or situation can be tackled with hope of success or survival.

Physiological 'Sources'	Instinct	Appetitive Experience	Appetitive Behaviour	Sign Stimuli	Consummatory Behaviour
Physiology of Alimentary Canal; Digestion; discarding of waste materials; etc.	(8) EXCRETION (a) Defaecation (b) Urination	Tension of bowels and desire for relief. Tension of bladder and desire for relief.	Possibly(?) seeking a place for defaecation and urination.	Internal Causal Factors.	The act of defaecation; the adoption of a crouching posture. The act of urination; possibly a crouching posture in the case of females.
Physiology of Growth of nerve tissue; maturation.	(9) GENERAL ACTIVITY (bodily and mental) (i.e. spontaneous; for its own sake; from general inner vitality.)	Over-all feeling of exhilaration; 'Feeling Fit'; General inner excitement; Restlessness; Desire positively to seek and encounter stimuli; desire for active, vigorous movement and manipulation of limbs.	General, undirected, 'non-utilitarian' restlessness and robust activity. Seeking stimulus; seeking the response of others; seeking companions; seeking any kind of excitement.	Not specific; probably mainly dependent upon internal factors. But perhaps aroused in adults by contact with new people, new places, fresh experiences, a breaking away from the customary environment.	In infancy: the general kicking and throwing about of limbs; grasping and throwing of objects; bubbling with lips; repeating early sounds of vocalisation; crawling; romping; smiling. In childhood: standing; balancing; walking; running; hopping; jumping; climbing; dancing about; inability to keep still; also—vocalisation: being robust and noisy; shouting, whistling, singing. In adults=similar, but usually confined to socially provided games and sports, forms of exercise and recreation.
	(a) Play	do.	General, irresponsible, excitement-seeking behaviour. Perhaps seeking companions of own age.	Sight of, sound of, proximity of, other children + any objects in the environment which can be imaginatively manipulated.	In infancy: as above. In childhood: chasing and catching; hunting; pretended fighting; sexual play—curiosity, exhibition of body, stimulation by feeling, perhaps even pretended copulation; making shelters-homes. In general=imaginative and imitative of serious adult activities.
	(b) Curiosity	Perhaps desire for new experiences; variety; new excitements, etc.	Seeking new experiences; exploring new places; exploring the unfamiliar.	(a) Strange, unfamiliar things—if not fearful: but sometimes even then. (b) Perception of problems, of difficulties of manipulation, etc.	Investigating; searching; seeking knowledge of and mastery of newly encountered objects, places, people, etc. Questioning. Experimenting in manipulation, etc.
	(c) Hunting	Perhaps only aroused by		Sight of moving live creatures; sound of movement of animals in undergrowth, etc.	Hunting, chasing; catching; killing. Sometimes destroying; sometimes keeping and peting.

(1) THE INSTINCTS PROPER (PRIMARY IMPULSES)—Continued

Physiological 'Sources'	Instinct	Appetitive Experience	Appetitive Behaviour	Sign Stimuli	Consummatory Behaviour
Physiology of sexual organs, sexual hormones etc.	(10) SEXUAL ACTIVITY (a) Eroticism and 'Courtship' (i.e. in the animal, not the social sense).	Sexual excitation. Desire for gratification of erotic impulses; desire for proximity of, and intimacy with, opposite sex. (Sometimes with same sex.)	Seeking the company of, and seeking to appeal to, to attract, to impress members of the opposite sex. (Sometimes the same sex.) Display and assertion; submission; enveigling—by means of glances, gestures, motions of head and body; caprice; etc.	Mainly 'Secondary Sexual Characteristics': e.g.: Male: Deep voice, physical strength, strength and dominance of personality; perhaps facial hair; etc. Female: Smooth skin—lack of facial hair; treble voice; wide hips; developed breasts; etc. Both: difference in genitals.	Seducing (often with forceful, violent element, but perhaps usually following upon the tender elements of seduction); becoming physically intimate; touching; caressing; displaying; mutual stimulation; stimulation of all erotogenic zones of body; consummated in act of copulation. (Also auto-erotic behaviour in both sexes when actual sexual experience is, for manifold reasons, unavailable.)
	(b) Sexual 'Fighting'	Jealousy.	Keeping sexual partner, or love-object, away from potential or actual rivals.	Sight of member of same sex successfully attracting one's own sexual partner, or love-object. Or perception of, or awareness of, members of same sex who are, potentially, successful rivals.	Quarrelling with sexual partner. Feeling enmity and displaying threat-behaviour to rival; verbal quarrelling and physical threats. Possibly fighting, both with sexual partner and with rival. In general, trying to belittle rivals in eyes of love-object, and to keep love-object away from rivals.
	(c) Parental Activity	Possibly no distinguishable appetitive experience or behaviour until birth of offspring?		Sight of dependent human baby, especially (but not only) one's own. Short face in relation to large forehead, protruding cheeks, maladjusted limb-movements; perhaps the smile of the child.	Holding, nursing, fondling, playing with child. Breast-feeding. Protecting, and in general, caring for child: satisfying needs—washing, clothing, feeding, etc. Smiling, laughing, uttering infantile noises to the child.

Physiological 'Sources'	Instinctive Tendency	Appetitive Experience	Appetitive Behaviour	Sign Stimuli	Consummatory Behaviour
	(d) Home-making. Formation of Elementary Family	Desiring permanent presence of sexual mate, or love-object, and desire to protect and care for children.	Seeking or constructing dwelling-place and providing manifold domestic requirements.	(a) Sign Stimuli of sexual mate + desire for permanent presence. (b) Sign Stimuli of offspring + need to protect and care for. (c) Also: vicissitudes of material environment, making warmth, shelter, comfort and satisfaction of manifold needs necessary for survival.	Finding or constructing dwelling-place. Also: economic occupations to satisfy manifold needs. (i.e. in case of both sexes.) Perhaps no specific actions.

(2) GENERAL INSTINCTIVE TENDENCIES (EGO-TENDENCIES[1])

Physiological 'Sources'	Instinctive Tendency	Appetitive Experience	Appetitive Behaviour	Sign Stimuli	Consummatory Behaviour
Total, overall physiological functioning. Satisfactory degree of gratification of all *Instincts Proper.*	(1) PLEASURE-PAIN (This 'polarity' derives from the seeking for gratification of all the instincts proper; and includes the fundamental tendency to safeguard individual survival.)	The desire for pleasure; for a state of over-all satisfaction and well-being. The desire for Physical and mental equilibrium and harmony. The desire to avoid or to resolve pain, conflict, dissatisfaction, frustration.	Seeking gratification and easy comfortable situations over-yielding over-all contentment. Avoiding difficult, disquieting, troublesome, uncomfortable situations.	Those of all the Instincts Proper, but selective now, within the context of habit and sentiment formations.	Adopting comfortable postures in all kinds of activity. Avoiding, and, when possible, refusing troublesome tasks. Seeking and taking the easiest, least disquieting way out of situations. General care to avoid pain, discomfort, and conflict. Effort to provide oneself and love-objects securely, sufficiently, and permanently with all the conditions making for over-all contentment: e.g. warmth, shelter, food and drink, clothing, human companionship, protection from fear, danger, disease, etc.

[1] Note qualifications in text: p. 306.

(2) GENERAL INSTINCTIVE TENDENCIES (EGO-TENDENCIES)—Continued

Instinctive Tendency	Appetitive Experience	Appetitive Behaviour	Sign Stimuli	Consummatory Behaviour
(Physiological source no longer applies.)				
(2) ATTACHMENT-AVOIDANCE (This 'polarity' attends the process of accommodation to the material and social environment; involving the affective aspects of human learning.)				
(a) Attachment. Attaching oneself emotionally to (identifying oneself with), Persons, Groups, Places, and shared Social Symbols, in the context of which satisfaction has always been found. (E.g. affective aspects of individual's accommodation to the 'structure' of social facts'; the Social Tradition; the complex of Social Symbols.)	Feeling: 'at home'; secure; emotionally satisfied; at ease; all expectations well-known, familiar—can be taken for granted. Deep-rooted feeling of 'belonging' to 'a certain place and a certain Social Tradition.	Living and working within this complex of material and social features about which sentiments are formed; to some extent devoting oneself to its maintenance and continuity; preparedness to sacrifice for continued existence of the Social Tradition—even to extent of one's life.	Familiar sights, sounds, scents, etc. (i.e. of the material and social environment) in context of which the earliest instinctual gratification was attained; and—later: Symbols of many kinds: Words and names; Totem; Flag; Uniform; Badge Crown; National Anthems; Religious Emblems or Symbols, (Cross, Saints, etc.); Leaders +portraits and caricatures of; etc.	Living permanently (or for by far the greater part of one's life) in the same place, with the same group of people, and moving in the same circles of society. Centring all activity, and building all one's life, about certain people, places, social values and social tasks. Behaving casually, happily, with a maximum of ease, confidence, and lack of self-consciousness. Feeling a profound, satisfying loyalty towards certain people, places, social groups, and social institutions; and tending to uphold and defend their character or reputation in the face of adverse criticism; tending to deny (tending not even to perceive) all faults that might be attributed to them. The tendency—even in advanced philosophical thought—to arrive at conclusions, a *Rationale*, which justify one's own group: its beliefs, values, and institutions, etc. Tendency to strive for those goals, to achieve that kind of character, appraised in one's own Social Tradition.

Instinctive Tendency	Appetitive Experience and Behaviour	Sign Stimuli	Consummatory Behaviour
(b) Avoidance. Avoiding, dissociating oneself from, looking askance at, people, places, groups, and Social Symbols which are strange: in the context of which satisfaction has not been found, and is not certain to be found; and which may in fact be opposed to, or may endanger the continuity of one's own 'Social Tradition': that context of people, places, groups and social symbols to which one 'belongs'—the context of one's deepest feelings and most deeply felt values.	Feeling oneself a stranger; feeling 'alone'; feeling 'out of place'; emotionally tense; hypersensitive and self-conscious; cautious, suspicious of others, insecure; nothing can be taken for granted—there is no structure of familiar expectations; uncertainty; lack of confidence in self and others; feeling of inferiority; feeling of being on the defensive. Desire to escape or to avoid all this, and to get back to one's familiar environment.	All strange peoples, races, social groups, social classes, and social symbols. (Outsiders; 'Out-Groups', etc.)	Avoiding strange places, peoples, social groups, social classes, and social symbols. Avoiding strange manners of living. Tendency to regard strange manners of life as being curious, even comical, and inferior to those of one's own social group. Tendency to characterise people of 'outside' groups in simple caricature-like terms, and, by and large, to deny virtuous qualities to such groups, or, at least, to be very chary or grudging in attributing good qualities to them. When living among other and strange groups: behaving cautiously, with constraint, without confidence, self-consciously, etc.

Instinctive Tendency	Appetitive Experience and Behaviour	Sign Stimuli	Consummatory Behaviour
(3) POSITIVE AND NEGATIVE EGO-TENDENCIES (a) Positive	The desire of the Ego to meet the flux of external circumstances positively, to master them and utilise them for its own ends; the desire for a positive active solution of its own problems, and the effort to shape environmental features to conform with its own desired pattern of life. A positive striving to solve its three-fold task of coping with the external world, the instincts, and the secondary impulses.	The details of the constantly demanding flux of the external world: i.e. the physical and social environment; and the continual instinctual demands from within.	Positive activity in dealing with, and attempting to master, the problems encountered in the material and social environment. The positive extension of reason in order to meet these problems. Also, a positive, constructive, creative attitude towards the growth and development of one's personality throughout one's lifetime of experience; attempting to manipulate the material and social environment towards this end. (Possibly the basis of the 'Rationalist-Humanist' life; or the 'Ethical' aspects of Religion.)
(b) Negative	The Desire of the Ego to withdraw from the continuing flux of circumstances; to retire; to give up the struggle; to despair; to escape reality; to seek an earlier state of things when these conflicts did not exist; or to believe in a future state of things when these conflicts will not exist.	do. ... together perhaps, with the perception of the apparent transience and insignificance of man in the world.	Resigning oneself to the necessitous facts of the material and social environment. Tending to withdraw from the task of actively grappling with external problems, and of trying, positively, to mould one's personality; and to find deeper contentment in an inner life of emotion, imagination, phantasy, or religious faith. At the extreme = to despair, and to wish to have done with life completely. Conviction that the world is an eternal flux of problems, an enigma, beyond human power to influence or control, and the feeling that the important issues of life are rather to be found in an inner life of faith. (Possibly the basis of the 'ascetic' element of religion; of worship; and of some artistic creation.)

(3) THE SECONDARY IMPULSES

The secondary impulses cannot be listed, as they vary in accordance with the structure of social facts into which the individual is born. Even so, what is of importance about them can be said from our theoretical basis.

The secondary impulses are of two kinds : (a) INHIBITIONS—which operate in order to control or repress the instincts proper, and (b) ASPIRATIONS—which tend to direct the moulding of the individual's personality in accordance with that constellation of valued human qualities (the 'operative ideals' of the particular society) to which the individual is introduced during his infancy and youth.

The secondary impulses are established in the individual personality in relation to predominantly affective, non-rational processes. As the individual grows, it is probable that rational criticism will increasingly be brought to bear upon them, so that some degree of modification of them must be expected. Nonetheless, the elements of instinctual striving are basic to the initial formation of the secondary impulses; and all subsequent reflection will, of necessity, start from this basis of affectively established 'norms' and 'ideals' which are closely related to the structure of social facts of a particular society.

CHAPTER IX

SOME IMPLICATIONS OF THIS INQUIRY

OUR concern in this inquiry has been the reconsideration of the concept of Instinct: an examination of its validity at the present day and the extent to which it is of use in Comparative Psychology and in the study of man. This task has now been more or less completed. Our discussion, however, contains many implications for other spheres of investigation. As Ernest Jones has remarked: the study of instinct is of importance in that it comprises a 'border-land territory', touching upon many related questions of great interest. All the implications we shall raise would repay much further thought, but they require a more detailed treatment than can be afforded them in a closing chapter. Still, our task would not be rounded off satisfactorily without some mention of them.

Perhaps we should point out that this piece of work has not been undertaken for its own sake, nor even for the sake of Comparative Psychology as such, but chiefly in order to explore the possibilities of establishing a reliable basis of psychological theory which would prove useful in the context of wider sociological theory. This interest, and some of the reasons why we have considered the task to be of importance, will emerge, it is hoped, during this final discussion of the few following pages.

1. *The Implications for Comparative Psychology*

It has become clear during the course of our discussion that the concept of Instinct is of central importance and utility in the comparative study of animal species. The 'Universe of Discourse' of Psychology is the positive study of experience and behaviour, and entails the investigation of *all* experience and behaviour manifested in *all* forms of organic life. In *all* animal species, without exception, a certain instinctual endowment (comprising some degree of correlation of the several features we have been at pains to clarify) is established by heredity; and we can now see that a classificatory scheme of *levels* of experience and behaviour, or 'levels of psychic organization', can be constructed for comparative purposes on the basis of the *degree of rigidity* of the inherited correlation of these various features of instinctive experience and behaviour. At one end of the scale we should range those species in which the correlation of the instinctive components was rigidly established by heredity and was completely adequate for behaviour within a very specific ecological niche. At the other end of the scale, we should range those species in which the correlation was but loosely established by heredity: comprising definite conative and appetitive elements, but leaving perceptual and behavioural components capable of a high degree of modification in accordance with individual experience, and thus achieving plasticity of accommodation to a changeable environment, or to a variety of environments.

In this way, Comparative Psychology can be seen to be an established natural science, companion to Biology.

In all probability, there are quite significant correlations to be drawn between aspects of experience and behaviour at the various levels of such a classificatory scheme. To take the example of the place of emotion in the experience and behaviour of species: it can most probably be established that when the several features of instinctive experience and behaviour are rigidly correlated by heredity (among species low in our scale) then emotion probably never, or only in the very slightest degree, arises in experience, and can be held to have no biological function to perform. When the features of instinctive experience and behaviour are *not* so rigidly correlated by heredity (among species high in our scale, and especially in man) then emotion becomes a much more noticeable feature of experience and has a positive function to perform (in connection with the preparedness for selective activity, and the degree of plasticity of behaviour). This can be stated in another way which will help us to introduce a further correlation which arises from Freud's work. The less rigid the correlation of the several features of instinctive experience and behaviour established by heredity, the greater is the task of the organism of 'binding instinctual excitations' and of 'raising the cathectic process as a whole' in preparedness for action, whilst the process of accommodation to the environment (the process of learning) takes place.

Freud's point suggests a further correlation of interest which Comparative Psychology might investigate profitably. It may prove to be the case that the emergence of a 'consciousness of self' (the emergence of the 'Ego-Element' in the experience of the organism) is directly proportional to the degree of rigidity of the correlation of features of instinctive experience and behaviour established by heredity, and the corresponding degree of the task of 'binding instinctual excitations' until adequate behaviour is learned. And it is probably only at those levels of psychic organisation at which the emergence of some degree of 'Ego-formation' can be established that we can speak, for example, of the relative degree of 'perceptual' and 'conceptual' elements of learning, or of 'personality' or 'character' formation, and the like. It is important to see that this question of the emergence of the Ego-element in experience must be considered one of *degree* as we ascend the comparative scale of species. There is no reason to suppose that the emergence of the Ego-element (or, indeed, of the Super-Ego element) in experience is entirely a human phenomenon. It may also occur, in varying degrees, in other animal species; and especially among the other higher mammals. Similarly, among human beings themselves, this may be to some extent a matter of degree among individuals, and may correspond closely with what we now term 'levels of intelligence'; and it might conceivably vary in degree, even in the same individual, at different stages of development. But we shall return to these points presently, when we consider the implications of our discussion for Learning Theory.

These, clearly, are very big questions which cannot be pursued satisfactorily here. But at least we have seen that (in view of the comprehensive universe of discourse of Psychology, and the necessity for some basis of comparative study) some classification of 'levels of psychic organization' is necessary, and in this connection the concept of instinct is of central importance and utility.

It should be rewarding, for the purpose of establishing a reliable basis of this kind for Comparative Psychology, to reconsider the work of writers such as Lloyd Morgan, and especially Hobhouse, whom we have dealt with briefly in our early pages; and to work over critically the various levels of mental development which they postulated. Even if their classifications prove to be inadequate in some ways, it should be possible to build soundly upon a careful critique of the basis which they have constructed. Perhaps, at this point, it might not be out of place to register a plea for a serious attempt in Psychology to reconsider in an exhaustive and critical way the entire literature on questions of this kind, rather than to engage in the prevailing scramble for 'originality': our contemporary badge of academic honour. In this way, much superfluous and trivial involvement in polemics might be avoided, and a systematic tradition and a commonly agreed body of knowledge, and discipline of method, might be built up.

2. *The Implications for Learning Theory and the Concept of Intelligence*

By and large, the study of *learning* has been approached far too much from the point of view of the strictly *cognitive* elements involved.

The tendency has been to regard perceiving, remembering, problem-solving, etc., as consisting of essentially *cognitive* processes, and as though, taken together, they constituted a sphere of study in its own right, whilst the question of the affective elements of experience has been, from the point of view of learning, relatively disregarded. In contrast to this view, the point which our findings emphasise is that the *affective* aspects of experience are of the most fundamental importance in the learning process. We might, indeed, go further, and suggest that it is possible that we are suffering, in Psychology, from a false and mis-leading conceptual dichotomy between the *cognitive* and the *affective* aspects of experience. Our knowledge of instinct, and our concept of primary *instinct-interest* or *instinct-meaning*, lead us to suggest that cognitive and affective aspects of experience (whilst we conceptually distinguish one from the other) are *not*, strictly speaking, *separable parts* of a process in the actual context of experience at all, but are *actually the same thing*: the felt significance of the whole relation between impulse and object. Whilst we conceptually distinguish between perception, cognition, and feeling, in actual experience they are 'all of a piece'.

Before elaborating this point, we might stop to note that considerations of this kind might lead us to an improved and extended conception of the nature of 'perception' and 'cognition'; for these have too thoughtlessly and rigidly been confined to the mode of operation of the *sense-organs*, and we have correspondingly limited our notions of perception and cognition strictly to what we have called *sense-perception*. This has had its repercussions in extreme phenomenalist positions within the empiricist tradition of philosophy, in which 'sense-data' have become the fundamental irreducible units of knowledge. This suggested widening of our notion of perception and cognition would accord with our actual experience, for we know that we 'sense' things about other people (what they are feeling, what they are thinking about, what their intentions are, etc.) without any strict reference to sense-perception as it is naïvely conceived. And this would bring up for consideration some of the intriguing remarks of Freud: such as his notion that, somehow or other, human individuals can communicate with each other, or be aware of each other, at the unconscious level, without the conscious being involved at all. It may be that the difficulties which an extreme phenomenalist epistemology encounters when attempting to account for certain kinds of human knowledge rest, quite simply, upon the falsity of this fundamental premise as to the nature of human perception and cognition.

But to return to our point that primary meaning is a *felt* significance of the whole relation between impulse and object:

During the experience of the individual, this felt relation between impulse and object may be modified in certain ways, and the behaviour undertaken in the service of this 'instinct-interest' may also be changed. In a word, *learning* will take place in order to deal with specific environmental conditions; but, even in this process of learning, the *affective* elements of experience are always fundamentally involved. As Lloyd Morgan says: modifications of the primary elements of experience and behaviour occur in accordance with the 'psychological values', or 'feelings of satisfaction and dissatisfaction'; (as Freud would put it, in accordance with the Pleasure Principle).

The fundamental *core* of the process of *learning* in *all* species, including man, can be regarded as the accommodation of the individual to the conditions of the physical and social environment in accordance with, or guided by, the *affective* elements of experience: (*a*) stemming from primary 'instinct-interests', (*b*) developing into what we have called 'general instinctive tendencies' (which we may also term Ego-tendencies in so far as they extend into, and are related to, the degree of Ego-formation in the species), and (*c*) in the case of man (and perhaps in some of the other higher mammals) involving the establishment within the personality of 'secondary impulses' comprising inhibitions and aspirations. The most important core of the learning which takes place in human individuals does not consist of conscious, conceptual, cognitive processes, but of *affectively* established attachments to, or reactions against, those objects, people, or symbols in the familiar physical and social environment in the context of which the earliest instinctual gratifications were achieved. And it is of the utmost importance to remember that much of this accommodation to the environment will take place at the unconscious level and especially during the earliest years of infancy in relation to the deepest *affective* ties of the individual in the early family situation. In these years of completely dependent childhood, these affective ties will be of the nature of what Freud has termed 'object-cathexes' or libidinal attachments to objects. As the earlier writers put it: they will be of the nature of deep-rooted sentiments and habit-formations established about those objects in connection with which the primary 'instinct-interests' were felt and satisfied. Subsequent necessitous learning imposed impersonally from the institutional framework, and to which the individual has to adapt himself more consciously (such as general education in schools, and the instruction and training necessary in preparation for certain social roles) will always be super-imposed upon an already established body of affectively-oriented learning, and will always appear superficial (in the strict sense of being on the surface, impersonally imposed, and without deep personal significance) to the individual when compared with the deep-rooted and massive content of this earlier affectively-oriented learning process which really amounts, as our inquiry has shown, to the formation of the very foundations of his personality.

If followed through, these suggestions would lead us to the reconsideration of a most important problem: what is the nature of 'intelligence'? We cannot give this question the treatment it deserves, but we might at least indicate the implications for this question which emerge from our inquiry, and, later, we shall be able to point out some of its further implications for Educational Theory.

In the past, we would suggest, the study of 'Intelligence' (as well as the study of perception, cognition, etc.) has been approached too much from the point of view of the specifically cognitive attributes. Intelligence tests are constructed predominantly about the ability to perceive relations; and pose problems the solution of which depends upon the perception of these relations. It has always been a favourite matter for controversy—as to what it is that the intelligence tests really measure, and we know that it is held that some general factor, 'G', emerges during individual performances in these tests, and that individuals can be graded upon this basis. Now we do not wish to argue against this fact at all. What we wish to dispute are some of the assumptions which often go with the acceptance of this fact. What we wish to suggest, following upon the discussion of our earlier pages, is that a 'level of intelligence' may refer *not* to a given and relatively unalterable capacity of the specifically cognitive, conscious, thought-processes of the individual (even though it emerges, or is indicated, during the exercise of these processes), but rather to the state of organisation of his personality as a whole.

In order to make our point of view clear, let us state the same thing with the aid of Freud's terms.

The level of intelligence discovered in an individual (his degree of success in manipulating and resolving problems in a test) may refer *not* to any *given*, and relatively unalterable, quality or capacity possessed by the conscious Ego, but to *the degree of order, integration, and discipline of his entire personality*. It may reflect the degree to which the Ego has satisfactorily resolved the conflicting demands of the Id, the Super-Ego, and the outer world of reality; and the degree, therefore, to which it is more consciously free to meet, and tackle objectively, newly encountered problems. What we are claiming is that the 'level of intelligence' of an individual is probably very intimately related to the extent to which the Ego has successfully resolved its problems and has established conscious knowledge of, and control over, the conflicts to which it has been subjected.

It may appear from this that we are merely saying the same thing as orthodox intelligence-theory in different terms: namely, that the individual with a high intelligence quotient, who can perceive relations clearly and solve intelligence-test problems, is, of course, the individual who can cope with his personality problems more successfully than can other individuals with a lower intelligence quotient. But this is not so. For when we say above: 'the conflicts to which it (the Ego) *has been subjected*'—we are stressing the fact that the actual intensity of conflict, and the content of this conflict, with which any individual Ego has to grapple is *not* of his own making or of his own choosing, but stems from factors of his early environment over which he had no control. Thus, a particular family upbringing; an early imposition of dogmatic religious beliefs; an early life in a poor, over-crowded slum tenement; barriers to education (including, we must emphasise, not only financial barriers, but, for example, attitudes of amusement or scorn directed towards 'academic' studies, or scholars, and, on the other hand, attitudes regarding as 'manly', 'practical', 'sensible', the desire to start work as soon as possible, to earn a wage, to join adult groups, to behave in adult ways with adult mannerisms, etc.) may result in the circumstance that the personalities of particular individuals are predominantly focused abouts or absorbed in, these early established affective constellations (loyalties and deep attachments to early encountered attitudes and values) and the conscious area of the Ego's knowledge, control, and freedom to meet new problems objectively is always minimal.[1] In a more rationally oriented family environment (shall we say among the professional groups) the desirability of conscious knowledge, foresight, and control on the part of the individual over the various factors in life is stressed early; there are always expectations of and concrete opportunities for future extended education, with perhaps concrete expectations of definite chosen careers beyond that; so that the emerging Ego of the child has, in all probability, not such a deeply-impressed set of affective attachments, out of which he has to find his way.[2] At a certain age, the child in the latter social circumstance may well give a more efficient performance in intelligence tests than the child in the former social circumstance—and this, not only because of overt facts such as wealth, oppor-

[1]This point may have a bearing, for example, on the psychology of the criminal. The criminal may find an integration of personality in his criminal role which is much more satisfying to him, in terms of his early affective constellations, than are any of the normal, respectable, social roles that are open to him.

[2]In the one case, the constellation of emotional ties will have been impressed as something permanent; a permanent framework of emotional and attitudinal reference and satisfaction; whereas, in the second case, the emphasis upon a permanent emotional constellation will be minimal, and the importance, for the Ego, of conscious adaptability to changing patterns of circumstances will be stressed.

tunity, verbal facility and the like, but also (and, we claim, more deeply) because of the different introjected constellations of affective attachments and their different intensity. It may well be, then, that the idea that 'intelligence' is *there*, and discoverable in certain grades each of which deserves a certain kind of education, may be mistaken; and we might be nearer the truth in thinking that EDUCATION ENGENDERS INTELLIGENCE. By this, of course, we do not mean the education of school years only—but the education which proceeds throughout the developing life of the child in the enlightened home, and which (*a*) avoids any unduly intense and dogmatic Super-Ego formation, (*b*) avoids the establishment of too strong a set of emotional ties to the family itself, and (*c*) from the outset *helps* the emerging Ego to extend its conscious knowledge, foresight, and control over the many aspects of experience which, sooner or later, must be encountered.

This question is of great importance not only for its own sake, but because of its relevance for practice. If intelligence is regarded as a given factor, relatively unalterable, and distinguishable at a certain age, then this has quite definite implications for educational theory. Children can be graded fairly reliably from a certain age onwards, and appropriate levels of teaching can be provided for them. This, as a rule, will be closely related to the subsequent recruitment of children to careers of comparable levels of social status in the wider society. If, however, intelligence is regarded (as we have suggested it might legitimately be regarded) as an indication of the degree of organisation of the personality as a whole, then this view has equally definite but very different implications for educational theory. It implies that the 'level of intelligence' of any individual permits of some degree of change if the vicissitudes at the root of his personality development (the affective constellations with which he is preoccupied, and which militate against the extension of the conscious power of the Ego) can be uncovered and to some extent changed. Similarly, it implies that, since these most fundamental learning processes begin before the child ever attends school, it may well be that the process of education should be extended more and more into the sphere of the early family situation. But again we will leave these considerations until we come to our section on Educational Theory.

A further point which must be mentioned here, and which is of the greatest importance in connection with the emphasis we are now laying upon the *affective* aspects of the learning processes, is that which has been called the 'Critical Period Hypothesis'. This hypothesis claims that there are critical stages of development in the growth and maturation of the individual when learning processes are more deeply significant for subsequent personality development than are learning processes which might take place during other, relatively quiescent periods. In these periods (which correspond with bio-physiological stages of growth and development) the individual is subjected to definite constellations of *affective* experience, and such accommodations to the environment as are made during these periods are of basic importance for the formation and development of personality. The first four or five years of life of the human child constitute an important period of this kind. It is during this critical period that deep-rooted object-choices will be made which will have the most important determining influence upon subsequent attachments to objects, people, and symbols (including beliefs and attitudes of mind) and in which fundamental 'secondary impulses' (inhibitions and aspirations) will be established at the unconscious level. Similarly, the period of adolescence is one of critical importance: when the affective constellations established during the infantile period are reactivated with the onset of adult sexuality proper, and when the objective demands of the social structure have to be encountered, making necessary qualitatively new adult responses.

3. *The Implications for Social Psychology*

All that has been said so far is of fundamental importance for Social Psychology. Let us define the sphere of Social Psychology as the study of the reciprocal influences existing between the various features of Social Structure and the formation of Individual Personality (which entails the study of experience and behaviour in various kinds of groups). Our discussion of the nature and extent of instinctual experience in man, and our derived theory as to the place of the affective elements of experience in the process of accommodation to the structure of social facts, provides us with a firm basis of theory in Social Psychology: a theory with which we can approach the empirical study of personality development in any human society, or in any sub-group within such a society. In this connection, we have merely extended the suggestions of Freud: mainly by claiming that the libidinal ties of members of groups may be established not only in relation to the *leaders* of groups, but also to social symbols (the complex facts of the social structure as subjectively experienced).

The theory of the instincts permits us to take, as a given basis of motivation in the members of *all* human societies, the 'Instincts Proper' and the 'General Instinctive Tendencies' which we have enumerated. The Freudian theory of the development of the human personality, coupled with the chief elements of social structure (which we shall mention later) permit us to postulate the formulation of a Super-Ego in the members of all human societies, and to postulate further that the secondary impulses then established will comprise inhibitions and aspirations. We can now go further, and state that the *content* of the Super-Ego formation (the *particular* pattern of inhibitions and aspirations in individual personalities living within a particular social structure) will differ strictly in accordance with the structure of social facts into which these individuals are born. We have here a clear and reliable theoretical approach to the problems of Social Psychology: (*a*) a theory as to the basic impulses common to all men, (*b*) a universal theory of personality formation, which is (*c*) related to the features of social structure—about which, as we shall see shortly, clear theoretical statements can be made.

It may be that our approach would require an elaboration of particular techniques rendering the theory useful for empirical research, but, on the face of it, this would not appear to be a very difficult task. Within the theoretical schema we have outlined *all* the detailed factors involved in any particular social situation could be clearly enunciated and clearly placed for the purposes of empirical research. For the sake of clarity, and since we cannot undertake a detailed discussion of this question here, a diagrammatical representation (Diagram 2, p. 330) of our theoretical schema is given. On the right of the diagram are features of the Social Structure, and these must be regarded from two points of view: (*a*) as *symbols* of the social structure *subjectively experienced* by the individual; in relation to which sentiment and attitude formation will take place, and (*b*) as the detailed *objective structure of social roles*, some of which the individual will be *compelled* to occupy, and between some of which he will have to exercise a definite choice. Subsequent conflicts in the personality can then be discussed in terms of subjectively established sentiments, habits, inhibitions, aspirations and the like, on the one hand; and the objective, necessitous conditions and requirements of the variously structured social roles on the other. This diagram may be more fully appreciated in the context of our following remarks on Sociological Theory.

Before closing this section, we should mention that our suggested approach does *not* (*a*) ignore, rule out, or regard as being inconsequential, the facts of such *genetic* variations as may exist between races, social groups (e.g. castes), or individuals—though this, in any system of explanation, is an extremely difficult factor to take into account. Nor does it (*b*) ignore the existence of rational and purposive activity among individuals and groups in social life. Rational and purposive activity obviously does exist to some degree; but in accordance with our inquiry, all we are supposing in this schema is that the *affective* aspects of human

experience are of fundamental importance in the process of the accommodation of individuals to their social environment, and that the
rational and consciously purposive elements always arise within this
context and are always concerned with certain elements within it. All
we claim for our approach is that, in respect of any social situation, the
factors upon which human beings exercise their reason and towards
which they behave purposefully can all be adequately framed within
such a theoretical scheme.

4. *The Implications for Sociological Theory*

The question as to the place to be assigned to Psychology in Sociological Theory is one which has been discussed often, and upon which
sociologists are still not agreed. It is again, therefore, a question which
we cannot hope to resolve in this final chapter. Nonetheless, we wish to
suggest briefly the ways in which we think that our inquiry contains
implications of importance for sociological theory.

In the first place we have been able to establish reliably the view that
certain 'instincts proper' are inherited by men, and that they are common
to all members of the human species. We have also been able to indicate
the 'general instinctive tendencies' which can be held to be operative in
all human communities, and within any social groupings within such
communities. These instincts proper and general instinctive tendencies
we have attempted to classify. In addition, we have seen how the work
of Freud provides us with a theory as to how human beings (given this
instinctual endowment) accommodate themselves to their physical and
social environment.

In a word, we have been able to state a theory of the instincts which
establishes reliably the bio-psychological basis of human nature in all
human societies and which clarifies the processes involved in the
'socialization' of the individual within any social framework. This, we
claim, is of importance for sociological theory, and we shall try to say,
briefly, why we hold this view.

It is impossible to attempt, within a short space, an adequate statement of the views of the main sociologists on this question of the place
of Psychology in Sociological Theory. What we may simply assert is
that—whether or not sociologists have, in their methodological writings,
assigned a place of importance to psychology—they *all*, without exception, refer to, or imply, psychological assumptions and propositions in
their own actual pieces of investigation. Even Durkheim, who adopts an
extreme position in arguing that an explanation of 'social facts' or
'collective representations' can never be reduced to propositions about
individual psychology, does, nevertheless, presuppose some basic psy-

chological sub-stratum upon which structural facts exert their influence; and some of his findings really terminate in psychological propositions, and rest upon psychological assumptions: as, for example, in his 'SUICIDE', which concludes that individuals who are closely integrated with their social group feel a greater degree of security and are less likely to commit suicide in the face of rapid changes of circumstance, than are those individuals who are only loosely integrated within any social group and who, left more to their own unaided resources, are more a prey to insecurity and individually experienced intensities of conflict when rapid changes of circumstance occur. Other writers, such as Vico and Max Weber, really require a basic psychological theory for their systems of explanation, though they do not themselves provide one. Vico holds the view that the Human Sciences are more satisfactory and complete than the so called Natural Sciences in so far as the latter can go no farther than generalisations referring to 'phenomena' (in the Kantian sense) whereas in the Human Sciences, besides observing the external facts of human behaviour, we are able to add an inner inter-pretation of these external observations in terms of our own subjective experience and the insight which it gives us. Similarly, Max Weber proposes an 'Understanding' type of sociological theory where social situations are 'interpreted' in terms of certain categories of social action (framed in subjective terms), thus rendering this social situation 'intellig-ible'. But the psychology assumed in this system of interpretation is never made explicit and remains a rough and ready affair in which we render a situation 'intelligible' by interpreting it in terms of motives and feelings with which we are familiar. Other writers—in particular Auguste Comte and John Stuart Mill—have argued for the Inverse-Deductive Method in sociological explanation. This involves on the one hand a basic Psychology—an empirical, experimental science; and, on the other, what we might call provisionally Sociology—comprising empirical generalisations on the level of Social Structure, or (to use Durkheim's terms) 'Social Facts'. Between the two levels of generalisation come the 'Middle Principles', consisting of the propositions of Ethology[1] (the science of Human Character; very similar to what we would now call Social Psychology) which is, for Mill, a deductive science stemming from the established empirical generalisations of Psychology. The empirical generalisations inductively established on the structural level are regarded as sociological 'Laws' when they receive deductive support from (1) Psychology and (2) Ethology. In the most recent sociological system of Talcott Parsons there is something of this combination of

[1]To be distinguished from 'Comparative Ethology', the term recently adopted to refer to the study of Animal Behaviour.

generalisations referring to the objective interrelationships between the variously structured roles of the social system on the one hand, and generalisations referring to the subjective aspects of the process of 'socialization' (framed mainly in psychological terms) on the other.[1]

DIAGRAM (1): AN OBJECTIVE VIEW OF A HUMAN COMMUNITY

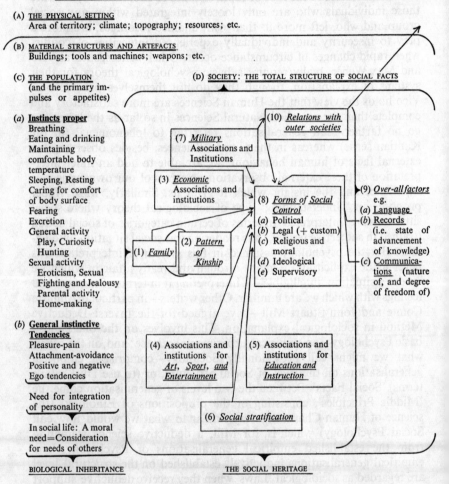

(A) THE PHYSICAL SETTING
Area of territory; climate; topography; resources; etc.

(B) MATERIAL STRUCTURES AND ARTEFACTS
Buildings; tools and machines; weapons; etc.

(C) THE POPULATION
(and the primary impulses or appetites)

(D) SOCIETY: THE TOTAL STRUCTURE OF SOCIAL FACTS

(a) **Instincts proper**
Breathing
Eating and drinking
Maintaining
comfortable body
temperature
Sleeping, Resting
Caring for comfort
of body surface
Fearing
Excretion
General activity
   Play, Curiosity
   Hunting
Sexual activity
   Eroticism, Sexual
   Fighting and Jealousy
   Parental activity
   Home-making

(b) **General instinctive Tendencies**
Pleasure-pain
Attachment-avoidance
Positive and negative
Ego tendencies

Need for integration
of personality

In social life: A moral
need = Consideration
for needs of others

(7) *Military*
Associations and
Institutions

(3) *Economic*
Associations and
institutions

(1) *Family*

(2) *Pattern
of
Kinship*

(10) *Relations with
outer societies*

(8) *Forms of Social
Control*
(a) Political
(b) Legal (+ custom)
(c) Religious and
   moral
(d) Ideological
(e) Supervisory

(9) *Over-all factors*
e.g.
(a) Language
(b) Records
   (i.e. state of
   advancement
   of knowledge)
(c) Communica-
   tions (nature
   of, and degree
   of freedom of)

(4) Associations and
institutions for
*Art, Sport, and
Entertainment*

(5) Associations and
institutions for
*Education and
Instruction*

(6) *Social stratification*

BIOLOGICAL INHERITANCE   THE SOCIAL HERITAGE

We shall adopt the view (though we cannot here defend it) that some system of explanation on the lines expounded by Mill would be the most

[1] See Parsons' treatment in 'The Incest Taboo in Relation to Social Structure and the Socialization of the Child', *British Journal of Sociology* (June 1954), pp. 101-117.

satisfactory, and that, with care, the best contributions of the other theorists could be worked into this scheme. What we are now suggesting is that whereas Mill was able to propose the methodological skeleton only of his scheme of sociological explanation, we are now in a position to clothe this skeleton with flesh and blood. Firstly, the theory of instincts which we have outlined gives us a sound basic psychology. Secondly, resting upon this basis, but with continual reference to the structural facts of the social situation, the Freudian theory of personality development gives us a basic theory of Social Psychology (Mill's *Ethology*). Thirdly, a systematic description of the chief elements of social structure, an analysis of the functional interrelations existing between them, and a detailed comparative study of social institutions and of societies, can provide us with the empirical generalisations on the strictly sociological level.

In order to indicate briefly the system of sociological explanation that this would imply, we can here attempt only the simplest kind of exposition with the aid of diagrams.

Diagram (1) represents an OBJECTIVE VIEW OF A SINGLE HUMAN SOCIETY. A *population* with certain *primary impulses* meets the challenge of a particular *physical setting*, giving rise to the *chief elements of social structure*. All these are facts which we could observe and objectively describe; and this includes, it may be noted, the functional interconnections between these chief forms of social organisation and their institutionalised relationships, and the variously structured social roles which are involved. Diagram (2) (p. 330) is an indication of the SUBJECTIVE ASPECTS OF THE SOCIAL SYSTEM. In terms of our earlier discussion, it represents our approach to Social Psychology (Mill's *Ethology*), indicating the way in which individuals, given a certain instinctual endowment, will accommodate themselves to the structure of social facts. The elements of social structure presented on the right of the diagram must here be regarded in the two ways we have mentioned: (*a*) as *Symbols* of the complex structure of associations and institutions in relation to which subjective attachments are established in the individual during his experience and his upbringing, and (*b*) as a definite number of *objective roles*, variously structured in complexity, some of which the individual will, of necessity, have to fulfil, and between some of which he will, of necessity, have to choose. Diagram (3) (p. 331) is simply a representation of THE KINDS OF PROPOSITION AND GENERALISATION WE WOULD BE ABLE TO MAKE ABOUT THIS SINGLE HUMAN SOCIETY. The set of propositions—(3)—under the heading of Social Structure, are those which would enter with a comparative study of human societies, and which thus complete the area covered by Sociology.

This whole subject (of extreme interest) is one which requires a much more extensive discussion than we have been able to devote to it here. We have, however, been able to indicate fairly clearly how we think the findings of our inquiry would be of use in this connection.

DIAGRAM (2): SUBJECTIVE ASPECTS: AN APPROACH TO SOCIAL PSYCHOLOGY

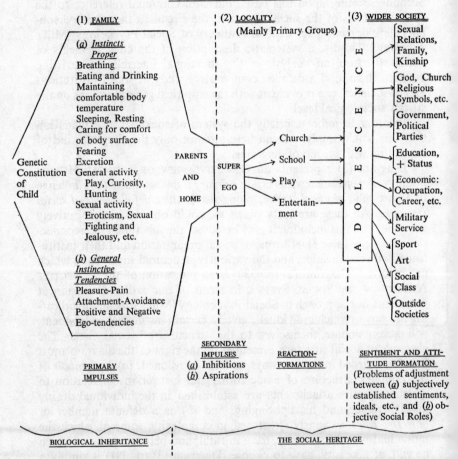

5. *The Implications for Moral and Social Philosophy*

This section will be brief since we do not wish to maintain that our inquiry has made any actual contribution to moral and social philosophy as such. At the level of inquiry on which we have been engaged, this would be impossible. We wish to suggest, however, that our discussion does provide a new and interesting *point of departure* for moral and social philosophy, and, it might be added, a coherent framework for the elaboration of such a philosophical inquiry.

DIAGRAM (3): KINDS OF PROPOSITION WE CAN MAKE ABOUT HUMAN COMMUNITIES

(A) ON HUMAN GEOGRAPHY
Climate; Topography; Resources (actual and potential); etc.

(B) ON MATERIAL STRUCTURES AND ARTEFACTS
Buildings; Tools and machines; Modes of production; Weapons; Works of art; Religious images; etc.

(C) ON THE POPULATION
(its nature, number, and numerical trends)

(1) QUALITATIVE
(a) *Biological:* Genetics, Race, Differential fertility, etc.
(b) *Physiological and anthropometric*
(c) *Psychological:* Instincts, Innate capacities, Modes of perception, Cognition, etc.

(2) QUANTITATIVE
(d) *Demographic-statistical*
Numerical trends: Fertility, Mortality, Migration
Total/working population
Age-groups, Sex-groups
Aggregations, etc.

(E) ON SOCIAL PSYCHOLOGY
Personality⟵⟶Social structure
+The subjective interpretation of Social Action.

(D) (1) ON SOCIAL STRUCTURE
(a) Description of existing associations, institutions, customs, etc. (including operative ideals)
(b) Analysis of the functional relations between the above elements of social structure

(2) ON BOTH HISTORICAL AND CONTEMPORARY studies as above

(3) ON COMPARATIVE STUDIES of societies, including:
(a) The classification of societies and elements of social structure. (Social morphology)
(b) Comparative studies giving
(i) 'Uniformities of co-existence'. (Social statics)
(ii) 'Trends of Social Change'. (Social dynamics)

(F) ON MORAL AND SOCIAL PHILOSOPHY
(a) Ethics and what society *ought* to be. The ends of policy
(b) Social philosophy
(i) What social conditions can best approximate to these ends
(ii) A critique of our methods of studying society

The theory of the instincts; the theory of the formation of the Super-Ego—the content of which is largely determined by a particular Social Tradition; and the fact that certain features of the Social Tradition can be regarded as *necessary* elements of social structure—to be found, though in various forms, in all human societies; indicate certain points of importance for Moral and Social Philosophy. These may be listed conveniently as follows:

(1) We can now hold that the primary human impulses (the instincts proper and the general instinctive tendencies) towards the ordering of

which human value judgments and moral prohibitions and exhortations are directed, are common to all members of mankind. The basic impulses underlying moral conflict, and, indeed, the fundamental nature of moral conflict (the continual and forceful threat of the primary impulses to disrupt the order and control of the secondary impulses) are common to all human beings.

(2) We now have a psychological theory of how the human 'conscience' or 'Super-Ego' formation comes to have the element of genuine and compulsive aspiration as well as elements of inhibition. This aspiration is, in fact, a derivative of the earliest love attachments of the child and the earliest tendencies to idealise the loved object,[1] which, when introjected with the commands and prohibitions of the parents, becomes a genuine aesthetic element in the personality, involving a desire to *become* the ideal personality that the Super-Ego prescribes. This lends psychological support to the tendency of most moral philosophers to recognise an element of the beautiful in the good, an element of positive aesthetic creativity in moral endeavour, and to view the ideal as being something which, though it involves inhibiting control and abnegation, and though it always has to be striven for and perhaps may never be attained, is always, at the same time, *desirable*.[2]

(3) The moral judgments operative in any social system (those values which become, in varying constellations, the content of individual Super-Egos) will also refer necessarily to the existing elements of social structure; the many roles and expectations involved in the structure of associations and institutions and the several forms of Social Control; as well as to some ordering of the impulses and the erecting of ideal standards. Whilst this structure of social facts will differ in particular details from society to society, the chief elements of social structure (as indicated in Diagram 1 above) can be considered as basic functional requisites which must necessarily be provided by the structure of *any* society; and, therefore, we may expect basic, common elements to be found among the moral systems of all human societies as well as elements of diversity. We may expect to find common elements in human value judgments and moral rules *both* from the circumstance that they refer to the ordering of basic impulses which are common to all men,

---

[1]Emulating many psycho-analytic writers, let us quote a poet in support of our contention! Shakespeare tells us:

'Love is too young to know what conscience is,
Yet who knows not conscience is born of love?'

[2]Since we have the poets in mind, we might point out how the poem, 'A Grammarian's Funeral', by Robert Browning, is saturated with the feeling to which we are here drawing attention.

and from the fact that they refer also to elements of social organisation which are necessary and common to all human societies.

(4) We have, therefore, reasonable grounds for expecting that a comparative study of moral systems may reveal certain common evaluations which a subsequent rational examination may be able to elucidate considerably. Further than this, we have promising grounds to suppose that a rational ethic comprising an account of the good life with reference (*a*) to the best ordering of the basic human impulses in the context of the claims and counter-claims of individuals participating in social life, (*b*) to the most desirable pattern of fulfilment of the various components of the human personality, (*c*) to the conditions of social life and organisation appropriate to the achievement of the good life, and (*d*) with corresponding implications for positive social and political policy within the present context of social development—can be achieved.

Here, too, we must leave what would be a most interesting and rewarding inquiry with but these few suggestive remarks.

6. *The Implications for Educational Theory*

The implications already traced for Learning Theory, for Social Psychology, and for Sociological Theory, suggest that we may be in the position, shortly, of being able to explain adequately the way in which the socialisation of individuals takes place within any particular context of social structure. In discussing the implications of our inquiry for moral and social philosophy, we have indicated a starting point for an attempt to construct a rational ethic comprising certain ideals and their implications for social policy. Assuming work in these two spheres to be carried to a successful conclusion (no small assumption!) we would then have before us: (*a*) a knowledge of how what actually is the case in a given society has come to be what it is, and a knowledge of the functional interdependence of the many social facts in this present situation, and (*b*) a knowledge of those ideals in the light of which social policy ought to be guided, and a knowledge of how the existing fabric of society should be manipulated in order to approximate as closely as possible to these ideals.

What we wish to suggest, finally, is that (given such an agreement of the ends we wish to attain) our inquiry also contains implications for the practical tasks of social policy. These implications all fall within the sphere of Educational Theory, and are extensions of what we have already discussed under the heads of Learning Theory and Social Psychology.

In the first place, it follows from the 'Critical Period Hypothesis',

and from our insistence upon the fundamental importance of the
affective aspects of the learning processes, that one of the most important periods of education is that of the first four or five years of the
child's life. This means that learning processes of fundamental importance for the formation of the individual's personality have already
taken place before the child ever attends educational institutions proper.
Consequently, the early family situation is one upon which educational
theory should increasingly focus its attention; and this clearly implies a
closer tie of co-operation between parents and teachers—or, perhaps,
some degree of compulsory attendance at nursery schools coupled with
a close co-operation between parents and nursery school teachers. This
suggestion is of particular importance if it is the case that the 'level of
intelligence' a child attains is closely correlated with his total personality
organisation and, consequently, with this earliest patterning of his
affective responses and attachments.

Similarly, it may be the case that we should pay more attention in
education to the period of adolescence; particularly with regard to the
task of bridging the gap between the individual's long period of dependence in the family and in school life, and the new responsible adult roles
he is required to fill in the wider society. It may be that, at present, we
terminate our process of education at the very period when it is most
important that we should continue it.[1] We know that, among the
simpler societies, public ceremonies and initiation rites at the age of
adolescence are widely found. The passage of the individual from the
status of childhood to the status and obligations of responsible adult-
hood is publicly recognised and, in a sense, socially shared by all the
members of the society. In our own complex but (for the individual)
fragmented industrialised society, individuals are left very much to rely
upon their own resources at this period. As Freud has pointed out, it is
a period of unsettling intensity, when the onset of adult sexual excitations is particularly demanding and actual physiological changes are
taking place; and when, simultaneously, the individual is called upon to
make some of the most important choices of his life: choices of career,
of the direction of further education or training, etc. (or, very often, the
problem of finding the least ugly and frustrating of the drab and
unpromising set of social tasks which are available to him). It may be,
then, that—in some way—education should be continued during this
period of adolescence. This, of course, need not take place in schools,

[1]To include our earlier point as to the importance of the first four to five years of the
child's life, we might say more fully: it may be that, at present, we begin our process of
formal education too late (when the fundamental adjustments of the infantile period *have
already taken place*), and terminate it too soon (when the problems of adjustment of the
adolescent to the pattern of adult roles *are just beginning*).

but perhaps in part-time colleges—such as those suggested in our own county-college scheme which, unfortunately, is being so little implemented. But other schemes might be considered with a greater emphasis upon linking the education of the childhood period with the tasks of adult social life and introducing the young person to the range of social tasks which is open to him. Thus, we might introduce Social Studies more widely into the syllabus of various schools, and reconsider the most desirable structure of an 'academic' education with perhaps a more explicit reference to its social implications. Perhaps, also, the two or three years following school might be spent in organised educational and work groups, relatively mobile, which were recognised by industry, and, indeed, by all spheres of employment, but during which period individuals would be under no obligation to make hasty, permanent, and binding choices. Following this relatively wide introduction to the actual variety of tasks in social life, individuals would have to choose and compete for the jobs of their choice, and could be helped (with advice, information, and training) to prepare for them.

It follows, too, from what we have had to say about the concept of 'intelligence' and its possible relation to the affective responses in the early family situation and the development of the total personality, that every care should be taken throughout a person's educational career to see that these factors are explored, uncovered, and improved where possible, and that his manifest 'level of intelligence' (i.e. the degree of efficiency of his performance in such tests as are accepted and in use at the time) should be reviewed carefully. In view of the present practical difficulties experienced within the educational system in meeting and implementing the requirements of even the 1944 Act, such notions seem Utopian; but (practical difficulties or no) there seems to be no doubt that, ideally, there should be a much greater degree of co-operation between home and school, and, if possible, a mutual interchange of knowledge between teacher and parent. It is clear that the present-day controversy in connection with 'Comprehensive Schools' is a problem in point. In this connection much research of great value might be done in attempting to correlate 'levels of intelligence' with kinds of locality and kinds of family background, and in discovering whether such levels do in fact permit of change and improvement during the course of a child's school career by a kind of 'therapeutic' uncovering of any adverse early affective patternings such as might be reflected in lack of confidence, anxiety, undue timidity, or undue intimidation by authority, etc. At present, political antagonists argue *a priori* that comprehensive school education must be either successful or unsuccessful; but the fact is that it has not yet been adequately tried or studied, and we require much more extensive investigations before we can arrive at reliable conclusions.

Finally, we might say something with regard to the problem of achieving certain ends of education; and we speak of these not entirely in terms of academic attainment or of vocational training, but also in terms of character-formation in the light of the ideals which we wish to be respected and desired among our adult citizens.

In this connection, our discussion again places emphasis upon the importance of the earliest affective experiences in the family situation, and—through this first channel—in the subsequent social environment: the primary groups of neighbourhood, locality, and school. We have suggested that the core of this process of accommodation of the individual to his social environment consists of his affective attachments to *symbols* of the social structure as subjectively conceived. Individuals do not experience the social structure as a rationally clarified set of organisations and interrelationships, but as a set of symbols, ideas, words, propositions, to which they are introduced via the affective ties with their parents and the influential people of their early social setting. By symbols, it must be understood that we do not mean only religious signs (such as the cross), national emblems (such as a flag or national anthem), political signs (such as a Party emblem or a Party slogan), school signs (such as caps, blazers, ties), but also all *words* and *relationships* themselves—Mother, Father, Lover, Parent, Family, Marriage, God, Love, Lust, Theft, Murder, Adultery, and so on: each of which have, for the growing individual, a definite status or evaluation within his experience, and a definite set of expectations and moral obligations. It follows from this emphasis, that—if we have common ends of education in view—we should consider more carefully this primary affective process of accommodation to social symbols during the early years of childhood.

We are not suggesting here any policy of dogmatic indoctrination, although, of course, the danger of this has to be admitted. We know that such a course of establishing early affective attachments to symbols is indeed the method of indoctrination utilised by all the propagandist agencies of our present world: the Catholic Church, the Communist Party, the Nazi Party (as it was), the fanatical Anti-Communist groups of the United States, and, indeed (to some degree), every social group in the world, large or small, that wishes to establish a permanent influence upon the minds of the young. But we are far from suggesting this kind of thing in the form of a simple dogmatism. What we are suggesting is that the whole question of the importance of this fundamental aspect of education should be considered seriously in connection with the achievement of the kind of adult character and adult attitudes we want among our citizens. We all see the necessity of *some* sort of character-training and *some* sort of direction of the attitudes of the young, and this can quite well be conceived within the framework of an enlightened and liberal education. Indeed, perhaps some of our earliest recommendations in connection with this point would be *negative*—in that they would be directed towards the *removal* of some of these early affectively-toned symbols.

But let us take an example.

In these days of international unrest, we are continually hearing complaints about the anachronistic nature and the rigidity of national barriers and of narrow patriotic loyalties. We need to establish a world outlook, it is said, an international attitude of mind, so that we can see the problems of the world as problems of interdependent communities of people who have common interests and common aims, rather than viewing them as the intractable problems of suspiciously competitive nations and alliances of nations. Well? The question is: how are we to produce such an attitude of mind among our citizens? One thing at least follows quite clearly from our inquiry. If definite and consciously designed symbols of world unity or world community were presented to all children (in all countries) continuously from their earliest years, as the fundamental objects of loyalty; embodying qualities of reverence and aspiration; and if the symbols of national groups, and of all other smaller groups, were presented simultaneously as *subsidiary* symbols within the context of the larger, more important ones; then it is probable that within a generation or two a considerable step towards the establishment of a world outlook could be achieved.[1] Considerations of this kind suggest that Comte's ideas on establishing a world religion based upon Humanism are not so improbable as they are often regarded, and we may remember that Graham Wallas expresses similar views in his book *Human Nature in Politics*.

If people object and term such methods propagandist, we must reply that all such attempts to establish emotional attachment to fundamental values and symbols are propagandist, and we have to choose between good propaganda and bad. It is also propagandist, for example, to introduce such affectively-toned symbols as National and Religious

[1]It must be noted that we are not claiming that Education *alone* would be sufficient for the establishment of a sense of international community. Many other difficult and detailed changes of social structure would also have to be achieved. But, given these changes, education could quickly achieve corresponding attitudes. And even without these changes, such education might at least help in promoting the awareness for the need of such changes in contemporary social structure.

symbols to the untutored and immature minds of children.[1] The British Broadcasting Corporation frequently provides Christian 'Services' in its programmes for schools. It is extremely unlikely that the B.B.C. would entertain a rigorous talk radically criticising the Christian Religion and, say, the way in which it is enmeshed with the justification of the constitutional place of the Royal Family and the Church of the Realm. Our schools would not allow the teaching of a sceptical approach to the supposed truths of Christianity; whereas they carry on without question, and largely with support, the usual practice of hymn-singing, saying prayers, reading passages of scripture, and the like, in school assemblies, on school 'speech-days', etc. What are these things but the uncritical acceptance and implementation of a certain kind of propaganda? Symbols such as the Crown, the pictures of the Queen and her consort, of the Royal Family, appear in our newspapers every day and in our popular magazines (especially in our Women's Magazines) every week. They are features of our radio and television programmes perpetually, and they continually figure on the newsreels of our cinemas. What is this but propaganda? The presenting of the Cross, the figure of Jesus, the figures and the traditional stories of the Saints, as affectively charged symbols to the impressionable minds of young children, and the inculcating of habits of praying to these symbols: what is this but propaganda? And this, of course, applies not to our own social tradition alone, but to the religious (or ideological) and political symbols of all present-day nations; and, further, to every small local group which wishes to fasten to itself support and loyalty for its cause.

If such methods as we suggest are not employed for the achievement of an *international* community of outlook, it is not that nations and other groups are not persuaded of their efficacy, but, on the contrary, that they *are* so persuaded, and that they cannot relinquish their own hold on the employment of these methods because of the risk of losing their own traditional unity and solidarity. UNESCO might well wish to undertake such an educational policy in all countries with the aim of widening international understanding and goodwill, but would, without doubt, be unable to do so because of the obvious lack of co-operation among member states. In this case, as in many others, it is not that we do not in these days know enough about social processes in order to approximate by means of social policy to the ends desired, but that we are unable to put our knowledge into practice because of the expedient policies of the existing structures of power in the world.

[1]The importance of simple, affectively established symbolisation need not refer, as we are here referring it—to the important early years of personality-formation alone—but also to the modes of maintaining social cohesion among adults.

In this inquiry the reconsideration and the restatement of the theory of instincts itself has been our major task, and has occupied by far the greater part of our attention. Nonetheless, the possible extensions of our theory into other spheres of investigation do appear to be of the greatest interest and importance. Here, however, we have been able to make only the very briefest remarks about them, and they must be left over for subsequent work and discussion.

BIBLIOGRAPHY

(List of Books and Articles to which reference has been made.)

ALLPORT, G. W. *Personality: A Psychological Interpretation.* Constable & Co., London, 1947.

—— 'Motivation in Personality: Reply to Mr. Bertocci.' *Psychological Review,* vol. XLVII, 1940.

Annual Review of Psychology, Edited by C. P. Stone. Annual Reviews Inc., 1952, 1953.

ARMSTRONG, E. A. *Bird Display and Behaviour.* Cambridge, 1947.

—— 'The Nature and Function of Displacement Activities'. See Symposium: Physiological Mechanisms in Animal Behaviour, 1950.

BENDIX, R. 'Compliant Behaviour and Individual Personality.' *American Journal of Sociology.* November 1952.

BENEDICT, R. *Patterns of Culture.* London, 1935.

BIERENS DE HAAN J. *Animal Psychology for Biologists.* 1929.

BERNARD, L. L. *An Introduction to Social Psychology.* New York, 1926.

BIRD, C. *Effect of Maturation upon the Pecking Instinct of Chicks.* 1926 and 1933.

BOWLBY, J. 'Critical Phases in the Development of Social Responses in Man and other Animals.' *Penguin New Biology,* 14, and *Prospects in Psychiatric Research.* Blackwell Scientific Publications Ltd. Oxford, 1952.

BREED, F. S. *Development of Certain Instincts and Habits in Chicks.* 1911.

BRUN, RUDOLPH. *General Theory of Neurosis.* International Universities Press Inc., 1951.

CARMICHAEL, L. 'Development of Behaviour in Vertebrates Experimentally Removed from Influence of External Environment.' *Psychological Review,* vols. XXXIII and XXXIV. 1926 and 1927. See also *Symposium on Heredity and Environment.*

CRAIG, W. 'Oviposition induced by the male in Pigeons.' *Journal of Morphology,* vol. XXII. 1911.

—— 'Appetites and Aversions as Constituents of Instincts.' *Biol. Bulletin,* vol. XXXIV. 1918.

CRICHTON-MILLER. *Psycho-Analysis and its Derivatives,* 2nd edition. Oxford University Press, 1950.

CRUZE, W. W. *Maturation and Learning in Chicks.* 1935.

COGHILL, G. E. *Anatomy and the Problem of Behaviour.* Cambridge, 1929.

DARWIN, CHARLES. *The Origin of Species.* Thinker's Library Edition. Watts & Co., 1929.

—— *The Descent of Man.* Thinker's Library Edition. Watts & Co., 1946.

—— *The Expression of the Emotions in Man and Animals.* Thinker's Library Edition. Watts & Co., 1948.

DREVER, JAMES. *Instinct in Man*. Cambridge University Press, 1917.
—— 'The Classification of Instincts.' *British Journal of Psychology*. January 1924.
FABRE, J. H. *The Wonders of Instinct* (English translation of papers from *Souvenirs Entomologiques*). Duckworth, 1928.
FIELD, G. C. 'Faculty Psychology and Instinct Psychology.' *Mind*, 1921.
—— *Moral Theory*. Methuen, 1921.
FORD, E. B. 'Genetics'. *Scientific Thought in the Twentieth Century*. Watts & Co., 1951.
FREUD, SIGMUND. 'Character and Anal Erotism.' *Collected Papers*, vol. II. IV. 1908.
—— 'The Transformation of Instincts with special reference to Anal Erotism.' *Collected Papers*, vol. II. XVI. 1916.
—— *An Autobiographical Study*. 1927.
—— *Beyond the Pleasure Principle*. 1922.
—— *New Introductory Lectures*. 1933.
—— 'Instincts and their Vicissitudes.' *Collected Papers*, vol. IV. IV. 1915.
—— 'Some Character-Types met with in Psycho-Analytic Work.' *Collected Papers*, vol. IV. XVIII. 1915.
—— 'Neurosis and Psychosis.' *Collected Papers*, vol. II. XXI. 1924.
—— 'Civilized Sexual Morality and Modern Nervousness.' *Collected Papers*, vol. II. VII. 1908.
—— *An Outline of Psycho-Analysis*. 1940.
—— 'Repression.' *Collected Papers*, vol. IV. V. 1915.
—— 'Certain Neurotic Mechanisms in Jealousy, Paranoia and Homosexuality.' *Collected Papers*, vol. II. XIX. 1922.
—— 'The Economic Problem in Masochism.' *Collected Papers*, vol. II. XXII. 1924.
—— 'Formulations regarding the Two Principles in Mental Functioning.' *Collected Papers*, vol. IV. I. 1911.
—— 'The Unconscious.' *Collected Papers*, vol. IV. VI. 1915.
—— *The Ego and the Id*. 1923.
—— 'On Narcissism: An Introduction.' *Collected Papers*, vol. IV. III. 1914.
—— *Group Psychology and the Analysis of the Ego*. 1921.
—— 'The Infantile Genital Organization of the Libido.' *Collected Papers*, vol. II. XX. 1923.
—— 'The Passing of the Oedipus Complex.' *Collected Papers*, vol. II. XXIII. 1924.
—— *The Future of an Illusion*. 1927.
—— *Civilization and its Discontents*. 1930.
GESELL, A. 'The Ontogenesis of Infant Behaviour.' *Manual of Child Psychology*. New York, London, 1947.
GINSBERG, M. *The Psychology of Society*. Methuen, 1944.
—— 'The Place of Instinct in Social Theory.' *Studies in Sociology*. London, 1932.
—— 'Emotion and Instinct.' *Studies in Sociology*. London, 1932.

GINSBERG, 'Basic Needs and Moral Ideals.' *Proceedings of the Aristotelian Society*. 1947.

—— 'On the Diversity of Morals.' *Huxley Memorial Lecture*. 1953.

—— *The Idea of Progress*. Methuen, 1953.

—— *Psychology and Sociology*. See *Further Papers on the Social Sciences: Their Relations in Theory and Teaching*, Edited by J. E. Dugdale.

GRAY, SIR. J. 'The Role of Peripheral Sense Organs During Locomotion in the Vertebrates.' See Symposium: Physiological Mechanisms in Animal Behaviour, 1950.

HEALY, BRONNER, and BOWERS. *The Structure and Meaning of Psycho-Analysis*. New York, 1931.

HINGSTON, R. W. C. *Problems of Instinct and Intelligence*. Arnold, 1928.

HOBBES, THOMAS. *Leviathan*. Everyman's Edition. Dent, 1949.

HOBHOUSE, L. T. *Mind in Evolution*. London, 1901.

—— *Morals in Evolution*. Chapman & Hall, 1951.

—— *Theory of Knowledge*. London, 1896.

—— *Development and Purpose*. London, 1927.

—— *Social Development*. London, 1924.

—— *The Rational Good*. London, 1921.

HUME, DAVID. *A Treatise of Human Nature*. Everyman's Edition. Dent, 1949.

JAMES, WILLIAM. *Principles of Psychology*. Macmillan, 1890.

JENNINGS, H. S. *The Behaviour of the Lower Organisms*. New York, 1923.

JONES, ERNEST. 'Psycho-Analysis and the Instincts.' *British Journal of Psychology*. January 1936.

—— 'The Classification of the Instincts.' *British Journal of Psychology*. January 1924.

KALMUS, H. *Genetics*. Pelican, 1948.

KATZ, D. *Animals and Men*. 1937.

KEPNER, W. A. *Animals Looking into the Future*. 1925.

LEWIN, KURT. *A Dynamic Theory of Personality*. McGraw-Hill Book Co., 1935.

—— *Principles of Topological Psychology*. McGraw-Hill Book Co., 1936.

LINDESMITH, A. R. and STRAUSS, A. L. 'Comparative Psychology and Social Psychology.' *American Journal of Sociology*. November 1952.

LORENZ, KONRAD. *King Solomon's Ring*. Methuen, 1952.

—— 'The Comparative Method in Studying Innate Behaviour Patterns.' See *Physiological Mechanisms in Animal Behaviour*. Cambridge University Press, 1950.

McDOUGALL, WILLIAM. *An Introduction to Social Psychology*, 29th edition. Methuen, 1948.

—— *The Energies of Men*, 7th edition. Methuen, 1948.

McGRAW, M. B. 'Maturation of Behaviour.' *Manual of Child Psychology*. New York, London, 1947.

MEAD, MARGARET. *Sex and Temperament in Three Primitive Societies.* Routledge, 1935.

MILL, J. S. *A System of Logic.* Book VI.

MITCHELL, T. W. *Problems in Psycho-Pathology.* 1927.

MORGAN, C. LLOYD. *Introduction to Comparative Psychology.* London, 1894.

—— *The Interpretation of Nature.* Macmillan, 1905.

—— 'The Natural History of Experience.' *British Journal of Psychology.* 1909.

—— *Habit and Instinct.* 1896.

MYERS, C. S. 'The Comparative Study of Instinct.' *British Journal of Psychology.* September 1945.

PARSONS, TALCOTT. 'The Incest Taboo in Relation to Social Structure and the Socialisation of the Child.' *British Journal of Sociology.* June 1954.

PLATO. *The Republic.* Everyman's Edition.

RAVEN, J. C. 'The Instinctive Disposition to Act Intelligently.' *British Journal of Psychology*, vol. XLII. 1951.

RITTER, W. E. *The Natural History of Our Conduct.* New York, 1927.

RIVERS, W. R. *Instinct and the Unconscious.* Cambridge, 1924.

ROMANES, G. J. *Animal Intelligence.* London, 1882.

—— *Mental Evolution in Animals.* London, 1883.

RUSSELL, BERTRAND. *Problems of Philosophy.* Oxford University Press, 1951.

—— *The Analysis of Mind.* London, 1921.

RUSSELL, E. S. *The Behaviour of Animals.* 1934.

SCHNEIRLA, T. C. 'A Consideration of some Conceptual Trends in Comparative Psychology.' *Psychological Bulletin*, vol. XLIX. November 1952.

SMITH, F. V. *The Explanation of Human Behaviour.* Constable, 1951.

SPITZ, R. A. and WOLFE, K. M. 'The Smiling Response: A Contribution to the Ontogenesis of Social Relations.' *Genetic Psychology Monograph*, vol. XXXIV. 1946.

Symposium: F. A. Beach, L. Carmichael, K. S. Lashley, C. T. Morgan, C. P. Stone, W. S. Hunter, 'On Heredity and Environment.' *Psychological Review*, 1947.

Symposium: C. S. Myers, C. Lloyd Morgan, G. F. Stout, H. Wildon Carr, W. McDougall, 'Instinct and Intelligence.' *British Journal of Psychology*, 1910.

Symposium: C. Burt, P. E. Vernon, J. Drever, E. L. Thorndike, C. S. Myers, T. H. Pear, 'Is the Doctrine of Instincts Dead?' *British Journal of Educational Psychology*, 1941-43.

Symposium: Lorenz, Tinbergen, Armstrong, Gray, etc., 'Physiological Mechanisms in Animal Behaviour.' *The Society for Experimental Biology.* Cambridge University Press, 1950.

THORNDIKE, E. L. *Educational Psychology.* New York, 1927.

*THORPE, W. H. 'The Modern Concept of Instinctive Behaviour.' *Bulletin of Animal Behaviour*. February 1948.

—— 'The Definition of Some Terms Used in Animal Behaviour Studies.' *Bulletin of Animal Behaviour*, No. 9. March 1951.

TINBERGEN, N. *The Study of Instinct*. Oxford, 1951.

—— *Social Behaviour in Animals*. Methuen, 1953.

—— 'Fighting and Threat in Animals.' *Penguin New Biology*, 14. April 1953. See also *Physiological Mechanisms in Animal Behaviour*.

WALLAS, GRAHAM. *Human Nature in Politics*, 3rd edition. Constable, 1920.

WATSON, J. B. *Behaviourism*. Kegan Paul, 1925.

*I very much regret that Dr. Thorpe's recent and excellent work: 'Learning and Instinct in Animals' appeared when this book was already in an advanced state of preparation, so that I have been unable to make extensive use of it. It does not appear that Dr. Thorpe's present views, and his detailed review of recent evidence, make necessary any great amendment of the summary account of Comparative Ethology presented here; but the reader should certainly refer to his work for a thorough-going discussion of Ethology, and especially of some of the more controversial areas of ethological theory, e.g. the great complexity of 'appetitive behaviour'; the difficulties which still attend the conception of the 'hierarchical organisation' of instinctive mechanisms; the degree of permanence and irreversibility of 'imprinting', etc., etc.

INDEX

345